SALOMÉ
HER LIFE AND WORK

ANGELA LIVINGSTONE

Salomé
HER LIFE AND WORK

MOYER BELL LIMITED · MT. KISCO, NEW YORK

Published by Moyer Bell Limited, Mt. Kisco, New York

LIBRARY OF CONGRESS CATALOGING IN PUBLICATION DATA
Livingstone, Angela
  Salomé: Her Life and Work
  Bibliography: p. 246
  Includes index.
  1. Andreas-Salomé, Lou, 1861-1937–Biography.
  2. Authors, German–20th Century–Biography. I. Title.
PT2601.N4Z68 1984   838'.809 [B]   84-29615

ISBN 0-918825-04-0

From left to right on the preceding pages:

Lou with Andreas, taken to mark their engagement, 1886
Reproduced by courtesy of Insel Verlag

Lou Andreas-Salomé, taken in 1897
Mary Evans/Sigmund Freud copyrights

Lou Andreas-Salomé, taken in 1934

First published in '1984 in the United Kingdom (England)
by the Gordon Fraser Gallery Limited, London and Bedford
Set in Monophoto Ehrhardt by Keyspools Ltd, Golborne, Lancs
Printed and bound by Butler and Tanner Ltd, Frome, U.K. (England)
Designed by Peter Guy

Contents

Prefatory Notes   6

Acknowledgements   8

CHAPTER ONE   *Introduction*, 9

CHAPTER TWO   *Childhood and Adolescence*, 15

CHAPTER THREE   *Paul Rée – Meeting with Nietzsche*, 32

CHAPTER FOUR   *Marriage and Travels*, 59

CHAPTER FIVE   *Essays on Religion*, 74

CHAPTER SIX   *Books on Ibsen and on Nietzsche*, 87

CHAPTER SEVEN   *Meeting with Rilke*, 99

CHAPTER EIGHT   *Rilke, Göttingen and Middle Age*, 121

CHAPTER NINE   *Essays on Love and Woman*, 133

CHAPTER TEN   *Meeting with Freud*, 145

CHAPTER ELEVEN   *War-time, Pscychoanalysis, Rilke and Freud*, 164

CHAPTER TWELVE   *Psychoanalytic essays*, 181

CHAPTER THIRTEEN   *Three Last Books*, 189

CHAPTER FOURTEEN   *Growing Old*, 197

FICTIONAL WRITINGS   *Early Fiction, 1883–95*, 204

Fiction, 1896–98, 208

Fiction, 1902–04, 213

Late Fiction, 1915–19, 216

Appendices

A   Nietzsche's 'Columbus' Poem, 221

B   Rilke's Letters to Lou compared with his other Letters, 222

C   Lou Andreas-Salomé's influence on Rilke's Work, 222

D   Lou Andreas-Salomé on Hauptmann, 225

E   Lou Andreas-Salomé's writings about Russia, 225

F   Lou Andreas-Salomé's writings on Art, 227

G   'Hymn to Life', 229

Notes   229

Translations & Abbreviations   237

References   238

Bibliography   246

Index   253

PREFATORY NOTES

The main part of this book is an account of the major events in Lou Andreas-Salomé's life and of her major non-fiction works. Her fiction, which she did not consider important yet which stands in an interesting if indefinite relation to her personality and life, I have treated in a separate section – as being of lesser significance now than her intellectual writings and of more interest if taken together than if divided up chronologically in the main text. I give there accounts of her longer fictional works and of samples from the collections of shorter ones.

Discussion of her non-fictional writings on certain subjects (Russia, art, etc) is relegated to Appendices. This is because, though interesting in themselves, they tend to repeat ideas expressed elsewhere and would have overburdened the main text.

NOTE ON TRANSLATION

Translation of quoted material, from German and from Russian, is my own, with the following exceptions: (1) quotations from Freud's works are taken from the Standard Edition of the Complete Works; (2) quotations from Freud's correspondence with Abraham and with Jung are taken from the published English editions. Apart from these, everything, including passages from the work of Nietzsche, and passages from such works of LAS as already exist in other English versions, is translated by me from the original.

NOTE ON USE OF NAME

On most occasions I am calling the subject of this book by her Christian name, firstly because she was herself particularly attached to it and used it prominently, secondly because, while not a feminist, she was a very independent woman whom it seems wrong to call by her father's or her husband's name, and thirdly because the other possible alternatives have distinct disadvantages: there are inappropriate connotations to 'Salomé', 'Andreas-Salomé' is long and awkward, and 'Lou A.-S.' sounds cold.

NOTE REFERENCES

Asterisks refer to end notes, which provide background information on persons and events. Superior numbers refer to bibliographical sources listed under 'References'.

FOR PETER STERN

ACKNOWLEDGEMENTS

My first and chief thanks are due to Dr Ernst Pfeiffer, of Göttingen, who, as Lou Andreas-Salomé's last friend and confidant, and as faithful keeper of her 'Nachlass', has allowed me to read numerous unpublished materials in his private collection and talked to me about her willingly and helpfully on the several visits I made to him during 1977–1983. I am grateful to Dr Pfeiffer for permission to refer to, and to reproduce in paraphrase, parts of the unpublished materials in his possession. I am respecting his request that I should not quote directly from them.

My thanks go also to Dr Konstantin Azadovsky, of Leningrad, who lent me manuscripts of his own forthcoming works on Rilke, allowed me to copy out a highly valuable new document (Lou von Salomé's first letter to Gillot which he had discovered in Leningrad) and helped me with encouragement and exchange of views; and to Dr Joachim Storck, of the Deutsches Literaturarchiv (Deutsche Schillergesellschaft, Marbach am Neckar).

Several friends have helped me and I would like to thank Simon Kingston (who asked me to write this book and has been a constant encouragement); also Wyllis Bandler, Susan Biver, Frank Cioffi, Irene Frowen, Sonia Livingstone and Elizabeth Rikh, for commenting on parts of the unfinished draft; and, above all, Sarah Symmons-Goubert for generously advising on the entire typescript at a crucial moment.

My work was assisted by the award of a Research Fellowship from the Leverhulme Trust Fund in 1979, which enabled me to take four months' unpaid leave from my University teaching, as well as by a financial grant from the German Academic Exchange Service enabling me to make research trips to Germany in 1979 and 1980.

The Department of Literature, University of Essex, helped me by letting me take two terms of sabbatical leave to work on this book and by awarding money from its Research Endowment Fund in 1980 to pay for my journey to Leningrad in connection with it. The Inter-Library Loan section of the University of Essex Library has been a great help, getting numerous books from abroad at short notice.

The author and publishers are grateful to Insel Verlag for permission to use copyright material, in particular from *Lebensrückblick*.

CHAPTER ONE

Introduction

'No woman has radiated a stronger or more direct influence in German-speaking lands in the last 150 years than this Lou von Salomé from Petersburg.'[1]   KURT WOLFF

The hazy greatness which surrounds the name Lou Andreas-Salomé usually emanates from other names accompanying it, luminous among them Friedrich Nietzsche, Rainer Maria Rilke and Sigmund Freud. It is occasionally thought, when she has been heard of only as someone with famous friends, that Lou Andreas-Salomé was one of those collectors of geniuses in whom the essential thing is their 'remarkable flair for great men'[2]; but this says almost nothing about her. A glance into her correspondence makes one ask not only what it was in her character and life that led to this astonishing series of encounters, but also what it was that enabled her to be so unambitious in relation to them, to remain so secure and independent a personality. When one discovers that she was herself a celebrated thinker and writer in her time, one is led to ask, further, what was her own philosophy? What ideas did she hold – in particular on the topics she wrote about most and best: religion, sex (in both senses of the word) and psychoanalysis?

These topics are directly linked to the main themes of her biography. Her unusual experience of love and, closely interwoven with this, her unusually intense experience of religion, were the factors which more than anything else influenced her character and determined the events of her life. Preoccupied by these two experiences, she moved from one kind of inner liberation to another, to become at last the forceful and — as she was often called — 'sovereign' person whom one meets in most of her non-fictional writing and correspondence. As for the third theme, the study and practice of psychoanalysis were the culmination of her career and the cause of her personal fulfilment.

Of particular importance is the book she wrote on Nietzsche – a considerable work in itself and one showing how deep was her engagement with the philosopher, despite the brevity of her friendship with the man (which lasted less than eight months). To us the names of Nietzsche, Rilke and Freud are likely to stand out with something like equal prominence, but to her they were certainly not of equal importance. Moreover, if we read her memoir, *Looking Back* [*Lebensrückblick*], we find there three other men, all of them fairly distinguished but none winning fame, whose importance to her was much more profound and lasting, though they must appear to posterity as a mere necessary background to the meetings with the great. These are Pastor Hendrik Gillot, Dr Paul Rée, and Professor F. C. Andreas. Her relationship with these men, who all passionately loved her, were inwardly most dramatic. Each relationship started with a kind of instantaneous, irresistible recognition and each was highly unconventional. At seventeen, she worshipped her teacher as if he were God; at twenty-one, she set up house for four years with a man she was glad she could never be in love with; at twenty-six, she made a marriage that would last for forty-five years and yet never be consummated.

Because Gillot, Rée and Andreas were such an important part of her formation, I have dwelt on these early encounters at far greater length than any later ones excepting those with Nietzsche, Rilke and Freud. Beside them the latter three may even acquire a certain plainness. Nietzsche (whom Lou met in 1882 at a turning-point in his thought) was after all to her merely a brilliant older scholar, a teacher, helper and temporary friend; the effect she had on him was immense, but she was later to say that she could think him out of her life.[3] With Rilke (whom she met in 1897 at the very beginning of his career as a poet) she had a fairly normal love affair, deeply important to her, lasting three years and to be followed by nearly three decades of friendship; but again the drama, the immensity of feeling, were chiefly on his side. And with Freud (whom she got to know in 1912 when, having expounded his fundamental theories, he was turning to work on new ones) it was, one could say, no more than an excellent twenty-six-year friendship and, to some extent colleagueship; in this case there was really no drama on either side, unless sheer depth of gladness can be accounted dramatic; again what is most noteworthy about the relationship is the eminence of the man. If sections of this book are dominated by her acquaintance with these influential persons, it is for the sake of our interest in them and may well be out of proportion to their significance in her life.

Another element of disproportion is that at least one relationship of great importance to Lou Andreas-Salomé is neglected – that with Dr Friedrich Pineles, known as Zemek; this is because almost nothing is known about it. And only perfunctory mention is made of the large number of other gifted and well-known people she knew with various degrees of closeness. Names of distinguished men cluster round hers throughout her biography, so numerous that some commentators assume she knew everyone, and reel off lists of friendships almost at random: one[4] tells us she was a friend of Kafka (in which there is not a gleam of truth), another[5] that she counted 'among her friends' Turgenev, Tolstoy, Strindberg, Rodin, Rilke and Schnitzler, whereas she never met Turgenev, scarcely knew Rodin or Strindberg, and had only

the slightest acquaintance with Tolstoy. But a true list of her friendships would be remarkable without any such additions, for during five
decades she made acquaintances in artistic and learned circles in Berlin,
Munich, Vienna, Paris and Petersburg, and the full story of them would
be something approaching a history of modern European culture.

A more than ordinary strength of character, eluding definition, seems
to have carried Lou Andreas-Salomé through her life. One might
perhaps see it as a matter of powerful will, and suggest that she knew
astoundingly clearly what she wanted and made sure she got it; one
could, alternatively, see it as a matter of great faith and trust and say, as
she sometimes said, that she was governed all her life by something she
had no control over. At the age of twenty-one, she wrote: '*Goals* have
not been a choice for me, and I have *never* really known the feeling of
choice, but have found in myself something very like the necessary
working of natural forces.'[6] At seventy-five, she told a visitor that she
could not understand why, when she had done the most obvious and
natural things, catastrophes resulted;[7] she could have said the same
about benefits resulting from her actions. Whatever it was — will, fate,
or the belief in fate, or perhaps belief in herself – it was something
which others always sensed in her and were attracted by. Nietzsche
called her 'courageous as a lion';[8] Rilke said: 'she moves fearlessly
among the most burning mysteries, which do nothing to her ... I know
no one else with life so much on their side';[9] her friend Helene
Klingenberg said of her that she had 'an enormous readiness for life, a
humble and most courageous attitude of holding herself open to it';[10]
Anna Freud said of her after her death: 'the unusual thing about her
was what ought actually to be quite usual in a human being – honesty,
directness, absence of any weakness, self-assertion without selfishness.'[11] Recent critics who did not know her have sometimes felt put off
by the very qualities that attracted her friends. D. Bassermann, for
example, who was fascinated by the 'natural force of unbroken power'[12]
in her and describes her as 'daemonically primordial' and also (lifting a
phrase from Freud's obituary of her) 'without any feminine frailties and
almost without any human ones', adds that she was a 'virago, lacking
only a bit of real humanitas to be a figure out of antiquity'. Of course,
not every acquaintance liked her (though all except Nietzsche's sister
were in some way very drawn to her). Rilke's friend Loulou Albert-
Lasard evoked her uncommon vitality and powerful gaze, but also
wrote with sarcastic humour that whenever Lou Andreas-Salomé
travelled to any big town she would first write to all the luminaries
living in it so as to have them lined up on the station platform as her
train steamed in.[13] But both the idea of the virago and the image of the
gatherer-up of great men at railway stations are belied by the impression of peacefulness and receptiveness she made on so many. Freud

called her an 'understander par excellence';[14] people continually came to tell her about themselves; she was 'such an apt student that her teachers appear to have grown wiser in her presence':[15] she was a patient and successful psychoanalyst. Few people can ever have been loved, admired, worshipped and clung to by so many others as she was.

Telling her life story, I have relied whenever possible on the way she told it herself, opening up and expanding the accounts she gave (mainly in *Looking Back*). Where she affixed ornate labels and provided compound wrappings, I have tried to decipher the labels and to undo the parcels. Some empty areas I have populated with names, dates, places and books. But, for the general view, I have usually taken her at her word about herself; she said these things happened and had these kinds of importance, and there is no reason to suppose it was otherwise, despite (to mention the most energetic of her posthumous depreciators) Rudolph Binion in his *Frau Lou*, which, from an unexplained position of antipathy, treats her throughout as a subtle liar about herself. One thing that makes Lou Andreas-Salomé difficult for us to appreciate, and which may have made up one of the strands of that antipathy, is the peculiar pathos of her style, which is especially conspicuous in her memoir. It has been called an example of *Jugendstil* (or art nouveau), by which may be meant an excess of the heavily decorative, a certain amount of rather humourless idiosyncrasy in the invention of new forms, and a habit of hinting at things of indescribable mystery and unfathomable significance. These qualities her autobiographical writing at any rate does have; it is somehow swollen, it is naively sententious, and it is unnecessarily secretive. But as this is so very different from what is reliably reported of her personality, I think one has to keep in mind that none of it could have been true of her voice, and one should listen for something more vivid beyond the thick curtain of the written style. In certain works, such as the *Three Epistles to a Boy*, and in many diaries and letters, one does overhear the persuasive fluency her speech itself must have had. In her *Freud Journal*, especially, one glimpses the rapt process of responsible and elaborative thinking that must have made her conversation absorbing. In the stories and novels one looks in on the passions that lay like a warming and threatening fire beneath her academic pronouncements. But in general her writings are not adequate to convey what she was. People called her a 'genius', but these are remote from being *works* of genius. There is a lush wordiness in nearly all she wrote which ranks it far below any grandeur.

On the other hand, taken together, the writings add up to something worthwhile. They are impressive for a certain sustained and unbothering vigour, as well as for the consistency of thought in their wide ranging over different subjects. They are interesting, too, as the work of a woman dedicated to an intellectual life at a time when this required

more courage than it does nowadays, and of a woman thinking alone.
The trouble critics often had in categorising her arose from the
solitariness of her thought. While other notable women attached
themselves to causes (social reform, perhaps, or female emancipation)
or to an eminent husband, perhaps to a brilliant salon, or, as actresses
and dancers, made their person their gift, Lou Andreas-Salomé, who
appeared to be always purposefully moving in a definite direction,
actually had no cause. She joined no movement, was wholly unpolitical,
was neither a feminist nor an anti-feminist (though she occasionally
satirised feminists and was called a reactionary). She did not link her
life to that of a great man and she was, more than anything, cerebral – it
was her mind that she gave. When, at fifty, she became an adherent of
psychoanalysis, she was not so much joining a movement as finding in
that movement a roof, a house, for the family of ideas she had already
borne and brought up, an edifice of names for an already assembled but
loosely labelled world-roaming luggage of thoughts.

As well as her major essays, she wrote a great deal which I treat as
minor work – especially about poetry and drama, and about the Russian
character and Russian culture. She also produced a multitude of
fictional works — indeed she spun out words all her life as naturally as a
silkworm spins silk. The fiction was received with a great deal of praise.
One critic said in 1898: 'the fictional work of Andreas-Salomé has the
effect of hymns in the thunderous sounding of an organ. It rings out full
and stirring, and dies away in tones celestially light'.[16] As literature, it
has not much to offer us now. None the less, it is interesting as soon as
we become interested in the personality of the author, for it contains
image after image of the girl and woman she felt herself to be, of the
girls and women around her, and of the men who fascinated and
disappointed her. I am therefore giving – in a final, separate section –
full accounts of most of her fiction.

Lou Andreas-Salomé held the principle that women ought not to let
their writing be central to their lives, and this guided her own
behaviour. If one had asked her why women have not achieved things
comparable to the achievements of men in the arts, sciences and
philosophy, and also why she herself did not try to become the much
better writer she doubtless could have become (to judge by many signs
and by Nietzsche's saying she 'could learn to write in a day'[17]), she
would probably have answered, to both questions: lack of ambition.
This, she told Freud, was 'a great lack but a legitimate one in women,
for what use is ambition to us?'[18] The whole business of devotion to
perfection in artistic achievement would have seemed to her (for herself
at least) a sort of sidetracking, and a denial of the fullness of experience
that she already enjoyed and that she believed she enjoyed *as a woman*.
She was, above all, utterly glad to be female. And I think an important

benefit from studying her life and her work is that they acquaint us with someone who, in spite of the moral and professional constrictions laid upon women in her time and in spite of her own emotional problems, found no conscious disadvantage in being a woman. She was convinced that women are the happier and the superior sex; she worked at theories to establish this, and never cursed her lot, nor laughed at it.

CHAPTER TWO

Childhood and Adolescence

'My childhood full of lonely reverie'[1]

At her home in Germany in 1904, Lou Andreas-Salomé recalled the
feeling of freedom she had had in her childhood.[2] She thought it due to
a double unawareness. She had been unaware of Russia (where she was
born and grew up) as the country that would later mean much to her;
and she was unaware of her family as people she would later love. If she
had loved her family and country then, it would surely, she thought,
have hindered her whole development. But had she been *too* free? This
reflection touches on two important aspects of her early life: a solitude
that came from independence of her surroundings; and something like
an instinct for freedom, which meant the postponement of love and its
attachments. Although her childhood was spent amid good fortune – a
very high degree of culture and comfort, kind parents giving discipline
and liberty in intelligent proportions, brothers to play with, good
schools, pleasant holidays, beautiful places – she said later that, whereas
most people felt their childhood to be the best time of their life, for her
it was the least good.[3] This was because she spent so much of it creating
and wrestling with a complex inner world of her own. Because her
mind's world demanded so much attention, she became withdrawn and
alone. Unusually self-vigilant, unusually plunged in thought and
dream, she was also, from the start, strangely confident of her right to
be and do whatever she wished. Her unhappiness was related to her
independence and to strong inner experiences that cut her off from
family and country.

FAMILY AND HOME

She was born as Louise von Salomé in a German-speaking family*
living in Petersburg, the capital of Imperial Russia, three weeks before
the announcement of the abolition of serfdom, in February 1861. Her
father, Gustav von Salomé, was a Baltic German of Huguenot extrac-
tion, born into the French nobility of his ancestors. After a military
education in Petersburg, he had been made a member of the Russian
nobility as well, since distinguishing himself during the 1830 Polish
uprising. He had quickly risen to General, subsequently holding

equally high positions in the Civil Service. He had been on friendly
terms with the Tsar Nicholas I, and he moved naturally in the highest
society. He was fifty-seven when his daughter was born. Her mother,
who had some Danish but mainly German blood and had been born in
Petersburg, was thirty-eight. Louise was the youngest of six children,
the only girl. Two boys died young; of the three who grew up Alexander was twelve years older, Robert nine and Evgeny three. The mother
had hoped for a sixth boy, but the father was glad of a girl.

Petersburg was a city of splendour and squalor; the von Salomés saw
its splendid side. They lived in a magnificent apartment in the General
Staff Building, across from the Winter Palace, residence of the Tsar,
and they spent summers on their estate in Peterhof, where many
aristocratic families and the Tsar too had summer houses. Altogether,
life in that misty northern city (Dostoyevsky's 'most deliberate city in
the world') whose lovely buildings had been forced up by the will of one
man over swamps and the myriad bones of labourers – bringing Russia
all at once into contiguity with Europe – was for Lou von Salomé
scarcely like living in Russia at all. 'St Petersburg', she wrote, 'this
attractive combination of Paris and Stockholm, gave the impression –
despite its imperial splendour, its reindeer-sleighs and illuminated ice-
houses on the Neva, its late springs and its hot summers – of being
purely international.'[4] The twenty years she lived there were years of
social and intellectual change for Russia, with the reforms of the 1860s
and the growth of radical political movements, as well as the emergence
of Russian artists and composers, and the most famous of the novelists.
Tolstoy's two great novels and all of Dostoyevsky's were written in
those twenty years. But although she read some Russian literature, and
although something of the Populist movement reached her at school,
Lou's education and experience were predominantly German.

From the beginning, Germans had been by far the most numerous of
the foreigners living in Petersburg and showed the strongest tendency
to form colonies. United by language, they were also, more widely,
joined to the French and Dutch communities by religion: Lutheranism
and the Protestant-Reformed churches. There were Tartars, Swabians
and Estonians among the servants in the von Salomé home, and young
Lyolya (she was called by this Russian diminutive of her name) had a
Russian nurse and a French governess. It was a grand and patriarchal
home life, with coming and going of high military personages. 'I grew
up in the midst of officers' uniforms', she wrote,[5] great balls in the
winter and other receptions in the large rooms 'over-high as in
churches'. But, in the grand house, family life was warm. Lou depicted
her parents as fine-mannered, authoritative and affectionate, sincere
and religious; after their marriage, they had been converted to pietism,
a movement in the Protestant church which sought the revival of deep

sentiment along with strict observance. She also recalled her mother as
a physically brave woman who would gaze fascinated at a knife battle
and who at the age of eighty-two had to be restrained from going out to
watch the fighting on the streets (in 1905), yet who was content to
devote herself to home and family; and her father as a man of passionate temperament, in his youth an enjoyer of all worldly joys, occasionally bursting out in rage, but trusting, open-hearted, chivalrous and
faithful. At atmosphere of fidelity and love developed in her a trustful
disposition and a permanent gratefulness. Later in life she offered an
analogy for the way she acquired these attitudes: once she saw blue
gentians growing in a forest and considered picking some for a sick
friend, but then, because deep in thought, decided against it; on her
way back she found the bunch of gentians in her hand. Thus she spent
her childhood distracted by thoughts of her own, later to find that in a
trance she had gathered something valuable to bring away with her – by
her own action, yet against her decision, as if some benevolent power
had been looking after her. This is what she felt all her life: that she was
looked after, that something vast and mysterious prompted her actions.

Lou recalled being fond of both her parents, yet the childhood
incidents she later recorded about her mother show only hostility.
Once, watching her mother swim, she called out: 'Dear mother, please
drown!' and to the reply 'But I'd be dead!' she called again: 'Never
mind!'[6] Her mother rarely hugged her, her father often did. With her
father she had a 'secret bond of affection'.[7] Still tiny, she went out
walking with him, holding his arm like a lady and taking enormous
strides to keep up; when their dog caught rabies, her terror was that she
would catch it and bite Papa.[8] She always remembered his gentleness
and kindly tuition. A story she wrote in later years[9] seems to record her
feelings about her parents: in it the father, coming home too soon for
the mother to tell him he is to punish the little girl for a misdeed,
gathers the child up and takes her to a travelling fair: among the
jugglers, rope-dancers, trained monkeys and roundabouts, she is so
happy that she resolves to stay there with him forever, and he agrees: he
will wear a snake round his neck and lead a bear on a chain and together
they will wander over the country, sleep in a caravan, eat roasted
chestnuts by the roadside. From this Paradise the mother is excluded.
But they have to go home, and there is mother and the question of
punishment. In fact, however, both Lou's parents were lenient with
her, and her mother was later to say: 'Rarely can a young girl have had
everything so much her own way as she had.'[10]

With her brothers she got on well despite hot tempers, and they
remained friends in later years. She acquired, with them, the confidence
of 'belonging among older male persons' which was one of the most
important things she kept from her childhood. It 'radiated out forever

onto all the men in the world,' she said,[11] and: 'When I went abroad as
a young girl the whole world seemed to me populated by brothers.' Yet
'it is most striking that in spite of such brothers ... and in spite of my
parents' harmonious marriage and pious fidelity towards their children
as well, I was nevertheless so bitterly lonely amongst them all and
devoted to an absolute life of fantasy as my only happiness'.[12]

There were daily pleasures. She could wander into the servants'
quarters and be given slices of cake; for 'growing pains' she was given
red-and-gold morocco-leather slippers and was carried; she would put
on dancing shoes and go sliding over the parquet floors of their huge
hall, liking the solitude as well as the movement. And there was the
pleasure of the regular journeying to the dacha in Peterhof, where
Lyolya climbed trees and played in her summer-house and raked up
leaves in early autumn, a very little girl in mauve knitted bonnet, eager
and happy.[13] But the pleasures she knew best were inward ones. She
knew two kinds of inner reality – one that simply happened to her and
that concerned God, the other that she deliberately cultivated and that
concerned people.

GOD

The first kind of inner reality was connected with faith in God and the
loss of it. This came to seem to her the dominant experience of her
childhood and is described again and again in her diaries, stories, essays
and reminiscences. 'My earliest memory is my acquaintance with God.'
The God she knew was solely *hers* – 'wholly for me alone and wholly
secret.'[14] He took her side in every dispute, listened with infinite
patience to everything she told him, and she told him everything
(prefacing each piece with 'As you know ...') in an attempt to raise the
external world to the reality that God and the internal one already had!
Protestantism does stress an individual and solitary relation to God; but
the God invoked at family prayer meetings seemed quite a different
one. At most, he was her own, dressed up stiff and formal in his Sunday
clothes and without a glance at her; nor was her God to be found in the
church. He was like an invisible grandfather, with pockets full of gifts,
known only to her, present in her solitudes, to whom she not only told
her life but also listened so intently that she was sure he spoke back. For
a long time she didn't notice that he was invisible and inaudible.

She said that she lost this belief while too young for a lucid encounter
of reason and faith, or for a chance to work out a compromise. 'God'
vanished one day when she realised that he didn't answer her. She told
this story twice.[15] One winter a servant told her he had seen two people
standing outside her own little summer house on the family estate; she
worried about them. When a couple of months later he came back
and told her they had mysteriously vanished, only their buttons, ribbons

and pipes remaining on the ground, she was very distressed, and, that night, demanded for the first time that God should tell her something in clear words: namely that – as she dimly guessed – these were not real people, for whom she had responsibility, but snowmen. No voice came: 'Like lightning, unbelief fell into my heart.'[16] Now faith was replaced by a severe time of gloom. The world lost its soul, the very vegetation became papery and she went into a frenzied increase of imaginative activity, while also building a substitute world of objective knowledge: late in the cold Russian nights, she would be sitting up in bed secretly reading, carrying out private study programmes. Her memoir, *Looking Back*, rarely gives dates or ages; the study time was clearly later than the age at which snowmen could be taken for people; but this activity seemed to her a direct consequence of the earlier incident.

Another consequence she repeatedly referred to as good was that – again because it happened so young – the *feeling* of faith, outliving the thing believed in, remained for ever, childish and irreplaceable. The self she had been projecting into God's imagined sympathy survived, too, with an unfaltering confidence in it; and she felt she kept from the original and early forfeited faith a 'prejudice against guilt',[17] as if she had learnt from the very beginning the relativity of all bidding and forbidding and hence the inappropriateness of guilt feelings about obeying and disobeying. None the less, for many years the vanishing of God meant loneliness, obsessive fantasising, a deep and long *basso continuo* of misery to everything she did.

FANTASY

About the second kind of inner reality she also wrote a great deal, later on, coming back to it so often[18] that it is clear it constituted for her a central part of what childhood *was*. It lay at the foundation of most of her fiction. This was the practice of a kind of imagining which had its origin in walking about streets or looking through windows and selecting from the faces of passers-by the ones she could dream up tales about. Without finding anything out about their owners, she would 'preserve' the faces only, allotting each a name, a history, a character, a set of feelings and ambitions, a fate. If a glimpse of one face was too slight, she would complete it from the features of another – 'till a whole bundle of people contained just one complete person.'[19] She looked after them, giving them, according to their appearance and need, the best things she could find in the shop-windows, and she wove them into families and lifetimes: this one was a sister or wife or daughter of that one, this old man was the same person, seventy years later, as that little boy, these others were his ancestors and descendants. Summers in Peterhof interrupted this intense dreaming, which needed streets and strangers, until one day she identified her 'people' with the flowers brought on trays to be planted in their dacha grounds; as different ones were brought, through summer and autumn, she kept finding different acquaintances to greet in them.[20] She was happier still to find, back in the snows of Petersburg, that her half-imaginary acquaintances were now colourful and fragrant from their transmutation.

Lou Andreas-Salomé was to be much preoccupied with the status of daydream, with the reality of what is ordinarily called unreal, and all this would go into her theorising about love, faith and art, and later into her study of psychoanalysis. The tangible sufficiency of a not-quite conscious, not-quite external world was her first remembered experience.

Once she came home and chatted about all this, until a cousin interrupted: 'You're telling lies!' and she stopped and thenceforth kept it secret.[21] The secrecy was partly what made it into a burden. For it all grew and grew in her head, becoming obsessive. Endlessly she would follow people down streets, checking and memorising their features; before going to sleep she recalled the stories about them. They became so numerous that she had to layer them in her memory: the ones invented earlier, with their more infantile fates and motives, were stacked further back, their existence sanctioned by their having continued through so much of her own life (for it went on for years) and their having become indistinguishable from actualities. At last she tried to unburden her memory by writing the whole thing down, starting with dates, names and numbers, but it made such a vast diagram of clues, with connecting lines in every direction, 'half script, half network',[22] that the responsibility for all those lives felt still heavier, since she alone could decipher it. At the time this began, she had an unquestioned belief in God, and her invented world was suffused with a 'fine glow' because each person in it had been held in God's hands.[23] When she lost this belief, it became solely a burden – now she herself must bear it all. If *she* should die – so she tortured herself in a feverish attack of measles – they would all come to ruin.

In an autobiographical novel (*Ruth*) Lou Andreas-Salomé depicted her young heroine making up people in this very same way and sometimes even avoiding or terminating real conversations in order to complete a piece of imagining. Thus it could take the place of reality. But what was it she was doing? Was there a kind of pity in it? Was it the practice of power? A neurotic obsession? In *Looking Back*, she insisted that she felt no maternal fondness for her created people: neither did she ever play in motherly fashion with dolls, though her brother Evgeny did. In another novel (*Struggling for God*), the girl called 'Märchen', or 'Fairytale', who in many ways represents Lou's adolescent self, is described as admirably free of softheartedness:

Just as she grasps everything inanimate with a poetic inwardness that strangely elevates its significance, so, without any ado, in the contemplative tranquillity of the artist, she remakes the human being into those figures that fill her mind and populate her every solitude. She penetrates into characters and conditions with a deep and subtle understanding, but it is with an artist's gaze and grasp, not merely with sincere benevolence; she is interested in *what* people are; *that* they are is far less significant to her. Not that she is bad or heartless – she would certainly not deliberately harm any one of them. She *thinks* people — that is her way of being egoistic: the way of other egoists is to do them harm.[24]

Lou was indeed always to see herself as engaged in a special kind of egoistic and proto-artistic activity, the half-inventing of a better-shaped world from the actual world's transitory and disorderly data; the half-transforming into something of her own everything that was prescribed and alien. It is interesting, and sharply honest on her part, that she admitted to understanding first, and loving second – and to being so absorbed in thinking that it looked like heartlessness. A curious godly benignity may be in it too, for although it didn't result in art (for which we customarily forgive artists their personal absorption or withdrawal) her strenuous daydreaming was an attempt to take everything and everyone under her mental wing. Possibly the reams of fiction which she did write, from her early twenties through into her early forties, should be regarded as a safer continuation of the childhood fantasies, safer because expressed conclusively in a form that no longer inhibited her life.

DISTINCTION AND BELONGING

Lyolya was not encouraged to brood over the poverty of most Petersburg inhabitants. Beggars provided a lesson not in human equality or social facts but in arithmetic and how to combine generosity with propriety: she must not hand over her ten-copeck piece but exchange it with her father for two five-copecks, to give one and keep one.[25] She belonged to the higher order of people by wealth, rank, nobility, and also by nationality; for, being a German, she knew that somewhere she had a smoother, more cultured country altogether, not chaotic like Russia but composed of neat towns and villages, well-tended meadows, tasteful constructions. The family religion may have felt like a distinction, too. Her mother disliked the barbaric, collective nature of Russian Orthodoxy; the individual pieties and strictnesses of Protestantism were more civilized and dignified. So the child had this essential, proud difference from the start. And all her life she had a guiding notion of excellence, an unyearning preoccupation with the 'lofty', 'the highest', 'high points' — not necessarily of accomplishment but of feeling and thinking, of something that flowed from sheer good fortune. This preoccupation is the more remarkable since so easily and so young she was to give up all aristocratic prestige and comfort and to choose for her life-companions not the rich and noble but the talented and original.

Another central motif was home, not the need of home but a grateful certainty of being at home. The social and geographical aspect of this was that she felt at home in a class, a family and a place. Not being quite at home in Russia (rather like not quite loving her family at the beginning) was a paradox with no disaster in it; it meant she was at home somewhere else. There is also the metaphysical aspect of home. This is hinted in the fact, as she tells it in *Looking Back*,[26] that as a child she had not believed mirrors when they told her that she had an outline, was limited and not mixed with her surroundings. When God vanished from her he vanished also from the universe which she herself (in defiance of the mirrors) always unlimitedly *was*, and so this gave her a new solidarity — in deprivation — with the entire world. She felt (her italics):

> *a then darkly awakening sensation, never again ceasing, conclusive and fundamental, of immeasurable comradeship – in fate ... with everything that exists.*[27]

Thus her loss of belief in God gave her the world, and the loss of it so young meant she kept the feeling of God, and thus, according to her infinitely optimistic interpretation of her life, she actually kept everything worth keeping.

EDUCATION

Lou von Salomé had a studious, introspective adolescence. Feeling different from everyone else, she kept away from the family balls and other social occasions – her 'whole thinking and striving developed in opposition to all family tradition'.[28] With school friends she rarely discussed her thoughts, and she felt full of age-old experience in contrast to their 'rosy' superficiality and amorous nonsense. At eight she had been to a small English private school, later to 'the big school, where I learnt nothing',[29] the *Petrischule*, a Protestant-Reformed Gymnasium, where her classmates had been a mixture of nationalities, the Petersburg foreign communities joining with Russian pupils. One reason she learnt little was that in her later school years, when Russian was the compulsory language of instruction and Lou, who spoke German and French at home, felt her Russian was not up to it, her father arranged for her to *hospitieren* (attend lessons without doing homework or exams), laughing and saying '*She* doesn't need the compulsion of school'.[30] Two exercise books remain from this period,

one in German, one in French. In the first are essays on German
literature (several on Schiller) and on general themes; she got marks of
four or five (the top mark in Russia was five). The other contains
discursive notes, or essay-plans, on the Académie Française, French
epic poems, French theatre, Descartes and Pascal. These are clever,
elegant compositions, a little but not very wayward, and not strikingly
original. The handwriting is beautiful in a fine, neat, assertive way.

Social-political questions, even at their most urgent, seem never to
have become quite real to Lou. She was fourteen when the first
movement 'to the people' took place, that idealistic attempt of young
Russian intellectuals to help peasants and workers by going, in their
hundreds, to work with them in villages and factories. The passionate
theorising that went with this penetrated into the secondary schools;
everyone talked about it. Lou was excited by it, too, 'especially as
despite connections with the previous tsar, the parental house was full
of anxiety about the reigning political system, that is after the reactionary change in the "tsar-liberator", Alexander II, after he had put an
end to serfdom';[31] and later on she kept hidden in her desk a picture of
the revolutionary, Vera Zasulich (who, in 1878, tried to assassinate the
Governor of Petersburg because of his cruelty to political prisoners,
thus initiating a series of terrorist attacks); mainly, though, she was
aloof from such things. Had she not been (she was to recognise), she
might then have made lifelong connections with Russia, and her whole
subsequent life would have been different: perhaps she would never
have left. But she was preparing to go abroad and to lead a life of her
own. She was also going through a love experience that was to deter-
mine the nature of her emotional life for a very long time.

HENDRIK GILLOT

At seventeen, Lou was hating her confirmation classes with Pastor
Dalton, the family pastor. He too was worried about them ever since his
unassailable statement that you can't even *think* of a place where God is
not, had been assailed by this pupil: 'yes, you can, Hell'.[32] When Lou
heard one Pastor Gillot spoken of as the most brilliant and most
unorthodox Protestant preacher in Petersburg, she went to listen to
him. She immediately 'knew' that he was for her. The most important
of her later relationships were to begin with just such moments of
instant recognition. In Gillot she felt she had found at last 'a human
being' and 'the quintessence of all reality'.[33] She wrote to him. The
letter is the first central document of her character. It was impeccable in
its politeness:

Respected Herr Pastor,
You will certainly skim these lines with some bewilderment — please
forgive me for burdening and disturbing you with them...

but also bold in its request: to be allowed to write to him whenever she was tormented by intolerable doubts and questions. She introduced herself:

> The person writing to you, Herr Pastor, is a seventeen-year-old girl who is lonely in the midst of her family and surroundings, lonely in the sense that no one shares her views, let alone satisfies her longing for fuller knowledge. Perhaps it is my whole way of thinking that isolates me from most girls of my age and from our circle — there is scarcely anything worse for a young girl, here, than to differ from the rule in her likes and dislikes, in her character and her views. But it is so bitter to close everything up in oneself because one would otherwise give offence, bitter to stand so wholly alone because one lacks that easy-going agreeable manner which wins people's trust and love.[34]

She explained that she had lost her 'literal' faith, and now, repulsed both by the surrounding dark orthodoxy and by the sober rationalism of 'our day', was groping for the truth, that no one had suspected her rebellious thoughts until the confirmation crisis, that she had thrown off reverie, shyness and all received principles, in fact all restraints, that she would love to attend his sermons if only she was not prevented by her family's adherence to Pastor Dalton, whose views seemed to her blind, intolerant, narrow-minded – all calculating cleanliness. With an impassioned rhetoric she said:

'I *cannot* let myself be blindfolded . . . You can imagine, Herr Pastor, with what desperate energy a person goes in the direction where the light beckons . . .' begging him not to misinterpret her request, for 'even in a girl there can live a wild untameable longing for everything ideal, and it can so repress every other thought that only one resolve stands unshakeably before her: at any cost!'

Pastor Gillot responded welcomingly and Lou went to visit him. As she later said that the essential story of the ensuing acquaintance is told in her novel *Ruth*, the main events of the novel can be taken as true — except that it omits the specifically religious solemnity it had for her. Ruth slips her chaperone to reach the unknown teacher's house and presents herself to him breathless with emotion, imperious in her need and certainty, yet with voice faltering from fear. The teacher says 'you come to me?'[35] and accepts her both into his spiritual tuition and his fatherly arms. For Lou, in addition, he became someone who took the place of the God she had lost years ago; she did not merely respect, but worshipped him.

She became his unique and special pupil, although she did not tell her family. To judge by the *Ruth* version, the lessons may have begun with some ferocious breaking of her will, as if she had first to be tamed; whereby it is important to realise that she wanted just this – to be forced out of her fantasies and into intellectual reality. As a man of terrible thoroughness, able to look into others' souls so fiercely they felt they stood naked before him, opponent of all fantasising, representative of the 'unbounded direction towards clear development of the understanding',[36] Gillot demanded of Lou that she give up her daydreams and do so by bringing them all to him: she must hand over every detail of her imaginary world. Letters to Lou from an older relative speak of the struggle this caused in her: 'How dreadful the conflict in you must have been, before you wholly gave in ... How difficult this "bowing" was for you in particular, I do know, as I know you so well!'[37]

This painful yielding and absolute trust – and the subsequent disappointment – were the decisive experiences of her adolescence. In 1900, she thought back to her early youth, recalling the tireless inward inventing and working away at herself which was like the endless gnawing of a mouse, and remembered how Gillot rescued her from it. She had been trapped in the heavy darkness of her fantasy world. In one go, he released her from it all. Not only his teaching with the stress on logic and learning, but his enormous personal influence, was what rescued her. The disturbing aspect of it was that, shifting her devotion from the fantasies to the teacher, she began to worship the teacher as God.[38]

The lessons were emotionally and mentally so demanding that in one of them she fainted. For Gillot offered, along with command and rigour, also love and personal closeness: she was sitting on his lap when she fainted. It is probable that many lessons took place in this manner – in *Ruth* there is much stroking of hair, and enthusiastic or tender embracing. Only later, it seems, did the feeling become on his part erotic, but the intensity of feeling which was there in them both from the start – in *Looking Back* she calls it a 'love relationship' – actually damaged her health, as did the extremely strenuous study programme he set her.

It was by no means just an alternative course of preparation for confirmation. Gillot took Lou through the whole history of philosophy, with lectures on the origins, history and transformations of religion. Doubtless these were based on the massive tome by Otto Pfleiderer, *Philosophy of Religion on a Historical Foundation*, which had recently (1878) been published and which Gillot was translating into Dutch. Pfleiderer's comparative approach gives more importance to the human need for religion and the variety of forms it has taken than to the exclusive claims of one of those forms. His opening motto is from Schiller: 'Behind the veil of the religious life lies religion itself'. Gillot also read Kant with Lou (in Dutch, which she learned to please him) and among the non-Christian thinkers he touched on she was most attracted to Spinoza, 'the one thinker to whom I had, still almost a child, an intuitive and almost worshipful attitude'.[39] And now – to apply a sentence from *Ruth* – 'so rapidly did she get used to forming her thoughts with logical acuity, and giving them an energetic direction towards knowledge, that it was as if she had never lived in the fantasy world of dreams.'[40] Indeed the lessons prepared her so well for her subsequent study in Zurich that Nietzsche, who met her straight after it, found her able to hold her own in philosophical talk with him.

In February 1879, Lou's father died; he was 74 and had a 'wonder-fully easy' death. Now that she need not fear hurting him with her religious rebelliousness, she told her mother about the lessons, appar-ently on Gillot's prompting. Eavesdropping the interview that followed between mother and teacher, she heard the former say, 'You're taking on a great responsibility for my daughter.' He replied, 'I *want* to be responsible for this child.' Her mother was upset, and storms took place. 'You ask me to be loving towards her,' she wrote to the relative who was Lou's confidante, 'but how is that possible when she has such a stubborn character and always insists on her own will in every-thing?'[41] But, even though outraged by Lou's decision to leave the church (an affront to her and indeed to the Petersburg Protestant community), her mother gave in to her wishes; the lessons continued.

Gillot seems to have 'recognised' Lou in the same way as she recog-nised him; but his sexual passion found no welcome in her. When she learnt that he had begun to make 'family arrangements for a union with me', the shock to her was that of a second loss of God – and she expressed it in the same violent way: 'With a single blow, what I had worshipped dropped out of my heart and senses and became alien.' It was also a human failure – in him, who now revealed himself as having a mere man's needs and weakness – and in herself, for 'when the decisive moment unexpectedly demanded that I bring Heaven down to Earth, I failed [*versagte*].'[42] Later she saw this failure as due to the inhibitions of her Nordic temperament: the body was erotically disturbed but the soul knew only love for a lord, or, as she herself put it, her love was directed to something beyond and bigger than the man. She also undoubtedly foresaw with what force she would be subjected to him if she did accept his proposal – she would never have been free again. For, as many of her fictional works were to indicate, the stronger the desire the stronger the subordination, and this, above all things, she did not want. In fact, Lou was never to yield herself sexually to a man until, by age and position and accomplishment, she was free of the risk of subjugation.

With a belief that her love life was over for ever, she refused Gillot, and she wrote, then or a little later, a poem called 'Death-plea' ['*Todes-bitte*'],[43] in which she offers herself to him in her coffin and tells him to stroke the hair of her corpse and kiss her dead mouth. (She herself has called the poem 'arch'.) And she fell ill, a pulmonary haemorrhaging, while at the same time feeling an increase in courage, a certain release and joy. Gillot had freed her to herself, opened life's gate for her, and sent her out through it 'boyishly ready' rather than 'girlishly depend-ent,'[44] and now she left her miserable childhood years and entered 'the wonderful years of my youth abroad',[45] for her uneasy but amazingly accommodating mother took her to Switzerland for cure and study. Gillot, whose interests had always been 'over the border', had also been her definitive 'derussification'.

To live abroad, she needed a passport, hard to get when one wasn't a church member; Gillot arranged a special permit for her through a service in a Dutch church where he had a friend. This ceremony, one Sunday in May 1879, not only got her the passport but marked her separation from and permanent connection with Gillot. The text he used was Isaiah 43: 'Fear not, for I have redeemed you; I have called you by your name; you are mine.'[46] He had in fact changed her name to 'Lou'. In *Ruth*, the teacher says to the girl as she goes abroad: 'I'm not setting you free, when I let you go. From the distance you shall belong to me doubly. Your promise is for your whole life.'[47] Lou may have understood Gillot's words to her like this. But they were no longer the words of God, rather of God's priest, blessing her on the path 'to everything lofty and beautiful to which I aspired.'[48]

ZURICH: POEMS

She now spent a year in Zurich with her mother, staying in the house of friends. Though not a registered student, she attended university lectures on logic, metaphysics and the history of religion. She got on well with the venerable professor, Alois Biedermann (author of *Christian Dogmatics* (1869), which argued the need for a transcendental realism). Professor Biedermann was delighted with her 'unusually intensive mental striving'[49] and said she made the impression 'of a fundamentally pure being who had, however, with exceptional energy concentrated solely on mental development' – he called her 'almost unwomanly' in her mental directness and independence of will, in both of which she was (he underlined the word) 'a *diamond*'.[50]

Some of Lou's notebooks of the Zurich period remain, filled with detailed notes from philosophical texts and her own earnest comment-aries on them. She also wrote poems, both then and earlier. Although she tried to get some published, she did not consider herself a very serious poet and later scarcely referred to the poems which did appear in various journals; they seem rather to have rubbed off her life by a natural friction and to have scattered. It is characteristic of the early poems that they express not so much moods and sentiments as desires, intentions, promises and demands: the twelve lines of the 'Death-plea'

are almost all in imperative mode. The manner of the poems is elevated
and their subjects are large and vague: tremendous love of life, desire
for experience, search for a path, need for space. There is a vital,
immediate voice in them and a vigorous syntax and structure.

Although it is not clear that any of the poems are worth preserving for
their own sake, two at least should be mentioned for their biographical
importance. Each contains programmatic statements about Lou's
attitude to life, and each was to mean a great deal to Nietzsche. 'To
Pain' ['*An den Schmerz*'][51] moved him to tears every time he read it and
had a 'complete power' over him.[52] Its twenty-four lines maintain that
Pain and Battle are not destructive but come to remind the spirit of its
strength: 'It's struggle that has made the greatest great,/Struggle for the
goal, on impassable paths'.[53] The other poem, 'Prayer to Life' ['*Lebensgebet*'] pleased Nietzsche so much (especially its last two lines) that he
set it to music. It was written soon after Lou left Russia, when she was
ill.

Truly, the way a friend loves friend
Is how I love you, riddle, life –
Whether I've rejoiced in you or wept,
Whether you've brought me joy or grief.

I *love* you, with your sorrow too;
And if you must destroy me, still,
I'll tear myself from your arms, as friend
Tears himself from the bosom of friend.

I clasp you with my strength entire!
May your flame kindle me, your riddle
Even in the ardour of the battle
Only more deeply plumb my depths.

Millennia-long to be! to think!
Enclose me fast in both your arms:
If you've no happiness left to give me –
Well then! you still possess your pain.[54]

This desire to accept all that life could possibly bring, Nietzsche was to
call heroic. Such an attitude of acceptance has ancestors in, for example,
Mörike's 'Prayer' ['*Gebet*'] and Goethe's 'Blessed Yearning' ['*Selige
Sehnsucht*'], from both of which it also greatly diverges. Mörike's poem
starts: 'Lord, send what Thou wilt/Whether pleasant or painful,/I am
delighted that both/Spring from Thy hands',[55] but it ends with 'pious
modesty of contentment' ['*holdes Bescheiden*'] – very different from
Lou's summoning of cosmically huge pleasures and torments. The
comparison with Goethe – 'I will praise the living thing/That longs for
death in flame'[56] – points up the powerfully erotic quality of Lou's

poem. In the way she emphasises the word 'love', in her imagery of
clasping and being clasped, of being set on fire by another's flame and
of wanting her depths to be plumbed, and in the whole readiness to
receive pain and even destruction in the intense embrace, her poem
resounds with a specifically female sexuality, which is not so much
disguised as vigorously re-channelled towards an idea – the idea of life.
It is interesting that to the man who offered her his physical love Lou
wrote a poem offering her imagined corpse in return, whereas here, in
relation to an abstraction, she seeks the most fierily passionate embrace.
This prayer without God, which is also a love poem without a beloved,
shows what an urgent, painful and triumphant fight Lou must have
waged in herself in order to close off her love life for ever, as she
claimed she did, and to wrench the newly awakened energies (without
looking at them too closely) into intellectual directions.

Possibly, too, just as she had thought in her childhood that mirrors
lied when they told her she had a precise outline and gave her an exact
counterpart of herself, so now she suspected both falsehood and
captivity in any relationship that would mean reflection of one limited
person in another limited person. To avoid that, she sent her love out
not to a man but to something far more vast and diffuse, something she
could think of as wholly and uniquely intoxicating: life itself, the very
sensation of it. Thus she transcended the conventional preoccupation of
a young woman of her time and background: to whom could one give
one's heart? whom should one marry? how soon would one settle
down? as well as the alternative preoccupation: by what means, by what
exertions, could one assert oneself *against* that convention? Something
in her so impetuously denied the conventional that she avoided being
fixed even in a posture of defying it; 'Prayer to Life' expressed that
impetus.

IMPRESSIONS OF LOU

In a photograph taken when she was twenty-one, Fräulein von Salomé,
in a dark, undecorated dress, high at the neck and with sleeves to the
wrist, and with her hair drawn fiercely back from her serious, pale face,
combines a preoccupied gaze with a slightly pouting crossness. She is
tall and proud, awkward and defensive. The head looks masculine,
firmly handsome, not quite related to the slim figure. She looks as if
there are people she wouldn't like to know; all the same, one would
have liked to know her. She looks resolute and unsmilingly opposed to
her own beauty, and though her face was once described as having an
'ancient Roman expression', it is not at all the face of one who braves
the public scene but is private and intent on something of her own.

Nearly everyone who knew her in her first year or so abroad admired
her exceedingly, and practically all those who recorded their im-

pressions noted an extraordinary strength of intelligence. (In this, and in the way she effortlessly attracted everyone to her, she is rather like Isabel Archer in Henry James's *Portrait of a Lady*, which was published this very same year, 1881.) It was, of course, an astonishing thing to meet a young and charming woman who was not concerned to exert any charm but that of her mind, but it is still remarkable how many were convinced her mind was an exceptional power to be used for great purposes. She was 'really a genius and of quite heroic character', she had pushed to the furthest horizon of the thinkable and was 'a genius in mind and character!'[57] She was too 'peculiar as a girl' to be understood in a hurry: she 'understood the world like a man' and was 'a lovable, winning, genuinely feminine being ... who has renounced all the means that women use and has taken up the weapons with which men conduct the battle of life, with a certain bitter exclusivity. Sharp judgment on everything ... no trace of forgiveness, a cold, unfortunately too often negative and analytical philosophising ... but she is too amiable, sincere, friendly, for the cold of intellect to suppress the human being in her.'[58] How was it she 'always seemed to represent something unattainably lofty and holy?'[59] She had 'superior assurance ... fineness of tact ...', was 'a quite exceptional creature ... So much cleverness in a 21-year-old girl's head would almost arouse a shudder if genuine tenderness and the most perfect morality were not combined with it. She is a phenomenon that scarcely seems possible, until one sees her in her pure effect ... She is a person of genius'.[60]

According to a much later acquaintance, she had already shown genius in coming abroad at all: 'the atmosphere of the aristocratic German colony of St Petersburg to which her family belonged was very much the indoor air of a nicely warmed but tightly closed-in drawing room. It was the first sign of real human genius that she succeeded in breaking out of this atmosphere not by smashing the window and running away but by the quiet force of her will.'[61]

The three main experiences Lou had left behind – the Petersburg community, the privacy of her own God and of her intensely cultivated inner world, the relationship with Gillot – all had in common both a certain exclusive narrowness and a sort of supremacy, a sense of having the best that there was. Renouncing these three things meant choosing experiences that were opposite to these in being wide and all-inclusive: instead of the tight community – all of Europe; instead of God – the whole godless world; instead of love – all men as intellectual brothers. Yet these latter experiences were also similar to the earlier ones in that Lou still sought the top, the best, in them all – that same thing, I think, that she was to call (when writing of Ibsen) the 'wild'. The 'wild duck' meant to her the free and natural aspiration to an ideal. Whether it was continued good luck, or a strange shaping of life's possibilities by her peculiarly firm and hopeful approach to them, it is hard to say, but she now did find, again and again, something of what she had originally had: a world hers by right; men as brothers; repeatedly a distinguished scholar ready to be her teacher.

Lou Salomé with Rée and Nietzsche, taken in
a photographer's studio in Lucerne, 1882
Reproduced by courtesy of Insel Verlag

CHAPTER THREE

Paul Rée – Meeting with Nietzsche

'Sharp-witted as an eagle and courageous as a lion.'[1] NIETZSCHE

In the first days of 1882, hoping the southern climate would improve Lou's health, her mother took her to Italy. They spent three months in Rome, arriving there in February. Italy was no occasion for meeting Italians, nor for sightseeing. Lou was shown monuments and watched carnival celebrations, but she was seeking minds, not buildings or events, and Rome was

> a background indistinctly painted with all sorts of ruins, and in front of it an experience of sheer future and youthfulness, a beginning of youth after its first precious but almost tragically difficult years . . . The clearest thing I saw of Rome was its sunshine.[2]

In that sunshine she straightaway found the very thing she was hoping for: great friendship. In fact, a chain of friendships: first with the famous *idéaliste*, Malwida von Meysenbug, then through Malwida with the philosopher Paul Rée, and then through both of them she made friends with Friedrich Nietzsche.

Malwida von Meysenbug*, like the von Salomés a German of Huguenot descent, was a friend of many distinguished people (she was Nietzsche's 'best friend in the world') and was herself distinguished as a feminist writer who put her energy into promoting 'noble' relations between the sexes. She was also a great fosterer of intellectual communities. Five years previously she had arranged a rather notable one when she, Nietzsche, Paul Rée and a gifted student, Albert Brenner, had spent some creative months reading, writing and discussing together in a villa in Sorrento which Nietzsche called their 'monastery of free spirits'. Educated girls now gathered in Malwida's salon in the Via della Polveriera, to read together and to hear lectures from invited speakers. Lou von Salomé joined these gatherings.

Malwida liked Lou immediately. She saw in her what Lou saw in Rome: youthful promise amid unimportant ruins, sunshine, a future; and felt a tenderness for her she had rarely felt for any young woman. Moved by her poems, she told Lou she had a great task and was destined for a noble blossoming,[3] and described her to others as richly

gifted and lovable, 'a wonderfully gifted girl'.⁴ She was so sure that Lou
had the very mind, the very enthusiasm that were adapted to furthering
the cause to which she had devoted her own life that she called her 'a
high apostle of our new belief'⁵ – that is, of belief in the emancipation
of the female intellect and in a new kind of relationship between man
and woman. Her rapid conviction about Lou foreshadows Nietzsche's
that Lou was the perfect furtherer of *his* ideas (oddly, as Nietzsche's
ideas were not Malwida's). But Lou did not consider staying close to
Malwida. She quietly said no to a career in feminism as she had tacitly
said no to all paths, conservative and emancipatory, open to her in
Russia.

On 17 March, the philosopher Paul Rée came to give a talk to the
group of intellectual girls. With her way of immediately recognising the
people she wanted, Lou recognised Rée as soon as she saw him. He was
a lucid, well-informed and thorough thinker. He was self-conscious and
affectionate. He was, above all, someone with whom friendship would
carry no risk of her falling in love. She thus chose him for herself (or
responded to the sense of predestination towards him) in much the
same way as she had chosen Gillot, though that was love while this was
avoidance of love and felt more like liberation from her fate. They made
friends and plunged into talk.

PAUL RÉE

Rée, the son of a rich Pomeranian landowner, was then thirty-two. He
seems to have been the born academic even if, because of his Positivism,
he never got a university post. From boyhood he had been devoted to
moral philosophy, and by 1881 was the author of two well-received
books. *Psychological Observations*, published anonymously in 1875, was
a collection of elegantly sceptical aphorisms, more damning than La
Rochefoucauld's, on humanity in general and on scholars, women and
social mores especially. Lou referred to them as 'these grey-haired
sentences'.⁶ *The Origin of Moral Feelings*,* published under Rée's name
in 1877, was the first major statement of his philosophy. Through this
he won his renown as a Positivist, that is, as a clever exponent of a
scientifically- and evolutionarily-minded rationalism. Its virtues are its
pleasant lucidity and its exemplariness.

Neither the graceful cynicism of his first book nor the cold demolition
of feelings he was planning in his second had prevented Rée from
leaping around his room with delight when Friedrich Nietzsche wrote
to him to thank him for a copy of the former. This was still 1875, a time
when Nietzsche was withdrawing from Wagner and from metaphysics
towards a cooler rationality, just such as Rée was practising. Rée
meanwhile was seeking another mind's light and warmth. When he met
Lou, his close friendship with Nietzsche had lasted seven years, and

when he arrived in Rome that March he came from Genoa, where he had spent five weeks in close companionship with Nietzsche.*

Everyone liked being with Rée: he was reliable, kind, brotherly and down-to-earth; he forestalled requests, lent money, thought up remedies, sent messages to relatives (he kept in touch with Nietzsche's mother and sister). He was a perfect balance of cleverness and niceness. His melancholy was less well noticed. But an uncomfortable estrangement from his own principles showed not only in his jokes about them but, more significantly, in his constant self-criticism and earnest enquiry into his own motives for this or that action, such that one might scarcely believe the same man had spent years arguing the absence of free will and reducing all motives to the evolution of self-interest. One of his psychological observations had run: 'Intellectual shortcomings sometimes look like virtues of the heart'[7] and this, like some others of its kind, may well have been directed at himself. He was Jewish and hated himself for it (he fainted when his Jewishness was first mentioned in Lou's hearing).[8] He was a gambler, and had come more directly from the casinos at Monte Carlo when he arrived that day in Rome, and he sometimes felt degraded by this passion. He felt unlikeable and he carried a phial of poison about with him in case of an impulse to suicide.

The friendship with Lou saved Rée from his melancholy side for several years. It was a friendship that began and continued in intense talk. At the very beginning, much of the talk was exchanged while he accompanied her home late at night from the Meysenbug salon. They talked of philosophy, of their lives, of Nietzsche. Malwida disliked Rée's theories ('his views are fundamentally wrong')[9] as much as she liked his personality, and was afraid he would lead her protegée astray philosophically. She soon feared he was leading her astray in other ways, too. Lou had put so much into her love for Gillot and had been so shaken by her disappointment in him that she had decided her love life was closed off for her whole lifetime,[10] but Rée, though he believed one should not marry and bring new people into this bad world, hadn't got feelings and theories united: he approached her mother and proposed marriage. Lou naturally declined. Rée got a talking-to from Malwida, who finally decided that he would have to depart since he could not control his will; but he stayed and he controlled it, firmly persuaded by Lou, who was merely angry with him for making such a mistake, and whose own will was fully under control. She loved their nocturnal walks and took pleasure in defying the conventions; but her behaviour (whether proper or provocative, or both) was guided by the certainty that love was out of the question. She wrote an aphorism that went: 'When someone falls unhappily in love with a woman, the degree of her friendship for him can best be judged according to whether she counts his love as one of her happy or her sad experiences.'[11] For her this had been a sad one. But she won Rée over to sexless friendship and now proceeded to challenge convention more heavily with a plan for their living together.

What she wanted was to set up a small intellectual community. The first and dominant version of this was that it would consist of herself and Rée only, with many visiting friends. She was, oddly enough, convinced of the feasibility of this by a dream, in which she had seen 'a pleasant study full of books and flowers, flanked by two bedrooms, and, moving to and fro between us, comrades in work, a cheerful serious circle.'[12] Another version, which for a while took the place of the first, or caused it to be postponed, was that Rée, his friend Nietzsche, she herself and an older woman for chaperone, would live together in a university town, attending lectures, discussing ideas and writing.* Had this been realised, it would have been Sorrento over again, only with Lou in Albert Brenner's place. Both plans contained a challenge not only to propriety but also to sexuality: just let it *dare* be felt! Both also laid emphasis on the equality of all concerned: in Nietzsche and Rée, Lou thus perhaps meant to overcome Gillot, replacing master and lover with comrades – just as loving (as it turned out) and on one side even more exalted.

The first plan was very like what they later did. But the 'trinity' with Nietzsche never became actual, although it was definitely enough conceived of, even before Nietzsche arrived, for locations to be considered – Genoa, Vienna, Munich, Paris ... – and for it to be referred to as their 'Winterplan'.[13] Again, Malwida von Meysenbug was anxious for her young friends and worried about the misrepresent-ation of her principles they seemed bent on bringing about. Of course she understood the charm of the Winterplan but she was appalled by the flouting of opinion, and even more by the personal risks it meant taking.

LETTER FROM LOU IN ROME TO GILLOT

Opposition also came from another quarter: Gillot. Lou had written to him about it, expecting him to be pleased that she had friends he might have chosen for her, and that she was putting an idea into practice, not just imagining it. But he said it was unrealistic and just as buoyant with fantasy as any of her earlier ideas. She kept a copy of her reply to him that 26 March, which amounts to another central declaration about herself. It starts indignantly:

I've read your letter at least five times, but I haven't yet got the hang of it. What, in the name of the three devils, have I done wrong? I thought this was the very thing to make you full of praise for me ... But now you assert that the whole idea is just as fantastic as any of my earlier ones ... and that I cannot properly judge men who are men who are so much older and superior like Rée, Nietzsche and others. But you're mistaken about this.

This is unceremonious, self-assured and colloquial: she did not cultivate respect for her elders. 'Nietzsche, Rée and others' were all, she implied, her equals. (People of her own age were often astonished by her light references to 'Malwida' and 'Malwida's circle'.) 'The essential thing', the letter went on:

(and for me the *humanly* essential thing is *only* Rée) is something one knows either straightaway or not at all. Anyway, he is not yet completely won over, he is still somewhat bewildered, but on our nightly walks between 12.00 and 2.00 in the Roman moonlight ... I expound it to him more and more successfully. Malwida too is against our plan, and I am sorry about this, for I like her enormously. But it has been clear to me for a long time now that basically we always have something different in mind, even where we agree. Her usual way of expressing herself is: 'we' may not do this or that, or 'we' must accomplish this or that – and I've no idea who this 'we' actually is – some ideal or philosophical party probably – but I myself know only of 'I'.

So far this sounds a typical (and remarkably modern) rebellious voice. But what comes next is Lou's main and original statement about herself:

I can neither live according to models nor shall I ever be a model for anyone at all; on the contrary – what I shall quite certainly do is make my own life according to myself, whatever may come of it. In this I have no principle to represent, but something much more wonderful – something that is inside oneself and is hot with sheer life, and rejoices and wants to get out.

In conclusion, she queries Gillot's hopes for her: don't all his loving and lofty expectations really amount to a wish to see her caged and tamed?

You also write: you had always thought of this sort of wholehearted devotion to purely intellectual goals as a 'transition' for me. Well, what do you mean by 'transition'? If any other goals are supposed to stand behind it, such as would make one give up the most magnificent and most hard-won thing on earth, namely freedom, then I want to stay forever in the transition, for I shall not give that up.[14]

Her defiance was conscious of no precursors. Indeed, had she looked for any, they would probably have had to be male ones, and it is interesting that Lou wrote almost as if there were no sexual discrimination going on at all. In fact, throughout her life she never said anything indicating resentment of male privilege. *All* conventions should be challenged, she implied, not just those which restricted women. Above all, she was, despite her indignations, happy. The happiness may have been somewhat emphatic, but it is very persuasive: 'I am sure nobody', she wrote, 'could become happier than I now am.'

NIETZSCHE'S MEETING WITH LOU

Nietzsche was dedicated to thought. He was often ill. These circumstances, and his life as a *fugitivus errans* – he was forever searching out some Swiss or Italian spot with a healthy enough climate – made lasting acquaintances difficult for him; moreover, nobody ever fell in love with him. He very much needed both a secretary – as he became increasingly blind – and a wife, though he often said he would not marry, for he hated to be woven up into the civilised order of things. Perhaps he knew that he ought not to marry. If he had syphilis, as is now generally believed, it is unlikely he did not know about it. But then it is likely that for short periods he thought he was cured. Sometimes the attacks of illness held off for weeks on end, and in the spring of 1882 he felt better than ever before. At times he asked his friends to look out for a wife for him and once (1876) unthinkingly proposed to a young lady by employing as go-between the man she was already engaged to. He also wanted someone who would be the 'heir' to his philosophy: this was the word he was to use again and again of his hope regarding Lou von Salomé.

Malwida von Meysenbug and Paul Rée seem both to have felt that Lou would be the ideal companion and fellow thinker for Nietzsche. Rée wrote to him about her and Nietzsche replied: 'Greet this Russian girl for me if there is any sense in doing so: I lust after souls of this kind. I even plan to go out on the prowl for them – I need them because of what I want to do in the next ten years. Marriage is another matter – I could agree at most to a two-year marriage.'[15] Some days later, a letter from Malwida von Meysenbug brought the suitability of Lou much closer to him. She was 'a very remarkable girl' who in her philosophical thinking had reached the same position as Nietzsche himself – 'that is, practical idealism, leaving aside all metaphysical preconceptions ... Rée and I agree in wanting to see you some time together with this extraordinary creature'.[16]

Lou was leaving Rome at the end of April to travel north through Milan, but was ready to change route in order to meet Nietzsche; she was astonished and aggrieved when he suddenly set off by boat for Messina, comparing himself to Christopher Columbus voyaging to the edge of the earth – a perfect climate was as important as perfect company, and he told Rée about the lovely Messina air and the pleasure of picking oranges. Rée wrote back to say long live the oranges, but how could he do it? He *must* meet the young Russian, who was 'an energetic, incredibly clever creature with the most girlish, even childlike, qualities' and who was always able to forestall his (Rée's) arguments![17] Whether or not he received this letter in time, Nietzsche left Messina and arrived in Rome on 24 April meaning to go on to Switzerland. He met Lou von Salomé that day or the next.

The meeting took place in St Peter's Basilica. Here Rée had been using one of the smaller chapels to work in (to think 'ardently and piously' and write his next atheistic book), and Lou was with him there when Nietzsche came in. She recorded his first words to her: 'From what stars have we dropped down to each other here?'[18] Later she described him: of middle height, thirty-eight years old, he made little impression from a distance, but, closer, one saw the very expressive smile. He spoke strangely soundlessly (though listeners to his lectures have called his voice magically compelling). Lou liked the way his half-blind eyes didn't spy out or blink or try to penetrate, but seemed instead to protect an inner treasure. She noticed his thoughtful, solitary gait and his incomparably 'beautiful and noble' hands.[19]

For Nietzsche, this meeting was part of a grand aspiration: to come down from his philosophical solitude, to give up breathing the icy male electric air of the summits of intellect and try living amongst other people. Like Zarathustra, weary of his wisdom after ten years in the wilderness, he said: 'I no longer want to be alone, I want to learn to be a human being again. Ah, in this *pensum* [task] I have almost everything still to learn.'[20] He could sigh over himself, and also laugh at himself – 'how near and strange it seems to me, old hermit that I am!'[21] But it was a solemn turning point for him.

Eight months earlier Nietzsche had experienced in Sils Maria (high up on a mountain) what has been called his Damascus day, when he first conceived of the 'eternal return of all things' – his conception of a metaphysics without a *Jenseits*, a world without otherworld, and without inherent values. Endurance of this nearly unendurable idea (so it undoubtedly was to him) made him finally a *Ja-Sagender*,* an accepter and lover of his fate. He had conceived the figure of Zarathustra and planned the 'poem' about him, though he didn't begin writing it until after the entire episode of his acquaintance with Lou von Salomé. He was beginning to consider himself a seer and singer, as well as the herald of new values. He had just written the very fine book *The Gay Science*, which records his radiant mood of January 1882 and commends the strengths of the 'higher' human being. He was increasingly inspired and uplifted. None the less he had remained close friends with the earthbound Rée, and a sign that the new visionary phase was different from the earlier Wagnerian one was the importance the music of *Carmen* had for him. So Wagner was replaced as composer-friend by Peter Gast,* as music by the 'idyllic' Bizet, and now as love by Lou von Salomé. Nietzsche was starting a great creative period when Lou crossed his path, and the place he marked out for her in his life was correspondingly sublime. Her influence upon him, too, was correspondingly important.

ORTA, LUCERNE

During their few days together in Rome, Nietzsche read out parts of *The Gay Science*, fell in love with Lou very fast and asked Rée to convey to her a proposal of marriage (again not knowing to what extent the messenger was himself involved). To avoid hurting him, Lou sent answer that marriage would mean forfeiting a pension she was entitled to (Nietzsche had little money, so this reason had some weight). Separate travelling brought Rée, Nietzsche, Lou and her mother to the mountain town of Orta, north of Milan. Here on 5 May Lou and Nietzsche climbed the Monte Sacro. It was probably on this height that Nietzsche told Lou 'in a quiet voice and with all the signs of deepest horror'[22] his doctrine of the eternal recurrence. Monte Sacro remained a treasured memory. Nietzsche had there the most enchanting dream of his life;[23] he was amazed by Lou's intelligence and 'free-spiritedness'. His hope rose high; he must speak to her again, and he appointed a meeting in the Löwengarten in Lucerne. At this meeting (on 13 May) Lou must have talked both tactfully and ardently, for afterwards marriage was not mentioned again, yet their friendship prospered and Nietzsche went on believing he had found his 'alter ego' in her. He intended now to work towards his highest goal with her help; never had he 'willed higher or acted more sublimely'.[24] A token of his hope in her was his taking her from Lucerne to Tribschen, where he had spent unforgettable times with Wagner, and talking to her, with tears, about that now finished friendship.[25]

Perhaps the Löwengarten conversation was reflected in the surprising photograph the three friends had taken of themselves in Lucerne: Lou kneels in a cart, wielding a flower-decked whip, the two men stand harnessed to the cart by ribbons. It provokes questions: is the woman being carried by the strength of the men while she spurs them on to *their* achievements, or is she lashing them along on a glorious journey of her own? The faces do not answer: Lou's is attentive and strained, gazing obediently at the camera, yet also unexpectedly sensual-looking and faintly mischievous; Paul Rée is ill at ease; he faces the camera and tries to smile, but also averts his eyes and wears an acid expression of self-dislike (Rée, who was quite handsome, thought himself ugly); only Nietzsche looks pleased to be photographed. As if acting out his character, he gazes with wide-open, visionary eyes ('seven-eighths blind' as he was) upward and out of the picture.

Lou and her mother went back to Zurich, then to Hamburg and Berlin. The mother now meant to take the daughter home, but Lou meant to stay in the West and realise her eccentric study plan. There was a great deal of conflict and argument. Lou's mother firmly told Nietzsche a few months later that she was against the idea of their planned life in Paris and that she did not see a woman's life in 'the striving for mental perfection, at least in the way my daughter seeks it',[26] and considered Lou's physical frailty to be the result of excessive mental effort. She was evidently a power to be reckoned with, and it says a lot for Lou's determination that she could once again defeat this strong-willed mother, who had after all the whole force of convention and opinion on her side and was further supported by her son Evgeny, who came from Russia for this very purpose. Finally (Lou wrote mildly in her memoir), 'the last fights burned down' and she won her point, helped by Rée's obvious trustworthiness and by his own mother's availability as chaperone. Mother and brother went back to Russia. Lou spent the next month or so on the Rée estate in Stibbe.

LETTERS TO LOU FROM RÉE AND NIETZSCHE

That May and June in Zurich and Hamburg, Lou received many letters from Paul Rée, all intimate, warm and caring. He now used the 'Du' form of 'you' (Nietzsche never did), called her 'Lu' and '*Schneckli*' [little snail], and himself her '*Häusli*' or – in his local idiom – '*Hüsung*' [little house]. This pair of images reflects a truth. No one knew Rée's 'supraterrestrial kindness' better than she did, Lou said later: 'I, who sat in it like a young bird in its maternal nest'.[27] Rée was a godsend to her: he gave moral support, intellectual stimulus, the attention of a whole family of brothers, practical help and – ever since his love was rejected – endlessly patient companionship. He offered her a home on his parents' estate, and was himself the perfect emotional 'home', from which she could venture into great thoughts and great talk, and to which she could return for recuperation. 'The most essential use that I can be to you', he wrote to her in August that year, 'will always consist in my being your "*Hüsung*"; that you have a home in me. Someone on whom you can securely rely in the great world, who, except for his book, regards you as the sole task of his life.'[28]

At the same time Nietzsche, too, was writing to her, and for a month her wish for a shared life of study – as holy as the Trinity – with two distinguished philosophers was strangely beset by the love letters the two philosophers kept sending her. There is nothing possessive in Nietzsche's letters. Though often fervent, they have a largeness of gesture, a generous-heartedness, that makes very sad reading when one knows how it was to end. His was no familiar love, but expansive and lofty. When Lou told him (in one of the very few of her letters to him that are extant) that, when ill in bed, she had his book *Dawn* for company, he wrote back:

> I too have dawns around me now, and not printed ones! Something I no longer believed possible, to find a friend for my *ultimate happiness and suffering*, now seems to me possible – the *golden* possibility on the horizon of my whole future life. I am moved whenever I so much as think of the bold and rich soul of my dear Lou.[29]

Thus Lou's two friends offered embodiment, with unforeseen elaborations, of the two main patterns of thought she had kept from her childhood. The motif of home was represented in Rée, and that of the highest possible aspiration towards excellence in Nietzsche.

What she felt about the two of them may be indicated by observations in the letter to Nietzsche containing the remark about *Dawn*. She compares his book with Rée's. Interested in the different effects the two books had on 'people like Fräulein von Meysenbug', she asks why, despite their both attacking the 'eternal' truth of morality, and Nietzsche's doing this far more thoroughly, such people prefer Nietzsche's book. He and Rée are alike, she says, in that they are 'like two prophets, turned to the past and the future, whereby one of them, Rée, discovers the origin of the gods, and the other destroys the twilight of the gods.'[30] Yet they are different in that Rée's ideal egoist moves towards a comfortable life, while Nietzsche commends the heroic life. Lou visualises two persons representing the two ideas: Rée's egoist and Nietzsche's hero. Although she does sum up Nietzsche's position in words coming very close to the last lines of her 'Prayer to Life' ('if one has to do without a happy life, there is still the heroic life') – the most notable point is that she does not express personal commitment or enthusiasm for either of the philosophers and does not exactly *admire* them. All her intensity went into the exercise of comparison: she was interested in someone's ideas, in what lay behind them, what they led to, how they differed from someone else's. She was like some unusually intelligent reviewer at the performance of a philosophical play who takes notes, weighs things up and is deeply concerned intellectually, even professionally, but who is not moved, and not really affected.

Nietzsche often underlined the word 'teacher' in his letters to Lou. 'You know that I wish to be your *teacher*, your guide on the path to scholarly *production*?'[31] Yet he hardly considered whether she wanted him as a long-term teacher, and seems to have been living in a sort of inebriation. 'She is astoundingly well prepared for precisely *my* way of thinking and my thoughts',[32] he wrote to his friend Peter Gast, and to her he wrote:

to tell the whole truth, I am now looking for people who could be my heirs; I carry something around with me which is not to be found in my books at all – and I am seeking the best and most fruitful plough-land for it. See my *self-seeking*![33]

One would think she must accept this: the most abstruse secrets of the greatest contemporary philosopher – for her alone! But, although she had great trust in Nietzsche's teaching power, Lou did not want another ecstatic pupildom. She wanted to learn, but not to follow or to submit. And she may even have felt offended (was she a fine piece of ploughland?), may have wondered whether he really meant her, or simply someone like her. She was sufficiently baffled at one point to think that he wanted her secretarial devotions. Nietzsche was too full of his golden vision to try to get to know her in any ordinary sense. All too clearly he wanted her not as new inspiration, or pointer to a new purpose, but as the missing, perfecting, component of a design already drafted. Her coming into his life was no deflection of it. She was what he had been looking for; he said of her poem 'To Pain': 'It sounds like a voice I have been waiting and waiting for since my childhood.'[34] His overestimation of her coincided with his overestimation of Gast, whom – by all other accounts a mediocre musician – he saw as a 'new Mozart', exaggerating not only his talents but also, as with Lou, his own affinity with him. His talk of his own self-seeking was surely a warning to those around him that meant not, 'Look out, I seek my own advantage' but 'Can you accept me, even seeing the enormous concentration that is necessary for me?' The pun in it meant, 'Don't join me if you cannot understand *this*.' But Lou did understand; *Selbstsucht* in that sense was her word too, and this kind of concentration was just what she and Nietzsche had in common.

Another word Nietzsche underlined was 'friend'. He asked Ida Overbeck to make sure Lou realised that Paul Rée was a better friend than he was, and was pleased with the wonderful new quality his friendship with Rée had gained through their loving the same woman. They were devoted, he said from the beginning, to their high-hearted friend Lou with '*identical feelings*' and with 'very great confidence'[35] in each other; it was a 'Pythagorean friendship' with the very strange motto 'φιλοισ παντα κοινα' ('Friends have all things in common'). 'But we can still laugh at it, can't we?'[36] Rée did not laugh, and did not always answer. He felt differently; his egoism was more straightfor-ward: happy to see Lou again, and wondering how he, an anti-moralist, could invoke moral categories, he developed the theory that he was entitled to a special one-man morality whereby Lou became, implicitly, the goddess or Beautiful Lady of his unique realm. This meant he could be false with all others, so long as he was honest with her. This was a stance she must have admired, since one of her aphorisms runs: 'To be *wholly* moral in one special sphere, to be *wholly* true towards one person, lends more dignity than universal morality and universal truthfulness.'[37]

After various plans to meet Lou again came to nothing (he was ready to alter all his plans to suit her), Nietzsche at last moved to the quiet village of Tautenburg, in Thüringen, where his sister had set him up an 'idyllic nest' for the summer. Here he invited Lou to visit him. She agreed and he exclaimed: 'Now the sky is clear above me!'[38]

BAYREUTH

1882 was the year of the last Bayreuth festival in Wagner's lifetime: the first performance of *Parsifal*. En route from her stay with Rée to her stay with Nietzsche, Lou von Salomé stopped in Bayreuth and attended the opera, encouraged to do so by Nietzsche himself although he knew she would meet people there who were hostile to him. She went more from interest in people than from love of music. Although Malwida looked forward to the effect of 'Bayreuth's artistic treat' upon her, she understood nothing of it; she was deaf to music. In the circumstances, a refusal to pretend to like the music showed an appealing independence. Yet reading their correspondence with this in mind, one is struck by the fact that it was precisely the *musical* in Nietzsche that Lou never responded to, and it is significant of his inebriation that Nietzsche did not take her music-deafness adversely. For he himself was, as he said, 'very, very much a musician'. He composed; he played the piano with passion; as a student he is said to have escaped from a brothel by playing the piano there; *The Birth of Tragedy* was 'music' for those dedicated to music; he had loved Wagner and he could not do without a composing friend; and he responded to Lou's 'Prayer to Life' by setting it to music.

Lou was now swept into a world of people after her quiet weeks in Stibbe. This change, from rural bookwork to a round of social gatherings and meetings with people concerned with the most advanced art or thought of the times, was to become a pattern in her later life, which was blessed by just this kind of alternation. In Bayreuth Lou met Nietzsche's sister Elisabeth for the first time and said (foreseeing no calamity) 'She is now almost mine, too.'[39] She met Wagner and his wife Cosima, and was a welcome visitor to their house 'Wahnfried'. She made several closer acquaintances, in particular the young philosopher Heinrich von Stein and the artist Paul von Joukowski. Von Stein* she found interesting but fanatical; the thirty-seven-year-old Joukowski was a more cheerful person, with whom she got on well, perhaps through his Russianness (he was the son of the famous Russian Romantic poet, Vasily Zhukovsky). Joukowski had for two years been wholly under Wagner's spell; he was an intimate of Wagner's family and had designed the scenery for *Parsifal*. A solemn hero-worship thus made up a large part of the atmosphere in which Lou von Salomé was now immersed. There were some light moments; a characteristic one was Joukowski's altering her dress for a party, sewing it while it was on her, so that she was accused of flirting ('innocent lamb that I was!', she recalled years later). Paul Rée, to whom she wrote everything, swore sadly to remain her friend should there ever be 'such an unpleasant event' as her marrying Joukowski. But Lou had not changed her attitude to marriage.

Elisabeth Nietzsche was thirty-six, prim and conventional and in no sense a philosopher. Unmarried, she was devoted to her brother as her only source of significance, and she was thoroughly alarmed by the phenomenon of Lou. She left hostile accounts of Lou's behaviour in Bayreuth, in which the prejudice is patent enough, for example:

> In Bayreuth she was led astray by vanity to make a European scandal out of her success with the two foolish hermits; she told everyone whether they wanted to hear it or not that Nietzsche and Rée wanted to study with her and that the two of them were going wherever *she* wished.[40]

Through this we can glimpse the uninhibited girl, naturally excited from conquering such hearts and minds, and no doubt also from the sheer respect she found herself getting for her friendship with Nietzsche, talking away with carefree eloquence. Elisabeth told her brother what she thought, and Nietzsche now lost his great confidence in Lou with astonishing suddenness. Three weeks before, he had described her to Gast[41] as 'sharp-witted as an eagle and courageous as a lion.'* Now he wrote to him:

> One day a bird flew past me, and I, superstitious like all solitary people ... thought I had seen an eagle. Now the whole world is trying to prove to me that I am making a mistake, and there is a real European scandal about it.[42]

He called himself 'the deceived' and telegraphed Lou to put her off from Tautenburg. Distressed by her reply, he sent a sad little letter:

> I wanted to live alone. But then the dear bird Lou flew over the path and I thought it was an eagle ... Come after all, I am too unhappy, for having made you unhappy. We'll bear it better together.[43]

JENA

Lou's stay in Tautenburg began badly. It was preceded by an explosion of hatred between herself and Elisabeth. This was in Jena, where they had broken their journey. In a tense conversation, Elisabeth had used some phrase like 'saint and ascetic' of her brother, at which Lou burst out (perhaps with examples) that Nietzsche was neither of these things. According to the account she later gave Pfeiffer, Rée had told her of Nietzsche's remark about the unlikelihood but not impossibility of a *wilde Ehe* ['wild marriage', a living-in-sin arrangement][44] with her, as a warning against any approaches Nietzsche might make, and she may have mentioned this now. The guardian of the philosopher's reputation was incensed, the legatee of his gay wisdom offered angry remarks in return, accusing Nietzsche of egoism and (if we choose to believe parts of Elisabeth's account) of madness, of not knowing what he wanted, of intending to use her and of wanting sex, like all men who talk of intellectual friendship.[45] Strained with animosity, they still travelled to Tautenburg as planned and put up together in a house near where Nietzsche was staying.

Now Elisabeth became Lou's 'deadly enemy';[46] she came to see the eagle as a poisonous worm that had to be annihilated. Her envious unhappiness exaggerated everything, from the bits of anti-moral conversation she kept overhearing to the fact that Lou did not tidy her room or bother enough about clean linen. She was revolted and infuriated, and saw in Lou what she feared her brother's philosophy really amounted to: egoism and love of evil.[47]

TAUTENBURG

At the beginning of the shared three weeks there was a bad quarrel involving them all; then 'a small tragic scene' every five days.[48] Yet, although he shed innumerable tears, in the very midst of the quarrels Nietzsche continued to admire Lou's way of thinking and her way of retorting to accusations; and between the quarrels they got on extremely well. Nietzsche's health was unusually good, he was able to talk for ten hours a day; afterwards he felt he had been through a 'convalescence'. When Lou worried that she was taking him from his work, he said: 'I have it so seldom and I enjoy it like a child.'[49] They spent whole days together, talking as they walked in the pine forests, with hopping squirrels and filtering sunshine; they ate together under a lime tree outside the inn. Some evenings they spent sitting on the bench by Nietzsche's cottage, and others in Lou's room which was darkened by having a red cloth tied over the lamp to save Nietzsche's eyes. Lou felt that whoever saw them took them for a couple, and told Rée so in the diary she honestly kept for him. Both were delighted with their conversations. Lou spoke of the 'meeting of similar thoughts, similar feelings and ideas, we can almost communicate with half-words'[50] and said Nietzsche told her they had 'lived and thought in the same way as each other.' Nietzsche later told Overbeck that the most useful thing he had experienced that summer was his talks with Lou: 'Our intelligence and tastes are related at the deepest point ... I wonder if there has ever existed before such a *philosophical openness* as exists between us.'[51] He was even more delighted than she, for while she analysed him quite critically in her diary, he was solely admiring: 'I have never known anyone who could draw from their experiences so many *objective insights*, or anyone who knew how to derive so much from everything they'd learnt.'[52] He felt they shared a sibling brain.[53] As for Lou, she was afterwards judged to have grown mentally by several inches during her stay with him.

But Tautenburg did not become Trautenburg [Betrothal-burg] as Rée feared it might. Lou did not want to unite herself with Nietzsche in any way at all. The breakdown in her relationship with Gillot had come from his mistaking her adoration as a desire for union with him, and she was still the same person. Moreover, she harboured no sexual aspirations. One of the characters in her novel *Struggling for God* says: 'Friendship between the sexes is a noble artificial bloom, said to demand considerable gardening talents. I once read that it even needs a small amount of physical antipathy.'[54] The last sentence is from one of Nietzsche's aphorisms but she took this view herself, and not only with regard to individual antipathies. Years later[55] she put the view that it was a great mistake to do away with the traditional prizing of virginity in middle-class girls: virginity could lead them to productivity, even to heroism. Nietzsche seems to have thought similarly. In Tautenburg he wrote a series of aphorisms for Lou, one of which (repeated in *Beyond Good and Evil*) runs:

> The enormous expectation in regard to sexual love spoils a woman's eye for all distant perspectives.[56]

As Lou expected neither sexual love nor, therefore, anything from it, this was praise of *her* distant-perceiving eye and its chilly cause. Mentally she was inflammable, physically not – and she was glad of it. When she told Elisabeth, during one of their rows, that she would be able to sleep in the same room as Nietzsche 'without insurgent thoughts',[57] Elisabeth was furious that such a matter could be mentioned. She ought to have been reassured to hear of such iciness.

The matter was less straightforward to Nietzsche. His feeling for Lou was passionate. 'Her intelligence and doubtless also her femininity tore Nietzsche to the highest heights', writes C. A. Bernoulli, who argues that Nietzsche desired Lou hotly 'only indeed not sensually' and claims that this was his one and only great, mature passion, a passion for possession: 'In the Lou-experience Nietzsche's androcratic self-awareness reached its fullness'.[58] It has also been argued that Nietzsche fled his own sensuality, being insecure about women, who had a

directness and uninhibitedness which he lacked;[59] and that he was
happy with Lou precisely because he saw her as being perhaps as
inhibited as himself. He insisted to his friends that this was no love
affair: 'we are *friends* and I shall hold this girl and her trust in me as
holy.'[60] But in some sense he was quite certainly in love and we can
even quote the indignant Elisabeth: 'the poor blinded lamb ... has
never been half so enthusiastic [begeistert] about any female creature.'[61]

What is remarkable is that, in Tautenburg, Lou too was convinced of
the great kinship between herself and Nietzsche. Their conversations
were unrecordable because so much depended on things only half said,
silently shared, needing no more than hints. Most especially they had a
similar religiousness, and they talked a great deal about this. Developing a thought Nietzsche had jotted down for her, Lou said both were
'freethinkers in the most extreme sense' – in whom religious feeling, no
longer related to the deity, is directed back to oneself where it can
become the heroic power of one's being, the 'urge to give oneself up –
to a great aim'.[62] Fragments of Nietzsche's writing preserved from that
month[63] indicate that they probably talked about such things as the
readiness for absolute self-destruction, good and evil ('every good
derives from an evil'), cruelty (the desire to be hurt by the beloved),
love of self as desire for self-destruction, marriage (being for 'stunted
half-people') and again and again the religiousness of the free-thinker.
Horrified, the eavesdropping Elisabeth recorded the gist of their
conversations: 'What was a lie? Nothing! What was a breach of faith?
Nothing! What was the most shameless talk of the most shameful
matters? Nothing! What was doing one's duty? Stupidity. What was
the most disparaging talk about loyal friends? Right judgment. What
was pity? Contemptible!'[64] How could she know that Nietzsche's 'We
must free ourselves from morality' was followed by 'in order to be able
to live morally' – or indeed what this paradox might mean? As Lou
herself said, 'if anyone had overheard us, he would have thought it was
two devils in conversation.'[65]

Lou decided that heroism was Nietzsche's most essential quality and
thought he would one day emerge as proclaimer of a new religion, with
heroes as its disciples; she felt she was close to him in this. He thought
so, too, and when he lent her his essay on Schopenhauer* he must have
felt she would respond well to his ideal of the man who 'takes the
voluntary suffering of truth upon himself', for this was how he saw her
– as someone who suffered joyfully for the sake of knowledge.

Lou's diary suggests they shared their most profound insights. 'We
kept coming' she said, 'to those dizzying spots where one had once
climbed alone to look down into the depths.'[66] But she also came to feel
that they were, in some hidden depth of their being, worlds apart from
each other. She had begun to sense in Nietzsche that which, twelve

years later in her book about him, she would define herself as being against. In one of the later summations of her views in *Looking Back*, we read: 'I must confess: if reverence risked disappearing from mankind, then any kind of faith, even the most absurd, would be preferable to that.'[67] Nietzsche often expresses a fundamental awe but he means the awesome conception of the world without any human meaning or possibility of faith, and Lou certainly did not follow him in this. For her, the godless universe was always full of something valuable and wonderful. She was beginning to perceive the strange strength of Nietzsche's nihilism, felt it was a hidden and dizzying chasm in Nietzsche himself, and realised that she and Nietzsche could end up as enemies.

They talked of doing some work together. But Nietzsche also began encouraging Lou to do independent work, to be her own kind of writer. He had remarked, to Gast, that 'she has an unbelievably definite character, and knows exactly what *she* wants – without asking the world or bothering about the world.'[68] Now he told her that she should 'go forward and seek quite independently – and never be only a learner, but learn by creating and create by learning.'[69] Of course, in this very advice he was likening her to himself.

LOU'S TAUTENBURG WRITINGS

Lou's studies and writings hitherto had been remarkably systematic. Her chief interests had declared themselves: the nature and function of religious feeling and (though at this time still secondarily) the special nature of woman. Reading an essay of hers on the subject of woman, Nietzsche said in solemn and emotional tones that it would be a pity if she did not build a '*monument* of her full and most inward spirit'.[70] This was despite his finding its style atrocious. He told her that all literary production repelled him unless it was excellent. He also told her she could learn to write in a day, and wrote down ten pieces of advice for developing a good style, starting: 'The first thing needed is life: the style must *live*.'[71] Writing must be an imitation of speech (he obviously had in mind a good speaker, but there is every indication that Lou was this); above all, one must avoid lengthiness, unfelt thoughts, the lure of the poetic, and the temptation to utter those things which the reader can guess for himself. His advice to feel the punctuation and the pauses in ones writing as *gestures* seems to have pointed beyond her talents. None the less her later style (when it misses its pitfalls of poeticality, repetition and over-explicitness) does at least *live*, and was possibly aroused to vitality by Nietzsche's attention.

Two pieces of her writing remain from the Tautenburg period. One is her discursive diary, the other a collection of some 190 aphorisms (the form favoured by both Rée and Nietzsche), to which she gave the strange title *Stibbe Nest-Book*.[72] She had begun it before Tautenburg, but submitted it there to Nietzsche. Twenty-three of the aphorisms he corrected or wholly rewrote; on others he put marginal comments, often quite teacherly, such as 'obscure', 'impossible expression' or 'make it sharper'. He also numbered some of them, apparently selecting the best for preservation. An example of his complete rewriting is Lou's sentence:

What does not enter our feeling [*Empfindung*] does not long occupy our thinking.

This he rewrote as:

What brings neither pain nor joy finds only brief lodging in our heads

– an introduction of wit and image. An instance of his radicalising the syntax is his treatment of her sentence:

Sometimes the size of our conscience stands in inverse ratio to the size of our brain.

When pruned and shaped by Nietzsche, this became:

Big conscience, small brain; that's often the case.

In general, Lou's aphorisms show talent and a certain maturity, and they indicate her main preoccupations. One (much influenced by her two preceptors) is the non-transcendental origination of the metaphysical, as in:

To the metaphysicians: question-marks are not holy mysteries.

and (an aphorism on which Nietzsche wrote 'obscure'):

Metaphysics ... is the glorification of lack of intelligence.
Religion is the glorification of lack of strength.

She points out prejudices, mental limitations, inhibitions and the mistake of saying 'I' of those impulses which happen to be the most frequent in us. An aphorism in which we hear the clearer voice of Lou von Salomé herself and which, with its dense question-begging and partial question-awareness, is particularly interesting, is the following:

There's no harm in being godless if you're really rid of God.
[*Es schadet nichts, gottlos zu sein, wenn man Gott nur wirklich los ist.*]

The unadorned conversational tone, the irreverence verging on rudeness – 'if you're really rid ...' – recalls the letter to Gillot in April. But it is a complex sentence. On the one hand, it seems to be praise of the Rée-type, which does succeed in being completely atheist (though the possible dryness and vagueness of life without God is suggested by the unfocused, what-does-it-matter gesture of the first three words) and impatience with Nietzsche, who in her opinion does not. (Another of her aphorisms, 'Hatred of God is the final resonance of love of God', emphasises this impatience.) On the other hand, the small g for 'gottlos' and the capital G in 'Gott ... los' (which some re-phrasing could have avoided) hint that it is right after all not to be able to be free of God; indeed, that it cannot be done. These ideas were taken up in Lou's Tautenburg diary and then again and again throughout her life.

'Woman' is a lesser theme in Lou's 1882 writings, as if she were keeping away from the question until she was securely established, so to speak, as a man. Some statements show her distancing herself from her sex, such as 'Women's thoughts are born of the heart'. The lost essay on woman must have contained ideas not unlike Nietzsche's own as, after praising it, he wrote a couple of pages for her on the subject,[73] apparently neither polemically nor didactically, and added thirteen suggestions for further thinking. He wrote, for instance, that women need a strength outside themselves, so they *invent* that strength and then lean on it as if it were really there; they are therefore more important than men in creating religions. (Something of this view reappears, stripped of its mocking aspect, in Lou's own later theory of religion: the Deity, while not 'really' there, has a beneficial effect upon its inventors.) Further, according to Nietzsche, woman feels perfected only in obedience; she is altogether determined by the state of pregnancy; she is more barbaric than man ... (Again, Lou later agreed with the letter but not the spirit of these remarks: pregnancy may be all-determining but that is no inferiority; women may be more primitive but this is paradoxically a higher stage they come to after passing the level of men.) The last third of the *Stibbe Nest-Book* is mainly about love, marriage and friendship. On marriage, the little she has to say is fiercely rejective (like Nietzsche's own remarks). It is a killer of love; married partners are 'trivialities to each other'. In love, she says (unlike Nietzsche), women are higher than men in that they come to sensuality last (men start from it). Love is ranked well below friendship, which has to be protected from the risk of vanishing into it and, worse, into sensuality, for 'no way leads from sensual passion to spiritual sympathy, though it does from the latter to the former'. Self-knowledge, the means of preventing this risk (and its product), is the chief value.

Psychologically-based comparison was what Lou was best at. She said 'I would like to have been inside the skin of all human beings', and she was still much exercised with comparing her two suitors: Nietzsche's 'religious' devotion to knowledge, which engaged the whole man, and Rée's total 'truth to himself', which split the man apart.[74] This difference is seen in their styles, with Rée trying to convince his reader through the head, Nietzsche aiming at the whole man; and also in their attitudes to work, with Nietzsche being possessed heart and mind by his, Rée *possessing* his, able to break off from it, watch in hand. Despite the praise for Rée, it is Nietzsche who comes off as the richer and deeper personality. Yet she was to reject him and live with the lesser man – indeed, had already decided upon this – no doubt because Nietzsche was too like herself for her to develop freely, and also too much an authority above her.

She also compared Nietzsche with herself. They differed in how they lost Christianity: Nietzsche abandoned his when he felt nothing more of it, but she lost hers by a rational insight and kept the feeling of it. And they differed in their sense of goals: while Nietzsche changed from one goal to another, she moved as if by natural necessity towards one goal only. This was not to say that she did better, for she had no choice:

> *Goals* were for me no *choice*, as I have never actually known the *feeling of choice* but found in myself much analogy with the necessary working of natural forces – which is why the doctrine of the freedom of the will never specially tickled me.[75]

This last was an arrow shot at Rée (for whom the question of the will's freedom was a chief preoccupation), but what is more interesting is her sense of herself as not making choices but living in accord with powers just as necessary as the laws in the natural world. So there was never any agony of freedom for her, and in fact she never talked of a purpose, though often of 'directedness' towards one. Directedness, without definition of the direction, has its dangers; Lou did not reflect whether her heroic religious atheist might not devote himself to wicked purposes, or make others do so. The diary even ends with her trying out definite positions of amoralism: 'there is no longer evaluation of the *directions* people set out on, but there is a *greatness of strength*'.[76] Elsewhere she had said, 'Strong natures are usually *true* natures', and, 'The greatness of a person is his intensity',[77] which might mean 'What we call great is really only intense', but asks to be read the other way: 'It is the intense people who deserve to be called great.' Like Nietzsche, she was worlds behind Yeats's observation that the 'worst are full of passionate intensity'. 'Religious', even along with 'godless', always somehow entailed 'good', and she never had to doubt the goodness of that which 'directed' her.

LEIPZIG

All the time Lou was noting down her thoughts for Rée, he was writing love letters as sensual as a platonic lover could dare to be. His jealousy was tenderly expressed: 'Just you wait, little snail!' – but he told her to call a halt to the friendship with Nietzsche. She came back to him at the end of August, and now Nietzsche missed her and once more began to write to her. Compared with Rée's, his letters were rather like short, vigorous walks past beauty spots rather than long sittings indoors in the lamplight. Their difference was the more telling when they happened to hit on the same idea. Each, for instance, had the idea of making Lou immortal. Rée was apologetic and helpful about it and sent her a volume of La Bruyère in case her vocation should turn out to be the writing of character sketches; Nietzsche, who had set to music the 'Prayer to Life', which Lou had given him upon leaving Tautenburg, said lightheartedly: 'That would be a little path on which we both *together* would reach posterity – other paths excepted.'[78] He was thus ready to share his own immortality with her (which is of course partly what has happened, although the song is forgotten). They still called themselves a Trinity and planned the winter of study (now at last with the approval of Malwida von Meysenbug). They were together again for three weeks that October in Leipzig, where Lou was 'wholly absorbed in the study of religious history';[79] they went to the theatre and received visitors, and Nietzsche wrote to Lou's mother, success-fully pleading that she be allowed to stay abroad. When she left Leipzig he gave her a remarkable poem he had written or rewritten, for her (Appendix A), and went on declaring: 'she is prepared, as no other person is, for the hitherto unexpressed part of my philosophy.'[80] Yet, after they left Leipzig on 5 November 1882, Nietzsche never saw either Lou or Rée again.

There remains some uncertainty about just what happened. Elisabeth had told her brother – probably in several stages – about the row in Jena, saying that Lou had slandered him, failed to respect his feeling for Wagner, set in motion vile rumours about him and had only wanted to exploit him. Nietzsche had at first defended Lou so vehemently that he had a violent row with his mother early in September and temporarily broke with his family altogether, recognising that he had 'the Naum-burg virtue against' him. But then, towards the end of November, probably poisoned by repeated doses of Elisabeth's hatred of Lou and perhaps especially provoked by her news that his two friends were mocking him, he turned violently against Lou. Three things were distressing Nietzsche. In Leipzig he began to realise that he had conclusively lost Lou to Rée; he was now hearing Lou progressively undermined and slandered by his sister; and he risked losing his sister too, and the whole security of his family. For a while he still hoped to maintain a relationship with Lou and begged her to 'create a clear sky', saying he would renounce proximity if only she would remain what he believed her to be, a creature with a 'higher soul'. But he too had by now done his share of slandering, trying to set her against Rée, and she did not reply. He had to admit that she did not need him, and he wrote to Malwida von Meysenbug: 'I am, it seems to me, superfluous to her rather than interesting: the sign of a good taste!'[81] But now he fell into a raging despair, and switched all his ideas of her to their opposite.

Suddenly, instead of an angel, she was a devil. Far from being the unique heir of his philosophy, she understood nothing of it. Her 'self-seeking' was the kind without holiness. Instead of representing his ideals, she was a caricature of them, clever but ignoble. (One wonders if he had foreseen all this, for one of the notes he made in Tautenburg went: 'Whoever has beheld the ideal of a human being, experiences the actual human being as its *caricature*.'[82]) In sum, 'she unites in herself *all* the human attributes that are the most repulsive and loathsome to me.' She was now not worthy of her poem, 'To Pain'; she was a revengeful school-girl, a cat nature, a beast of prey masquerading as domestic animal, she was a brain with an appendage of soul, she lacked industry, cleanliness, bourgeois decency, she was sexually immature, had a cruel sensuality cunningly deployed against men's, she had enthusiasm but no love except for God, she was faithless, shameless, goalless, treacherous, ungrateful – and 'incapable of the courtesy of the heart'.[83] Some of his criticisms (uncleanliness, for example) obviously stem from Elisabeth; some suggest a delayed hurt to him as lover; some would appear partly true: she was capable of enthusiasm but without love (yet) for people. But the abundance, pain and danger of his raving was chiefly due to his having to recognise what a mistake he had made. There was not anyone else in the world like him, after all: for a while he had dreamt the stupendous dream that there was. As he said a year or so later: 'The peculiar misfortune of the last two years consisted most strictly in the fact that I thought I had found someone who had exactly the same task as I had.'[84] He cursed Lou – at least in drafts of letters (which, if sent, may not have reached her, since Rée was trying to protect her from them), and warned her, melodramatically: 'If I banish you from me now, it is a frightful censure of your whole being ... You have caused damage, you have done *harm* – and not only to me but to all the people who have loved me: this sword hangs over you.'[85]

LOU'S SUMMARY OF THE YEAR 1882

Very few of Lou von Salomé's letters or writings of this time have been preserved, but there is a letter she wrote to Rée in Berlin that New Year's Eve.[86] It shows how remote from the centre of her life Nietzsche was, and how close Rée was. What a good year we have had together, she says, and reminisces about her arrival in sunny Italy the previous January, the walks and talks in Rome with Rée, the 'Orta idyll', its Monte Sacro and nightingales, the days in Lucerne, the beginning of their unusual relationship as friends after her mother returned to Russia: 'a relationship such as perhaps exists nowhere else in such intimacy and such restraint, just as perhaps never before, or very rarely,

have two people made a bond so imprudently and yet so prudently.'
She recalls how she arrived in Stibbe, alone and unknown, and he made
it into a home for her, and how then (Tautenburg is not even mentioned!) she and Rée, hand in hand like two good comrades, confident of
not being misunderstood, entered the big world, where they were now
so firmly nested, and were proving that their relationship was viable.
How well they had succeeded in making people accept it; like a garden,
their friendship had blossomed with thousands of blooms. Lou's
happiness had nothing at all to do with Nietzsche.

NIETZSCHE AFTER THE RELATIONSHIP WITH LOU

Nietzsche's feelings about Lou and Rée were to undergo further
extreme changes: Elisabeth chose a later moment to inform him that
Rée, too, had behaved vilely. Nietzsche (apparently the puppet of his
sister) thereupon raged against Rée, wrote insulting letters, threatened a
duel and threw in some vulgar abuse of Lou: 'this dry, dirty, nasty-
smelling monkey with her false breasts'.[87] (Again, doubtless the
influence of Elisabeth, who found Lou physically revolting and
reported with disgust that she could even move her ears one by one like
an animal, as well as the skin of her head.[88]) Yet a month later he was
recalling Lou as someone whose will and originality destined her for
greatness, 'a creature of first rank – what an eternal shame it is, about
her'.[89] A meeting in August 1883 with Overbeck (who found him 'half-
raving') made him feel calmer and able to recognize the ill-will of his
sister. By January he was apparently thinking unrealistically of his sister
becoming reconciled with Lou;[90] by April he was glad to think of how
he had helped develop Lou's mind and wondering how he could
recompense her and Rée for the harm done by Elisabeth.[91] His
repulsive and brutal sister had harmed him by shortening his friendship
with them, for, he told her in the spring of 1884, he did have something
in common with Lou and 'of all acquaintances I have made the most
valuable and full of consequence is the one with Fräulein Salomé. Only
since knowing her was I ripe for my Zarathustra ... Lou is the most
gifted, most thoughtful creature one can imagine – naturally she also
has some dubious qualities. *I* have some, too ... You can't sense what
consolation Dr Rée was to me for years – faute de mieux, it goes
without saying, and what an incredible benefit the communion with
Fräulein Salomé was to me!'[92] A year later, he saw the books that Rée
and Lou had published. By now quite calm, he commented that Rée's,
though admirable in form, was boring and false, while Lou's *Struggling
for God*, though girlish and in some ways absurd, was serious and lofty,
'and if it is certainly not the Eternal-Feminine that draws this girl
onward, perhaps it is the Eternal-Masculine.'[93]

Nietzsche's last remarks about Lou – in *Ecce Homo*, shortly before his collapse at the end of 1888 – were wholeheartedly laudatory again: he wrote of his musical composition, the 'Hymn to Life', that the text was 'the astounding inspiration of a young Russian woman who was my friend at that time, Fräulein Lou von Salomé. Anyone who can draw any meaning from the last words of this poem will guess why I preferred and admired it. They have greatness. Pain is *not* considered an objection to life.'[94]

In February 1883, in the midst of his despair (intensified when Wagner died), Nietzsche wrote, in ten inspired days, the first part of his prophetic book *Thus Spoke Zarathustra*, for which the relation with Lou had made him 'ripe'. In June, with similar inspired speed, he wrote the second part. In *The Gay Science*, he had commended the philosopher who could laugh and dance; now, in the figure of Zarathustra, he *is* that philosopher. There is pain in the book, and some of it is a direct reflection of his disappointment in Lou von Salomé. In the second part he repeats the words of Emerson he had quoted to Rée the September before in reference to Lou's effect on him: 'all experiences useful, all days holy, and all people divine.'[95]

Thus my purity once spoke, in a happy hour: 'all creatures shall be divine to me'.

Then you assaulted me with filthy spectres; alas, whither is that happy hour now fled!

'All days shall be holy to me' – thus spoke once the wisdom of my youth: truly, the speech of a gay wisdom!

But then you enemies stole my nights from me and sold them to sleepless anguish: alas, whither is that gay wisdom now fled?

Once I longed for fortunate bird-signs: then you led an owl-monster across my path, an untoward sign. Alas, whither did my tender longing then flee?[96]

But the cheerfulness of the book is also due to her, both to the ecstatic hope he had first felt about her and to the effort to surmount the subsequent grief.

Probably, if my soul had been bright and cheerful all year, I would have chosen – for artistic reasons – darker, harsher and more sombre colours for the first two parts, considering what the *conclusion* is like. But this year the solace of more cheerful and airy colours was *essential to my life*; and so in the second part I have leapt about almost like a clown. The detail of it is incredibly full of personal experience and suffering which only I can understand – I felt many pages to be almost *bleeding*.[97]

There are also passages, especially in Part Three, written the following year, which can be read as declarations of love he would have liked to make to her (and possibly did make) and as a narrative of the pursuit of that love (which did not occur).

ELISABETH'S ACCOUNTS OF LOU

Although the remainder of Nietzsche's life did not affect Lou, she carried with her for the rest of her life both the fame of having been his friend, and exposure to criticism and controversy about it. Elisabeth, whose own letters and outraged explanations to friends had caused the evil rumours about her brother to be spread, later wrote her account of what had happened, giving her view of Lou von Salomé in several publications. It is worth remembering that Lou, who kept well out of all controversy and never attempted to justify herself or to answer Elisabeth publicly, certainly knew that her character was torn to shreds in books that many people were reading. Even before coming to the distortions contained in the body of her attacks, one is put off by the introductory falsehoods, such as that Lou was Jewish, was ugly, and was aged twenty-four in 1882. In 1904 Elisabeth's book, *The Life of Nietzsche*, described the meeting of Nietzsche and Lou as a lamentable error, and claimed that Nietzsche could not endure people like Lou with their feeble devotion to enjoyment and comfort. In 1905 her article, 'Nietzsche Legends', in *Die Zukunft*, said a series of nasty things about Lou, among them that her book on Nietzsche was an unsuccessful attempt to win back Rée's benevolence. Her 1915 book, *The Lonely Nietzsche*, had a chapter on Lou giving a vicious detailed account of the Jena row, and all sorts of dubious facts such as that Rée paid for her living in Germany and that she had had an unsavoury affair with a priest in Petersburg. Finally, following a short and not fully accurate (though uncritical) piece in 1920 about Nietzsche's setting of her 'Hymn to Life', there came her 1935 book, *Nietzsche and Women*, in which the whole story was raked over again.[98]

Others, too (friends of Elisabeth), attacked Lou over the years. Fifty years later (in May, 1932) Freud wrote to Lou: 'Often and often I have felt angry on finding your relationship to Nietzsche mentioned in a way that was obviously hostile to you and could not possibly be in accord with the truth. You have endured it all, you have been much too noble; won't you finally, in the most dignified manner, come to your own defence?'[99]

NIETZSCHE'S INFLUENCE ON LOU

Acquaintance with Nietzsche, his views and standards, and his unparalleled evocation of the struggles and rewards of the life of the mind, had considerable effect on Lou's development. It corroborated her intellectuality and her self-confidence as a thinker, and the romantic

habit of being enraptured by thoughts. Nietzsche particularly encouraged her to think about religion and told her she had a vocation in
this sphere. Many of his ideas and occasionally his very formulations
recur in Lou's thought over the next few years. Then the fact that she
knew both Nietzsche and Rée so closely and at the same time, minds so
opposite in their approach and intention and yet so similar (for a time)
in their preoccupations, meant that she was impelled to think as much
about *them* in relation to their philosophies, as about their philosophies.
She could work out for herself the nature and cause of their tremendous
differences; and validate each (since, as men, she admired both of
them). This was the beginning of her lifelong concern with psychology,
and her understanding of all ideas in psychological terms, a concern
which eventually led her to Freud and psychoanalysis. Further,
Nietzsche's original estimation of her – an extraordinarily high
estimation from an extraordinarily gifted man – *must* have influenced
her self-esteem, however little she chose to say about it. She now always
knew that she could have been the 'inheritor' of a great philosophy, and
must have pondered how much there was in herself that fitted his ideal.

The theory of the 'Superman' (or 'Overman') does not exclude
women. The word *Übermensch* applies to both sexes and the attitudes
extolled are available to all. The passages about war or manliness are to
be construed metaphorically; and if women may be more compassionate and sentimental than men, yet the debilitated society which
aroused Nietzsche's contempt was a society men had made. Passages
explicitly about women do appear to exclude them from the possibility
of superhumanity, for woman is either the soother of the superior man
or a deceitful creature he has to control; but passages about the qualities
of superhumanity say almost nothing about women, either including or
excluding. Nietzsche did not despise women. He admired, for example,
Cosima Wagner, Ida Overbeck, Malwida von Meysenbug. In Lou he
saw – as he did not see in any man – many qualities the 'higher' human
being was to have: devotion to knowledge, welcome of pain and
spurning of convention and comfort, the orientation to optimism,
adventurousness and the 'higher soul'. The Superman's motto 'become
what you are' was enjoined upon her with a conviction that she could do
it. Nietzsche did not think: 'but this is only a girl'. It has been suggested that, in creating the Superman, Nietzsche was merely translating
Lou into the masculine, since she had, simply and without any fuss,
that 'feeling of life amid the nothing' which was really the state he most
longed for.[100] Yet this would mean a consequence worse for Nietzsche
than the failure to win over a brilliant and beloved female mind. It
would mean that Lou's existence undid his very philosophy. If by mere
fortune, by the generosity of nature, she could be it all – vital, self-
creating, unconventional, happy; the *opposite* of the mediocre, unim-

pulsive type he loathed – and yet live as if there were nothing to 'overcome', she would be an annihilating caricature: the Overman without the Overcoming!

Much of Lou's subsequent life could indeed be seen as being lived in accord with Nietzsche's seminal precepts. For she arranged her character, as he said one should, to 'give it style'.[101] She affirmatively *was* someone; she avoided the stability he warned against ('let your habits be short')[102] by vigorous alternations of contemplation with action; she knew, loved and taught the high achievements of feeling and the ecstatic possibilities of thinking. She never blamed herself, but always felt she was essentially *right* – that is, in Nietzsche's terms, felt herself to be the source of values. Neither did she blame others, nor pity them; there are plenty of instances of her helping others, but not of her feeling sorry for them, in the distracting and futile way Nietzsche attacked. And if she sometimes damaged people by her forceful irruption into their lives and by her naive attractiveness, she also gave them a tremendous amount (just as Nietzsche urged: 'a blessing *and* a danger to neighbours')[103] and gave, apparently, with that sheer straightforwardness he called 'the bestowing virtue'.

In particular, Nietzsche's description of 'the noble type of man' in *Beyond Good and Evil* (1886)[104] accords in many points remarkably well with Lou's character and thought. 'everything which he knows to be part of himself, he honours': one may think of Lou's later theory of a good narcissism. 'In the foreground stands the feeling of abundance, of a power that wants to overflow, the happiness of high tension': her essays on religion come to mind. 'The noble person also helps the unfortunate, but not from pity, or almost not; rather from an urge begotten by an over-abundance of power': this could be said of many of her relationships. 'Belief in oneself, pride in oneself' is true of her, too, as is the view of the noble person as one who above all knows how to *respect* – to respect, for example, age and tradition. And when, after an account of the opposite type, the slave (pessimistic, suspicious, sceptical valuer of pity and patience), Nietzsche gives the 'final fundamental distinction' between the noble and the base person (the base longs for freedom while the noble does *not* but practises reverence and devotion), this chimes in again with Lou's perennial guiding enthusiasms for reverence and devotion [*Ehrfurcht, Hingebung*] and with her many statements about neither feeling free nor wishing to feel free. (Of course, she made other statements insisting on her freedom, as in the letter to Gillot, but these meant freedom from conventionality, and do not contradict the statements about obeying a deeper necessity.) Perhaps it is only because she so thoroughly possessed in addition the instinct for happiness (which Nietzsche associated with slaves) that she must still have looked to him like a confounding or a parody of his ideal.

CHAPTER FOUR

Marriage and Travels

'Nichts bedürfen, alles dürfen'
(To need nothing, to be permitted everything.)[1]

For the next three years, Lou and Rée defied propriety by sharing their home without being married. At the same time, they defied the alternative expectation by *not* setting up an unregistered 'marriage' but realising Lou's dream of the ideal cohabitation: a close but passionless intellectual friendship. Just possibly, it was Rée's theoretical ideal as well, despite his original passion for Lou and his recurrent jealousies, for he had once written: 'When, in our relations with a noble, spiritual, deeply likeable woman, we finally obtain intimate possession of her as well, we always lose more than we gain'.[2]

Though they spent part of the winter of 1884–5 in Vienna, where Lou's favourite brother, Evgeny, was starting work as a doctor, they had chosen the more discreet, if more difficult, Berlin as their home. In Berlin, they had to contend with the indignation of landladies sceptical of their unprovable purity, but Vienna was worse, where the landladies were only too welcoming to a lovely young couple apparently living in sin. To protect their reputation, they selected acquaintances with care, avoiding both the good-bourgeois and the Bohemian circles and making a group of friends among 'natural scientists, orientalists, historians, philosophers'.[3] These were all youngish men (Lou was the only woman and by far the youngest in the group), many were university lecturers, and some were, or were to become, well known for their work. The learned friends gathered regularly, at first in the flat of the philosopher Ludwig Haller, and later in Lou's and Rée's home, to talk and to read to one another from their current writings. Among them* were at least three who subsequently made considerable names for themselves: Georg Brandes, the Danish critic and historian of literature; Hermann Ebbinghaus, to become known as a pioneer in experimental psychology, and apparently one of Lou's unsuccessful wooers; and Ferdinand Tönnies, the distinguished sociologist, conversationally the 'most brilliant man' Lou had met after Nietzsche, who also wooed her, admiring her 'extraordinary cleverness', 'delicacy of feeling' and 'most perfect morality'.[4]

This was no *salon*, no drawing-room reception of clever men by a woman more talented socially than intellectually. Lou von Salomé, who constantly studied and wrote (she was then writing her novel *Struggling for God*), was very much one of them, as well as their female centre-point. Indeed, if it is true that she was jocularly known as Excellency (the title she had in her Russian passport) and Paul Rée, odd though it sounds, as Maid of Honour,[5] it could almost seem a *salon* run by Rée, with Lou as one of the chief men.

Lou later described the atmosphere of their Berlin circle.[6] It was the time when the great post-Kantian systems, faced with the new Darwinism, were in decline, so it was a down-to-earth period, she thought, yet with its own idealism, as it was inspired with the sense of having to sacrifice great thoughts for the sake of terrestrial truth. There was also the beginning of a fundamental concern with psychology, which meant the beginning of an age of humility, or of 'the special pride of superiority in the establishing of human inferiority.' And all the time she felt Nietzsche standing there unseen in the midst of them, with his earth-philosophy, his psychologising and his heroism. The big difference she felt between Nietzsche and her present milieu was that, in the latter, science and passion were kept strictly separate. That was in fact what she appreciated most; it was 'the healthy clear climate I was striving for'.

MARRIAGE

Paul Rée had made a number of vain attempts to obtain a university post. In 1885, at the age of thirty-six, he embarked on the study of medicine, which took him for a time to Munich. There is little evidence of what was happening in his relationship with Lou at this time but the two had clearly grown somewhat apart and no longer shared their home. Lou continued to study, to write and to meet people of distinction. She rejected several offers of marriage. But some time during 1886 she was called on by a stranger, one Fred Charles Andreas, a specialist in Oriental languages, at that time teaching German to some Turkish officers in the boarding-house where she lived.[7] He was determined to marry her. On 1 November 1886 she became engaged to him and the following June they were married.

Whether a casual paucity of information makes it seem so, or the silence preserved about it corresponds to the actual astonishment, Andreas does seem to have dropped straight out of the sky into Lou's life and to have obtained her by some amazing force, amazing her if only with the feeling that he was indisputably the man she had to marry. She later wrote of him as both a wonder to her, essentially unfamiliar, and as also familiarly and wondrously bound to her from the beginning of time. She gave no explanation of how she came to meet him or how their acquaintance developed, no word of anything of that sort of intellectual affinity and influence that had linked her with Gillot, with Rée, with Nietzsche, or would later link her in different ways with Rilke and Tausk and Freud. As if revealed by lightning or sent by miracle, there he suddenly was, and she went without will into an extraordinary marriage.

It was a great grief to her that through it she lost Rée's friendship – indeed lost Rée altogether. In old age she still spoke of this loss as 'the irreparable'.[8] They had intended their unusual relationship to last for ever and Lou hoped, even after her marriage, to keep Rée as a lifelong friend. But some time in the spring of 1887, after a long night of talk with her, he departed in thunderous early-morning rain, leaving a note – 'Be merciful, don't look for me'[9] – and she never saw him again. His withdrawal she explained as being due to the self-hatred which he could keep in check only while she was with him, as well as to her inability to tell him (she felt it would have belittled Andreas) that she intended her marriage never to be consummated.[10]

THE IDEA OF COMPULSION

Throughout Lou's life, and through all her thinking too, a pattern can be discerned which consists of the strongest self-assertion along with the most absolute self-giving. Her mother had found her invincibly wilful at the very same time that Lou was 'recognising' Pastor Gillot as her fate and giving herself almost wholly away, mentally and emotionally, as if to something greater than human. Her marriage to Andreas shows the same two elements: an irrational compulsion to give and bind herself for ever, as though she were being forced by something much more mysterious than love – thus again the ineluctable recognition – and yet at the same time an absolute selfwill in her refusal to sleep with him.

Both these things might seem signs of an unusual freedom: surely she both *chose* Andreas (out of the many she could have married) and *decided* to stay a virgin? She said she experienced both, however, as necessities. To show the absence of rational choice in the question of virginity, she recorded a violent incident from early in the marriage.[11] One afternoon a sound woke her from a sleep. It turned out to be the rattling in the throat of her husband, whom she was in the process of strangling! He had tried to take possession of her while she slept and, *while she slept*, she had mustered the strength to kill him. So she told it, implying that this was (somewhat understandably) his last attempt. Silence then fell upon that aspect of their relationship, which was symbolised by her not wearing a wedding ring.

Lou saw her marrying, then, as an act of strange obedience. 'My love for my husband', she wrote in a long diary note in 1888,[12] eighteen months after marrying, began – I cannot express it otherwise – with an inner command ... It is not at all a question of a binding together, but of being already bound, a question as to whether there is something in us through which we are actually already married. ... It is a question of knowing whether one already belongs in the other person (not just *to* the other), and belongs, in an almost religious, or at least purely ideal, sense of the word.

She could not, of course, find adequate words: 'command', 'bond', 'religious', 'ideal': these scarcely convey what it was like, yet they do indicate something that was undoubtedly there, and something, moreover, which was surely the same thing as made Lou unusually attractive to so many people, and to so many poets and philosophers among them. Somewhere in the mystery which she sensed in Andreas, and in her insistence on acknowledging it and living by it, lay the mystery that made her what *she* was. Many years later, in *Looking Back*, she again wrote about the strange compulsion of her marriage, rather more conclusively, but even more impenetrably:

Only someone who has known him wholly and deeply ... will be able to sense what this word 'compulsion' means. What effected the compulsion was the power of the *irresistible* to which my husband himself succumbed.[13]

She described it as something gigantic, overcoming them both, and simultaneously tender and helpless, like a bird that must not be trodden on. 'The creaturely' is the nearest she came to finding a word for it.

But then there was the other compulsion – not to give her body to him. This, she said, was like (more than any apparently comparable cases) her own earlier refusal to go through with the church confirmation: that, too, had been due to a strong inner necessity, for after a dream in which she had heard herself interrupt the confirmation ceremony with a loud '*No*', she had realised it was quite impossible to force herself to do, even *pro forma*, something others demanded.[14] Neither could she make love to her husband *pro forma*. She argued to herself that married love and sexual love were quite separate things: 'by God, I have never understood why people who are in love in a predominantly sensual way get *married*'.[15] These are genuine thoughts, and perhaps one should leave the matter there, as something inexplicable, a deep and imperious certainty. But it may be relevant to look at Lou's early fictional writings, where sex is often depicted as overpowering, sudden, destructive and bringing subordination, and to consider that subordination was something she had a powerful instinct to avoid. There is no question of her ever disliking men; men were always her friends, and her theories about friendship between the sexes were as

important to her as those about love. But she resisted that instinct
which could wholly subdue her to a man. According to the fictional
work, a 'full' marriage would mean full slavery – firmly to be foregone
because deliriously desirable.

This is especially the import of the story *An Aberration* (written ten
years later, it is true, but perhaps harking back to those years), which
shows a conflict in a young woman which Helene Stöcker, always an
intelligent commentator on Lou's work, summed up, in her review of
the story,[16] as that between a 'passionate desire to be conquered as a
woman and at the same time the most outspoken urge to develop herself
further in individual freedom'. One has to shift the reference of 'desire
to be conquered' from the sexual to the magical (the irrational force of
the 'creaturely') but then the phrase does have its application to Lou
herself. Stöcker notes: 'that he was a man who had to fit the woman into
his life according to his will ... that was the enchantment!' and
something of this too is echoed in Lou's own later account of her life:
'With great naturalness I adapted myself ... to his way of life, as
seemed necessary to him for his aims. I was even ready to leave Europe
for this purpose, when at first it seemed we should go to Armenian
Persia and then to the monastery region of Echmiadzin, near Erevan.
Our external mode of living, too, was defined more and more in
accordance with that of my husband'.[17] But Stöcker's concluding
observation is the most apposite: 'Nonetheless she, the story's heroine,
knows that she would never be capable of enduring the love of a man
who *really* wanted to spellbind her onto her knees or violate her in her
individuality; and so she is condemned to swinging eternally between
the two poles of feeling.' Helene Stöcker pondered whether the higher
woman of the future might love *less* absolutely, so that love could
become an 'episode' in a woman's life, as it already was so often in a
man's – a thought Lou too was to entertain, with mixed hope and
horror.

We must return to Lou's expressed feelings at the beginning of her
marriage. In the diary note of 1888, she contrasted her relation to Gillot
with that to Andreas: the former had been a case of one person kneeling
to another, the latter was 'two people kneeling together' – to something
higher than both. The implication is that passion (present in her feeling
for Gillot and likely, she said, to have carried her away in any maturer
relationship with him) did mean kneeling. So did she marry Andreas
partly because she did not desire him? She liked his body (whereas in
Rée she had sensed the 'physically alien'[18]) but she liked it as 'creaturely', and thus not in an erotic way. Perhaps there was also a quasi-
incestual hesitation: he was of fatherly age in relation to her, and she
later noted that she could well seem to have been affected by 'those
inhibitions which so many women know of and which have nowhere

been described better and more clearly than in the findings of psycho-analysis.'[19] She added: 'However, the experiences of my later youth contradict here the correctness of such classifications', but this is unconvincing. 'Later youth' must refer to the experience with Gillot, precisely the experience of recognising that she *was* held back by such inhibitions and could not overcome them. And if Andreas stirred the old piety with which she had once believed in a paternal or grandpat-ernal God and had later loved Pastor Gillot, then this naturally kept him in the category of those who may be loved but may not be possessed.

ANDREAS

Fred Charles (or Friedrich Carl, as he later became) Andreas, was a short dark bearded man with very intense eyes. He was forty years old when he met Lou von Salomé. He was the son of a German-Malayan mother and an Armenian father, a Prince Bagratuni who had changed his name. Born in Java, Fred went to school in Germany and Switzer-land, studied Classical and Oriental languages (he knew an immense number of languages and dialects and specialised in Pahlavi) and spent six years in Persia,* where the study of inscriptions in bright sunshine damaged his eyesight. Back in Berlin, he had to give private lessons for some years. Soon after his marriage he became Professor of Persian at the newly-founded Oriental Seminar in Berlin and, in 1903, Extraordi-nary Professor of West Asiatic Languages at the University of Göttin-gen. Although he came to be regarded as the best Iranologist of his age, his reputation was largely based on promise. His perfectionism made him hesitate to publish and at seventy he was still talking of his future work. His colleagues found this sad or infuriating, but to his wife it meant that he remained young; right up to his death at eighty-five he had an exceptional vitality and charm, and his whole life was 'unaffec-tedly turned toward the extraordinary'.[20] He was a passionate teacher who would immediately plunge new pupils into the thick of his own research in a way that made them feel magically at home in it. In Göttingen, students came to his house for classes, which often went on all night, with, according to the topic, either wine and sandwiches or tea and cakes, served by Andreas 'with Oriental care'.[21]

Her own life Lou once described as 'full of Sundays'; her husband's, always overworked and restless, she called 'Sundayless'.[22] There was also something in his way of life that led her to describe him in violent terms: his fifteen years in Berlin without suitable pupils were a 'murder' of him; when once she conveyed a colleague's request to write an essay about himself he was so disturbed that he put down his cup (she wrote) as if needing his hands free to fight, perhaps to kill.[23] She saw him as always likely to burst forth in some desperate way: 'his

whole sphere of feeling was more capable of vibration than is common';
and he carried a knife. The only recorded instance of his violently using
a knife was, however, against himself. Just before their engagement, the
two of them had been talking (perhaps about the intended permanence
of her virginity) when he grasped a knife from the table and, with a
'calm movement', stabbed himself in the chest. Lou ran and got help,
but the doctor thought it was she who had done it.[24]

Through his exceptional sensitivity, Andreas had a remarkable
closeness to animals. He could get sparrows to chirp with him and
engage cockerels in crowing competitions; he once stripped naked to
deceive his dog (testing him as a watchdog) that he was a marauder,
whereby both, the absorbed creeping man and the bristling-haired giant
Newfoundlander, looked (to Lou) like two beasts of prey stalking each
other in the night.[25]

Under her husband's influence Lou came to cherish plants and
animals and altogether to admire the 'world of the not-yet-human';[26]
also to wear rough-woven clothes, eat vegetarian food, spend hours in
the open air and walk barefoot in fields and woods. But their mental and
emotional lives were lived in the main quite separately from each other.
Their work was separate – although some of Lou's essays refer to
Persian religion, her thought did not greatly alter through living with
Andreas – and the way married people change and develop through
years of being rubbed and polished against each other ['*Abschleifung
aneinander*'[27]] was unknown to them. So little did they ever sit talking
'of an evening, round the lamp', that when, in her late sixties, she lay ill
in a clinic and he, over eighty, visited her for the specified hour each
day, they found themselves involved in real conversation for the first
time.[28]

TEMPELHOF, SCHMARGENDORF, FRIENDS

They had set up house in Tempelhof, a suburb of Berlin, where they
lived for five years, at first in Andreas's bachelor flat and later in a grand
but dilapidated house they rented in the same suburb, with a garden
full of elms and huge rooms that reminded Lou of home in Petersburg.
From Tempelhof they moved in 1892 to another Berlin suburb (or
outlying village, as it then was): Schmargendorf.

It was in 1892 that Lou made one of her two long-lasting friendships
with women. Frieda von Bülow, five years older than Lou, was an
eccentric, gifted and moody person whom Lou described in one of her
novels[29] as fighting against the melancholy and masochism that came
from belonging to a family too old and too noble. Frieda was an
explorer: she had been in Zanzibar with the colonist Carl Peters, with
whom she was in love and helped to found medical stations; she went
back there in 1893 and wrote a number of novels set in colonial Africa.

She and Lou saw a great deal of each other, at intervals; they travelled together in Europe and corresponded regularly until Frieda's death in 1909. Lou's second close friend, whom she met in 1896, was Helene Klingenberg (born von Klot-Heydenfeldt, a Baltic baroness), three years younger than herself. She lived from 1899 in Berlin with her husband Otto, an architect, and their children. Lou stayed with Helene on most of her visits to Berlin after she had herself moved out of the city. Rilke once described Helene's family as 'very lovely and mature ... very secure and dear and good';[30] Lou, who never had children of her own, was emotionally close to Helene's children and valued the warm domesticity of Helene's home.

Most of the Andreases' acquaintances lived in out-of-town parts of Berlin similar to Schmargendorf. An animated social, literary and artistic life went on in these suburbs.

In Erkner lived Gerhart Hauptmann with his wife ... and three small sons ... there too Arne Garborg and the charming flaxen-blond Hulda Garborg. In Friedrichshagen lived Bruno Wille, Wilhelm Bölsche and the two brothers Hart, who soon drew a whole trail of people there after them – Ola Hansson-Marholm, August Strindberg and others ... I still remember the first gathering at our house, on the flowery terrace and in the dining-room behind it I see Max Halbe ... Arno Holz, Walter Leistikow, John Henry Mackay, Richard Dehmel ...[31]

Others Lou came to know at this time were Fritz Mauthner, the philosopher and novelist, their neighbour in his Grunewald house; the editor, Maximilian Harden, her friend for many years; Otto Hartleben, Eugen Kühnemann and many other writers; and the theatre producers, Otto Brahm and Max Reinhardt.* She continued her friendship with Ebbinghaus and others from the years she had spent with Paul Rée. She and her husband knew well Gerhart Hauptmann, chief dramatist of the Naturalist movement, and his wife from October 1889, and met them occasionally up to 1894. (In 1900, after a six-year gap, Lou met Hauptmann again and introduced Rilke to him.) Whereas with Rée she had avoided the Bohemian and literary world, with Andreas she did just the opposite and threw herself into it with energy, enjoying the society of writers and contributing to their debates both in talk and in print: this was the time of her first prolonged involvement in writing and being published.

Meanwhile Paul Rée, who never got in touch with Lou again and is said to have hated her memory, had gone on to a different sort of life. He finished his medical studies and became a doctor on his family's estate, where he lived very simply, treating the poor without payment and often paying their hospital fees himself. In 1900, when the estate was sold, he moved to Celerina in Switzerland, and there devoted himself to the poor and the sick, so that he soon became known locally as a saint. He died at the age of 51 in October 1901, by falling from a rock in the mountains.

LEDEBOUR

Only once in those years did Lou's resistance to the sexual danger almost slacken: in her relationship with Georg Ledebour.* Ledebour, later very important in the German Reichstag, was working as a journalist when, in 1892, he met and fell in love with Lou. He had edited the *Berliner Volkszeitung* with Franz Mehring in the 1880s, then had joined the staff of the social-democratic paper *Vorwärts*. He was forty-two, a Marxist and a freethinker '*von Hause aus*'. He ran educational courses for workers. He impressed people as 'absolutely fearless'[32] and selfless, as a powerful, clever and sarcastic orator, as an enjoyer of fights and a man able to be unjust and tactless but having both magnanimity and modesty, a great strength of character.

Ledebour fell in love with Lou and, guessing that she was not really a 'wife', declared his love. Discreetly, indeed cryptically, Lou confessed in *Looking Back* that her feeling responded to his.[33] Andreas was furiously jealous and there were scenes of murderous rage. A description of the undertakings, the meetings, the passionate correspondence of that year cannot and need not be given in detail. There are two important things to be said. First, this marital crisis, which was felt so strongly that not only did Andreas plan suicide but his wife turned it into a double-suicide plan, marked a deep change in their relations and the beginning of the enormous freedom that characterised Lou's whole life thereafter. Second, the very little she said about Ledebour in *Looking Back* does hint at the special importance of the temptation he presented to her. At that moment she was offered something which, given Ledebour's realistic exhortations and appeals to her esteem for 'knowledge' (what did she *know* of love?) as well as his tenderness (he was attracted by her Brunnhilde-like defiance) must have been desperately tempting: it was the offer of the abundant happiness of normality. At that moment she might have gone away into a splendidly normal marriage, one starting from a shared passion, perhaps producing children, and very likely involving some sort of politically active life as helper of a prominent husband. She rejected all that out of fidelity to the inexplicable kinship with Andreas, and doubtless also for the sake of an unconventionality which guaranteed her independence – perhaps in ways she did not even then quite foresee.

She does not seem to have done any brooding over this, or blaming of herself or anyone else, and at the end of her life, when she remembered Ledebour (who had remained so angry that years later he had sent back a letter from her unopened), she said, as if none of it had ultimately mattered: 'These lines greet him'.[34] Yet it had mattered. It had been an important turning-point. Clearly enough, Lou did not want that total married union with a man which is generally regarded as desirable and normal. Perhaps, despite the difficulties she went through and the pain it meant to herself and to others, she should be seen as pointing to another kind of ideal love life altogether. In his recent biography of Nietzsche, C. P. Janz, attempting to understand the phenomenon of Lou von Salomé, recalls that according to Aristophanes in Plato's *Symposium*, love was the result of God's slicing the originally spherical and self-sufficient human beings into two halves, so that each, ever after, ran around looking for its other half. He adds: 'From this conception/of love/Louise was very distant.'[35] This is certainly true, but when he relates this to Lou's being 'never mature for marriage'[36] and insufficiently aware of her one-sidedness (halvedness), and when he says that her not seeking total union with another human being showed her wanting in something vital, he neglects the possibility that she was living by a different model. In fact the very selection of the Aristophanes passage is arbitrary. Socrates' view of love, put a little later in the *Symposium*, may be more appropriate. According to Socrates, one should learn to separate the lovable – the beautiful – qualities from the loved person, and finally reach the point where one can love Beauty itself, seeing only instances of it in individuals who happen to be beautiful. Beauty is an ocean, the beauties of particular men mere water droplets in it. This view suggests an admirable wholeness in the individual lover – he is mature not when he feels himself a half in need of another half, but when he is sufficiently whole to revere the absolute and to love its examples without being bewitched by them. Not that Lou was exemplarily Socratic, but there is a better parallel to be found here than in the Aristophanic view. It could be argued, for one thing, that it was from a desire for something bigger than could inhere in any individual that she preserved herself from exclusive passionate attachment to any one man, and that much later, when she gave herself in love to particular men, it was because she then felt free to acknowledge in them fragments of a loveliness which she inwardly cherished as indivisible. For another thing, she later argued vehemently for the bisexuality of every human being, and seems always to have felt the presence of man and woman in herself, not sliced asunder but still in the original paradisal conjunction, and to have resented all approaches to her which acknowledged the woman only.

All she ever wrote about herself, and all she wrote about the nature of woman, suggests she did think in ways compatible with Socrates' way: she did feel complete in herself, and she described femaleness as essentially self-sufficient, impersonal, occasionally opening up to admit another being but only 'for the sake of *better* completion'[37] (my italics), and apt to contemplate the eternal harmony of things.

NATURALISM

In the years 1889–90 Lou Andreas-Salomé was writing her first
scholarly book, a study of Ibsen's female characters. This was published in 1891 and was very favourably received. Somehow Lou always
arrived at the heart of things just when that heart was beating especially
strongly. Her participation in German literature took place at the very
moment when that literature was undergoing a remarkable rebirth.
This was taking place largely in Berlin, and it was mainly the work of
the young men who gathered in Friedrichshagen. These were the
avant-garde dramatists, poets and novelists, theorists and thinkers, of
the movement known as Naturalism. The years 1889–92 were the
Berlin movement's heady years.[38] For a year, Lou and Andreas were
members of the 'Verein Freie Bühne', the theatre club ('free from
considerations of theatre censorship and of earning money'),[39] set up in
1889 for the semi-private production of plays too daring to be performed on the public stage. It flourished vigorously for four years. Lou also
wrote articles for the associated periodical, *Die Freie Bühne*, which has
lasted to this day.[40] Moreover, her book on Ibsen appeared just at the
time when Ibsen was replacing Zola as the preferred model. Both her
interest in Ibsen and her connection with – and forthcoming book on –
Nietzsche qualified her, in advance of her personality, for a significant
position among the Naturalists.

There was an optimistic spirit among them which suited Lou well.
Their interest was declaredly away from the past and towards everything present; they felt modern. In biology, the theory of evolution and
natural selection; in psychology, the idea of the Unconscious and
beginnings of ideas about the minute dependence of the mind's
workings upon physical factors: these contributed to the vision of a
world in which the absence of God and of free will was compensated by
the wonder of all phenomena and by the sense that things were going
forward. The determinism implied by evolution theory mattered less
than its idea of an endless improvement. Many spoke of the emergence
of a higher type of man, or Superman,* and in general the influence of a
more or less misunderstood Nietzsche was felt.

The *Freie Bühne* proclaimed that it wanted to attack falsehood,
examine the 'finest interrelationships of modern art and modern life',[41]
promote an untendentious art ('morality begins exactly at the point
where art ends')[42] and to bring art closer to science – 'the basis of our
whole modern thinking is the natural sciences'[43] – by demonstrating,
for instance, the universality of causation. Lou could agree with all this,
though she was not especially interested in their more detailed artistic
programme. She shared too the general admiration for Tolstoy at that

time (Tolstoy was a recurrent presence in *Die Freie Bühne*) though again, she did not share the socialism of many of the Naturalists. Nor did she as yet contribute to the newly prominent 'woman question', unless the novel *Ruth*, which she was then writing, a dreamy, ardent re-telling of her experience with Gillot, be regarded as dealing with it. (Some did read it this way and saw it as showing how the cruel difficulty in the way of idealistic girls was that their sensualist teachers took advantage of their admiration.)

Her interest in religion grew during her Naturalist period; of the eight substantial articles she wrote on religion between 1891 and 1897, six appeared in *Die Freie Bühne*. But her ideas conflict with what most of the Naturalists were writing. ('Culture should rid itself of both religion and ecstasy,' wrote Heinrich Hart in 1891.[44]) Lou was developing ideas she had long held, and had been encouraged in by Nietzsche, so she was not concerned to learn from her new acquaintances in this sphere. But she did learn from them something of natural science – not its method, but at least an admiration for the physical world seen in some of the detail that the new physics, chemistry and especially biology were revealing. In this, the main influence was Wilhelm Bölsche.

BÖLSCHE

Bölsche was a biologist before he became a literary theorist. When Lou met him he was preparing his three-volume work, *Love-life in Nature*,[45] a popularisation of evolution theory, which, as friend and neighbour, Lou must have discussed with him. In this romantic – scientific work, which Freud was to mention with praise,[46] Bölsche makes a grand survey of the biological knowledge of his time; his theme is the interconnection of human, animal, plant and unicellular creatures through the phenomenon of self-propagation, to which, in all its varieties, he gives the name 'love'. From the basic bacillus, even from the inanimate matter out of which it arose, and which – as Bölsche stresses with Goethean delight – shares so many attributes of our love-life: election, attraction, adhesion, division, reformation; to Raphael's Sistine Madonna and Child, the world is harmoniously and ever-changingly united in love, in sexual energy. 'In the original bacillus already lurks the human being.'[47] Nothing is ugly in the world of this very visual book, where we see as in a film the beauty of the massively and awkwardly copulating ichthyosaurus, and equally the magnified beauty of the tapeworm making its placid idyll in the laboratory of the human gut and doubly 'loving' – by budding from itself and by its buds producing male and female features which proceed to a mysterious intercourse in the dark flesh of the pig. Nothing is ugly, and nothing is gloomy; evolutionism is optimism. That life has adapted itself to changing conditions for millions of years is proof that there is nothing to fear: man will adapt himself to the cooling of the sun. In all life, moreover, there is individuality, and even in non-life: crystals, snowflakes, planets, stars, the earth – each is an individual, and what is admirable in human personality is its sharing this universal condition of being rounded off into singleness, a finished unit within a vastly unified cosmos. Following Haeckel (Germany's foremost Darwinist philosopher) Bölsche suggests, further, that every cell has a kind of consciousness, a psyche, and that memory may be a basic attribute of matter.

Later, in an article called 'Physical Love' (1898), Lou gave her view of the first volume of Bölsche's book. She admired the layout, the pictures, the bold theme (though disliking the linking chatter) and was very enthusiastic about the grand demonstration that the same laws underlie what we call higher and lower manifestations, particularly the idea that sexual love is a refined form of eating, and parturition a refined form of excretion. Her emphasis, like Bölsche's, is of course not reductive but redemptive, and this is very much the way she was later to approach psychoanalysis: it enabled the forbidden and the rejected to be redeemed, restored to beauty or value. 'Physical Love' developed an interesting notion: that, as reproductive method had evolved from the protozoon's total union to the sophisticated division of labour among the organs of the mammal, and as, emotionally, humans were still at the state of total union (that is, in love we yearn not for a part of the beloved but for 'him' entire), so further development was likely to lead to just such a division of labour in the mental as took place in the physical, and it would become possible to love with a specialised bit of the self, while the rest would go on being occupied with other concerns. She did not consider that this would be better. In fact, this is a good example of her frequent theme that more advanced does not mean more valuable – on the contrary, the very balance we have now, between the specialised body organs and the non-specialised mental experience of love, is probably the best thing we possess.

Through Bölsche, Lou Andreas-Salomé became knowledgeable about the metamorphosis and variety of biological phenomena, which she was henceforth often to draw on, and he was important to her in articulating, with the advantage of a scientist's authority, the same grateful wonder in the sight of a universe from which the traditional object of religion has disappeared, as she herself now felt. The otherworldly is in fact marginally but definitely allowed for in Bölsche's other influential book, the mainly rigorously positivistic *Scientific Bases of Poetry*, where, although he states that 'Everything we humans see is physical, even the psychical, in so far as it is always linked to something physical',[48] he also argues that this very observation is an opening into something else. Establishing laws, the scientist constantly comes up against limits – he notes invariable parallels and connections but cannot say how they come about. This is enough for Bölsche to speculate that there is another, unknowable, world 'behind' the one we study. 'Of that world in itself we know nothing at all, except that it exists. But much lies in this'. The point at which the scientist, the rationalist, has no more to say, was for Bölsche the exciting point, and he was cautiously ready to allow a whole sphere of 'miracle' at this point. Here too he influenced Lou, who in her way thought the same.

PARIS, VIENNA, MUNICH

Lou Andreas-Salomé led an intense social and intellectual life in the later 1890s, in three major cities, Paris, Vienna and Munich, in each of which she reached a significant stage in her emotional development. By now well known as the writer of several books and many articles, she was received in literary circles for her achievements as well as for her personality. The experience with Ledebour had led to an acknowledge-ment between herself and Andreas that they could not live together all the time, and this meant a series of lengthy separations. So the uncon-ventional marriage not only confirmed her inward freedom but also forced her out into greater freedom of movement and acquaintance.

In the spring of 1894 she went to Paris, the first cosmopolitan city she had lived in since Berlin. She met a number of writers there, mainly the visiting Germans and Scandinavians: for instance, Knut Hamsun ('who looked like a Greek God'), Hermann Bangs (who, though ill, had an inward 'sparkle'),[49] and Frank Wedekind,* with whom she spent a lot of time and had an embarrassing misunderstanding when he mistakenly assumed she would welcome him as a lover. She also got to know the Russian colony in Paris, introduced to it by a compatriot, a Russian doctor called Savely, of romantic background and incredible physical strength. Savely took her to stay with him in a hut near Zurich, where they lived for a while on milk, cheese, bread and berries, and climbed the mountains barefoot. They also did some writing together.[50] There is no statement or evidence of anything beyond a friendship, and this, given Lou's views and feelings, is undoubtedly what it was. In October she went back to Schmargendorf, to the joy of both herself and Andreas, and from now on the pattern was often repeated: she would leave, stay a long time in another town, be vigorously involved in friendships and cultural life, then return to the peace of home and the glad, conciliatory embrace of her husband.

From April of the following year (1895) she spent several months in Vienna, a city she characterised as a 'matching of intellectual and erotic life'.[51] Here literary society was opened to her through her Berlin friends. She met and liked the writer Peter Altenberg, and called on the aged author Marie von Ebner-Eschenbach. But the most interesting of her literary acquaintances there was with the group consisting of Arthur

Schnitzler (who had just become celebrated for his *Liebelei*, performed for the first time that year), Richard Beer-Hofmann (known for his *Novellen* of 1893 and to have great success with his play, *Der Graf von Charolais*), Hugo von Hofmannsthal (then only twenty but already known as a precocious poetic genius) and the dramatist and animal story writer, Felix Salten, made famous by *Bambi*.*

The next year, 1896, Lou spent a long time in Munich. Max Halbe has called the 1890s the era when Munich flourished in three spheres: beer, carnival and art. As regards the last of these, it was a time when 'everything that was young and hopeful and wanted to spread its wings gathered in Munich as if by appointment.'[52] Lou thought, too, that there was no specially 'Munich' type of life; instead she found there a community of 'all the nationalities of Germany'.[53] She met old friends there (Max Halbe himself, Frank Wedekind and others) and made new ones, among them the novelist Jakob Wassermann, and August Endell, the artist craftsman and architect, who was particularly active in the *Jugendstil* movement. Here once again Lou was involved (at least slightly) in the beginning of a new direction in art: Jugendstil, the German equivalent of art nouveau, had begun to develop in Munich precisely in that year, 1896, when its two main periodicals, *Jugend* and *Simplicissimus*, were founded.

In Vienna Lou felt an attraction to Richard Beer-Hofmann which seemed to her a second (after Ledebour) testing of her capacity for sexual love.[54] Though nothing came of it but a lasting affection, she was now increasingly impelled by a yearning which drove her onwards into a sort of late adolescence. In 1897 she was once again in Munich, where she met the young poet, René Maria Rilke. He became her first lover and was to be an intimate friend for nearly thirty years.

CHAPTER FIVE

Essays on Religion

'everything rare, strange, privileged, the higher man, the higher soul, the higher duty, the higher responsibility, fullness of creative power and lordliness'.[1] NIETZSCHE

When Nietzsche encouraged Lou von Salomé to philosophise about religion, he was recognising an inclination she showed long before she met him. Faith and loss of faith had been her main childhood experience, history of religion had been her main study with both Gillot and Biedermann. She went on thinking about religion all her life. Her theories about art, love, femaleness and Russia are all closely related to her religious views. More specifically, though, during the years 1891–8, and still under Nietzsche's influence, she devoted eleven long essays to this subject.

  Some of the essays are more scholarly, some more personal. All suffer from looseness of expression and structure; one would like to rewrite them concisely, put in paragraphing, and request some references and facts. She often talks of history, of developments and changes, without mentioning time or place, and sums up literatures without naming a book; she seems carried away by ideas too pressing to allow time for detail or proof. None the less, all are worth reading: in addition to their interest as part of a contemporary debate, there is in these writings a forthrightness and vitality which greatly commend them. Forthrightness is not a quality of Nietzsche's; if what Lou Andreas-Salomé took from Nietzsche was the confident glorification of the individual mind, the habit of thinking evolutionarily, and the assumption of a responsibility for 'culture', what eluded her in him was the whole of his irony and paradox. Nietzsche could praise intelligence while showing the ambiguity of all its achievements, but Lou was uncomplexly enthusiastic, and the uncritical confidence of her style gives, to put it mildly, a tolerant restfulness to ideas that in Nietzsche are utterly demanding.

  Lou Andreas-Salomé's study of religion amounts to a study of religious feeling. The 'death of God' is central, for her argument usually starts from the conviction (still novel in her time) that 'God' has a history: he was born, he lived and he died. The big divergence from Nietzsche is that, in her theory, God also has an after-life. The object of faith has indeed disappeared (ceased to be believed in), but while it was there it caused the growth of feelings which would otherwise never have come into being, and these are the most valuable feelings we are capable of. Her concern is to describe and promote these feelings.

Like Nietzsche, she is dismayed at the banality with which some Bible critics and 'free-thinking' writers approach matters so serious as the shattering of a great tradition,* and scornful of their inability to *feel* what they were doing. She would have shared the attitude of George Eliot, who had translated both Strauss and Feuerbach into English and been in the forefront of debates in England about Darwin, yet still said that to her 'the Development Theory and all other explanations of processes by which things came to be, produce a feeble impression compared with the mystery that lies under the processes', and also that she cared 'only to know, if possible, the lasting meaning that lies in all religious doctrine from the beginning till now'.[2] Lou, though, spoke less of a 'lasting meaning' than of an everchanging meaning, itself the product of change.

THE BACK-EFFECT

Lou's central ideas are set out in her first long article, 'Realism in Religion' (1891). The divine has a history, and its history has two stages: in the first the gods were created and were worshipped, though without the inner devotion that appears only in the second. First of all, man made God. Then the man-made God made plain man into god-made man – that is, into man with a need for God, a need not merely to explain the mysteries of nature but to satisfy the idealism that had developed in him through his evolving relationship with the God he had made.

This is not a concern with ethics; it is not a matter of people having changed through *behaviour* resulting from their faith, nor of evolution of feelings towards other people; it is solely a concern with the feelings that are addressed to the Deity and that survive its demise. This idea is elaborated repeatedly in Lou's essays on religion, as if she is forever engaging with something she can never finally express. Man creates gods. Then the gods influence man. Whereby it is most characteristic that she does not say 'the idea of the gods', or 'the idea of God', influences man.

The formulation is perhaps most succinct in her essay 'Jesus the Jew' a few years later:

If one starts from the human being instead of – as one used to – from the God, then one realises almost involuntarily that the actual religious phenomenon first comes to be present in the *back-effect* of a godhead – no matter how it arose – upon the person who believes in that godhead.[3]

She was to become known as the propounder of the theory of the 'back-

effect' (*Rückwirkung*). As late as 1955, Karl Kerényi quotes this
sentence (on which he bases a large part of his inquiry into the history
of religion) and comments: 'Here that precise borderpoint is identified
at which a science of religion becomes possible; at which the religious
already exists ... The science of religion begins with the concern with
what Lou Salomé calls the "back-effect".'[4]

REALISM IN RELIGION

This first article started with the need for a new approach to religion.
No naive belief, nor positivist denial, nor the current matter-of-fact
efforts to rescue something of Christianity for 'modern man': instead an
approach which would start from the fact of religious *experience* – a
'psychology of religion', an exploration of the obscure areas of religious
mood and impulse which are not (*pace* Paul Rée) explained away by
their origination in error.

Lou discusses here a recent book about religious experience and dwells
on two affective moments in the unnamed author's account of this:
humility and pride. She has a lot to say about pride in this context.
Christian writers usually stress humility – Rudolf Otto, for instance,
speaks of 'creature-consciousness', the sense of one's own abasement, of
being overpowered by something other than oneself, the feeling 'I am
nought', and calls the feeling of identification of the personal self with
the transcendent reality not 'pride' but 'bliss'.[5] Lou Andreas-Salomé,
by contrast, dwells on the exhilaration of the very swing from 'I am
nought' to 'I am all'. Seeing it another way, from 'I am all' to 'I *have*
all'; or again, in another image, of the friction between these opposite
attitudes:

> Neither the sincerest humility and self-prostration before an ideal
> conceived as divine, nor the most full and satisfying enjoyment of all
> self-assertive powers for themselves alone, is able to produce the
> religious affect. Only the two together in enigmatic self-contradiction
> yield that friction from which suddenly, hot and vivid, the flame leaps
> out.[6]

She often uses pairs of words, like '*Demut*' and '*Hochmut*' ('humility'
and 'pride') and claims there is in all of us this inebriant seesawing
between 'the awareness of weakness and helplessness in the face of all
reality and the pride of being, as a human, in a certain sense superior to
it all'. These combined, she says, make up our highest feeling, which is
also described as 'the knowledge of our limit, and at that limit the
exaltation that grows beyond it'.[7]

This is not equally available to everyone. Fascinated with the idea that
evolution means ever greater individuation, she sees the desire for God
as an increasingly individual desire, leading to ever more individual

God-creating. I make a God for *me*. So, as well as collective God-making, followed historically by the back-effect of the shared God upon people in general, there is also an individual God-making, with consequent lasting effect upon 'Me'. Indeed, the 'greater' the individual personality, the greater its capacity to pray to what is conceived as the holiest. Echoing her Tautenburg diary notes, she states:

> The religious affect is thus also the characteristic sign of all *great egoists* – taking greatness here in the sense of a *force*, not as a mere selfish *direction* of the being.[8]

This is what religion always is, she says, for it aims at 'egoism' and the individual, its chief and reckless question being 'What must I do to be blessed?' (In German, as in Russian, 'blessed' and 'blissful' are the same word.)

Lou sounds like Nietzsche when she upbraids her author for becoming too theoretical and adapting his own experience to the existing theology. One would like to take each thing he says he values and ask 'How do *you* stand in relation to this: was it the ladder for *you* to climb up by toward yourself . . .?'[9] and she quotes Zarathustra: 'Let yourself be in the deed, as the mother is in the child: let this be *your* word about virtue!'[10] The conclusion of the essay is Nietzschean, too – a vehement page or so on most people's inability to care about what is going on. Religion is increasingly enfeebled, God is vanishing behind abstractions, and yet

> Nothing is more amazing than the ease, even the pleasure, with which nearly every cultivated person of today is capable of swallowing down the vastest helping of doubts – so long as they're 'modern' ones – without getting the slightest spiritual discomfort from it; they are like conjurors who swallow swords.

And she adds:

> *May* it tear us to bits! If only we *were* less conjurors and more real people who feel in their innermost life the things that they think and do.[11]

One has to keep in mind that what she laments is the disappearance not of faith, but of feeling. The courage to *feel* the loss of God is more creative than any clinging to His image, and only from courage will great personalities be born. By implication, the purpose of our existence is the production of great personalities; this is a part of Nietzsche's thought that she has made her own.

'HARNACK AND THE APOSTOLIC CREED' AND FOUR OTHER ESSAYS, 1892–5

Between 'Realism in Religion' and the important 'Jesus the Jew' of

1896, Lou published five other articles on religion. Two were in 1892, the polemic 'Harnack and the Apostolic Creed' and the self-indulgent 'God-creation'. The latter is an autobiographical piece, less well argued than most. It could have been entitled 'self-creation', for it seems that the projecting of the self into an invisible being, wholly believed in as existing 'out there in the real', is what the 'religious' means; and the article is written in a spirit of somewhat complacent gratitude for having had, in infancy, the naive and sober certainty of the existence of – such a – God. It is hard to grasp that she is *not* saying that God is only a projection of the self. But the essay is anything but a coolly reductive exercise. When she says 'This involuntary blending and exchanging of the most intimate ... with the most lofty – this conception of the intimate *as* the lofty, already contains the characteristic basic element of the religious', she is conceiving of that 'loftiest' as somehow really existent. If it slides out of the categories of subjective and objective, without clarity as to whether a third category is intended, or a transcending of these two, then this appears to be a non-definition essential to the experience.

'Harnack and the Apostolic Creed' is much more interesting and Nietzsche's influence is palpable in it. It praises the courageous, godless life and distinguishes between the few who can live such a life and the many who cannot. Un-Nietzschean, though, is the way Lou Andreas-Salomé does not scorn the 'many'; in fact the article is written in their defence, and for their protection. It is her response to a tract by the Protestant theologian, Adolf Harnack, just published in its fifteenth edition, widely on sale and a talking-point in many circles.[12] As an inquiry into the origin and varied history of the apostolic creed, it angered the orthodox and delighted the free-thinkers. Andreas-Salomé, while approving of its historical approach, curiously enough argues for orthodoxy, and asserts that not only are Harnack's revelations unlikely to shake the rigours of orthodoxy, but they *ought* not to shake them.

Her argument is ingenious. Precisely because religious forms sprang up in consequence of human wishes and needs – because, that is, they are not about something objectively there (here she appears to say straight out that there is no God), they are vulnerable and might disappear; but religion is good for us, we evolve and deepen through it. Rigid, even petrified dogma, and all the firm traditional forms, far from being a deathly element, have been – and for some still are – essential to the preserving of religious life. Even Protestantism needs some orthodoxy. Those who talk of individual assent, moral uplift and spiritual transport, rather than of doctrine and formality, are confused about the way religion arises: need creates God, then God creates in His believers specific religious feelings, but those feelings are not felt by all to the same extent and at the same time. For instance, not by certain simple people, or by people in despair and suffering. What these people may need in addition to our efforts to do what we can to improve the conditions of their lives (and this is one of the few places where she says anything of this order) is the consolation and support of firm doctrine. So while the stronger and luckier no longer need it, it must be kept for the weaker and less fortunate. This may sound a little like the view of Dostoyevsky's Grand Inquisitor, the benevolent dictator who, himself an atheist, spends his life promoting belief in God for the multitude who cannot do without it, only where he is burdened with anguish and the strain of keeping it all going, Lou's more developed and prosperous non-believer, who is to protect the belief for the others, is thought of as purely happy, the only true enjoyer of religion's natural and wonderful fruits. (Also, of course, she does not envisage either tyranny or Utopia.)

These true enjoyers should leave the church, she says, while (presumably) continuing to present church-protective arguments. Free-thinking has no business to be going on *in* the church. It damages the interests of the simple and the poor, and also dissuades stronger minds from leaving. Full of the enthusiasm they have gained from religion, these people should leave all beaten tracks and take their light into pathlessness (*'das Weglose'*) – all the dark places the church knows nothing of. Again we hear Nietzsche: the highest daring is that which explores places never yet made habitable by any kind of meaning. Lou's paradoxical and optimistic variant of this is that the most valuable thing religion gives us is the courage to explore the dark places without its help. Truth, she says, is a more jealous God than the Judaeo-Christian one, and you have to be ready to be destroyed by it.

The early 'history of God' is developed in two subsequent studies: 'From the beast to the God' (1893) outlines, among the early Semites, an evolution from tribal gods through animal totems to 'God' as 'king of the land'. 'The Problems of Islam', a year later, is an enthusiastic piece of scholarship (perhaps inspired by Andreas) arguing that the ancient Arabs, the very type of the original uncultivated human being, not yet religious, but lordly, proud and full of splendid virtues, were weakened by the humbling and levelling effects of the later Islamic culture; clearly with Nietzsche in mind, she writes of 'an original master morality and its destruction through the slave morality of religious culture.' Then, in 'On the Origin of Christianity' (1895), Lou is concerned with how the few plain facts of Jesus's life were transformed into legend and glory. But her main study of Jesus is the essay of 1896, which was to impress and influence Rilke.

'JESUS THE JEW'

'Jesus the Jew' re-states Lou Andreas-Salomé's main ideas and develops them to a new conclusion. The conclusion – which we are largely left to draw – is that Jesus belongs among the great unbelievers, the geniuses of unbelief.

Rehearsing her two stages in the life of God, she points out that while the first one is amazing enough, even more amazing is the second, when the idea of God may so drench someone's inner life that he grows into something greater than he could otherwise ever have been. By stressing Jesus's Jewishness – he was not the overcomer of Judaism but its sharpest expression – she is able to make him a forerunner of her great religious unbelievers. For, as a Jew, he believed God would manifest himself upon earth at the right time and believed this quite simply and practically – 'The Jew did not brood over his God, he suffered and lived and felt',[13] and trusted not in breath but in blood, that is not in a hereafter but in the keeping of divine promises on earth. Like some other martyrs, then, Jesus expected God's manifestation at the last moment: and at the last moment he found that it was not going to happen. He thus faced something far more terrible than did later Christian martyrs, for they were to die expecting Heaven, while he died expecting nothing. In this way she interprets the cry 'My God, why have you forsaken me?' as his *really* taking upon himself in that moment, just as we say he did, 'the suffering of all mankind'. For he suffered the suffering that lies in wait for us all when, having trusted in a personal God, we find out that there is none.

Although she does not explicitly connect Jesus with the ideal of the free-thinking genius, the conjunction of very great love with complete and sharply felt unbelief, and the fortitude in enduring the two together, suggest the connection. Jesus was essentially and solely the lonely genius, capable of the highest human feeling and so deep in it that nothing else mattered to him; he was not the founder of a new religion, although a new religion was, paradoxically, born of the events connected with him.

Religion in its whole truth and its whole illusion, embodied in a human being, bled away to death here on the cross, which, since then, strangely enough, has become the symbol of religion.[14]

The Cross (she ends the essay), whatever it may mean in Christianity, should really remind us

that it is always only the individual, the great individual who attains the peaks of religion, its genuine blissfulness and its full tragedy. What he experiences up there, the crowd below does not learn.[15]

'RELIGION AND CULTURE', 'FROM THE HISTORY OF GOD',
'ON THE RELIGIOUS AFFECT'

After 'Jesus the Jew' Lou published four more long essays on religion.

'Egoism in Religion' (1899) is largely a replay of former themes, but three essays of 1897–8 offer interesting developments of them.

According to 'Religion and Culture' (1898), all cultural activities originated in religion like children from one mother; and each, as it grew up and away, ceased to need parental guidance, so that the lonely mother was thrown back on her own resources: that is, religion became specialised, concerned only with the belief in God and visibly separated off from the rest of life. But the 'children' carried an invisible aspect of religion further and further along with them, and this emerges at peak points in the lives of individuals. For:

> Innumerable people have innumerable times applied the name God to something other than God; innumerable souls have let their most ardent pieties and enthusiasms overflow away from faith and into life ... God is not God but only a symbol for all that in human life that is too intimate, intense and dear to be called by a human name.[16]

Rather mysteriously, she says that religion's dream of salvation, the dream of God as the life of life, is perhaps only true and 'blessed-making' at the two extremes: deep below in the dark places where man was born as man, believing he derived from God; and high above on the summits of culture where he feels he is at last truly man – and gives birth to God.

Then, in part of 'From the History of God' (1897) and in most of 'On the Religious Affect' (1898), Lou Andreas-Salomé sets out what I will call her theory of sublime moods. Both these essays are written with an excitement that shows she is describing her own experiences. She is deeply convinced of the possibility of joy. Her tone is that of urging people to stop being dry-as-dust, to look upwards and to realise how intensely happy they could be. They should stop both protesting against old articles of faith and rehearsing old habits of belief, and should instead take a fresh look and see the whole phenomenon of religion anew, as someone might look again at his wintry old home in the spring.

'From the History of God' starts with another attack on the accommodations of the modern church to rationalism and science, and quotes Nietzsche's 'madman'[17] who cried out that 'we have killed God' and 'who will wipe this blood from us?'

It is followed by a weird account of the history of religion in five stages, unsupported by evidence. These she says go from intoxicated freedom in interpretation, through the demand for orthodoxy (not ossification but a necessary harness), then a stage of asceticism and self-humbling (which produces for the first time the 'objective godhead', or rather conceals for the first time its actually human origin), to another of mysticism, and finally to one of rationalism, in which the mysteries

are put to the test of reason. After this nothing much is left but a
dubious brew of allegory. Thus is the contemporary church – feeble
and droughted. It is this rationalistic dreariness that is now contrasted
with her account of what, in an age after the death of God, the
religiously-inclined person could be having. Her own theory of sublime
feelings is now presented as a contrast to the pettiness of those who
couldn't care less about the death of God. The sublime feeling (a chief
part of which is actually 'devotion') comes when external events, no
longer speaking in their everyday voice, appear to reveal themselves as
symbols, 'as if they were uttering something divine to us'.[18] The man of
a particular faith was able to give clear expression to this state; we
cannot. None the less, at such moments of self-communion [*'Einkehr
und Sammlung'*] we are totally concerned and participant; everything
becomes unified, peaceful, profound. (Although Lou does not derive
this mood from childhood or countryside, nor connect it with impulses
to perform acts of kindness, there is an obvious similarity to many other
accounts of an experienced quasi-religious peace, for example to
Wordsworth's 'serene and blessed mood' in which 'with an eye made
quiet by the power/Of harmony, and the deep power of joy,/ we see into
the life of things'.)[19] Now this mood, she declares, is not a sentimental
reminiscence of faith, but a new growth from the soil from which all
religion grows. And non-believers can in fact have intenser religious
experience than believers, for the latter may be hindered by the weight
of their fixed faith from daring 'to enter into all the hidden blisses
where the faithless person frequently feels and experiences something'.

'On the Religious Affect' then proceeds to distinguish two basic states
of mind. One kind is shared with people in general, the other is not.
Above the stable, indubitable and universally shared everyday moments
of our existences there tower, like mountain peaks over a great plain,
our lofty moments of beauty and ecstasy, which are *not* shared, and
which we don't feel any need to share, so confident are we of their
reality:

> Plains flow effortlessly into one another, but that which rises above the
> flat ground is separated – to the extent that it reaches upward – from
> neighbours and comrades; certainly the summits may be similar to
> each other in kind and in height, yet you will only get from the one to
> the other by a detour over the common ground and by climbing
> painfully up.[20]

Despite their tremendous separateness, we feel in those moments that
we are breathing 'the air of home'; what's more, we feel certain that
others have their own such experiences, and without needing even to
think about it (whether they do or not) we quite naturally seek to
express that experience in words or deeds. Not, she stresses, for the *sake*

of others, although it will turn out to have *been* expressed for them.

Mountain peaks are Nietzsche's frequent image, and when Lou writes here –

> then come the individuals once again to one another and they
> recognise and greet one another, and there goes a laughter from
> summit to summit . . .[21]

she echoes Nietzsche's 'republic of geniuses', in which 'one giant calls to another across the arid intervals of the ages, and, undisturbed by wanton noisy dwarfs creeping about beneath them, the lofty intercourse of spirits continues.'[22]

Unlike Nietzsche, she also conceives of the most extreme individuality as a moving away into the experience of something no longer to be called *self*. 'At these heights of our self we are released from ourselves.'

The essay culminates in prophecy. An epoch is to come in which all fragmentation and isolation will be overcome. A time of harmony and of blossoming when, instead of endlessly collecting pieces of new scientific knowledge like gathering gold coins into an enormous heap, we shall join together and begin to *spend* our wealth. All will come together 'and close into a whole, in art, science, ethics and life' and

> there goes a laughter from summit to summit, as if what had seemed,
> not long past, to be shapeless mountain-ranges rising up meaninglessly
> here and there, and just as meaninglessly plunging down to the flat
> plain, were being quietly shaped and arranged into a gigantic human
> building, like a temple, with the immeasurable sky above it.

An impracticable vision, yet not a vision of Heaven or the end of time. It is conceived evolutionarily and relatively; for it, too, she says, will pass away, and we must not mind that this will happen. Just as she put it in *Struggling for God*, she says here:

> What does it matter if late-following generations look back upon this
> as upon collapsed ruins and see in them only what we ourselves see in
> the highest dreams of past epochs: a mere symbol of our own highest
> dream?[23]

Is this Lou Andreas-Salomé's equivalent of Nietzsche's 'eternal recurrence of all things'? She endures, and makes a part of her scheme, the thought of the inevitable disappearance of all things. Since she is certain that happiness and perfection are not only definitely coming in the future in all their fullness, but are already intimated, already being enjoyed; since she herself already enjoyed their intimations with a peace and security such as Nietzsche never knew; the thought of Disappearance must be a far more desolating one than that of Recurrence would be. It is impressive to see how she accepts temporality and transience with a wave of the hand, with a light gesture, an almost aesthetic flourish, at the end of this solemn, ecstatic essay.

CONCLUSIONS AND QUESTIONS

On the central question Lou is never quite clear. She will build a complex argument leading to it but, reaching it, behaves as if it were not there: instead of the peak of a hill with a view all round, there is a cloud, into which she walks. I mean the question: given that we 'make' God, what can be meant by 'God's existence'? Does God exist or not? Repeatedly she argues that God came into being in the course of history, as the product of human wishing, willing, believing. Does it not follow that He is a figment, a fiction?

We postulate God, learn this *was* only a postulate, abandon it, but not before we have developed a whole range of valuable feelings in relation to it. That is, we have become religious beings, enriched and enabled. These feelings now need fresh objects, so we set up new ideals, something else to revere, love and work for – hence the best in our culture – and in our finest achievements we recreate God. For those who have not learnt that God was merely our postulate, the church with its dogma and mysteries should continue, but we luckier and cleverer ones already overflow with the best it was able to give us, and can now bear to know it was a beneficial error. But when she comes to the point of saying God was an error, and there is no God without us, she doesn't say it. Instead it appears, without scrutiny, that there is no difference between emotion about God, and God. It seems that God *is*, wherever He is needed, and He is needed not only by the weak as a prop, but also by the strong as recipient of their gratitude.

> It would be unendurable, indeed quite simply impossible ... to be without him in those highest moments in which one does not wish to be consoled and raised up by someone else's help but only to relieve one's heart of a gratitude such as only a God can receive ... However, at that point there never is such a lack, for there God is always.[24]

It is true that in 'Religion and Culture' she does say God is not God but 'only a symbol' for everything that is 'too intimate, intense and dear to be called by a human name';[25] but thereupon the question is begged again: *what* is too dear, etc.? What *are* we aware of in those moments? If no human name, then surely no human thing? And what does the end of that essay mean, saying religion is 'true' at the two historical human extremes? *True*? If only she would say something like: reverence proves there must be something to be reverent *to*; or even that when we create God through feeling, this makes Him really *be* there. But though these things are what she seems to mean, she prefers to keep the matter just turbid enough to make the reader feel he is forever floundering.

In many other writings, Lou talked quite unproblematically of 'God' or – often – of 'der Gott' (the God: easier in German because of the normality of the phrase 'der liebe Gott' which English would have to render 'the good Lord' or 'the dear Lord'). She found it easy to say of the Russian peasants not merely that they were very religious but that they were 'filled with God' and to say 'I love this land because God is in it,'[26] despite having spent the preceding eight years showing that God had died out. Sometimes she seemed to mean as pantheistic a concept as that God is 'everything': sunshine and meadows ... Sometimes, that God is happiness, or is the renewal of our sense of self, or is the certainty of meaning, or even that necessary trust in the world's meaningfulness which accompanies moral goodness. All this ought to introduce confusion into her theory, since if the religious feelings can themselves be called God, then God does not die, but survives whole. Perhaps this *is* the explanation of the confusion. Or perhaps there are always, to our imperfect understanding, these two meanings of 'God'; depending on us, and not depending on us. If she meant this, then she was close to experiences related by Tolstoy, as when Levin (in *Anna Karenina*) suddenly understands what 'God' *means* when he hears someone described as 'living for God' because he lives unselfishly; or as when, at the end of *Confession*, tormented by the question of whether God exists, Tolstoy alternately thinks 'he does, he doesn't', till he notices that each 'he does' coincides with a sense of life and joy, each 'he doesn't' with despair and senselessness.

The difference for Lou is that she did not have corresponding moments of despair and loss of meaning – or at least did not utter them. Much of her writing about religion prompts us to place her in the category William James had in mind when he wrote:

> In many persons, happiness is congenital and irreclaimable. 'Cosmic emotion' inevitably takes in them the form of enthusiasm and freedom. I speak not of those who are animally happy. I mean those who, when unhappiness is offered or proposed to them, positively refuse to feel it, as if it were something mean and wrong. We find such persons in every age, passionately flinging themselves upon their sense of the goodness of life, in spite of the hardships of their own condition, and in spite of the sinister theologies into which they may be born. From the outset their religion is one of union with the divine.[27]

But we should also bear in mind that the philosopher she most admired in her youth was Spinoza, and what she later came to see herself as doing was emulating Spinoza's attempt to think the Absolute, to unite – in thought – God and Nature 'without supernaturalising the natural nor dragging the name of his God down to the level of things'.[28]

Although it is true to say she does not discuss Spinoza in the essays on religion, he must have been a philosophical model no less than – and perhaps only reactivated by – Nietzsche (with his comparable attempt to 'think *totally*' and his greater contempt for those who did not do so). This must suggest more of an effort towards enthusiasm, a more conscious refusal to 'feel unhappiness' than would fit the healthy-minded worshipper described by William James. In her Journal of 1912, Lou writes of our coming to rediscover what 'more primitive people' always knew, namely that Joy is Perfection and she adds the name Spinoza in brackets. In fact what Spinoza wrote – in the passage she apparently has in mind – is not that joy is perfection, but that joy is 'the affect by which the mind crosses over to a greater perfection'.[29] It is most telling that Lou, forgetting this, set up an equation between happiness and sublimity, while behind it lay, as she also really knew, something else: the long transition to happiness, the effort of aspiration to the sublime, which she had made so earnestly in her youth and which remains tacitly present in all her writings on religion.

CHAPTER SIX

Books on Ibsen and on Nietzsche

'However far a person may reach with his knowledge, however objective he may seem to himself, he finally takes nothing away but his own biography.'[1] NIETZSCHE

Lou Andreas-Salomé's first scholarly book was her *Henrik Ibsen's Female Characters*, published in 1892, when she was thirty-one years old and German interest in Ibsen was at its height, especially among the members of the *Freie Bühne*. Lou was always involved in the theatre and had many friends among actors, theatre directors and playwrights, most notably Gerhart Hauptmann. During the first years of her Berlin period she published eight articles on contemporary drama in *Die Freie Bühne* and, subsequently, several more in various journals.*

The book on Ibsen, which established her as a writer, is not so much a work of literary criticism as a lengthy and enthusiastic psychological exploration. Lou writes of Ibsen's heroines almost as of women she has personally known, and is concerned with the works less as dramas than as stories. She often recounts the heroine's life from birth to death, as if her role is to fill out a picture that has been only partly given, to imagine fully the people Ibsen only sketches.

THE WILD DUCK

The image of the wild duck is central to her concern. Before bringing out the book, she published an essay (which then became the book's Introduction) on the six heroines she chose to deal with, likening them to six wild ducks which respond in different ways to imprisonment in an attic.[2] The two elements in this image that inspire her are the attic as a narrower 'home' (not necessarily bad) and the bird's wildness, taken as a symbol for all urges, all aspirations to whatever is higher, wider and freer than that home; as all sensing of and striving toward some boundlessness of world and mind. So the dichotomy is the familiar Romantic one between wild spirit and tame domestic comfort; contentment and ecstasy; the bourgeois life and the belonging in something infinitely more mysterious. In *A Doll's House*, Nora's wild-duck quality is her childlike ability to idealise, her expectation of miracles and, at the end, her released instinct for an ideal freedom. She is the duck which comes to learn that it belongs in a freer element and, at time of storm, flies out of the attic to find it. Frau Alving (in *Ghosts*) also learns of her real wild home outside, but no storm comes for her and she lives and dies in the tame unreality of the attic. Hedwig, in the actual *Wild Duck*, is not so much the duck itself as (rather vaguely) a blind bird which is its friend, the duck here representing all ideals and freedoms that are trapped in everyday dullness; this bird tries to fly *within* the prison (to live by ideals while in bourgeois conditions) but crashes against the barriers and falls dead. These first three are products of attic upbringing. The later three plays (*Rosmersholm, Lady from the Sea* and *Hedda Gabler*) show ducks which, having been brought up in the wilderness, come to *require* taming; these women, instead of idealising the men, realise their own ideals through them, and, instead of liberation, need self-devotion. But the taming can be overdone. Rebekka, for example, is a true wild duck which plunges to its death because it has become too bound up in the attic world of the domestic and honourable.

The book is more about this pattern of experience than about woman's lot as such; it cannot be called a feminist book. The author is sympathetic with all the male characters and does not argue that women in particular are unfairly caged by social conditioning. She scorns the ordinary marriage but not only because it is a trap for the wife: Helmer (in *A Doll's House*) is wrong to imprison his wife in marriage with him, but so is Gina (in *The Wild Duck*) wicked to surround her dreamer husband with dulling comforts. Lou does suggest that there may be something valuable (the 'wildness') in women that is found less often in men, but also presents women as the natural reconcilers of the ideal with the real. She is contemptuous of all mediocrity and lack of aspiration and wants the bourgeois life to be transcended by, or infused with, 'wildness'. Indeed, her welcoming of sheer aspiration makes her seem blind to other qualities. When, for instance, she analyses *The Wild Duck* as a debate between, on the one hand, Relling's idea of the sustaining lie that brings comfort to all and, on the other, Gregers' insistence on the obligation to face life nobly and without lies, bringing 'greatness' for the few, we find her admiring Gregers to a surprising degree:

He is obliged to learn that among average men, as they are, truth must always appear a robber, that it always takes more than it gives, because acceptance of its gifts presupposes the highest straining of one's strength, and so it must appear to the tame appetites of enfeebled house-animals as something savage, like a beast of prey.[3]

One senses Nietzsche's influence: at one point she sees Gregers coming down from the temple of ideality towards humanity rather like Zarathustra coming down from the mountain.

NORA, REBEKKA, HEDDA

Lou writes of Nora and Rebekka with a special warmth, perhaps because of her affinities with them. Her Gillot experience sounds through, in the account of *A Doll's House*, in her sympathy for the daydreaming young woman who has deified an older man (here the husband) yet longs to develop herself and (like Ruth in Lou's novel) secretly longs for him to recognise her as his equal. This, says Lou, is the 'miracle' Nora looks forward to. There is also a similarity to her own case in the climactic revelation of Helmer's callousness: it is like the loss of God. 'It all crashes down around Nora like the de-deification of a world'.[4] While sorry for Helmer, she considers Nora right not to be governed by pity but, for her own sake, to *go*; right, too, to refuse to be reconciled to a life of everyday prosaic effort like Frau Linde. Thus Lou sets herself rigorously apart from those who greeted the play's first performances with outcries about Nora's desertion of her proper role as wife and mother. She calls Nora's refusal 'childlike and manly' in its uncompromising recklessness, and says: 'What formerly knelt within her, credulous and devoted, now stands up straight and becomes virile'.[5]

Of Rebekka (in *Rosmersholm*) she uses the word 'daemonic' and describes her in terms that recall her own sense of being impelled through life by an inner necessity. Rebekka is the naturally free person, somehow beyond ordinary good and evil (she *has* to treat Beate as she does), and somehow bigger than everyone else, breaking or making those she meets with the splendid impersonality of a thunderstorm. She desires and gets power over others, yet she herself has no definite ideals – only her great strength (the opposite of both Brendel, who has ideals but no strength, and Kroll, whose strength is bound to a faith, while Rebekka's is free). Consequently she yields to alien ideals and becomes trapped.

A strong contrast to Lou's liking for Nora and Rebekka is her dislike for Hedda Gabler. She sees Hedda as another who damages the people round her, but who does it in the wrong spirit and without the right to do it, since she is no true rebel or seeker, but a wild duck who has crept meanly into an attic to eat at forbidden fruit: even the average person is better than this. Hedda is Rebekka's opposite:

She does indeed have a tendency to destroy but it has nothing in common with that daemonic elemental force of the Rebekka-nature, in which the storm of a great passion sends forth evil as well as good, bad as well as noble, indiscriminately and unrestrainedly.[6]

Lou Andreas-Salomé's characteristic method is to work out antitheses and parallels like these; she does more of it in comparing Rebekka with

Hedwig and with Nora. It is a method that works well for an analysis of the plays' psychology. At the same time, its cerebrality reveals an innate tendency to mystify, as when she insists that there exists a 'higher' way in which these opposites, these incompatible ideals and types, can be united, yet does not tell us what (outside a shared suicide) this might be.

THE BOOK'S RECEPTION

The book was highly praised by reviewers, among them Wilhelm Bölsche, who called it the best book yet written on Ibsen and the author a 'modern woman' (adding that 'as such, she is a problem' – she somehow baffled him).[7] Fritz Mauthner, who said the book was a key to Ibsen and was itself poetry, remarked that 'the old jokes about female writers would be very much out of place in relation to this writer. At no point does one miss sharpness and logic, and it is only right and delightful that it is a woman who has so well understood old Henrik's praise of women.'[8]

THE BOOK ON NIETZSCHE

Friedrich Nietzsche in his Works was Lou Andreas-Salomé's second work of sustained scholarship. It appeared in 1894 and was the first serious book on Nietzsche ever published. Several decades later, critics still acknowledged its importance. Karl Löwith pointed out in 1935 that it preceded Nietzsche's self-presentation in *Ecce Homo*, so 'All the more astonishing is the circumspection and maturity of the characterisation ... In the subsequent fifty years there has not appeared a more central attempt at a presentation.'[9] Bruno Hillebrand wrote in 1976: 'The first to look deeply into Nietzsche's life and thought was Lou Andreas-Salomé.'[10] The book is outstanding among her works – it is the most scholarly of them and written in a firm, impulsive prose, which, though often repetitious and sometimes obscure, is without gush, either Germanic or feminine. It is prompted by respect for Nietzsche as well as by a lively concern to distance herself from him: as in Tautenburg, twelve years earlier, warm admiration is to be found along with cool dismissal, both attitudes expressed with energy and intelligence.

A PSYCHOLOGICAL STUDY

Lou was indeed the first to grasp the intimate connection between Nietzsche's work on the one hand and, on the other, his temperament and way of life. Her approach is psychological. She starts, in fact, as if intending to reduce Nietzsche's philosophy to psychology, with the quotation from *Human All Too Human* given as the epigraph to this chapter. Then she quotes Nietzsche's letter[11] in which he said he liked her idea of 'reducing philosophical systems to the personal acts of their originators' but added the caveat: it is not that 'the system is no more than the person' but that 'the person may be grand even after the system is shown not to be.' This is what Lou means to say about Nietzsche himself. That 'in no one else do the outer work of the intellect and the inner image of the life so completely coincide'[12] is her main theme. His entire experience amounted to thought – his life was all 'a falling ill from thoughts and a getting well from thoughts.'[13] This was his peculiarity, his tragedy and also his grandeur. If Nietzsche made his own soul a model for the universe (this is her main criticism), yet it was a soul supremely worth attending to.

Lou was accused of presenting Nietzsche as a 'morbid weakling', but this is not true. Rather she saw him (though putting it less vehemently) as his friend Erwin Rohde did after reading her first – 1891 – essay on Nietzsche: 'It is clear to me now (although Lou veils this) that with Zarathustra the madness begins, but *what* a madness, and what fire it throws in shining flames over the world.'[14] Lou consistently evokes the power of Nietzsche's writing. Far more than mere ideas is experienced by his reader: 'While we hear thoughts contradicting each other, we see worlds sinking away, new worlds arising'.[15] His true originality, she says, is in the way he takes on and puts off his ideas, and discovers

> those inner experiences and products of thought-worlds which we otherwise only brush with our understanding without exhausting them in their depths and thus without becoming creative through them ... The least touch felt by his spirit was enough to release in him a fullness of inner life – thought-experience.[16]

Laudations recur throughout the book. She speaks of Nietzsche's unequalled ability to find the finest formulations for the finest nuances of thought, of the living force of his ideas, which can be contradicted but not killed, of his 'delicate and expert hand', of his infallible instinct for discovering lacunae in knowledge, of his scrupulous honesty, his genius. 'Even his errors open up an infinity of new perspectives'; and 'no other writer has been able to transform thought so completely into lived experience.' What is more, she shows that it would be wrong to imagine him sitting pen in hand at his desk: he wandered among mountains and seashores to think out his philosophy: a living man, not a mere scholar! Even in the main points of her criticism she finds ways to appreciate him: though he replaced God with himself – thus going very wrong – his whole engagement with the 'death of God' made him the most representative philosopher of the age. She believes him to be immensely beneficial in expressing the state of the contemporary mind which is, she considers, the mind of the free-thinker which is still burning and struggling in the grip of religious problems, and in which a religious hunger, deprived of food, cannot be fed by the crumbs of modern knowledge. Nietzsche depicts that mind's insatiable appetite and inexhaustible endurance – 'this is what is great and shattering in his philosophy'.[17]

What follows is a summary of the psychological process which Lou identifies at the root of Nietzsche's work. One should keep in mind that her description of this process is accompanied by extensive and (in their context) convincing quotations from his books, and also that, however much the particular judgments seem to put him in his place, his great talent and importance are constantly taken for granted and implied.

NIETZSCHE'S ENIGMA AND METAMORPHOSES

The first chapter offers an account of Nietzsche's temperament. The second, under the heading 'His Changes', discusses the works of what Lou defines as his first two periods, according to the three-fold division of his life's work which she was the first to make. The third and last is a presentation and criticism of the 'system' contained in the works of his third period.

The metamorphoses in Nietzsche's development are due to the central 'enigma of his being' – his extraordinary need of suffering. For other people, pain and illness are an interference; for Nietzsche, they belong 'zur Sache', they are 'the thing itself'. He moves through an alternation of illness and recovery which he *needs*. In illness he is tortured by a desire for health; in health he is sent back into illness by a desire for illness. It is a biography of pain. With little regard to the fact that Nietzsche was afflicted by an actual recurrent physical sickness which he had to overcome in order to create anything at all, Lou speaks of 'the uncanny feature of Nietzsche's mental life which meant he could only find satisfaction in self-sacrifice and self-violation'[18] and derives the suffering he made such intense use of from a basic conflict in him between a need for God and a compulsion to deny God. What made this conflict insoluble was his insistence on difficulty. He abandoned Christianity because it was too comfortable; he left Wagner because he suited him too well. He was thenceforth driven by 'an obscure instinct' beyond every accomplishment and onward into more and more searing fires of search.

The first – 'metaphysical' – period goes up to the break with Wagner, which was also the break-up of all his early ideas. He found himself in ruins, sought a new ideal and found it, typically, in a new friendship, that with Paul Rée, and in the 'positivist' philosophy he called 'realism'. Positivism, his second main period, was valuable to him for its pain. In subjecting himself to Rée's influence, in undermining through 'explanation' all previously loved concepts (such as genius), he was deliberately hurting himself in order to force himself onward. In the whole of the second period his apparently sober fight against intoxication is 'solely an attempt to become intoxicated on the violence he was doing himself'.[19] (In the account of the friendship of Nietzsche and Rée, Lou certainly exaggerates Rée's influence and Nietzsche's dependence on him, but she notes that Nietzsche himself overestimated Rée, and does recognise Nietzsche's far greater creativity.)

The second period was a preparation for a return to his old ideas, but on a magnified scale. Its extreme reasonableness made possible the paradoxical switch to an exaltation of feeling and will. The third period – that of the five major works beginning with *Zarathustra* – Lou repeatedly calls 'mystical'. The positivist critiques which had led again and again to the insight that knowledge has narrow limits and that thought is reducible to the instincts from which it flows was superseded. Nietzsche now elevated those very instincts, envisaged an unlimited knowledge available through infinite feeling, and degraded all thought. He 'abdicated' from thought. 'Previously he did violence to his soul, now he does violence to himself as knower.'[20]

For he now uttered such things as: 'the falsity of a judgment is no objection to it'.[21] Lies are desirable and good for life; all values are arbitrary and depend on us, their makers. She sees Nietzsche in this third period as both crying out to be 'delivered from himself',[22] giving way to the sheerest self-expression, losing himself in a sort of wilderness of voluptuous thinking, and also as engaged in reconstructing the world as the image of himself. He 'luxuriates' in the thought of the philosophical individual as the world's creator, then posits this philosopher as a god: this is the 'monstrous divinisation of the philosopher-creator', who thinks he can do anything. When Nietzsche asks Why shouldn't the world that concerns us be a fiction? he adds, at the back of his mind: 'and be re-makable through an act of violence?'

NIETZSCHE'S MISTAKES

Lou's main criticism of Nietzsche's philosophy is that the main ideas of his 'system', while purporting to be about external things, are really the product of the universalising of his own internal self:

Not what the spiritual history of mankind is, but how his own spiritual history is to be understood as that of the whole of mankind, that was for him the main question.[23]

Master and slave, for instance, are both within himself; the decadence of culture stems from the teeming decadence of his own soul; the world is tragic because his life is tragic; the divinised philosopher-creator is himself. The model of an oscillation from extreme to extreme which explained the changing Nietzsche of the first two periods is applied in more static form to the Nietzsche of the third period: he now seeks to contain all possible opposite and warring ideas within himself and then to set over against them, taken as a totality, their single opposite, the Superhuman (or its herald, Zarathustra, whom she calls the Supernietzsche). His great mistake is to take the Superhuman for something outside himself. The division of 'dark soul' and 'light soul' is only a division within himself.

A further, moral, criticism she makes is that his hope for a new kind of human being who will be controlled, healthy, harmonious and serene, entails the horrible desire for a preliminary increase of disorder, debauch and cruelty. This is because the new man will be the great overcomer, and the more he has to overcome, the stronger he will be. (The worse Nietzsche's own self-torturing, the more exalted the half of him that can smile at it.) She cogently distinguishes the goal from the state of affairs that is to precede its attainment. She understands this in Nietzsche – without impulse, no control of impulse; without chaos, no dancing star – and defends him well against those who say he would promote a Cesare Borgia as such. But she laments his admiration for great criminals and his attacks on democracy, on civilised institutions, on kindness and pity. These are all the more lamentable in that the goal that should justify them is unattainable. For the Superman, in addition to being Nietzsche's psychical double, is a mere aesthetic image. An excess of something cannot give rise to its opposite, the inhuman will not produce the superhuman, except as an idea, a yearning. Nietzsche, she says, thinks that from the depth of anguish 'a boundless overpowering yearning for its *own opposite* should grow', but:

> As no gradual development brings the opposites together, as on the contrary they condition and produce each other by virtue of their oppositeness, there remains eternally an unbridgeable gulf between them; on the one side the living reality of human drives, intensified to the point of being terrible, stirred up to a chaotic state, on the other a mere illusory image, an easy reflection of an essence, to a certain extent a divine *mask*, which no independent reality inhabits.[24]

And Nietzsche is above all mistaken in thinking he had moved on into something new, something quite unprecedented. His reversal of values, Lou considers, is in fact an unwitting return to the religion he had left. He has arrived, in his mysticism, at the other side of the very island of Christianity from which he started out, without realising it.

Lou sees a connection between Nietzsche's final insanity and his whole work. Yet in this very thought (with which her book ends) we see her generous, if high-handed, admiration for him. She argues that numerous hints (his esteem for dream, intoxication and madness, the growing irrationalism) had pointed forward to that final state, and suggests two explanations: that he *chose* madness in order to reach the truth, having shown it to be reachable no other way, and alternatively that he had felt

it coming all along and therefore gave it advance place in his philosophy. She concludes her book with this ambivalent look at Nietzsche:
although he ended in a tragic delusion, in the 'gigantic apotheosis of
himself', it was all the same a sort of victory. She sees him as a man in
decline who heroically hides his decline in laughter.

A ... sovereign malice, which consisted in rejoicing in his own
sufferings ... runs like a heroic self-contradiction and like a heroic
laughter through Nietzsche's whole life and suffering. But the
powerfulness of spirit with which he succeeded in raising himself so
high above himself, contained in his eyes an inner justification for
seeing in himself a mystical duality, and in this lies his work's deepest
meaning and value for us too. We hear in his laughter a shattering
double resonance: the laughter of a madman – and the smile of a
conqueror.[25]

GAPS IN LOU'S UNDERSTANDING OF NIETZSCHE

Lou's view that Nietzsche came back to a substitute religion has some
plausibility. Plenty of Nietzsche's later statements look like a wayward
religiosity. Yet it dismisses with amazing nonchalance his own resolute
hostility to religion and quite neglects the fact that he was trying to
replace the traditional absolute with something that would be just as
absorbing of human energies and loves, while also being by definition
not God, and not absolute. According to her, he so much wished to re-
invent God that he tried to make himself into a god, thereby splitting
himself into two halves. She did not think of making her point without
bringing in 'deification'. She might have said, for example, that the very
effort to think the unthinkable thought – that to a world we know to be
without meaning we can give back a meaning – was the terrible error
that sent him, or let him go, mad. She prefers to insist that he was
religious, a view of him she had formed in Tautenburg. Whereas
at that time she had stressed their affinity in this matter, she has now
come to see the difference between them. For her, the lightning-like,
'rational' loss of God (in childhood and again in adolescence) had been
a misfortune, yet one which left her in an elemental union with
'everything' and with all the mental equipment needed for rediscover-
ing or redirecting the sense of divinity. For Nietzsche, the total
rejection of God left a meaningless universe and a feeling of emptiness
which he had to work hard to fill with some replacement. Although
Nietzsche actually proposed the Superman as one who endures the
emptiness, Lou saw him as a godly figure designed to fill it up.

A more serious gap is that which makes Lou Andreas-Salomé
constantly overstress Nietzsche's irrationality. She does not seem to
notice that the amount of lucid thought in *Beyond Good and Evil* alone

is more than most clever people can manage in a lifetime. And in *Zarathustra* she misreads Nietzsche's declarations about feeling, and about the 'intelligence of the body', as instances of his having himself given up all but bodily intelligence. Yet it is to an inspired rationality, not to mere will-power or leg-power, that Nietzsche addresses such remarks as 'Sayings should be summits, and those to whom they are spoken should be big and tall of stature'.[26] She constantly takes him too literally, does not note his metaphors or follow his meditations upon language. And altogether she misses the aspect of experiment, the 'What if . . .?', the approach that implies 'try out this thought, see if you can bear it.' Lou had not thought about the problem of language, its inescapable inaccuracy and arbitrariness, which nowadays looms up as a central theme in our culture, and which Nietzsche was one of the first to try to observe. How can it be observed, since the observation is made *in* language? And how are its consequences (the whole world a fiction, error a necessary component of our life . . .) to be endured? Nietzsche, trying both to observe and endure, had inevitably to practise many ironies, a multiple donning of witty masks and guises, and to make curious lateral leaps. Lou does not notice much of this, and her view that he sought suffering by seeking insoluble problems and resented solutions just because they brought things to an end, ignores the whole question of whether the world might really consist of insoluble problems, whether our solutions (and our language) might not suffice; and whether Nietzsche's 'heroism' did not consist in loading *this* thought upon himself. Her intellectualised commonsense, in many contexts powerful and attractive, can also appear abrasive. When she writes with an admiring pathos:

> Scarcely anyone accompanied this lonely, hardly fathomable, secret and also uncanny spirit, which imagined it carried something colossal and broke down from a colossal imagining[27]

the fundamental uncertainty of the matter quivers neutrally and elusively under the solemn certainty of her 'imagining' and 'imagined', even in this sentence, which *tells* of elusiveness and oddness. Nor does she take account of the many occasions where Nietzsche foresees and forestalls her kind of criticism; she does not consider what he meant by: 'Philosophy *always* [my italics] creates the world in its own image, it cannot do otherwise; philosophy is this tyrannical drive itself . . . to the "creating of the world", to the causa prima';[28] nor does she see that his masks and changes, and his aphoristic style, are an unprecedented attempt to philosophise without being caught in the ineluctable patterns of the philosophers.

Thus in this book Lou betrays her innate dislike for the insecure, the unshaped or unpatterned, which held her back from Nietzsche's deepest inquiry. She was also unable to feel the poetry in his more prophetic prose. In an autobiographical note, Ferdinand Tönnies recalled how in the autumn of 1883 he brought the newly-published text of Book I of *Zarathustra* to Lou in Munich and read it aloud: 'The pathos and the unction in it seemed to us somewhat comic. We thought the more genuine Nietzsche was to be found in those writings that were dedicated to the memory of Voltaire and had come into being under the influence of Paul Rée.'[29] And in *Looking Back*, remembering the years with Rée, Lou recalled the pleasure she felt in the healthy climate of their friends at that time, who differed from Nietzsche precisely in being able to keep their 'emotional tumults separate from their cognitive will',[30] whereas Nietzsche's psychical depths were the very furnace for his thoughts – a feature she (confusingly) called 'almost female'. In her book on Nietzsche she says something similar: that such things as the reducibility of ideas to instincts which, for his positivist colleagues, were merely a consequence of modern epistemology and did not weaken scientific method, meant for Nietzsche the most radical upsetting of everything. This, she implies, was most regrettable.

THE RECEPTION OF THE BOOK

So Nietzsche was right about Lou von Salomé's intelligence but wrong about her perfect aptness as his pupil or inheritor. He was right to expect a mental kindling between them, for she studied his work with intensity and wrote about it a more brilliant and rigorous book than she ever wrote about anything else. If Nietzsche is more interesting than he appears from her book, so he is than appears from anyone's book, and hers was the first of them all.

It was praised by friends (Bölsche called it a 'fine book' and the first systematic attempt to give a complete picture of Nietzsche's work[31]) and also by strangers: Henri Albert wrote 'Nietzsche cannot repeat often enough his low estimation of women and – cruel irony! – his work is most intimately understood – by a woman!'[32] It provoked a bitter fight in the pages of the *Magazin für Literatur*. Here Fritz Kögel, composer, author and recently-recruited collaborator of Elisabeth Förster-Nietzsche in the organising of her brother's archive, launched a 'massive slaughter'.[33] Heinrich Romundt, Kantian scholar and friend of Nietzsche since his student years, emerging from scholarly privacy, countered this with a strong defence. Kögel, who later changed his views,[34] wrote that Lou Andreas-Salomé misrepresented her acquaintance with Nietzsche as a long one, getting not only dates and facts but also Nietzsche himself completely wrong, showing him as a morbid weakling and omitting all his noble and heroic qualities: altogether the book was full of neurotic female psychology, wrong as only women can be wrong. Romundt, saying he was certain he spoke for many friends of

Nietzsche's, rebutted all these arguments, emphasising Lou's scholarly achievement in analysing Nietzsche's work into three periods, and countering Kögel's anti-feminine onslaught with the view that she had been sympathetic to her subject as only a woman can be.[35] Franz Overbeck (perhaps Nietzsche's closest friend) also thought Lou had not been open about the brevity of her acquaintance with Nietzsche, but he was disgusted with Kögel's unjust attack. Another friend of Nietzsche, Erwin Rohde, Professor of Classical Philology, had said on the publication of one of her essays on Nietzsche that were later collected to make the book: 'Never has anything better or more deeply felt and understood been written about Nietzsche.'[36]

The criticism from Elisabeth Förster-Nietzsche and Kögel that she deviously overstresses her relationship with Nietzsche is only insignificantly true. The quotations from his letters and the references to certain moments of their acquaintance are introduced not deviously, but ineptly: there *is* a disproportionate amount of correspondence quoted in the middle section. And it is true that the absence of firm statement as to how long she knew Nietzsche could make a reader think the acquaintance lasted for years. But the avoidance of dates and of firm facts is characteristic of all her writings; the same is true of her books on Rilke and Freud, with each of whom her relationship *did* extend over years. What's more, with a little rearrangement she could, if devious, have made the acquaintance with Nietzsche appear much longer still. Her reminiscences and quotations do make the reader realise that she not only knew Nietzsche and had privileged insight into his mind, but was also admired by him – she quotes bits that show his admiration and omits his criticism or fury. (She even manages to speak at length about his state of grief before the writing of *Zarathustra* without giving any sign that she was its cause.) But this is at worst an ordinary vanity. One could point out that just as she omits to let us know how badly she disappointed him at one stage, so she also omits to tell us how important she had been to him at another, and what an incomparable trust he had put in her.

CHAPTER SEVEN

Meeting with Rilke

'Be sign and oracle for me
And lead my life to festival.'[1]

RILKE TO LAS

While one may speculate as to the influence Lou von Salomé had on Nietzsche and how much the meeting with Nietzsche affected her life, there is no need for such doubts and guesses about her acquaintance with Rilke. She affected him deeply throughout his adult life, sometimes intensely and continuously, sometimes more remotely as an indispensable memory, but always vitally. It is equally clear that he was extremely important to her.

They met in Munich on 12 May 1897, introduced by the novelist Jakob Wassermann. The following day, Lou received a letter from Rilke. He had read her essay, 'Jesus the Jew', found it akin to his poem-cycle 'Christ Visions' and wrote in great excitement:

> What guided me deeper and deeper into this revelation was not mere interest but a belief, a trust that dawned upon me along the serious forward path, till finally I was filled with a kind of rejoicing when I found – with the gigantic force of a holy conviction – that the same thing as my dream-epics offer in the form of *visions* was here expressed with such masterly clarity ... Through this iron parsimony, through the relentless force of your words, my work became consecrated; in my own feeling, it received a sanction.[2]

The words Rilke used in this first letter to Lou were to mark the whole course of their friendship. 'Trust' and 'rejoicing' described his feeling; she was 'masterly' and 'relentless'; 'sanction' indicated her importance to his work.

On 14 May they met at the theatre, and by 30 May Rilke was wandering about Munich in the regal gold of a long midday, avoiding Lou's door but hoping to come across her somewhere – a chance meeting, like throwing a letter on the sea – and to give her a handful of roses with which (in a poem) he symbolised his helplessness towards her: 'As if with pale homeless children I seek you, and you'd be a mother to my poor roses.'[3] On 3 June he was calling her 'Du' and 'Sie' in the same letter; from the 8th she was solely 'Du'. The friendship had grown fast into a love relationship, which was to last for nearly four years.

Some of the circumstances in which Lou met Rilke look rather similar to those of her meeting with Nietzsche. When Nietzsche wooed her she was involved in the friendship with Paul Rée, which was non-erotic yet becoming as inviolable as a marriage, and all the while that she knew Nietzsche she was sheltered by Rée. When Rilke wooed and won her she was married to Andreas, which was just as non-erotic and more like an inviolable friendship, and through the long acquaintance with Rilke she was anchored by Andreas. With each meeting with genius, a stable if very unconventional attachment to a goodhearted non-genius. But she was now rather a different person. At the time she met Nietzsche she had been a brainy, boyish girl, twenty-one years old to his thirty-eight, and firmly armoured against passion; with Rilke, the age relation was reversed – she was in her late thirties and he twenty-one. She was now a much published author (at this time she was writing the stories that were to be published as *Children of Man*), of mature and practised intellect, and ready, through the Ledebour crisis and the mere advantage of age, to be disarmed sexually. And while Nietzsche was personally almost unimportant to her, a mere amazing crossing of lives' paths, Rilke was of paramount importance to her as a person, as a man. He entered her life with that 'necessity' she always so much respected. Love came to her, she said, with a great quietness and naturalness; it was a love which was 'not only without defiance or guilt-feelings, but comparable to the way you find something blessed, through which the world becomes perfect'.[4] Lack of guilt, through the feeling of a guiding destiny, was something she and Rilke had in common.

RILKE'S LOVE FOR LOU

Rilke had come to Munich from Prague* the previous September. Though he had published some collections of poems, edited a journal and written stories, he was not at all known and gave little sign of becoming one of the great poets of the century. The meeting with Lou was a decisive turning-point for him. 'Under her sign Rilke's way of living and his attitude to life acquired almost at a single blow their final forms.'[5] He fell in love profoundly; at her suggestion he changed his name from the effeminate René to the stronger Rainer; he altered the style of his handwriting, making it maturer-looking and more like hers.

Lou was, miraculously, the person he had been needing. One of his poems said he had a thousand questions like belfries waiting for the woman who would make them ring. All his bells rang in the first weeks of this love. His letters to her were both wildly tender and deeply awe-struck. All that year he was in love with Lou's superior confidence: 'How I've admired this in you, my love: this carefree trust in all things, this kindness that knows no fear.'[6] It was like having found Eternity. He exalted her, prostrated himself, begged for her blessing, wanted to know nobody but her, wanted to *be* her. His heart was a lamp before the Madonna's image. He knelt with upraised arms to receive her grace, and she gave endlessly: she was, he said, boundlessly generous. But Rilke was palpably a poet through all his effusions. In all their spontaneity, these letters – with their deification, hyperbole, antitheses – are like sketches for a book of Petrarchan verse; the boundless emotion is finely balanced and shaped.

Some day, in many years, you will wholly understand what you are to me. What the mountain spring is to the thirsting man ... My clear spring! How thankful I wish to be to you. I want to see no flower, no sky, no sun, except in you ... And the sunbeam coming dusty and simple to your borders grows clear and sparkling a thousandfold in the bright wave of your soul [*in Deiner hellen Wellenseele*]. My clear spring, I want to see the world through you, for then I see not the world, but only you, you, you.[7]

If Lou compared his letters with the equally self-humbling ones from Paul Rée long ago, she must have been glad of Rilke's lack of possessiveness. If she compared them with Ledebour's, she may have been glad they were so unchallenging and empty of hurt. Rilke was undemanding and utterly submissive, a man with whom she did not risk losing her inner independence. He saw her as mother and home. He recounted to her what wealth she had given him and talked of 'future' as if she had made the future possible for him. One senses – at least with hindsight – the strong talent moving among unrenewed words, soon to burst clear and renew them. He thought of that renewal and future as a ripening towards simplicity and summer:

I shall tell you this often, often. Even more simply and plainly my confession will ripen. And one day when I tell it to you quite simply, you will understand it simply, and then it will be our summer.[8]

She herself meant summer to him:

You my June night with a thousand paths
On which before me no initiate walked.[9]

LOU'S LOVE FOR RILKE

Most of Lou's letters to Rilke have disappeared. Later she wrote: 'If for years I was your wife' (something she never said of any other man) 'it was because you were something *real* to me *for the first time*.'[10] She recalled Rilke as 'glowing with dream-certainty' and having, despite his appearance, 'an inviolable delicate lordliness'; she liked his manly grace and the way body and person seemed one. They were closer than ordinary lovers, she said, and closer than married people, because (as if she foresaw Janz's Aristophanic criticism of her!) instead of being two halves trying to make up a unit, each was already a whole (she a mature woman, he a poet; or, perhaps, both conscious of male *and* female in themselves). They were thus more like brother and sister in an age before incest became sacrilegious.[11] It could scarcely have been put more strongly; yet she added that she could have said to him then what he wrote in the most famous of his poems to her: 'Put out my eyes: I can see you'.[12] It is a poem about a primeval union before all form and beyond personality. Cut off my limbs, destroy my senses, the poet says, but I will still carry you on my blood.

Years later Rilke wrote three powerful stanzas[13] about their love relationship at that time. The first of them speaks of a nec-plus-ultra of intimacy:

O only in the plunge towards you
my face is not exposed but grows
into you and darkly continues
infinitely into your protected heart

The second, even more fleshly, starts as if in mid-attempt to start, looking for an image that will be strong enough – perhaps a handkerchief held up to gathered breath, to stop it being breathed out? Then, no, pressed not against held breath but against a bleeding wound, to stop the life itself from streaming out. This was how he clasped her to him, and 'you became red from me'. He was entirely wound and blood, she was entirely bandage. This corporeal account of their abstract relationship is followed by an abstract meditation on the corporeal one. They made up in each other for what they had missed; 'Who can express what happened to us? We made up for everything for which there had never been the time.' He grew mature in 'every impulse of missed-out youth', while she had a kind of 'wildest childhood over my heart.'

WOLFRATSHAUSEN

That June, Lou and Rilke and Frieda von Bülow rented a small house in Wolfratshausen, near Munich, and later another in the same village, a peasant's home built into the mountainside. They lived in three upper rooms, with the cowstall underneath. Andreas and the dog joined them later for five weeks, and others came and went: Jakob Wassermann, August Endell, who made them a flag with the rather Wagnerian name Loufried [Lou-peace, cp. Wahnfried] painted on it. The Russian writer Volynsky, who had met Lou in Petersburg and was becoming her mentor in Russian literature, also came, and all seemed to have had a gay and peaceful life there, sharing meals and excursions, reading and discussing various works. As well as writing stories and pursuing

Russian studies with Volynsky, Lou read books on Italian art with Rilke and worked with him at his poems, later wondering if they had not destroyed too much in them. The two of them were in Munich again together in September, and then in Berlin, where Lou settled back with Andreas in their Schmargendorf home. Rilke, living in a nearby suburb, was for many months their frequent visitor.

DISCORD AND CONCORD

Those first years do seem to have been like a parallel marriage: they were together nearly all the time. Andreas's attitude is not recorded, though in another unnamed connection Lou once asked him if she should tell him all she was doing and he replied very firmly: No.[14] Things were not idyllic, however, between Lou and Rilke; discordant notes sounded from the beginning. Lou was not receptive to Rilke's poems of that time: despite their musicality, she found most of them guilty of excess of feeling.[15] (She did not see him yet as a great poet, though she loved him for being a poet.) Some of his letters she found excessive, too. But the main cause of trouble was that, between creative periods, Rilke suffered unmanageable attacks of depression and anxiety and apparently a kind of childishness. Lou tried to keep things cheerful and balanced, wanting to cure him of his irrational fears rather than accompany him through them. She made many efforts at reassurance, even at jocularity. The times when, despairing of the return of inspiration, he accepted her idea that he had best take up some other work, they called 'the decision to become a postman'.[16] Rilke must have been glad of her response. A chief theme of his poetry, running through his life, set out most painfully in *Malte Laurids Brigge* and finally coped with only in the last of the *Elegies*, is that of an unbearable degree of exposure to reality. In a letter to Lou, he later offered as a metaphor for his sensitivity an anemone he had seen, which had opened out so wide that at night it could not close again and (so he felt) had 'to receive the whole night'.[17] Rilke was too open: the merest perception – a fragrance, a musical note – could wound him. Others' pain – a blind man's, a widow's – reached into him as if into his flesh. Being a person at all, 'so exposed to the excess of influence',[18] was something he felt so intensely he could hardly bear it. The maturing of his poetry was the learning to bear it, the turning of his exceptional openness into an exceptional virtue. Lou helped him learn it as one who understood his thoughts without being horrified by them, and was aware of his depths without herself peering into them.

RILKE'S 'FLORENCE DIARY'

As her lover, Rilke may have had difficulty with the very qualities in Lou that he otherwise most needed. Her magnanimity, her understand-

ing and kindness may have diminished him. To acquire some independence and come back to her as an equal, he went to Italy alone in the
spring of 1898. Meanwhile Lou went to Petersburg, where her brother
Evgeny was fatally ill. On her way back, she stopped in Zoppot, near
Danzig, to wait for Rilke.

In Italy, Rilke kept a diary, addressed to Lou, rather as she had done
for Paul Rée from Tautenburg. This 'Florence Diary' was both a
collection of treasures for ardent presentation to Lou and also Rilke's
first act of spiritual exploration without her since their meeting. It was
important to him that at last he would be giving instead of receiving.
Something was to go wrong with this, but for two months the gift grew
and gathered.

Practically all of Rilke's writing to Lou (after the first love-affair
period) is the expression of crises, doubts, illness and fears, much more
dark and tormented than his letters to others (Appendix B). Most of the
'Florence Diary', on the other hand, is informed with pride and
happiness. He calls it the proof of his yearning, and declares at its
beginning that 'my joy remains alien and unfestive so long as you are
not its confidante'. The word 'festive' comes up again and again in it,
both in relation to Lou Andreas-Salomé, as on one special Sunday (22
May) when

> I felt so truly ceremonious: but I can have no festival without YOU.
> And so I pushed up my high armchair, dreamed YOU into it, sat
> opposite and read[19]

and also in relation to art: when the artist has achieved his needed
inwardness, then 'it becomes wide and festive in him'. Rilke was
seeking the festive, seeking himself and seeking the essence of art, and
these were all related. All were conceived as goals of a journey under-
taken in Lou's sight.

Concepts later central to Rilke's poetry are first elaborated in the
Diary. He begins to define the inner space he later named *Weltinnen-*
raum; he begins (near the end) to see himself as a disciple of 'things'; he
begins – perhaps the most important – to identify himself with the
artist, to see himself as continuing the work of past artists, or, as he put
it, his yearning continuing theirs. And along with this, meditations on
the Renaissance led to the hope that something as great might be
accomplished in his own age. The Renaissance was an immense spring,
and its summer might be realised in us: we – he meant *he* – might bring
to fruition its conception of all things as 'things upon the earth'. These
were indeed great thoughts and he was not deceived in his belief that he
was bringing back something valuable for Lou from Italy.

Some of the Diary employs a prophetic manner, apparently in
emulation of Nietzsche's Zarathustran style, and it is notable that,

towards the end, where he seems to find his own ideas more firmly, he shakes Nietzsche off and writes with naturalness and urgency. Nietzsche is also tacitly present in his disquisitions on religion, which are interesting in relation to Lou, both because they suggest her having brought Nietzsche's ideas close to him and because they show him developing thoughts alien to hers. Ordinary people differ from the artist, writes Rilke, not in their lacking depth of feeling but in their possessing religion for the containment of it. Religion is 'the art of uncreative people'. It had been a coincidence of ideas about religion that had initially brought Rilke and Lou together, but now, in this very sphere (and as if unaware of it), he was elaborating ideas foreign to hers. For her, art was always secondary to life, and highest among the life-experiences was always the religious. While sharing her sense of an immanent godliness and her opposition to established Christianity, Rilke here reverses her favourite idea.

He does not forget her for long at any point of the Diary. An inspired day ends with a sudden rushing back to her:

I so much wanted to come fast, fast, to you, for I know of something in me that you don't yet know, a new big brightness which gives power to my language and a fullness of images ... Something is deeply resounding from me.[20]

Another day culminates in a similar way:

You, who're magnificent, how wide you have made me. For if the Italian days bestowed treasures upon me, it is you who created room for them in my soul, which were crowded with dreams and my many anxieties. You have made me festive.[21]

What he had achieved was independence, yet without her he could not have achieved it. This fact and the way in which, laying out his thoughts, he repeatedly leaves her for divergent intellectual excursions yet comes rounding back to her before the next careful departure, are like the way a child plays and grows. He wrote:

What have I gathered all the splendour for,
throughout the day, of gardens and of lanes,
if in my night I can't display to you
how the new wealth enlarges me
and all crowns fit me?

and, the same day, a poem ending:

This isn't seen by you.
So all the festivals become untrue.[22]

REUNION AND DISAPPOINTMENT

The end of the Diary records a shock. High-intoned talk of pilgrimages deep into Lou's soul breaks off on his receipt of a letter from her, and everything becomes dark. Lou must have given some dread injunction or made some distressing announcement, after which it would be painful or difficult for him to return to her. She may perhaps have spoken of another lover or of feelings connected with her brother's death, or may simply have been less loving. Or could it have been to do with a pregnancy and, perhaps, an abortion? It has been assumed[23] that Lou was pregnant by Rilke and that she probably bore his child. But no evidence at all is offered. It has also been argued at length[24] that she had an abortion, but the evidence for this is drawn entirely from her fictional writings and so cannot be proof of fact. Both conjectures appear unlikely, since the Florence Diary contains so many eulogies of motherhood, before and after this date: had Lou lost a baby, in whatever way, Rilke would surely not have gone on blithely telling her that the supreme fate of woman was motherhood. And if she had a child, where is any further reference to it in the whole of her life?

What she said, what had happened, we do not know. The reunion in Zoppot was unhappy, and when, on 6 July, Rilke took up his diary again, it is one long account of neurotic sorrow and loss. The wish to surround Lou with the holy gift of his diary had somehow been disappointed. She had always surrounded him with her wealth, and now he had proved unable to surround her with his. He blamed circumstances, and also himself – as if he had gone to fetch medicine for a dying sister and forgotten to get it, carried away by games and pleasures. But what had she needed? Had she set him a task? All we see is that he was helplessly guilty, convinced that by being absorbed in his own growth he had missed doing the one really mature thing, perhaps without knowing what it would have been. He was trapped again in an old, bad mood he thought he had shed forever. Worse than humiliated – terrified – he used, of Lou, words in which, many times in the course of his life, he expressed his deepest existential fear: 'I hated you as something *too big*.'[25] Lou may simply have disliked the diary's Nietzschean tone or some of its ideas (elevation of the Artist, derogation of religion, disgust with the common folk); in any case the excitement about Italy and the Renaissance meant little to her. Yet she was surely trapped, too, by his backward turn. She could only act out her former role of patient listener, kind friend and helper, the altogether superior being.

When Rilke was feeling at his worst, Lou sensibly asked him what he meant to do. The question jolted him back to a decision: reconciliation, and a new self-humbling. Come what might, he could not do without her. Now the language of worship flooded back, even biblically ('though

my arm drop from your shoulders awhile, yet shall I fear nothing').[26]
Lou became as unattainable yet ubiquitous and unlosable as a Deity.
Within this now final humility and adoration, he re-asserted none the
less his brave new concept of the Artist.

They went back to Schmargendorf, and the greater part of the
following year was a recovered idyll of proximity – 'a twosome living in
each other'.[27] As before, both were occupied with writing. Rilke wrote
poems, essays on art, and stories, including the first of the *Tales of God
the Father*; it was a productive time for him. Lou, having finished
several stories and her novel *An Abberation*, was mainly writing reviews
and articles on culture, art, love and the nature of woman. She was also
preparing to start a new novel, to be called *Ma*. There were few periods
in her life when Lou was not spending a good deal of her time writing.
But if she did her writing in the spirit of her later expounded theories
(which say that woman, being less 'differentiated' than man, ought not
to take literary work as seriously as he does, that it is always marginal to
her and not a great act of self-expression for she expresses her self
elsewhere – indeed everywhere else), then she must have sat down to
write only when she could feel that the best of her powers had gone into
other things. Neither love nor cooking nor barefoot forest walks would
be sacrificed to this work; she might be central to it, but not it to her.
Once (in 1904) she wrote to Rilke: 'I too have let a work slip out of me,
while I was ill',[28] which shows much about her attitude to her literary
work. Rilke and Lou were also once again studying Russian language,
literature and geography together, so continuously that Rilke called
those months 'our stay in Russia'.[29]

The first actual stay there was soon to follow. On 25 April 1899 Lou,
Andreas and Rilke set out by train for Moscow, arriving there on the
afternoon of the 27th.

THE FIRST JOURNEY TO RUSSIA

Moscow in the 1890s has been recalled by Boris Pasternak 'in all the
splendour of her "sixteen hundred bell-towers"', with 'the look of a
remote, provincial town as picturesque as in a fairytale, but with
something of the legendary grandeur of the ancient capital and of the
Third Rome. Ancient customs were still observed. In the autumn,
horses were blessed in Yushkov Lane'.[30] All was to be violently
changed with the new century. The ancient bell-towered city, rich in
rites and blessings, was the Moscow Lou Andreas-Salomé and Rilke
were looking for. They arrived for Easter week and spent it participating in the religious celebrations and making visits, being well provided
with letters of recommendation. They called on the painter Leonid
Pasternak (father of the poet) and the sculptor Prince Pavel Trubetskoy, who had a studio in the Pasternaks' house. Pasternak was then

working on his illustrations to Tolstoy's novel, *Resurrection*; Trubetskoy had just finished two sculptured portraits of Tolstoy. The German guests were given an introduction to Tolstoy himself and they called on him for tea on Good Friday in his Moscow home.

Tolstoy at seventy was no old man: he would still ride twenty miles and come home to make love to his wife; and he was still hard at work on a dozen strenuous projects. All that year he was writing *Resurrection*, working against the clock. He completed drafts of instalments, got his family to copy them, sent them to his publisher, had them back, made alterations, and sent them off again; and it required more than writing: with his novel's departure scene in mind, he had been to the railway station to watch a group of exiles departing for Siberia. And he was deeply involved in public affairs. Just before their visit, he had been expressing his support for students treated brutally when protesting against brutality. A little later he was expressing fury with the Russian government for proposing an international conference on disarmament while increasing its own army. After finishing *Resurrection* that December, he launched into an exposure of the desperate poverty of Russian workers, an attack on the government's cynical peace-talk,[31] and other writings of this kind. In fact, Tolstoy's concern was with a Russia that could hardly have been more different from the one Lou and Rilke were concerned to discover.

Their conversation with him did not go smoothly. They tried to tell him how moved they were by the Moscow Easter: the praying crowds, the little chapels with dusky icons, the ecstatic believers there. Tolstoy, who for twenty years had been criticising the Russian Orthodox church and proposing a new form of Christianity, cleansed of ritual, was not impressed. He spent some effort, even anger, trying to dissuade them from 'honouring these superstitions of the people',[32] and was, in any case, more interested in Andreas's work on the Babids sect in Persia* than in the other two visitors. (He asked for a copy of Andreas's book,[33] which Rilke later posted to him along with a work of his own and one by Lou Andreas-Salomé.[34] Tolstoy wrote back, mentioning their conversation after all with pleasure, and saying he had read the first three stories by Madame L. Andreas, liked them and would read the others.)[35] But they were overwhelmed by the personal grandeur of Tolstoy, 'the eternal Russian', just as they were also overwhelmed by the Orthodox services they attended straight after visiting him. Rilke wrote later of how 'all the people thronged and ... the Ivan Veliky [the famous bell] beat at me in the darkness, blow upon blow. That was my Easter, and I think it is enough for a whole life: the gospel was given to me that Moscow night in a strangely large way, it went into my blood and into my heart.'[36]

The week in Moscow was followed by six weeks in Petersburg. The

'Russian' Moscow had been almost as new for Lou as for Rilke, and she
sometimes spoke as if she were visiting Russia for the first time. But in
Petersburg, too, she was now seeking more than it had held for her in
her childhood. Although their 'great step towards the heart of Russia'
was not taken until the following year, both Lou and Rilke cultivated
from the beginning a reverent admiration for all things Russian.
Another traveller in Russia[37] describes the white troikas of princesses
storming the Petersburg avenues on their way to concert and theatre
and flinging people into the dirt on either side, and how some of these
would raise their fists but most would cross themselves. Lou and Rilke,
when they saw such things, paid less attention to the insult than to the
fact that those insulted made the sign of the cross. But they had no
interest whatever in the fashionable class 'bowing and exchanging
smiles'[38] along the pavements, and were themselves the contrary of
elegant and smooth. An account remains of a visit they paid that May to
Fyodor (or Friedrich) Fiedler, a literary critic, who gives a rare, and
rarely unkind, description of Lou's appearance:

> She did not look very aesthetic: no collar, in a slovenly dress that
> showed her ankles – but nothing else of a decadent-symbolist-
> exaggerated sort. Getting on for forty; starting to fade. (A tiny bit
> pert.)

As for Rilke, Fiedler saw him as Lou's 'pageboy':

> her page . . . a very sympathetic youth with knowledge of literature and
> art. He doesn't smoke and doesn't drink and is so nervous that he
> won't join any large gatherings and is personally acquainted with only
> a few German writers.[39]

In Petersburg they had moved away from icons and churches to
modern art, and they had come at an important moment in the history
of Russian art. If in 1890 the main function of art in Russia was to
express ideas, in the next two decades Russian art became one of the
most cultivated in Europe. In painting, in ballet and in all the visual
arts a rebirth had begun. Two dominant names were those of the
impresario Sergei Diaghilev and the painter Alexander Benois; the first
number of the magazine *World of Art* had appeared in 1898, and the
first official 'World of Art' exhibition was held in 1899. Lou and Rilke
met artists connected with this movement, as well as some of the
Moscow group of 'Peredvizhniki', among them Ilya Repin.[40]

BETWEEN THE TWO RUSSIAN JOURNEYS

The three travellers left Russia in the middle of June; by the end of the
month they were back in Berlin. Rilke and Lou now became increasingly absorbed in Russian studies and were preparing for another,

longer journey there. Although they stayed six weeks that summer with Frieda von Bülow, she found herself robbed of their expected company, 'for they had now thrown themselves body and soul into Russian studies, and were learning all day long with phenomenal industry – the language, the literature, the history of art and the political and cultural history of Russia. When we met at meals they were so tired out and exhausted that they were no longer capable of stimulating conversation.'[41]

Rilke now discovered a Russian poet, the peasant Spiridon Drozhzhin, whom he read with the typical pleasure of someone learning a foreign language and able to follow poetry in it for the first time. He also read another minor poet, Fofanov, and later translated works by him as well as some by Z. Gippius, Sologub and Lermontov, and Chekhov's *Seagull*; he also wrote an article on Russian art. In all this Lou was his helper, both at Frieda's and back in Schmargendorf, where again Rilke shared in the life of the Andreases, walking barefoot in the woods with Lou even in January. Together they read M. de Voguë's *Le roman russe* and works of Tolstoy and Dostoyevsky.

That winter in Berlin, they made friends with a Russian woman of Lou's age, Sofya Shil, who worked and wrote (under the pseudonym Sergei Orlovsky) in Moscow. She was their guide on their second Russian visit. Sofya Shil was one of the many intellectuals devoted to Tolstoy's ideas: through Tolstoy she published books for the 'people', and she taught at the Prechistenka study courses for workers.

Apart from their Russian preoccupations and friendships, and their contacts with the 'House of Brotherhood' (*Dom bratstva*, a cultural and social centre for Russian émigrés set up in Berlin in 1892–3, with a Russian library, historical museum and church), both Rilke and Lou enjoyed a productive autumn. For Rilke it was an unprecedented period of inspiration and creation. In less than a month he wrote the first book of the *Book of Hours* (The Book of Monastic Life); in a mere week, the rest of his *Tales of God the Father*; in a single night, the poetic tale that made him suddenly famous: 'The Lay of the Love and Death of the Cornet Christopher Rilke'; as well as a great many poems. Lou meanwhile was writing *Ma*, as well as a number of stories set in Russia and later published as *The Land Between*; and an article entitled 'Thoughts on the Problem of Love', which was the first full statement of her views on sexual love and which augured badly for the continuation of her love-relationship with Rilke.

SECOND JOURNEY TO RUSSIA: MOSCOW

When they went back to Russia for a longer visit in May 1900, this time without Andreas, there were no disappointments: they felt 'indescribably at home in the kindness of these people'. The first three weeks, spent in Moscow, brought acquaintances on many levels: princes, museum directors, artists (they went to the Peredvizhniki centre at Abramtsevo), monks (at the monastery of the Trinity and Saint Sergius) and workers, for Sofya Shil took them to her courses and introduced them to four of her adult pupils. In a memoir of her friendship with them she wrote:

> It was interesting to be present at this rare contact between our peasants and workers and representatives of the most exquisite culture of Europe. The two of them were not interested in the Russian workers' first attempts to take an active part in politics, but in their everyday life, the village element in them, the healthy roots – the soul of the plough, not yet completely deformed by the town and the workers' barracks.[42]

The visitors asked leading questions and received answers that pleased them. A peasant from Smolensk told Rilke of the joy of working in the fields amidst larks and dew, though he was also deeply involved in politics and could have told them very different things. This is not to say that the peasant was not telling the truth about his field work or that the picture that Rilke and his companion got of Russia was false; they were just looking for a single aspect of Russia. Two impressions Lou recorded from those days are characteristic of what she and Rilke felt. Once, she noted the radiance in Rilke's face when a peasant woman kissed him and said, 'You too are only *narod*! [ordinary people]'.[43] And once, in the Tretyakovsky Gallery, they overheard a conversation between two peasants: 'Cows!' one said to the other, looking at a painting of *Grazing Cattle*. 'What of them? We know all about *them*!' 'But these ones are painted because they matter to you', said the other. 'You must love them, see, that's why they're painted, love them even if they don't matter to you.' Then, surprised by his own explanation, the peasant looked enquiringly at Rilke, who was standing beside him, and Rilke, deeply moved, broke out in stammering Russian: '*You know*'.[44]

But this was only one aspect and their error was to take it for the whole of Russia. Sofya Shil was gently critical of their inability to feel any distress about Russia's backwardness:

> Our friends from abroad experienced the journey to Russia as a festival of the spirit. How should one not be glad of such sympathy. But they sought and saw in our country an idyll, while storm clouds were gathering there and the first dull peals of thunder were rumbling. They saw in the people everything pure and bright and this was the truth. But they did not want to see the other truth just as true – the fact that the people were perishing without rights, in poverty, in ignorance, and that the vices of slaves were growing in them: laziness, filth, deception, drunkenness. When we spoke of this with deep

sorrow, we felt it was unpleasant to our friends; they wanted (very legitimately) gladness and miraculous peacefulness.

She also left an attractive account of their wanderings in Moscow:

The large, rather heavy figure of Luiza Gustavovna[45] [Lou] in her home-made 'réforme' clothes of strange colour, and at her side the thin young poet of middle height in his cardigan with its numerous pockets and an original felt hat ... This couple roamed about Moscow – through the Arbat, down side-streets and lanes – holding hands like children and calling forth smiles and stares. But they paid no attention. They often went and drank tea in cabmen's canteens, to listen to their speech and to talk. For the mornings they would disappear into picture galleries and museums. At service-times they were in the churches. They jostled their way along the Sukharev and Smolensk boulevards, they went into the darkest areas of the city. Everywhere they were looking for the genuine face of Russia. The further this was from literature and from Europeanism, the better. They made little use of my introductions to well-known writers. On the other hand, they were extraordinarily interested in the people who came to my Prechistenka courses for workers. Several times we arranged tea-parties and the foreign guests listened to the tales of our weavers and carvers.[46]

VISIT TO TOLSTOY IN YASNAYA POLYANA

On 1 June, they travelled by train to visit Tolstoy in his country home, Yasnaya Polyana. On the train they came across the ten-year-old Boris Pasternak, on his way to Odessa with his father; and it is because of this that the poet's autobiographical work, 'A Safe Conduct',[47] opens with a description of these two foreign strangers. The man, he wrote, had something inexpressibly special about him, as if he were 'a fiction in the midst of the unfictitious'. (Leonid Pasternak left a description of Rilke's childlike, pure, inquiring eyes and his noble bearing;[48] Sofya Shil described the amazing, even seraphic purity of his character, and said he seemed not of this world, and girlish, like the young Francis of Assisi.) The tall woman with him was probably 'his mother or older sister', and they got off at a little railway halt, disappearing into the huge landscape and the huge importance that was Tolstoy, and into, it seemed, oblivion, from which, years later, Rilke would re-emerge as one of the most significant figures in Boris Pasternak's life.

It is always interesting to hear what happens when great minds meet. At the meeting between Tolstoy, Lou and Rilke, the interesting thing is that nothing at all happened. There was no real communication, nothing but embarrassment and the reinforcement of some preconceptions. Nor can it be claimed that this meeting with Tolstoy was

important in Lou Andreas-Salomé's life. But some of its details should
be given, both to interrupt the intense seriousness of the Russian
experience, and to contradict those who repeatedly and hopefully assert
that she numbered Tolstoy among her 'conquests'. There are three
accounts by Rilke of the visit and several descriptive references to it by
Lou.[49]

In a letter to Sofya Shil the day after the visit, Rilke related how they
approached the house at Yasnaya Polyana like pilgrims, and were
greeted by the eldest son and then by Tolstoy himself, who seemed
small, bent and white.[50] They walked in the grounds for two hours,
with the son waiting in vain for his father to reappear. Back at the
house, Tolstoy's wife was highly inhospitable, being in a terrible mood,
throwing books around and shouting. They overhead angry weeping
voices, and then the soothing voice of Tolstoy, who at last came out to
them, asked a few questions and vanished again. Later he returned and
took a short walk with them through the park to avoid dinner. Though
hungry, they had a rich conversation with him (Rilke doesn't say what
it was about!) and they noted his vigorous way of picking flowers.

In a diary version[51] a couple of months later Rilke filled out the
account a little, describing their joy and apprehension, the villagers
staring as they arrived, and how at the door they had first seen searching eyes in a little old face behind the glass; then the door had opened
to let Lou in but violently shut behind her, leaving Rilke outside till
finally he, too, was let in. They had a long, boring wait in a room full of
paintings which they talked about with Tolstoy's son, then went out for
a walk, to return talking about flowers and trees. (All this is put
respectfully, but one guesses how they were forcing themselves to
respect every flower, bird and branch of the Tolstoyan estate!) At the
house, finding the old countess in her bad temper, they waited another
'anxious half-hour', overhearing the agitated voices and the weeping,
till Tolstoy came and 'coldly and courteously' asked Lou something,
then said to Rilke: 'What is your occupation?' 'I think I answered: "I
have written one or two things . . ."' and the story breaks off here;
clearly the confession about being a writer was the most painful and
memorable moment, the nadir in their feeling of being intruders.

After twenty-five years he described it again, in conversation with
Maurice Betz.[52] This time it is Tolstoy and his wife who at first were
having the row (perhaps Rilke and Lou could not acknowledge this of
their idol at the time). Only later did they hear more shouting and
Tolstoy's soothing voice. Tolstoy then asked them, in a loud voice in
which impatience mingled with irony, 'Do you want lunch with the
others or a walk with me?' Outside he seemed to become himself,
snatched up flowers, and talked of landscape, Russia, God and death –
in Russian, not all of which Rilke could follow though 'it all had an

elemental power and majesty', and Tolstoy looked like a prophet. In the same year (1925), Rilke told Charles Du Bos[53] about it all, stressing the pitiless note in Tolstoy's manner of questioning, and how afraid he had been that Tolstoy would ask him what he did, when he would have to answer 'poetry' and would be lost.

Tolstoy's avid plucking of flowers features large in Lou's several accounts of the visit – he picked them as if catching a butterfly, and smelled them as if satisfying an appetite, using each flower up. She tells the whole tale sparsely. Most of it (including the row) is left out, but she adds two points: that ('if I remember rightly') Tolstoy, upon hearing that Rilke was a poet, gave him a severe lecture against poetry, and that, as they left the house together, a little old peasant man, a pilgrim, appeared and bowed to Tolstoy, who silently returned the bow, walking on, while the pilgrim kept on bowing and bowing and bowing.

This was all there was to their meeting with Tolstoy. They meant little to him; the conversation was scarcely remembered; the great man was absorbed in domestic troubles; and the visitors felt foolish.

THE RUSSIAN VILLAGE, DROZHZHIN

In mid-June, after a fortnight in Kiev, which they liked far less than Moscow, Lou and Rilke travelled along the Dnieper to Nizhni-Novgorod and Yaroslavl; and a few versts from Yaroslavl they spent some days pretending to be peasants, living in a freshly built izba of fragrant timber, sleeping on straw mattresses, tending their samovar and suffering from gnats. They ate a 'terrible porridge' and met the local population, including the half-naked *yurodivy*, or holy idiot of the village; officials bothered about their passports, and a beggar was specially sent to them.[54] All this they liked, particularly the superstition and simplicity of it all; and they read art history and poetry in their izba. Returning to Moscow for a while, they set off next on another rural visit, which they valued very highly: to see Spiridon Drozhzhin* in his village.

Drozhzhin is now more or less forgotten, mentioned only in enumerations of 'peasant poets'. Born a serf, he had gone to Petersburg at the age of eleven to find work and had had a number of lowly jobs, till at forty-eight he had come back to his village, Nizovka, to spend the rest of his life working the land: a real peasant at last. He had been publishing poems since 1873 and was fairly well known and acquainted with Tolstoy and other writers. In photographs he is a small, thin, unkempt man with straggly white beard and a crafty, curious expression. Later, Drozhzhin wrote a lively and reverent autobiographical sketch, with glimpses of smoky huts and pancake-making, prayers and pilgrimages, fairy tales, poverty ... and a chat with Tolstoy soon after his return to the village. Tolstoy asked him about changes in the peasantry after the

reforms of the 1860s, and Drozhzhin, one imagines, gave straightforward answers – all very different from the talk Rilke had with Tolstoy.
Drozhzhin was Rilke's opposite, in temperament, in life-style and in
talent. He wrote fluent melodious poems full of fields, mist, birds and
reapers, snowstorms and forests, 'drops of dew', 'my native land', and
echoes of Pushkin, Fet, Nekrasov and Kol'tsov. They have no loud
faults, but they flow along like a rippling liquid, transparent and
carrying very little. It is understandable that Rilke, a beginner at
Russian, and in love with it, was enchanted with this for a while, though
it is strange that, translating them into German, he did not notice the
lack of content. That Lou, with her knowledge of Russian, did not find
them insipid confirms how little she was engaged with poetry.

Drozhzhin described[55] how he took his guests into his newly-built
izba (they seem to have been spared all old and dirty lived-in izby),
drinking tea with them and talking – Rilke in a Russian that was 'not as
correct as that of Andreas-Salomé but very comprehensible'; how they
looked at his books and garden, at field and river. Rilke asked where
cranberries grew and picked some for his souvenir book. In the evening,
Drozhzhin recited his own poems. He was still asleep when the visitors
were up and off for a barefoot walk – 'all morning they wandered in the
dewy grass, finding this, as they told me afterwards, very good for the
health.' The next day he thought he'd go with them, 'only not trusting
in the health value of barefoot walking in the dew for me, I put on my
high boots; we walked a long time in the dewy meadow, picking
bunches of various flowers.' Lou was impressed by the peacefulness of
the people in Nizovka, and by the way all their conversations there
'immediately reached the deepest things, the great problems, God,
death, spring . . .' Nevertheless, when Drozhzhin introduced them to a
neighbouring landowner, Nikolai Tolstoy (a relative of the writer), they
moved to his house and felt much better in 'this still very conservative,
old, genuinely Russian, deeply believing family'.[56]

They had been eleven weeks in Russia. After a rather sudden parting
from Rilke, Lou now went alone to stay with her brother's family in
Finland, and Rilke stayed on in Petersburg for three weeks.*

CHANGES IN LOU, AND A BREAK WITH RILKE

The first phase of Lou's relationship with Rilke came to a crisis and the
beginning of its end during their second visit to Russia. She wrote to
Sofya Shil, on 7 July, that she would like to persuade Rilke to stay all
winter in Moscow without her: 'it would be better for him than
Schmargendorf. I have my own nest there, while he's a free bird and
has a lofty flight ahead of him.'[57] In Rongas, she received an 'ugly'
letter from him; then a letter thanking her for her reply which, he said,
'touches me like a wave, so strong and resounding, surrounds me like a

garden and roofs me with skies'. He described his unbearable loneliness
and muddle, which 'must be foreign to you in the beauty in which your
life is again rounded off, in your new circumstances. Now I can hardly
bear the thought that in the great chorus around you *my* voice should
have been the alien one, the only banal one.'[58]

Anxiety, remorse, retrospection, self-flagellation, the endless flow of
words about worry, these were his world, not hers. He yearned, clung,
analysed, regretted, pressed towards her, while she was discovering new
things about herself and, as always, taking them as fate and command.

Lou had been overtaken by the novelty of her own development.
Fiedler may have thought her 'in the process of fading', but this was
certainly not how she felt, nor indeed how other men found her. The
late sexual awakening had set going a kind of late adolescence, with new
powers, new needs, new growth. As well as this, she was re-integrated
into her family, and altogether her experience of Russia was enabling
her to round off her conception of her life hitherto.

For one thing, she had been glad to come to know not just the simple
people but also the radical intelligentsia of Moscow and Petersburg,
people she met through Sofya Shil. She liked their kindness, spirit of
sacrifice and idealism, their way of combining social action with tender,
contemplative ideals, and she wrote interestingly of the baldness of
their homes, which was as if no one had the time to make a nest in
practical life[59] and as if their homes were there for everyone to use.
This pleasure was perhaps the greater since it brought back something
of her youth and gave it a sort of completion, or complement: as a
schoolgirl in Russia she had come across such people (an earlier
generation of them) but had never before come close to them.

In Russia Lou now found many things which she felt fulfilled and
released her. One such thing was simply the land itself. It was the first
time, she said,[60] that she had properly *seen* landscape, and she felt the
Volga landscape was somehow a completion of herself. It seemed to her
she was being changed from a user of life to one who was more of a
receiver of it, an observer and a listener. The land itself meant godliness
and roots and was, moreover, related to a certain idea of femaleness. It
is no coincidence that it was while she was in Russia that she defined
female beauty as 'lack of full development, lack of the complete
elaboration of all features and personal possibilities': where full
development begins, woman ends. Evidently she felt she was moving
back, to something that was both less sharply evolved, and also better.
She must have had in mind, too, an idea she had already expressed:
that, instead of trying to grasp things systematically, woman takes in
only what is particularly helpful to herself,[61] when she now said of the
Russian that he 'does not criticise, but simply nourishes himself from
whatever is good in what's offered to him'. These reflections led her to

realise, as she thought back to her youth, that Gillot had been her 'derussification'; and she went on to think further back than that to the tenderness of her Russian father, and thence to her own origination in Russianness. It was a discovery, or re-discovery, of her own childhood, an accomplishing of it such as she wanted to help Rilke to achieve with his. But he was not feeling the sort of things she was feeling. Her sense of fulfilment and of rest took her away from the ever restless Rilke.

A little later, on New Year's Eve 1900, Lou wrote: 'What I want from the coming year, what I need, is almost nothing but quiet – more aloneness, as it used to be four years ago.'[62] She felt certain that wherever she went from now on she would 'in a certain sense be wandering on along the banks of this river [the Volga], as if towards a home'. Surrounded by her family and her country and filled with her life's ease, she had again become for Rilke that something huge, strong, finished and benevolent for which his longing was edged with fear. (In *Looking Back*, she wrote, addressing Rilke: '*Without* any achievement there had fallen into my lap that by which you, for the sake of your achievement, were wrenched apart in all your depths.')[63] As on his return from Italy, he pleaded (in the second letter he sent her in Rongas): you're big and I'm small, and I've done wrong: how can I put it right? He described pretty things to her (some childhood squirrels) to win her back: he took on a winning tone. But Lou was above and beyond this. She hadn't liked the first letter, which she felt showed him to be almost depraved through the 'presumption of his prayers', and she did not like the second, which struck her as a relapse into the effusiveness of the beginning of their relationship. The break seems to have been all her decision, and had two reasons: he needed to be free of her, and he had become a burden to her.

Back in Germany, Rilke discovered in the artists' community in Worpswede a welcome for himself and a new source of creative work. But soon he was back with Lou in Schmargendorf, where, despite shared pleasures – social gatherings with Gerhart Hauptmann and others, discussions of Russian art, moonlight walks and forest rambles in frosty afternoon sunshine – things apparently got rapidly worse between them, or perhaps simply the decision to separate got firmer. That December, Rilke recorded again a tormented state of mind: haunting thoughts of burial, damp and rot, a state worse than being dead which he called a 'land between', irremediable loneliness and 'asthma of the soul'. With Lou, at the rehearsal of *Michael Kramer*, he sat 'churned up, ploughed up.'[64] But Lou, beside him, was happy; she had no regrets, the great recent experience of Russia lay around her like a radiant treasure, and she was pleasantly visited by recollections of the Nikolai Tolstoy household, about which she had begun to make a story, a novel whose very title, *Rodinka* ['dear mother country'; literally, 'a birthmark'] summed up what she had been to Rilke and what he lacked in himself. Another relevant reflection on titles is that Lou was at this time writing her volume of stories called *The Land Between*, which is how Rilke had named his near-mad condition of nightmare and loss of self. For Lou, this same word meant adolescence, time of hope and turbulence and growth. It also meant (one gathers from the setting of the stories) the experience of being between two homelands and belonging to them both. For him, failure and insecurity; for her, development and redoubled security.

LOU'S 'LAST MESSAGE'

At the end of February Lou wrote Rilke a strange valedictory letter,[65] the importance of which she marked by giving it a title. She called it *Letzter Zuruf*. This is best translated 'last message' to avoid the ambiguity of 'last call', but it means a call, a calling out *to* someone without need of reply. The letter has often been commented on and has sometimes been seen as cruel. One should bear in mind that for Rilke there was Worpswede, promising him a new life, and Clara Westhoff, whom he thought of marrying. Also that he himself must have realised that he could not stay with Lou any longer; and that, in her rather powerful way, she was trying to help him even while feeling forced into announcing his dispensability to her. It is a remarkable letter, which shows her once again rigorously formulating her own character, deciding what she was and would be – or, to put it according to her sense of necessity, recognising what she was inevitably becoming.

The letter opens with her confirming Rilke's view of her as happy and successful, as a mother with the aura of an earth-goddess:

> Now that everything is standing around me in sunshine and peace and the fruit of life has rounded ripely and sweetly, a last duty comes to me from the memory that is surely dear to us both – of how I was like a mother to you in Wolfratshausen. So let me, as a mother, express the duty which I took on towards Zemek, after a long talk several years ago.

The reference is to a doctor who had been Lou's friend since 1895 (his real name was Friedrich Pineles), and who had privately diagnosed Rilke's trouble without ever seeing him. He had uttered fears about the poet's future which Lou had promised to pass on. Now, as she waved Rilke away from her life, she told him of these fears, in view of his likely marriage:

> So long as you roam about vaguely, you answer for yourself alone; but in the case of your binding yourself, you must learn *why* I tirelessly directed you onto such a definite path to health. It was Zemek's fear of a fate somewhat like that of Garshin.

The analogy with the aristocratic Russian writer Garshin was not made lightly – Garshin had suffered fits of insane anxiety, in one of which, at thirty-three, he had killed himself by jumping down a stair-well, going through five days of agony before dying. And now Lou reminded Rilke of his own depressive, excitable, first over-timid then over-active states of mind which together they had named the Other in him, and told him that Zemek recognised this as a condition that could lead to spinal or mental illness. But this does not have to be!, she declared, observing that often, for instance at the time of writing the 'monk's songs' (the first part of the *Book of Hours*), he was wholly healthy. Thus she implied that he could *choose* health. She had been worried, furious, she told him, when she saw the old illness coming back, and it had harmed her, too. She had become 'distorted', tormented, strained, found herself going along beside him mechanically, unable to give warmth, nervously used up. She had kept pushing him away, and if *she* kept coming back it was only because of what Zemek had said, that is in the hope of healing him: 'I felt: you *would* get well, if you only stood firm!'

And then, she went on, something else happened, 'something almost like a tragic guilt towards you' (a phrase unusual for her, but grammatically arranged so that the guilt does not become quite *hers*: it came along, it was *a* guilt, and the word 'tragic' also saves it from being personal). This was

> the fact that, despite the difference in our ages, ever since Wolfrats-
> hausen I have had to keep on growing ... growing further and further
> into that thing I told you about so happily when we said goodbye –
> yes, strange as it may sound: *into my youth*! for only now am I young,
> only now may I be what others are at eighteen: wholly myself.

When Lou wrote to Gillot from Rome, nineteen years before this, she had really been an adolescent, and she had made her decision to refuse love for a lifetime, and to live for the intellect alone. Yet she had then written of self, of freedom, of the obligation to live in one's own way, similarly to the way she was now writing at forty, and in a similar tone of slight defiance: you oppose me, but this is what I am and what I intend and I am right! Thus she had driven away Gillot's last solicitude, and thus she drove away Rilke's wrongheaded adherence. The difference is that this time her vigorous strides were taking her not into a world of intellect but, having made that her own, into a world of love.

Either now or a little later, Lou entered upon a love relationship with Zemek which was to continue for many years, and this was presumably part of what she meant by having to grow into her youth. Intent on explaining to Rilke the truth of how she was changing towards him, she made no bones about letting him know how unimportant he had become to her: she called him a tiny speck in a vast landscape, and was ecstatic about that landscape:

> Without knowing it I was obeying the great plan of life, which –
> beyond all comprehension and expectation – already smilingly held a
> gift ready for me. With deep humility I accept it.

One has to admire the rather rare ability to seize the happiness that
came along, and to feel not merely glad but wholly right to do so; one is
struck both by her ruthless honesty and by her recognition of her own
ruthlessness. Later, she was to quote back to herself a sentence she had
jotted down at that time in relation to her treatment of Rilke, recognising it as a nakedly honest sentence: 'I am faithful to memories for ever;
to people I shall never be faithful.'[66] She was also being a consistent
individualist: each person had his *own* way and must find it, and so she
advised Rilke:

> go the same way towards your dark God! He can do what I can no
> longer do with you – and have been for such a long time now unable to
> do with full devotion: he can bless you to sunshine and ripeness.

Finally, saying that this *Zuruf* was all she could do now to save him
from the 'bad hour' Zemek had in mind, she reminded him of a farewell
note which at one moment in their separation, too overcome by emotion
to speak, she had scribbled for him on the back of a milk-bill:

> If one day, much later, you feel bad, then there is a home with us for
> the worst hour.[67]

Rainer Maria Rilke, taken in 1924

CHAPTER EIGHT

Rilke, Göttingen and Middle Age

'At home in happiness'[1]

Towards the end of June 1903 – two years and four months since the Zuruf letter, during which time he had married, had a child, and separated from wife and child – Rilke at last contacted Lou again.[2] He wrote from Paris, saying, timidly, who could tell whether he'd be able to come in the 'most difficult hour', but he would be in Germany in the next two months and longed to seek refuge with her. It was a humble letter and ended, as if to put himself wholly under her authority, with a request for the address of Dr Pineles. Lou's reply was friendly but firm:

> You can always be with us, in difficult hours as in good ones. All the same I suggest that this time we first meet again in writing. For two old scribes like us that doesn't mean anything artificial; and whatever you want to say to me will come, exactly as it used to come, to
> Lou[3]

At the same time she wrote to her friend Frieda that she had received a short letter from Rilke, which was just a cry for a reunion, but that a meeting with him was impracticable.[4]

RILKE'S CONFESSIONAL LETTERS, FROM 1903

Rilke's preliminary note had been short, but he now replied[5] to Lou's letter with one twenty-five times the length of hers. He was quite disproportionately grateful, saying he could read it for hours on end as if it were very long, and that he felt a soothing influence from it 'with all my senses': he thanked her for the kindness which made her recognisable among thousands, and he plunged into introspective confession. 'I am still a beginner at living, it's hard for me'.

This is the opening of the first of a series of long 'confessional'[6] letters so characteristic of Rilke's relationship with Lou, written at times of prolonged creative crisis in his life. In 1903 it was the crisis between the time of the *Book of Hours* and the period of his life connected with Rodin. He began by pouring out to her his immense dread of Paris and his fear of losing both his identity and his hold on reality. As before, he was wretched to think that his letter was the one black spot in her bright life, but the need to write to her was irresistible:

> Forgive me for coming into your clear days with my worry. I can ask no one for advice but you. You alone know who I am. Only you can help me and I feel from your very first letter the power that your peaceful words have over me. You can explain what I don't understand, you can tell me what I should do; you know what I should be afraid of and what not –: must I be afraid?

He apologised, made promises and assured her he would do all she said; he thanked her again and again, and he foresaw that now he was allowed to write to her, 'everything will be better'. The style is child-like. One would think this was the emotional Rilke whom Lou did not want clinging to her. Her reply, which opened with the authoritative and amazingly down-to-earth assurance: 'no reason to be afraid', and then gave details of how influenza (he had had an attack of it) often caused such states, might indeed show her controlling a certain impatience. On the other hand, he was no longer her recent or potential lover, and she was able to keep him at letter's length. So she now gave him a sort of official permission, indeed encouragement, to write all his bad states of mind to her, with the idea that telling them would alleviate them.

> This is what I think: that if you write everything out each time, about how you feel and what troubles you, this in itself may acquire some power to help. And perhaps too the fact that your letters come to someone who is at home in happiness. For even I never had any other power, Rainer, than that which is innate in all happiness.[7]

To his fears and self-searchings, she said little in direct reply; much of her letter consisted of news about her dog and garden. But these things were never banalities to Rilke. Through all the years of their friendship from 1903 on (especially after her move to Göttingen), he thought of Lou as the geographical centre to his life, of her house and garden – his letters frequently mention her garden – as the one safe point from which he might occasionally look at the world without fear. 'For see, I am a stranger and destitute, and I shall pass by. But your hands shall contain everything that once could have been my home, if I had been stronger.'

In the next five weeks, Rilke wrote nine letters to Lou, most of them very long, some well over three thousand words; and Lou wrote back three times, also at considerable length. Rilke's subject was Fear. Although he also wrote about his child, the little Ruth who lived with his wife's parents, about life with the Vogelers in Worpswede, and about his translations of the Russian epic poem, *Prince Igor*, the main thing he had to tell her was that he had felt the horror of existence: 'the

horror of everything which, in an unspeakable confusion, is called life'.[8]
He felt the traffic drive through him, he saw himself in the Book of Job,
he recognised his own poverty and fear in Baudelaire, he felt the
dreadfulness of Paris hospitals and of seeing a man with a swelling on
his neck. He saw other lonely people like tortoises, their comfortlessness
'in the overlarge town', and all the horror of rust and dust and 'fragments of people, bits of animals, remnants of past objects', old women
with hooks instead of hands, selling twenty pins or a ghastly old pencil,
madmen, beggars, and his own despairing involvement with them all. It
was now, writing to Lou Andreas-Salomé in July 1903, that Rilke began
to formulate the first part of his poetic task:

> If I had been able to *make* the fears which I experienced so intensely,
> if I could have formed things out of them, actual, quiet things . . .
> perhaps if everything had been better for me, quieter and kinder . . . I
> would have been able to do it: to make things out of fear![9]

Lou recognised before he did the change in him. Realising, with some
perspicacity, that she could at last cease countering a mere emotional
pressure from him and respond instead to what was starting to be great
art, she told him his letter had moved her so much she had forgotten
him while reading it, and that he was wrong to think he was simply
writing of what he had suffered helplessly, for

> They are all there: not in you alone any more, but from now on in me
> as well, and outside both of us as living and self-eloquent things, just
> as if it were a song that came to you.[10]

She told him that he was approaching health. 'Never were you so close
to health as now!' is the climax of her long and urgent letter of 22 July,
a letter he received as something 'new, unhoped for, good beyond all
measure', like bread brought to him undeserved in the wilderness.[11]
Meanwhile Lou was meditating in her diary:

> Reading Rainer's letters and his descriptions of poverty from Paris:
> the artist, who through his imagination shares the experiences of
> others, is rarely good, despite the sensitivity that identifies him with
> the suffering person; he suffers egoistically from the way all his own
> memories of suffering are drawn into the matter, and frees himself
> egoistically by repeating the suffering artistically, he goes one better
> than life. The 'good' man, the Jesus-man, rarely has much imagin-
> ation, it would weaken him.[12]

A born moral psychologist, she was again contemplatively comparing
two types of person and forbearing to judge in favour of either of them;
and she was exercising the readiness to think beyond the usual good and
evil which had so delighted Nietzsche and (by its naturalness to her) so
deeply disconcerted him.

More letters came from Rilke, full of restless loneliness, all of them punctuated with invocations of her name ('What should such a person do, Lou . . . Lou, what should he do? . . . Yes, Lou, I believe it myself . . .') and wrapped round with gratitude to her ('it is so infinitely much for me, to be allowed to tell you the everyday things as well . . . they order themselves in your sight').[13] And Lou now wrote Rilke a once-for-all declaration of support. For at the end of a long two-part letter[14] (in which she had been explaining to him how working with a sculptor was one cause of his feeling so bad) she pointed out that he was now defining himself marvellously, and added: 'I for my part am now certain what you are.' Given his own violent uncertainty as to who and what he was, even whether he was, the statement has almost a funny aspect, but it was meant very seriously indeed. It went on: 'and this is the most personal thing in the book [his book on Rodin] for me – that I believe us confederates in the weighty secrets of living and dying, united in the eternal truth that binds people'. It culminated in the following sentence: 'From now on you can rely on me.'

LOU'S HELP TO RILKE

It has been argued by Elsa Buddeberg in her biography of Rilke[15] that with remarks like these, and in general with her response to his letters, Lou took an attitude that was harmful to Rilke. She failed to understand either his need for poetic form or his relation to religion, since for her the highest experience of all was prayer, and 'prayer' meant spontaneous utterance continuous with 'life', while for Rilke it was utterly important that the hands of the praying person should be perfectly folded, as God had to be visible from them: God was made in the writing of the poem. In her view, Lou had not understood Rilke as maker, as poet. Nor had she realised that he was confronting the huge modern problem of loss of transcendence. Taking 'repose in God' to be the only desirable and possible religious experience, she constantly made everything harder for Rilke by reminding him of this kind of traditional idea. In short, according to Buddeberg, she was living in the nineteenth century while he, unknown to himself, was moving into the irreligious agony of the twentieth. Moreover, with her belief in cure, Lou translated Rilke's incurable *Angst* into the more trivial concept *Furcht*, which meant fear *of* something, fear that could be explained and removed, whereas Rilke's fear was the existential dread, and it needed not be cured, but increased, for a new truth to be found in it. 'Lou's tragic function in Rilke's fate was to block up with her person the access to the source of his fear'; through her 'the revelatory power of fear was broken'.[16]

Of course it is true that Lou Andreas-Salomé ranked religion (or, what was the same for her, 'life') higher than art. Especially after the Russian visits of 1899 and 1900, her idea of God was pleasantly unproblematic. There were visionary and existential margins she did not reach and, if to understand reports from the margins one has to have been to them, she did not understand them. She was indeed linked to her time by optimism and the assumption that everything was in some sense knowable and (with some courage) acceptable. Her habit was always to set things right, to explain them in prose, and to embrace the explained world joyfully. Rilke's approach was more like a habit of setting things wrong. He explored without stopping at explanation; he exposed and was exposed to non-existence. But to say this is neither to demolish Lou (who did not pretend to be a seer or poet), nor is it to agree that she must have harmed Rilke. It seems certain that, on the contrary, she was only helpful to him. For one thing, she encouraged him to utter his fears and made him realise that in doing so he was already creating. (He re-worked all the descriptions of Paris he had sent her and incorporated them in his *Notebook of Malte Laurids Brigge* – exactly the same incidents and emotions, if often in different words.) For another thing, more intangibly – and this is where one must disagree with Buddeberg – it would seem that she helped him become and remain the kind of poet he needed to be, by saving him from the destructive extreme of his dread, by taking enough edge off the terror to enable him to survive while still feeling it.

THE 'TOO BIG'

Lou was often to stress the wonderful unity of body and soul. To Rilke, a matter of the deepest dread was the disunity of body and soul. One and the same contingency (co-existence of body and soul) was perceived by these two people in opposite ways. Rilke was distressed that, for instance, bodily feelings are not directly involved in spiritual creation, and that there is no longer any myth that would give an accepting and celebrating place to the body. *Being* a body at all was frightening to him.* Now it seems that Lou came to stand for this anxiety – to be both what he was afraid of and what soothed the fear. This can be deduced from the way Rilke uses the phrase 'the too big' [*das zu Grosse*]. In *Malte Laurids Brigge*, the hero describes a horrible feeling he'd had in childhood fevers:

> It grew out of me like a tumour, like a second head, and was part of me, though it could not possibly belong to me, it was so big. It was there like a big dead animal which, when it was alive, had once been my hand or my arm. And my blood flowed through me and through it, as through one and the same body. And my heart had to make a great effort to drive the blood into the Big Thing: there was almost not enough blood there. And the blood entered the Big Thing unwillingly, and came back sick and bad. But the Big Thing swelled and grew

before my face, like a warm, bluish boil, and grew before my mouth, and already over my last-remaining eye stood the shadow of its edge.[17]

The account stemmed from Rilke's own real memories of the indescribable childhood fears which he had told Lou about in the first confessional letter to her in 1903: 'as of something too big, too hard, too near, deep unsayable fears' which held his heart over the void till everything familiar fell away and he was 'forced out of the world . . . into another uncertain namelessly anxious place', as when someone dies in a foreign land, 'alone, supernumerary, a fragment of other relations'.[18] In 1913, Lou wrote in her *Freud Journal*,[19] after conversations with Rilke at that time, that his horror of the 'big, hard and near' originated in fear of sexual manifestations at puberty, and was also connected with his feelings – mixed horror and rapture – about a large washerwoman who visited his home in his childhood (she repeated this in a 1917 letter to Freud).[20] Rilke's sexuality has been discussed elsewhere,[21] and I want to stress here only the recurrence of the image and the way it comes into Rilke's relation to Lou. He was possessed by thoughts of things stony, huge and over-close: he dreamt of an insecure gravestone reared up beside him; he called his will a 'reed against stone'; high buildings inspired terror; later the attraction to Rodin was to someone who worked fearlessly in the hard, physically close medium of stone, and this turned out to be too much for him, an 'over-big example', about which he used, to Lou, the same strange words: 'too hard, too stony, too big'.[22] The 'too big' meant something both beyond his control and yet connected with him so closely that his own blood ran through it and threatened him with imminent destruction.*

Yet this very same dread-imagery had been used by Rilke of Lou. During the bad time when he had come back to her from Florence, in 1898, he said: 'I hated you as something *too big*,'[23] underlining the words, as he often did. (He said, too, that he was 'only the smallest beggar on the last threshold of your being which rests on such broad safe columns',[24] – so she was also thought of as stony.) Now what is interesting here is that instead of saying 'I feared you' he said 'I hated you'. In relation to her, the fear was thus transformed into a manageable emotion. So she represented, in her physical size and fearlessness, the awful mystery of bodily existence, but at the same time she was a woman who loved him and whom he had possessed. She rescued him far more than a mother could. Large as the washerwoman, close as his own body, hard and alien as stone, she was yet also his mistress, his beloved. Surely it scarcely mattered, then, if she was not always right, or if indeed she did not (at the deepest) understand him. By speaking to her about his fear, he was communicating with it, in manageable, bearable, human ways.

Many sentences in Rilke's letters support this view, and it is borne out too by three poem fragments[25] he wrote after receiving Lou's 'last message'. In the first of these he says he is blinded and cannot see her; that is, he cannot see what is both his life and his death. It is telling that instead of saying, conventionally, that without her he finds death, he says that she *is* his death, as well as his life. The other two fragments relate her again to the idea of the 'hard, big and near': she had pressed as close to him as a hand does to the clay it moulds, she was 'the tenderest thing I'd met, the hardest with which I'd struggled' as well as 'the high thing that blessed me'. Thus in her the 'near' was a forming hand; the 'hard' was hopefully struggled with and was akin to the 'tender'; and the 'big' or 'high' (this 'high' came from his dream of the dangerous tombstone) blessed him. The loss of her took away this healing combination, so that for a while she became one half of it only, 'the abyss that swallowed me'.

Another objection to the suggestion that she was harmful to Rilke is the actual outcome of Lou's attitudes in Rilke's writing. Far from preventing him from transforming his anguish into art, her remarks helped him to achieve this. It was *after* receiving her placid self-description 'at home in happiness' that he dived down into accounts of his own trouble, as if needing the reminder that she was immune before he could put his vulnerability into words. It was *after* her pronouncement 'no need for fear' that he proceeded to discharge his great fear, to show her the inevitable need for it and to make art of it. He knew she wanted him healthy, yet he never tried to appear healthy to her; on the contrary, it was with her alone that he showed the whole extent of his illness, as if her insistence on health made this possible. Rilke was convinced that Lou did understand him in some sufficient way. Many times he told her, 'You alone know who I am.' And he did, finally, achieve all that he could. He did turn the Paris dread into *The Notebook of Malte Laurids Brigge*, did complete the great lament and affirmation of the *Duino Elegies* and the *Sonnets to Orpheus*, did with incomparable effort and success both express and overcome his existential suffering. One must conclude that if his insecurity is the hidden insecurity of all of us who live in the twentieth century without faith or transcendence, and if it is good that a hidden general condition be revealed and named by a poet, then Lou Andreas-Salomé was instrumental to a poet's becoming the beneficial namer and expresser of all our lives.

RILKE'S EFFECT UPON LOU

Rilke's influence on Lou's intellectual work is seen in her writings on love, on art and on Russia, as well as in her fiction of those years and afterwards.

The first and probably the most significant of these intellectual influences is that from about 1897 the focus of her writing shifted from the theory of religion to the theory of love. This interest and the acquaintance with Rilke's psychological troubles were a large part of what would lead her to study psychoanalysis. Secondly, her theorising about art – or, more strictly, about artistic creativity – was stimulated by her intimate knowledge of Rilke the man, far more than it had been by her knowledge of Nietzsche, who, no less a man of genius, was prevented from genuine mental intimacy with her by his requirement that she be a fellow-genius. Rilke needed her for what she was able to be: an understander and helper and repository of confession. His communication with her was uniquely open and full. Thirdly, her work on Russia, though not properly a result of the relationship with Rilke, was closely linked to it. Although she was the leader, they worked on the Russian thoughts together and shared for a time the same enthusiasm; she saw Russia partly through his eyes. Then, finally, her fiction showed in a general way the effect of the years with Rilke. The chief interest of Lou's fictional works lies in the images of herself that they contain and the atmosphere generated around these images. In the earlier works (*Ruth*, *From Alien Soul*) there is an atmosphere of solipsism almost impenetrably dense and suffocating. In later works (for instance many of the stories in *Children of Man*) it is far less oppressive – and this is doubtless where Rilke's importance to her emotional life is felt. One senses the release of her attention to more outward things. It is also noteworthy that the infinitely desirous heroines of the works before about 1900 are replaced by the more relaxed and more motherly figures in her three novels after 1901 (though still, it is true, 'intense' and conceived of always as in the midst of pressing problems and emotions).

More generally, some at least of the glowing mixture of rejuvenation and mature balance that informed Lou's life as well as her writing in the years following her meeting Rilke must be a consequence of the relationship with him, which freed her from a long, inhibiting enchantment. Her diary was full now of expressions of happiness. In 1900 she meditated, apparently with herself in mind, on the 'miracle' of the completely healthy person, the person with a basic power but without specialised talents. Not having to develop a particular gift meant being able to concentrate on, and to *solve*, the central problem of life itself. Such undiverted human power she compared to God's declaring, on the first Sunday, that the world was good. Later, as we have seen, she was to describe herself as someone 'at home in happiness'. Her diaries abound in such expressions. Thus one New Year's Day (1901) she noted that human beings should always live as if in preparation for festivities, festivals and radiant ceremonies, for these were the only true reality.[26]

GÖTTINGEN

At the end of 1903 Lou had moved with Andreas to Göttingen. He had
accepted the newly founded Chair of West Asiatic Languages at the
University there. They took a tall solitary house, to be called 'Loufried'
after the house in Wolfratshausen, high up on the 'Hainberg' overlook-
ing the town, with foxes at the end of its garden, forests behind it and a
path winding down to the town: this was now their permanent home.
Lou loved the house. On New Year's Eve 1903 she wrote that this had
been the year in which the house became hers, as, exactly three years
earlier, she had written that 1900 was the year in which Russia became
hers: 'After the big homeland, the small home'.[27] The surroundings
somehow reminded her of the Volga landscape, and she felt she had
been there a hundred years. Her diary filled up with weathers, seasons,
plants. She tended her forty-three fruit trees, walked in the woods with
her much-loved dog (there was always a dog), saw to her goat, chickens
and vegetable garden, and kept away from the town.

In May and again in July of 1905 Rilke came to visit Lou in Göttingen. Repeatedly she had put him off, then finally sent word: 'Dear
Rainer, yes, I can well have you here if it can be in Whit-week',[28] to
which he had replied: 'Dear Lou, I don't read it, I hear it as a tiding . . .
I know that this year is blessed'.[29] After this, though, he lived away
from her till the end of 1909. He had moved in as private secretary with
Rodin and begun a new kind of work, which the exchanges with Lou
had helped him towards, though it did not need her participation. (Yet
he could rather surprisingly tell her: 'the transposing of joy, *that* is the
goal of all artistic work',[30] which was very much her sort of idea.)

Lou was often ill, sometimes ailing for months, but she always read
and wrote a great deal. In these years she began her novels *The House*
and *Rodinka*. *Rodinka* contained her best memories and thoughts of
Russia. In *The House* everything – domestic, bohemian, routine,
adventurous – takes place in relation to the firm and central nest-like
home. Rilke is represented in Balder, the son who, unable to deal with
everyday responsibilities and his father's criticisms, goes to live alone in
foreign parts and devote himself to his art, writing passionate letters
back to the mother he increasingly worships as a goddess. The mother-
goddess lives in the house and is supremely at the centre of things,
while the poet-son is attracted to that centre only through her. She was
also writing several memoir pieces, two plays, a number of theatre and
book reviews, the first of her stories about children, and the essays on
love which were to be re-written in 1910 into her book *The Erotic*.

JOURNEYS AND VISITS

Essential to the stability of Lou's life at this time was its great diversity.
She was often away, in Berlin or Munich or Paris; each year she visited

her robust ageing mother in Petersburg (until her death in 1913); and she made many other journeys. One summer (1904) she went to both Italy and Scandinavia, and the following year to Spain. In 1908 she made a two-month trip down the Dalmatian coast. As she grew older she became not less but more receptive to external impressions and liked travelling more and more. So it was a life of regular contrast: the journeys in the summer, in the winter the excitement and society (especially the theatrical society) of the bigger cities; and home again in the spring to peaceful solitude and a firm programme of work. This is what she liked and what she had.

The day-to-day notes Lou kept of her activities in those years give a vivid impression of the variety of her experience. In February and March 1906, for instance,[31] her sojourn in Berlin was filled with: attendances at dress rehearsal and première of a play by Schnitzler and at a Moscow Art Theatre première; afternoons and evenings spent talking to poets, painters, playwrights, actors, theatre directors and critics of her acquaintance (among them Rilke, the Hauptmanns and the Leistikows); long talks to her close friends Helene and Frieda; and gymnastics and rest in her hotel room (often crowded with flowers which had been sent to her). The contrast between the kaleidoscope of culture and conversation in Berlin and the return to Göttingen was marked and welcome. Lou came home in good time for the April birthday of Alterchen ['little old one'], as she called her husband. He met her at the station and took her back to peace and quiet, to rural walks and weathers, and to her loved garden with its cherry blossom and the scent of narcissus.

Many of the holiday journeys were made in the company of Zemek – Friedrich Pineles. Lou's relationship with this rather ordinary man six years her junior seems to have been mainly sexual – 'she yielded to her senses'.[32] There is no sign that there was conflict or distress in it for her: she travelled with him far and wide and sometimes spent months in his company. But she rarely spoke or wrote of him and did not mention him at all in her memoir of her life. Meanwhile, in February 1905 the housekeeper at 'Loufried', Marie, bore Andreas a daughter, also called Marie. Although she wished the pregnancy had not been in her house, Lou shared the worry of it with Andreas.[33] She accompanied Marie to the clinic for the confinement, and took an interest in the child (whom Andreas could never publicly acknowledge as his), making a companion of her as she grew up.

CHILDLESS MIDDLE AGE

Lou had now found a *modus vivendi* with her husband; she had a lover who respected her marriage and her independence; she had many friends, an established reputation, work of the kind she enjoyed, and, although she was often anxious about Russia and her family there (she was saddened by the Russian defeat at Port Arthur in 1904), little was wrong with her own life. She declared herself glad, and not in the least regretful, about growing middle-aged. In 1903 she wrote down her thoughts about the second renewal of life which takes place when erotic feeling recedes.[34] Not only was this new phase valuable in itself, it was also a resumption of the aspirations of childhood which had had to be postponed when the erotic (the first 'renewal') had made its appearance. Lou was often to write in this spirit, and she had written to Frieda that being a woman, and accepting the predominantly erotic fate of woman, meant not being all the other things one was able to be as a human being.[35] So the middle years of life brought liberation, not loss. Indeed, she had come to see youth altogether as terribly limited by its preoccupation with sex, and the disappearance of this as the start of a bigger life.

Evidently Lou did not regret being childless. (She had at least one pregnancy by Zemek, which ended in a miscarriage, perhaps brought about by a fall from an apple tree,[36] or perhaps induced.) Once she expressed some high thoughts about not having dared to set a human being into the world,[37] but she told Rilke that she denied herself motherhood for reasons similar to those for which he avoided family relations: one needed to be more and more oneself, in a way that needed immense concentration. In her story 'Siblings' (written in 1919), she makes a boy ask his sister if she intends to become a 'studying or a suckling Madame – one with head-children or one with breast-children'.[38] After a talk with the artist Käthe Kollwitz (in Berlin in 1907) who spoke to her of the difficulty of combining a profession with being wife and mother, Lou wrote in her diary that for most women it was important to have both, none the less for *some* the truth was that abstinence in youth led to a later release of unsuspected inner wealths and powers. She remembered being taught at school, in connection with Joan of Arc, that 'there is nothing on earth so powerful that a pure virgin cannot achieve it'. She saw her non-motherhood as a continuation of the purity of the long sexual abstinence of her youth. In each phase it was a matter of not giving oneself away and not being subjected to something outside oneself, but of increasing what one already *was*, for the sake of strength and achievement.

CORRESPONDENCE WITH RILKE FROM 1911

Lou's inner stability and peace were evident in the rather new way she spoke to Rilke when at the end of 1911 their relationship was renewed with – on his side – its old intensity. It was at the beginning of his so-called 'After-Malte crisis'. In the *Malte* notebook he had hoped to write his fears out of himself, but instead he found he had written them in, and he asked Lou – for 'no one but you, dear Lou, can decide'[39] – whether this meant he was to be identified with his hero, or was it a new current that would eventually bear him onward; was it illness or convalescence? Thus he handed her almost a life-and-death responsibility for him. Once again he longed to see her:

> *If only we could meet, dear Lou* [doubly underlined] – this is my great hope now. I often tell myself that I am connected with the human only through you, it is turned toward me in *you*, senses me and *breathes at me* in you; everywhere else I seem to be behind its back and can't make myself known to it.[40]

Rilke was again writing in the language of deep psychic-existential need. By contrast, an increasingly hearty, commonsense tone marked Lou's replies to him, as if a fundamental security about herself as well as insight into what he was convinced her she could help, and made her feel completely comfortable in relation to him. She wrote with a new half-slangy affection, calling him 'dear heart (*Herzchen*) and 'dear old fellow' (*du lieber Kerl*); he was even 'an amazing lucky dog' (*ein unerhörter Glückspilz*)[41] because of his poetry, which – Lou insisted – made people happy. She had become more briskly persuasive, and despite her great fondness for him, she sounded less a friend and former mistress than a qualified adviser. 'Every least bit you have conveyed from your thoughts or memories is important to me and rich in insight,' she told him, continuing as if she were already the analyst: 'If ever you want to write me something from old, childhood–oldest, recollections, *do-it*, even if there is a brief resistance.'[42]*

Lou had been doing some reading in the then very new subject of psychoanalysis. In August 1911, at Ellen Key's house in Sweden, she met the Swedish psychotherapist Poul Bjerre. With him she went to the Third Psychoanalytical Congress, held in Weimar at the end of September, and there she met Sigmund Freud. She wrote in her diary that December: 'Working ceaselessly at psychoanalysis, with ever growing admiration for Freud's recklessness; I am getting deeper into it than through Bjerre. I can see where he comes to a stop. If one avoids that, springs gush forth.'[43]

CHAPTER NINE

Essays on Love and Woman

'Ultimately one loves one's desire and not the thing desired.'
NIETZSCHE[1]

'Always, in the woman's highest hour, the man is only Mary's carpenter beside a God.' LAS[2]

The chief concern of Lou Andreas-Salomé's writings shifted in the late 1890s from religion to sex, in both senses of the word: physical love and the difference between woman and man. Two more essays on religion appeared, but the main works of the decade or so between her meeting Rilke and then Freud are the two long articles called 'The Human Being as Woman' (1899) and 'Thoughts on the Problem of Love' (1900), and her book *The Erotic* (1909–10), which in large part re-states their theses. 'States' is an appropriate verb, since in this subject as in others her manner is authoritative and undoubting. She writes more as someone with privileged knowledge to expound than as someone with an enquiry to conduct. It is the opposite procedure to that of, say, Virginia Woolf who, watching a man and woman get into a taxi together, ponders: 'Perhaps to think . . . of one sex as distinct from the other, is an effort. It interferes with the unity of the mind', then wonders whether there are 'two sexes in the mind'. Lou Andreas-Salomé always starts out from the indubitable, and would never be so lightly untheoretical as to say, with Virginia Woolf: 'I like women. I like their unconventionality. I like their completeness. I like their anonymity',[3] although these very sentiments are also hers.

LOU ANDREAS-SALOMÉ AND THE EMANCIPATION OF WOMEN

Lou did not take an active part in the women's emancipation movement in Germany.* Yet friends of hers were involved, and she was often regarded as being connected with it – of value for the feminist cause though not one of its fighters. One of her friends was Helene Stöcker (1869–1943), who played a very prominent role in the radical section of the German feminist movement. Helene Stöcker was active in campaigns for women's education in the 1890s and in the Berlin Abolitionist movement (against prostitution); in 1901 she was one of the thirteen founder members of the German Union for Women's Suffrage, and in 1904 she led the breakaway group from the Abolitionists which subsequently developed the so-called 'New Morality' (campaigning for legal abortion and contraception, easier divorce, legal equality of man

and wife, rights for unmarried mothers). Despite their friendship and
mutual respect, Lou did not concern herself with these issues. Certainly
she shared some of the ideas put forward by Helene Stöcker, who was
strongly influenced by Nietzsche, interpreting him as a supporter of the
free and full development of female personality. As early as 1893,
Stöcker had published a level-headed article[4] in the *Freie Bühne*,
explaining that if women could not yet combine being emancipated
with being married, this was because men were trapped in their rigid
notions of women as either housewives or prostitutes, and declaring
that the many women who were now deciding to live without love were
doing so not from asceticism but because they discerned – behind the
'great bliss' – sheer imprisonment in kitchen and nursery. Lou herself
rarely criticised men, but this free and happy ideal was hers too and the
prison lurking beyond the bliss of love was the image that dominated
her 1898 novel, *An Aberration*.

In the early 1890s Lou was not yet writing about women's nature and
needs. Even her *Ibsen's Female Characters* was less about woman's lot
than about human freedom and ideals more generally. But she was well
aware of the issues being debated. There were increasing numbers of
theoretical (as well as fictional) works about women's needs, rights and
position in society published in the 1890s and 1910s. The question on
which Lou joined the debate was that of definition. Was woman
essentially different from man? Was she weaker, inferior, naturally
incapable of achievement (as Otto Weininger was shortly to argue in his
influential book *Sex and Character*, 1903)? Did she have the same
abilities and nature as man, at least potentially? Or did she have
different but equally valuable qualities? In two preliminary and slight
pieces on the question – a review of Ellen Key's *Misuse of Female
Strength* in 1898 and an article in 1899 called 'Heresies against the
modern woman' – Lou showed herself convinced of the profound and
necessary differences of female nature from male. She argued that
women should not be, and do not need to be, ambitious or competitive,
for (she often used this vegetative analogy) 'femaleness is a serene
blossoming'. A few years later, despite the complacency of this
conception, she wrote in her diary that she largely agreed with the book
Women and Economics by the American feminist (or sociologist, as she
preferred to be called) Charlotte Perkins Gilman. This was a powerful
attack on the Victorian notion of woman's role as exclusively maternal.
Lou read a German translation of the book in 1903. She commented
that it was the first book of this sort she had really enjoyed and she
regretted only that its writer wanted to liberate women for the sexless
work of the intellect; this left out, she said, the special instinctual world
of the woman.

In 1899 Lou was taken to task by the radical feminist Hedwig Dohm,

in an article appearing in *Die Zukunft*, 'Reaction in the Women's
Movement'. This identified the three most important 'reactionaries' as
Laura Marholm, who said woman should live for the man; Ellen Key,
who said she should live for the child; and Lou Andreas-Salomé, who
said she should live to develop her own special qualities. All were
convinced, thought Hedwig Dohm, of the superiority of the male
intellect and all were opposed to women's engaging in professional and
active life. She was fond of all three, especially the last-named, whom
she called 'Frau Lou' and criticised without hostility. She pointed out
Lou's total neglect of economic questions, as well as the contradiction
in her being professionally active while part of that activity was arguing
why women ought not to want such activity. At the same time, she
acknowledged the seductive power of her style (while also mocking it –
'her speech is through a tender veil, all flutes and harps . . .') and would
doubtless have agreed with the critic Ernst Heilborn, who concluded an
article of 1897 with the words: 'In short, Lou Andreas-Salomé is
interesting even when she is wrong.'[5]

THE HUMAN BEING AS WOMAN

Lou's first full statement of her view of woman opens with a lengthy
reference to Bölsche, introducing the analogy she had learnt from him
between the behaviour of one-celled creatures and human behaviour,
and her own notion of woman as the less differentiated being.* Which
does not mean less valuable: women are nobler and happier than men.
One way she argues this, with a rather subtle belittlement of the male, is
by developing the comparison with unicellular life. Following Bölsche,
she describes the evolution of egg-cells and sperm cells. Their differentiation resulted from the variation in size among the cells that split off in
their billions from the once fissively reproducing parent-cells. The
smaller ones were less complete and needed to join on to others; the
larger ones didn't need others. Thus came about the difference between
female and male reproductive cells. Now, Lou adds, the tiny male cells,
inadequate on their own, have to be very mobile, striving hard in search
of other cells to fix on to, while the large lazy female ones stay put,
perfectly happy, occasionally opening up to absorb one of the mobile
foreigners for the sake of better completion. Though she insists, 'to the
horror of all feminine emancipation',[6] that the female is thus the less
developed, her main point is that it does not *need* the male. A psychological parallel seems to arise indisputably from the biological account:
possessing in herself her own natural home, the female has a more
intact harmony, a more secure rounding. True, she does not venture
into the unknown, into the 'thousand vague possibilities of being and
living outside',[7] whereas the male cell is the cell of adventure and
progress, forced by dissatisfaction into permanent search, and therefore

forever finding new things and moving onward unpredictably. The latter might sound a noble enough mode of existence, but Lou makes the male (cell) look slightly silly: it is minute, and frantically dashes about in all directions. And as for nobility: the female is related to the male, she declared, just as a person of ancient aristocracy, with castle and landed property, is related to the upstart, who is rich in potential and sure of the future and who will indeed get further but who will see the ideals of beauty and fulfilment flying away from him again and again.

Yet the woman is not to be called less active than the man. In begetting, bearing, feeding and rearing the child she is wholly active, indeed masculine (a mixture of concepts that unfortunately prevents any equation of *feminine* and active). Nor is she passive even in conceiving the child, for, if one looks not at the sexual act but at the biological event it leads to, one sees that male and female bodies make an equal contribution: egg and sperm equally move forward to their meeting. The female then additionally becomes the earth for the growth of the seed. So Lou rejects the usual idea that woman is receiver, man the giver and begetter, and suggests a new construction. Rather than the male using the female for his pleasure and propagation, you could say, she suggests, that the female uses the self-giving male for her own development.

She proceeds to expound the different mental qualities natural to woman and to man. Woman's greatness lies in the absence of ambition. Instinctively she takes from around her only what she needs for the unfolding of her self: hence (and not from historical or social causes) her apparent dilettantism and non-achievement. Man goes for the logical in argument and thought, not because he is cleverer but because, being so volatile, he needs to anchor himself by adopting truths that hold for the majority, while woman, firmly anchored already, needs only accept the truths that are true for *her*. She thus seems more chaotic and selfish, but her way is the truer one, for

the essence of things is ultimately *not* simple and logical but manifold and outside logic – woman has a special resonance for this truth, and involuntarily thinks in an individual way from one case to another, even when she is schooled in logic.[8]

Woman's thought is like the original egg-cell – monistic, circular, warm, enclosed upon itself – and not, as man's is, like links of a chain going on into the unknown. Lou quotes (in her own form and not as Nietzsche re-cast it) the aphorism she once wrote into her Stibbe notebook: 'What fails to enter our feeling does not long occupy our thought', now applying it to women in particular. She also praises the more unified nature of the artistic man: like a woman, he is more influenced by 'that which darkly proceeds beneath all thoughts and will-impulses'.[9] She conspicuously omits to conclude that men as artists might be greater than women, for her tendency is to value the person who can be content with life only, with experience only, with *being*, and she sees what is great in the artist as precisely his womanly bond with 'that which darkly proceeds' and not as his production of work.

The unquestioned assumption that there is a female nature, and the idea that its chief quality is organic harmonious enclosure, accord with the conservative view of woman put forward in a number of works of those years, as for example in a much-read book called *Woman and Art* by Karl Scheffler, published in 1908. According to this author, man gives up an original unconscious unity-of-being which he once enjoyed, for the sake of making titanic efforts to re-create it in consciousness, while woman keeps that original unity, grows like a fruit, and is 'an organism closed in itself which seems silently to enjoy the happiness of existing'.[10] But Lou (avoiding, as so often, the readiest-made ruts of thought) escapes the pure banality of this view in that she sees the 'harmonious' (alternatively the 'chaotic'!) life of women as active, not passive, and presents it as indubitably preferable to the life of men. Her view of the differences between men's and women's kinds of preoccupation accords too with D. H. Lawrence's when he writes: 'For man is ever keenly aware of the multiplicity of things, and their diversity. But woman, issuing from the other end of infinity, coming forth as the flesh, manifest in sensation, is obsessed by the oneness of things, the one Being, undifferentiated.'[11] Except that she puts a thumb in the opposite scale: not man keenly aware and woman obsessed, but man gone too far in discrimination, woman calmly beholding the world's unity.

Lou does not disapprove of current demands that women be free to study and work, and is certainly not saying women should spend their lives as good wives and servants of men. Her emphasis is rather that the girl cannot be *harmed* by study and work, as she carries her home, her domesticity, wherever she goes, always complete, like the original egg. This idea of the female having a special 'home' quality about her (which tacitly contradicts Paul Rée's old conception of himself as her *Hüsung*) is another example of Lou's presenting unsentimentally, as a sheer strength, a quality praised by male writers in tones suggesting it is a weakness and a comfort to themselves.* What is wrong, says Lou, is that many women are being made to think they want emancipation when really they don't, yet fail to realise that they don't. The woman does not need the man in *any* sense, either to live with as a support or to compete with in work (whereas the man does need the woman, for without her he is homeless). It is wrong when women think they have to choose between being career-women and being hangers-on of husbands. Both these are cries for the man and both are dreadful mistakes:

women really want neither. She does not explain where the mistake comes from.

In every way, it seems from this essay, woman is luckier than man. He has the future, but she has eternity. And as for their relative beauties, the man is beautiful in resisting death, the woman in yielding to it, for she sinks back like a drop of water into the ocean. Which seems to mean that women do not die.

THOUGHTS ON THE PROBLEM OF LOVE

'Thoughts on the Problem of Love', a year later, is one of Lou's best-written essays. It has an urgency and excitement which give it coherence and relate its style to its subject. Here she analyses the erotic feeling: its intoxication, its rightful selfishness, its antagonism to fidelity, its analogousness to the experience of the artist. She also, unexpectedly, considers the possibility of loving without respecting. The essay speaks of the good effect sexual happiness can have on mental work and is itself perhaps a proof of this.

The sex impulse is different from all the other impulses. Its laws, its status, are all its own. This incomparability, a theme already outlined in the diary-note eighteen months after her marriage and emotionally expressed in the novel *Fenitschka*, now comes to be her most firmly-held idea about sexual love. Midway between the world of the individual and the world of society, sex confounds our usual categories: self-seeking and benevolence lose their opposition, egoism merges with altruism; the beloved is a separate person yet we seem to flow into him; the experience is finite, yet seems eternal.

These are not illusions. Lou argues their reality by claiming that in the erotic intoxication we perceive something we otherwise never would: we perceive how the mental arises from the material. It is as if we were watching an ancient theatrical performance: 'we are present at the birth of the psychical in all its glory out of the great all-embracing maternal body [womb] of the physical'.[12] That is, we see the original generation of mental energy. (Later, she compared this process with the transubstantiation of the bread and wine at the sacrament of Communion, and said the love-partner was like the priest at Mass: one can only half-guess what he is doing.)[13] The distinction between illusion and reality scarcely applies any more. If, in the light of everyday, the atmosphere with which the lover surrounds the beloved seems untrue, arranged by a yearning for beauty, yet one could also say that it is a 'truth' which has no everyday aspect at all. Indeed, Lou now declares, in one of her most interesting formulations: 'Certain things can be experienced only, so to speak, in stylised form, and not realistically.'[14]

The essay introduces ideas later to be gathered and developed under the heading of 'narcissism'. Central to these is that happiness is found not in being loved but in loving. To the happiness of loving, the loved person is merely an 'addition', a doubling and an echo. As thanks for the echo we heap the person with glorification, but the fact remains that we are fulfilled not by him but by our own condition:

> The passion of love is our deepest entry into our self, it is a thousand-fold solitude . . . The loved object is . . . only the cause that gives rise to this.[15]

To a certain extent, this seems a simpler version of Rilke's difficult praise of great unrequited love. But Rilke meant danger, exposure, adventure and 'the open', while Lou conjured up utter safety; her solitary 'intransitive' love goes deep into 'home'. This thought later turned into one of her best-known theories after her sojourn in 'Freud's school', and one of her last, concluding thoughts, some thirty years later in *Looking Back*, took the form of a vivid metaphor for this same relation of lover to beloved:

> When we love, we undertake with each other, as it were, swimming exercises with a cork board, whereby we behave as if the other were himself the very sea that bears us up. This is why he becomes as uniquely valuable to us as our primal home [*Urheimat*] and, at the same time, as misleading and confusing as infinity.[16]

'The Problem of Love' develops, too, a more serene version of Nietzsche's argument against pity: feelings such as pity which are directly concerned with the other person entail a narrowing of our self; love – which really is not concerned with the other person – is immensely valuable for unfolding the self and for growth.

A persuasive passage again compares the lover and the artist. The artist, too, 'overestimates', experiences wholeness and the disappearance of the alienness of things. And just as the artist has to wait for inspiration, so one has to wait for the erotic. One cannot force a way into this feeling. It is intermittent, and the intervals between its appearances are as hard to bear as those between creative moments for the artist. Lou has Rilke in mind, and describes these intervals as what they were for him: 'the most wretched hell in life'. One must be overcome by it, as by inspiration, she continues; there is no way of recovering it once it has gone, and the difference between the high pleasure of love and its absence is not of degree but of being [*Wesen*]. Sexual feeling is like nothing else, and nothing else can be invoked or used to make it happen.

In conclusion, she argues that it is possible to love with entire erotic intoxication and yet not to involve the whole self. People who expect one to love only a person one respects, and to resist any passion for someone unworthy, don't understand 'what gods are fighting there':

So it can happen that one feels a strong passion for someone whose bodily nature speaks a quite different language, symbolises something quite different from what his psyche on closer acquaintance proves to be true.[17]

We may be carried away by some single feature, like the shape of the back of someone's neck, which perhaps no longer corresponds to his character but is inherited from previous generations – like light from distant stars that have actually stopped shining. Even when we know this, that feature will kindle a fire in us. This she calls tragic, and says there is a tragic quality inherent in the erotic. Love is for the body as a symbol of the person, as an indirect way to the person, and 'it is always an unattainable star that we love.'[18]

THE EROTIC

Lou's book *The Erotic* was written in response to a request from the young Martin Buber and published in 1910 (the year in which she met Buber and made friends with him) in his monograph series, 'Society'. Most of it seems better said in the preceding articles. Buber, however, admired it unreservedly and said, when he received the copy, 'this is no mere "contribution" but a pure, powerful, essential piece of work!'[19] The conservative feminist writer Gertrud Bäumer* admired the 'unembarrassed and joyfully acknowledged urge to life'[20] in it and thought its arguments for constancy and restraint would be especially convincing coming from an author who was so obviously not a puritan and was so straightforward about the physical facts of sex. Its new material can be considered conveniently under the headings Individualisation, Idealisation and Woman.

INDIVIDUALISATION

Lou builds up a sort of conceptual pyramid, a great ascent from the broad base of the love that is shared by all living creatures (here is Bölsche's influence), up through the lower and the higher animals, to human beings, and still onward to the finest summits of human individuality. All are joined in love, but on the way up there is increasing need for novelty and variety. The more individual a person is, the more fastidious and the more subtle in choice – so the fewer are his possible points of contact with another person, and the more quickly he tires and needs to change. Hence the natural necessity of infidelity. The furthest development is thus seen in the Don Juan types. (We have to remember that for Lou the most developed does not mean the most admirable.)

On the subject of individualisation (which she once called her favourite idea) Lou wrote a curious passage about the joys available to the individual cells of the body. The happiness of the original single-celled creatures (happy because they reproduce by the merging of two bodies, and are thus immortal) is present in our own 'highest dreams of love'. A boy and girl in love desire that total merging and are bewildered to find they have to make do with a single bodily *part*. But then desire itself brings about something like the total merging again, as each separate organ, each cell of the body, in the sexual moment, 'remembers' its descent from what was once a single-celled animal. In this recollection all the cells are swept up into the excitation of the sexual ones.

> For they all of them come, so to speak, from the same nursery as do the inhabitants of the sexual organs, and each one of them could, after all, have played 'sex cell' if the devil of pride had not ensnared them in such far-reaching differentiation. Therefore that memory, by means of which the sexual is able to force itself upon them, is evoked in them powerfully, they forget how wonderfully far they have got meanwhile [a phrase echoing words of Wagner in Goethe's *Faust*], and indulge in an unforeseen yearning for the good old days of the first formations and separations in the mother egg.[21]

IDEALISATION

Idealisation is the process by which, in excitement or emotion, we create new values and realities. Here the key sentence is: 'Certain things can be experienced only in stylised form.' The lover's magnificatory fantasy brings about something real. The fantasy may even be more desirable than the person it is about. Idealisation is the rapture that makes us want to lift up, by means of a loved person, not only our spirit but the world itself; we make a sort of treaty with it – to stand together 'upon holy ground'. Lou calls this the beginning of holiness, the fundamental act of creation, and the 'great intoxication of rejoicing' [*Jubelrausch*]. 'For no other three things on earth are so deeply involved with one another as these three' (not faith, hope and charity but) – 'creating, worshipping, joy'.[22] She also names the beginning of the idealisation process 'God'. The holiness she is trying to evoke, the urge to idealise, is felt both at the bottom of the entire process, in the very first appearance of mind at all, and also at the top of it, in the gifted poet or thinker. (Again there is implied a pattern consisting of a large base, a slanting uprise of growth and a culminating peak. Both at the peak and at the base is the act of 'giving ourselves up to values over and beyond ourselves'.) *All* specifically human activity is to be thought of as erotic, and 'the ultimate image for all that happens is a marrying fertilisation and conception'.[23]

WOMAN

The bottom and the top of the pyramid of life – the point of the amoeba and that of the poet – are equally characterised by selflessness: the amoeba is pre-self, the poet goes beyond self. Lou sees woman as manifesting the selflessness of both these extremes, and thus as belonging to the whole pattern. Woman is selfless as mother, for 'mother-love is nothing but a sort of *power of incubating* [*Brutkraft*], a sort of continued *procreation*; it is nothing but a *warmth sunk over the embryo*'.[24] When the child is grown up and the mother sends it out into the world as someone 'alien' to her, she is again selfless in that natural, elemental way.

In the woman's love of the man, the same thing is true: however much she robes him in the illusions of her individual love, she always sees in him the 'child of man' [*das Menschenkind*], and however devoted or demanding her behaviour towards him, what she is really doing is making available to him the vast original warmth he once rested in. To rest in it again, in her, is his rescue from the cosmic loneliness of individuality. (It is remarkable how this view directly contradicts that of Rilke, who in the first Duino Elegy – two years after *The Erotic* appeared – wrote of lovers: 'Alas, with each other they only conceal their lot!')

Lou now points to the two female figures for which there are no male counterparts – the Madonna and the prostitute – and says that both are characterised by this same sexual selflessness. Their behaviour is related to something bigger, deeper and older than individual personality. The Virgin possessed by God yielded herself up with neither choice nor voluptuousness. So does the prostitute, who, although she is a carica-ture of that archetype, shows just as well the essence of the female sexual act, which is able to have extra-erotic purposes.

Lou's unquestioned conviction is that the sexual act is essentially a different thing for women and for men. For the man it is physiologically partial, temporally brief, spiritually indifferent. He may indeed go through some great erotic passion, but this will be the anomaly in his life, not its normal content. For the woman it involves the whole body and the whole soul, and it changes her by opening up to her her innermost self. The experience of passion is not anomalous but normal and continual. That we recognise this, Lou observes, is seen in our having set up the Madonna as the highest female saint. The saintly here encompasses the sexual – doubly, as it glorifies woman both as receiver of male love and as mother. Woman's best being is sexual, whereas a male saint is always ascetic: the best a man can be is *not* sexual. At the same time, 'sexual' *means*, for woman, something spiritual, as the same image indicates: 'Always, in the woman's highest hour, the man is only Mary's carpenter beside a God.'[25] Her union is with God, not with the mere man who helps her to the union.

Lou's strange prose – excited and abstract, bulky and rapid at once –

often seems to be persuading us that it is far less admirable to be a man, that person at once more definite and much more needy. But she repeatedly insists, rather against the thrust of her rhetoric, that she is not talking of a *merit* in woman, whose superiorities are the consequence of her lesser 'differentiation'. She argues, too, that if modern woman would only acknowledge these things about herself she could stop inconsistently trying to become as differentiated as the man (to develop her individual abilities) while remaining the supremely loving sex. She could instead develop 'a new fine shame'.[26] This would not be anything like the old prudishness about sex but would be a new self-discipline based on insight into the truth that physical love has to bring total spiritual involvement. More is not said about the new discipline.

This truth is both a hampering and an ennobling. A woman's self-development is obliged to go in an uncomfortable zig-zag line between her sexual and her individual being, each prospering at the cost of the other. Yet the whole zig-zag is an infinitely vital process[27] which makes even the least female fate significant, because in her sexual life *every* woman has to keep coming to terms with the generalised and universal 'all'. This 'all' is to her what the external world is to the man: while he struggles with that, she struggles with this. Examples are not given, but probably we are to think of men fighting wild beasts, cultivating fields, putting up buildings, confronting economic and political actualities, and to realise that women have just as much as all that, within.

There is a final way in which women differ from men, which (like all these differences) is their great good fortune. Their sexually active life ends earlier. Before old age, woman has the advantage of seeing the full flourishing of everything that grew in her throughout her life, and she can enter a calm state in which everything she has absorbed and acquired becomes visible in its fruition, like a 'hamster burrow before the onset of winter'.[28] So an ideally achievable human perfection is envisaged, which would be manifested in children were they not confused by immaturity, and would be seen in old people were they not confused by the approach of death. Whatever it is: wisdom, peace, self-assurance without activity, or a sort of 'oneness' with life in general, it can be achieved by women at the end of their sexual life and before their old age.

There is much in the book about marriage and about love's obligation (like religion's) to 'bend back into life itself'. For example, the four-teenth chapter, 'Life Bond', opens with a paragraph consisting of ninety-eight rather ethereal words[29] which could be rendered in these twelve: 'However lofty your love, you need to come down to earth again.' Despite a cautious regret for this need, the overt theme is that a love relationship on its own is never enough. Love has to give way to consideration of family, the sharing of work, and so on. This is what seemed to Gertrud Bäumer the most important message of the book. It is certainly less interestingly dealt with than are the more unconventional and daring ideas. But the view recommended is indeed that the erotic – complete in itself – is to be followed by marriage, which has got to be valuable enough for the erotic to be sacrificed. Doubtless Lou has in mind her own success in separating the two things; she writes with great assurance. Eros is momentary, marriage continues; eros thrives on idealisation, marriage is a matter of working hard at oneself – worthwhile because there is so much to be, she says, to one's spouse: lover, sibling, refuge, goal, defence, judge, angel, friend, child . . . At the end comes, however, a delightful reminder of the Nietzschean in Lou Andreas-Salomé, when, in the very midst of commending the ordinary marriage bond, she introduces the concept of the 'exceptional human being'.[30] For there are geniuses of feeling even in the sphere of everyday loving, people who discover the fullness of the *ordinary* and become guide-posts for everybody else.

Characteristic of the whole book is that it describes and lauds *things as they are*. As they already are, they are marvellous. Especially characteristic is Lou's delight and gratitude for the way things are for women.

CHAPTER TEN

Meeting with Freud

'I would never have thought that psychoanalysis could mean so much to someone else.'[1]   FREUD

The crowning episode in the career of Lou Andreas-Salomé was her encounter with psychoanalysis in the years 1912–13. She said that two things made her especially receptive to Freud's depth psychology.[2] One was the fact that she had grown up among a people of 'readily self-giving inwardness' – the Russians; the other was her experience of someone's extraordinary 'mental fate' – Rilke's. It has been said[3] that it was solely for Rilke's sake that she took up psychoanalysis: to make it available to him as a source of knowledge, while protecting him from undergoing it at the hands of a third person. Her pondering of Paul Rée's melancholy must have brought her to it, as well. Her interest had deeper roots, though, than these altruistic ones.

LOU'S AFFINITY WITH PSYCHOANALYSIS

Lou's preferred mode of thinking had always been psychological. The Tautenburg reflections, the books on Ibsen and Nietzsche, the fiction, the religious essays, all showed the same desire: to describe the mind's experiences. Her inclination was not so much to judge or select as to investigate differences, to compare, explain, set forth and synthesise. She wrote numerous comparative studies of people she knew – for example, of Nietzsche with Rée, of Nietzsche with Ludwig Haller, of Andreas with Rée, of Rilke with Poul Bjerre.[4] At the very beginning of her writing career, at the start of her *Stibbe Nest-Book* of 1882, she had jotted down two contradictory statements: 'Every happiness outlives itself. Every happiness dies of itself.'[5] They represented a question: What makes people so different that they can utter such different truths? And that led to a further question: How are they alike under their differences? In this concern she was a born psychologist.

   Psychoanalysis, in particular, suited her, for it promised to systematise, to make 'scientific', many of her own cherished ideas. Her idea of the erotic as a primary ground [*Urschoss*] of feeling,[6] to which and in which all living beings are related, now found a stricter name in Freud's 'libido'. Her interest in the phenomenon of idealisation was rearranged in the vocabulary of 'sublimation' and 'sexual over-esteem'. Above all, in Freud's concept of narcissism (to which she was to devote a long essay), Lou found the formulation for the ideal she envisaged, which combined self-love with the glorious unity of person and cosmos. Other intuitions she had had, such as that of an original masochism (the theme of some of her stories) or those about a universal bisexuality (discussed in *The Erotic*), also found their place in the context of psychoanalytical theory. Nietzsche once wrote down for Lou the sentence: 'To unlearn our *oppositions* – this is the task',[7] and Lou had taken this as her task: she now found its accomplishment in psychoanalysis. The very first lecture she heard Freud give impressed upon her that all values are continuous with each other and that classification into opposites is unreal. Good and bad, normal and abnormal, healthy and morbid, even bodily and mental, even real and imaginary, were indistinguishable in the Unconscious, and 'somewhere in the depths, aversion and love become only differences of degree,' she wrote in her *Freud Journal*.[8] Psychoanalytic therapy, in which quite ordinary people could free themselves from a snare and reach, as it were, beyond themselves, appealed to Lou's belief in self-transcension (not only for artists and saints). Moreover, Freud's confidence that the troubles of the self could be put right through an understanding of their causes coincided with what Lou admired in Spinoza, whom she called 'the philosopher of psychoanalysis' and of whom she said, 'for me it is a beautiful fact that the one thinker to whom I had a prescient and almost worshipful inner attitude, almost as a child, has come my way again here.'[9]

In more personal ways, too, Lou was well prepared for the study of psychoanalysis. Its esteem for infancy experiences, and for dreams and daydreams, supported her long pondering of her own fantasy-rich childhood and her conviction that 'one is and has, later, only so much as one has won for oneself there [in childhood]'.[10] Through Freud, she realised that 'the things we consciously experience take place at the foot of gigantic primordial formations to which the earth-masses originally crashed colossally down before their articulation into the landscape of foot-hills, lakes, woods and paths that we know now.'[11] The readiness to accept whatever life might bring characterised the adolescent Lou's statements about herself and found a fellow in the attitude of the psychoanalyst, who shrank back from nothing. '*This* was exactly what I needed',[12] she wrote, and recorded how glad she was to be forced to avoid 'pleasant psychology', frequently praising the exceptional uninhibitedness of Freud himself, who could face so much without either enjoying it or yielding to repulsion: it was a victory over himself. Further, the fact that she herself came to sexual love so late in life may have made especially salient for her the question of what is sexual pleasure; she pondered 'pleasure' throughout her psychoanalytical studies.

In these studies, Lou was defining herself still further away from Nietzsche, for despite the coincidence of many of Freud's insights with Nietzsche's, what she liked best in the Freudian theory was the affirmation she consistently found there of an ever-meaningful, ever-interpretable Unconscious, suggesting not the questionability but the discoverability of all things. Not the ghastly intuition of an ultimate vacuity requiring our desperate heroism, but the comforting vision of an infinite plenitude, requiring only our honest recognition.

THE PERSONAL IMPORTANCE OF FREUD TO LOU

Then there is the importance to Lou of Freud himself. That capacity for reverence for a great man, to which she had abandoned herself at seventeen only to find out its dangers, had never again been fully yielded to until, at fifty, she met Sigmund Freud. She could now re-enact the best in the Gillot relationship, for now she found herself admired, encouraged, taught and guided, but not desired. This time the teacher could remain the intact superior. It was a deep need of hers to find such a person, and yet another instance of her amazing good luck (or brave perception) that she did find him. Freud was to give her the security of a permanent friendship and continual intellectual stimulation – and indeed, work – and was to fill the place she had always wanted to have filled: of a man she could trust and look up to without reservation. Many of her ideas implied disagreements with his, but she took care not to let these become prominent. She consistently presented her ideas to Freud as their progenitor, and as if she had him to thank for them and knew he would always be pleased, whatever disagreements they contained.

Illness played a determining role in the lives of all three of her friends of genius. Through resisting illness, Nietzsche made himself a fighter and affirmer; languishing in it, Rilke explored and exploited his condition. The difference is that where these two pressed out moral and poetic insights from their sufferings, Freud when ill made himself into an object of sober study and used the illness to find out how to cure it. He became a describer and healer of illness, always above it or to one side, taking notes. It was in Freud the doctor that Lou saw the kind of attitude she most admired. And she liked Freud's commitment to discovering rather than inventing. She said his great ability was to leave an inquiry in suspense, not to brood over the inaccessible nor insist every time on a single explanation – perhaps thinking of Nietzsche's impatience with not 'being God' and of his all-explanatory 'will to power'. Freud had, she said, patience, clarity, seriousness, obedience to the will-to-know, complete honesty of thinking, and none of that 'aggressive wish to convert which corresponds to some urge to convince or to teach', adding in brackets 'e.g. to a Nietzschean "Be true to the

earth!" or other will-to-proclaim'.[13] Again and again she praised
Freud's use of rationality to track down the irrational (we remember her
finding that Nietzsche became irrational in this sort of search), and his
refusal to go beyond what the clear mind can recognise. At most, he
pointed to boundaries. This is what impressed her, and if it gave her the
opportunity to go some steps further herself, then this was another
advantage. Where Nietzsche's thinking had reached out boundlessly
and Rilke's concern with mental frontiers was to deny them, Freud's
mind had edges and left a space for *her* mind just outside them.

ARRIVAL IN VIENNA

At the end of April 1912, Karl Abraham told Freud that he had made
the acquaintance of Frau Lou Andreas-Salomé in Berlin 'and I must
say that I have never met anyone with so deep and subtle an understanding of psychoanalysis. She is coming to Vienna in the winter and
would like to attend the sessions there.'[14] That September, Lou wrote
to Freud:

> Ever since I was able to be present at the Weimar Congress last
> Autumn the study of psychoanalysis has not let me go, and the deeper
> I get into it, the more firmly it holds me. My wish to be able to go to
> Vienna for a few months is now fulfilled: I may, mayn't I, turn to you,
> attend your lectures and beg admission to your Wednesday evenings
> too? To devote myself to this subject further in all its aspects is the
> sole purpose of my stay there.[15]

He replied:

> If you come to Vienna, we shall all endeavour to make accessible to
> you the little in psychoanalysis that can be shown and communicated.
> I have already taken your participation in the Weimar Congress as a
> favourable sign.[16]

Lou arrived in Vienna on 25 October, in the company of her young
friend Ellen Delp,* and with a solemn feeling of fatefulness, as if all
that was to happen were invisibly sketched out. She was fifty and she
was making a youthful new start. There was a 'homely beginning': her
hotel chanced to be next to Freud's lecture hall and near his home, too.
As she looked for the hotel, she came across a member of the Wednesday Society, Ludwig Jekels, who told her the lectures were starting that
day. Freud himself accompanied her after the lecture part of the way
back to her hotel.

Although it seemed to her an attempt to put people off psychoanalysis,
the first lecture none the less gave her the desire to learn endlessly. She
was overwhelmed by Freud's cleverness in making the normal Unconscious comprehensible through study of the abnormal, overjoyed to be

initiated at last into the realm of empirical interpretation rather than philosophical speculation, and looking forward to something really new.[17]

From her first encounter with it, psychoanalysis was a joy to Lou. When Freud met her in Weimar he laughed at her eagerness to learn his new science, saying she behaved as if she were about to receive a Christmas present. Later, he was amazed that 'even after the most horrible things we talk about together, you still look at it as if expecting Christmas!'[18] Another festival-image he used of her (and one she often used of herself) was 'Sunday'. As she joined the group of male scholars at his Wednesday meetings, he reminded the group that their work must proceed as before, shying back from nothing – it would be the usual strenuous 'weekdays' except that now they would have a 'Sunday' amongst them. Lou said, of the material they studied, that 'however repulsive or abhorrent it might look in particular instances, for me there always remained a Sunday-quality behind all the weekday work'.[19] After two months of it she felt that, while she had previously been rather solemn, psychoanalysis was making her ever more cheerful and lighthearted.[20] It wasn't just from the interest of being in on a new science, but from the experience of being given something and 'one's own life becoming radiantly more and more comprehensive through the process of groping towards the roots with which it is sunk in the totality'.[21] In February she told Freud that receiving all this from him was 'the great joy of this winter' and working through it in herself would be 'the joy of this summer'.[22] Three years later she wrote to him that she was acquiring his work bit by bit, like searching for eggs in the garden at Easter.[23] This joy lasted for the rest of her life.

THE VIENNA PSYCHOANALYTICAL SOCIETY

Lou attended Freud's Wednesday discussion evenings from 30 October 1912 until 2 April 1913. These meetings, through which Freud had first emerged from isolation in 1902 and had begun discussing his ideas with a small group of friends, had been known since 1908 as meetings of the Vienna Psychoanalytical Society. It still had a fairly small and select membership – there were forty-two on its roll in 1912–13 (including four women), of whom about fifteen to nineteen (men) came to most meetings.*

Lou Andreas-Salomé could scarcely have begun her work at a more promising moment in the history of psychoanalysis. The main concepts and theories had been formulated, Freud's first major works were written* and he was working now on new themes for *Totem and Taboo* and the essay 'On Narcissism'; Lou was present at several stages of the discussion of these themes. The psychoanalytical movement had begun to be widely known. In 1908, the first International Psychoanalytical

Congress had taken place in Salzburg attended by forty-two people, half of whom were – then or subsequently – practising analysts, and who came from Austria, Switzerland, England, Germany and Hungary. Shortly afterwards the first psychoanalytical journal was founded; in 1909, Freud and Jung had visited the United States and lectured there with considerable success; in 1910 a second congress was held in Nuremberg and another journal and a congress bulletin were founded. The third congress was the one in Weimar that Lou had attended. Further periodicals were to be established in 1912, one of them being *Imago*, in which Lou would publish articles.

It was a significant year, too, for dissension within the movement. Three serious breaks had taken, or were taking, place. Alfred Adler had just departed and set up a rival group of his own. Not knowing quite how bad were the relations between Adler and Freud, Lou also attended Adler's meetings for a while, Freud agreeing on condition that she did not talk in either group of what she heard in the other. Wilhelm Stekel, another established member and partial supporter of Adler, was breaking with Freud, and Lou was present at Freud's announcement of his departure. The third rupture of that time, and for Freud the most painful, was with C. G. Jung, who was finally to leave him after the Munich congress in September 1913; the quarrel was going on during the time Lou was there, and there are several comments on it in her diary. So this was a time of success, growth, splits and changes in the movement.

OTHER FRIENDS IN VIENNA

During her stay in Vienna that year, Lou saw much of her Viennese acquaintances, among them Beer-Hofmann, Schnitzler and Salten. She also paid several visits to Marie von Ebner-Eschenbach, and met Brandes and Harden. She went to the theatre (attending the dress rehearsal, for instance, of Wedekind's *Pandora's Box* in February with a group of writer friends) and to the cinema several times with her friend Viktor Tausk and his sons, laughing at her own addiction to this new art form and wondering if it was destined to have a great future.

In photographs taken at this time, Lou was a tall, handsome, big-boned woman, with thick, wavy hair. She wore vast furs, looking rather forceful and challenging but at the same time magnificently female. More than once she found her hotel rooms overflowing with violets or with hyacinths, apparently from admirers. It seems that she had a love affair with Poul Bjerre, and at least a close and fiery friendship with Emil von Gebsattel.[24] Her diary notes show that she also developed a very close relationship with Viktor Tausk, who was certainly in love with her. All three men were younger than herself: Bjerre was thirty-five in 1911, Gebsattel twenty-eight and Tausk thirty-three. Other diary notes show that she often saw Zemek, too, who lived in Vienna. However, these were not grand passions – at least not for her – or vital experiences in the forming of her character or views, nor did major works spring from them. For her this was a time devoted mainly to scholarly study, though she was living a full emotional life with its share of happiness, excitement, conflict and pain.

STUDYING WITH FREUD

Lou did not usually speak at the Wednesday discussions. When she did, Freud would take up her remarks. But she felt at ease in this company. She called it a pure company of brothers and sisters ['*eine reine Verschwisterung*'].[25] 'Altogether I feel more at home and more comfortable each time I am with all these people around Freud', she wrote in her *Journal* for 20 November 1912,[26] and some weeks later, more critical but still appreciative and relaxed:

> I reflected again, as I have done so often, that quite apart from the value of the individual papers one feels oneself to be in such good company here, and that Freud's chairmanship and the unobtrusive guidance he gives to everything produces a very good kind of work, such as perhaps would not be produced by a similar number of more significant minds. And one would like to invite the best minds to these evenings, and one is grateful to sit here with him.[27]

Lou sympathised with Freud's dislike of much assertiveness among his colleagues and with what she saw as his sacrifice of a valued solitude for the sake of making his work public. The way he entered the lecture-room, leaning a little to one side, she interpreted as showing 'a will to solitude, a concealing of himself in the purposes that are most his own and which in themselves want to have nothing to do with a school or a public.'[28] But she was also impressed by his unexpected flexibility about his theories. For example, on the very first Wednesday,

> Freud seated me beside him and made a very sweet remark. He himself gave the paper. During the discussion we talked quietly together about various things. I was surprised how much interest he took in a view of neurosis as a disturbance between libido and ego instead of proceeding one-sidedly from the libido; when I observed that his books said something different, he said: 'my *last* formulation'. And this remained my impression in general: that the theories are not all conclusively tied up but continue to be regulated by experiences, and that what makes this man great is simply the man of research that he is, quietly striding onward, tirelessly working.[29]

Of Freud's colleagues, the men Lou came to know best were Karl Abraham, Max Eitingon, Sandor Ferenczi and Viktor Tausk (and, rather less well, Otto Rank). As well as Freud's lectures,* she attended Tausk's and some seminars by Hermann Swoboda (which she found clever but without deep insights). Later on, she worked with Ferenczi. But her chief experience was of Freud himself. She met him not only in lectures, on Wednesdays and with colleagues in the Ronacher Café, where discussions often went on late into the night, but also on private Sunday visits to his home, often staying till one or two o'clock in the morning. They talked, too, on their walks home from lectures and visits. Though he did not analyse her, Freud asked Lou a lot about her early life and she told him her experience of 'brothers' and many memories, including that of imagining the female genitals as jewels inside a mountain (and the related importance to her of the Russian word *zhemchug*, meaning 'pearls'). Freud charmed her with talk of his 'narcissistic cat' and discussed some of his ideas with her, especially those that were going into the fourth part of *Totem and Taboo* about the significance of parricide for civilisation. He discussed the other psychoanalysts with her, too, in particular Stekel and the problematic Tausk, and talked to her about his own life.

FREUD'S VIEW OF LOU

Ernest Jones writes that

it might perhaps be fair to describe [Freud's] view of the female sex as having as their main function to be ministering angels to the needs and comforts of men . . . [he] found the psychology of women more enigmatic than that of men. He said once to Marie Bonaparte: 'The great question that has never been answered and which I have not yet been able to answer despite my thirty years of research into the feminine soul, is "What does a woman want?"'

But to this remarkably silly question he adds that Freud was also interested in women

of a more intellectual and perhaps masculine cast. Such women several times played a part in his life, accessory to his men friends though of a finer calibre, but they had no erotic attraction for him. The most important of them were first of all his sister-in-law, Minna Bernays, then in chronological order: E. Eckstein, Loë Kann, Lou Andreas-Salomé, Joan Rivière, Marie Bonaparte. Freud had a special admiration for Lou Andreas-Salomé, her distinguished personality and ethical ideas, which he felt far transcended his own.[30]

As well as his personal regard for her, Freud may have considered that, as a well-known writer, Lou might help the psychoanalytical cause at a time when it needed influential allies, although before he met her he had been discreetly cautious about her abilities. The January before she came to Vienna, she had offered her article 'On Early Worship of God' to the *Jahrbuch* (the annual collection of research articles on psychoanalytical topics) and Jung, who was then its editor, wrote to Freud that 'Frau Lou Andreas-Salomé, of Weimar fame' wanted to send him a paper on 'sublimation' (instead of *Sublimierung*, she had mistakenly written *Sublimation*, then a chemists' term for a purification method), adding: 'This would be a step towards the "secularisation" of the *Jahrbuch*, a step to be taken with great caution but one which would widen the readership and mobilise the intellectual forces in Germany, where Frau Lou enjoys a considerable literary reputation because of her relations with Nietzsche.'[31] The manuscript arrived; Jung found it 'weird' and said ironically that there were 'tremendous things in it'. Freud (who hadn't read it) thought they ought not to decline it 'provided she contents herself with sublimation and leaves sublimates to the chemists. If it turns out to be idealistic chit-chat, we can reject it politely but firmly.' It was a relief to both when she decided to take it back. It is interesting that Jung's implied judgment of her here is so different from that of Karl Abraham four months later: clearly she talked about the subject far better than she wrote about it.

All Freud's subsequent exchanges with Lou are marked by great courtesy. If he criticised, it was so gently that she may hardly have noticed, and he soon came to think highly of her scholarly writing. He was forthcoming with every kind of help, lending her manuscripts and books, giving advice. In November he hoped she would send a contribution – presumably that same essay – to the newly founded *Imago* (which was in any case adapted to a wider public). It was published there a year later. When Lou once missed a lecture (this was early in November) he wrote to her:

> I missed you yesterday at the lecture and am glad to hear that your visit to the camp of masculine protest [i.e. Adler's camp] had nothing to do with the cause of your absence. I have adopted the bad habit of always directing the lecture at one particular person among my listeners, and yesterday I stared as if under a spell at the space that had been left for you.[32]

ADLER AND JUNG

Lou found Adler 'kindly and very clever'; she was disturbed only by the too personal way he talked about the current dissensions and by the fact that he looked 'like a button'.[33] She attended four or five of his sessions. Her short friendship with him helped her to see Freud's theories more clearly, and it may have been useful to Freud in that it gave him for a time an observer in the dissident camp.

In Adler's book *Organ Inferiority*,[34] much of which she admired, Lou was put off by three main things: the terminology of 'upper' and 'lower' and 'masculine protest', which led to a negative valuation of 'female';[35] the tendency to get rid of the dualism of mind and body; and the negative understanding of the psyche as something arising from a deficiency. Some months after her association with him she wrote him a statement of where she stood in relation to his theories, spelling out these fundamental objections. In his reply, he fiercely re-stated what he believed: '*The psyche is an inferior creature's ability to live.* It contains aggressive drives, expansive tendencies, and an orientation to what is culturally more highly valued, to the man.'[36] Adler accused the Freud school of stealing his ideas and going in for hushing-up tactics, and accused Lou of being unwary.

Much of the first part of the *Freud Journal* is given to rejection of Adler's and Jung's theories. Lou found both of them mistaken in their making a 'premature and therefore quite sterile synthesis'.[37] It now seems surprising that she wrote so little about Jung, whose conception of the Unconscious appears to be closer to hers than does Freud's. But she objected both to Jung's 'naive' attenuation of the concept of libido to include other than sexual drives and to his view of the Unconscious as something independent of the Conscious (strangely, since her own view of it implied a similar autonomy). At the same time, she liked certain things in Jung, such as his amplification of the concept of incest to that of a 'longing for the mother's womb'.[40]

Freud respected her views on these dissenters, and in 1914, after writing his *History of the Psychoanalytic Movement*, said he would have liked her to judge the whole Adler and Jung controversy.[38] Lou sent Freud the letters exchanged between herself and Adler and he told Karl Abraham[39] that they showed 'her insight and clarity in an excellent light', and did the same for 'Adler's venom and meanness'.

FERENCZI

Lou greatly enjoyed working with Ferenczi, whom to Freud she referred to as 'your most philosophic son'. She appreciated Ferenczi's passionate relation to his work, felt she shared with him a (non-sterile) 'synthesising' tendency and particularly welcomed his idea that the Unconscious contains more than repressed material (which she had heard Freud outline but not develop): this was extremely important to her, and she hoped Ferenczi would influence Freud in this. She was interested in the way Ferenczi's ideas and her own were so opposed to each other that they almost came round to making contact again. For, as with Freud, it was her essential optimism that made her clash with Ferenczi. Thinking it over, she discovered, intelligently, that the clash depended on nomenclature:

Everything that Ferenczi . . . entitles 'death-tendency' could also be called 'life-tendency' without anything being altered thereby except the entirely personal attitude. For that which might be conceived as existing behind the structures of life that alone are known to us could just as well be considered the *quintessence of the vital* as 'absolute *rest*' – from which only the first 'impulse to movement' remains unknown.[41]

She wrote this while working with Ferenczi in September 1913 and she added one of her early criticisms of Freud:

One cannot quite reject the thought that that tendency to 'death' and 'rest' which Freud sees as innate in, and the true being of, every living thing, which is only reluctantly stirred up into activity, does itself contain a somewhat neurotic estimation of life. Exactly the opposite conception has as much right as it has: everything that is organised and has entered the processes of existence is a part of the original vitality which constitutes its essence and from which it constantly derives.[42]

TAUSK

Viktor Tausk* was a particularly helpful colleague to Lou Andreas-Salomé in Vienna. He had been attending the Wednesday discussions since 1909 and, shortly after Lou joined them, became the first to lecture on psychoanalysis to the lay public. Tausk had a brilliant, excitable mind and he shared Lou's interest in literature as well as her love of Spinoza. He thought ideas through with her and came up with many inspired notions of his own. He was especially interested in narcissism and in August the following year Lou helped him work at a paper on this for the congress in Munich.

She first met this 'blond headstrong fellow'[43] a few days after her arrival in Vienna; they made friends rapidly and she grew very fond of him. That December, she accompanied him daily to the neurological outpatients' clinic, where they were permitted to analyse patients throughout the morning, both of them wearing white doctors' smocks. Tausk is mentioned almost as much as Freud himself in Lou's *Journal*. Here she pondered the difficulties in his character, starting with the meaning of his devotion to Freud and of Freud's impatience with him.* It has been argued[44] that Freud rejected and destroyed Tausk out of jealousy of his originality. This argument has been cogently countered by another,[45] which concludes that Freud simply found Tausk's character irritating. He was certainly a moody person; he was often distraught and strangely forgetful of words and facts; at one lecture Lou noted that he looked 'quite remarkably miserable'.[46] She thought she came to see the whole tragedy of Tausk's relation to Freud – it was that he would always tackle the same problems and move towards the same solutions as Freud, thus making himself into Freud's 'son' and at the same time hating the father for it. Besides this, there

was in him, she thought, a sort of blind, deaf urge to express himself at
all costs, due to his suffering so much under 'the burden of himself'.
She perceived tenderness, ardour and energy in him (all of which she
summed up as 'motherliness') and a promise of beauty of character if
he could only let it come forth; yet he seemed bent on self-destruction.
'It is all so painful to watch that one turns one's head and would like to
go away.' Part of the trouble was his unrealistic love for her, for 'he
deceives himself about me and fantasises'. She felt there was no way she
could be really helpful to him and she began to withdraw, though with
compassion, for she saw in him 'the struggle of the human creature' and
on several occasions called him 'Brother Animal' [*Brudertier*].[47] So
their friendship had stormy moments, and Tausk wrote several penitent
letters – parts of which recall Rilke in the wealth of loving names he
called her (including the supreme one, 'real') and in his admiration for
her unequalled vitality. He told her she had a genius for always learning
from life. The relationship was short; they parted after the Munich
congress. When the war began, Tausk went to the battlefront and wrote
a paper on war neuroses; from then on he lived a lonely, inwardly-
tormented life. In 1915 he told Lou, whom he still longed to be with,
that nobody would ever agree to take him on with his 'bit of neurosis',
and nor would she either, and rightly.[48] Four years later, on the verge
of a second marriage, Tausk put his head in a noose and blew his brains
out.

END OF THE STAY IN VIENNA

The last Wednesday discussion Lou attended was that of 2 April 1913
and she paid her last private visit to Freud on 6 April. Although she did
not make a farewell speech, she put in her diary the one she would have
liked to make. It was full of gratitude for the honesty of the group of
psychoanalysts and for their achievement in making life bow to
knowledge and academic knowledge bow to life, and ended with the
words 'For men scuffle. Women thank'.[49] She left Freud's house that
Sunday carrying roses and feeling joyful 'that I had met him on my
path and was allowed to *experience* him: as my turning-point'.[50]

After some days spent with Ferenczi in Budapest, Lou was soon back
home in Göttingen, where she felt like a snake, stretching and digesting
in the sunshine.[51] Rilke visited her: 'One day there was Rainer standing
at the garden fence in the evening twilight, and even before we spoke a
word we clasped hands across the fence. The whole of the time he spent
here made me so happy!'[52] She found him wonderfully united in
himself again, and they talked well; he gave her his poem 'Narziss'* and
they went away for a holiday together, during which Lou analysed
Rilke's dreams. That August she was in Munich with Gebsattel and in
Vienna with Tausk, and then in September she was at 'that disagreeable

Congress in Munich'[53] at which Jung broke with Freud. After this, she went to Dresden with Rilke and then to Berlin to see Eitingon, and home again. For Lou, all of 1913 was filled with formal and informal discussions of psychoanalysis.

THE FREUD JOURNAL

From October 1912 to November 1913, Lou Andreas-Salomé kept a copious diary (which I refer to as the *Freud Journal*, the title under which it has been published in English). This diary might be seen as her counterpart to one of Nietzsche's books of aphorisms: it consists of a collection of diverse reflections, usually related to particular seminars or conversations and given titles. They are short, quite carefully structured passages and written in a manner at once scholarly and personal; some are not without wit. The book is more accessible and more attractive than most of her longer articles, which again suggests her greater gift for conversation than for learned disquisition. Two of the Journal's chief themes are Woman and Narcissism.

WOMAN

Lou Andreas-Salomé's views on the nature and destiny of woman did not alter fundamentally through her acquaintance with psychoanalysis. She accepted as complementary to what she already thought most of Freud's (tentative) statements about the female, but re-arranged his ideas with her own emphasis and evaluation. She seems to have accepted without trouble the theory of the Oedipus complex, and its corollary: that while the boy rescues himself from battle with his father and from consequent defeat and castration by 'internalising the father', and thus initiating 'all the processes that are designed to make the individual find a place in the cultural community',[54] the girl – not having to avoid castration, which has already taken place – does not develop so strong a super-ego (or internalised father) and thus is not impelled into a strong involvement with the making of culture. None of this meant, for Lou, any inferiority in the girl. The very fact that she was not compelled to make the sublimations and searches that bring about culture left the girl freer, luckier; she remained whole, and 'her spirit is sex, her sex is spirit'.[55]

A discussion with Jekels one day gave Lou a sudden insight into the question of woman, sex and culture.[56] Jekels had said that 'even men', when they recollect sexual relations, dwell on what led up to the act rather than on the act itself, as if this were embarrassing to recall. Lou's insight was that it was not 'even' men but *especially* men who do this (most men, anyway) and that it was because their formation as cultural beings was bound up with the acquisition of a bad conscience about wish-fulfilments. But women give not a part but their whole self in the act of love and therefore, if they are to survive at all, cannot feel embarrassed or ashamed. This is so important – a matter of survival – that they apply all their cultural power (which men use for so many different things) to the cultivating of this single point. A woman who insists on fidelity, ethics, marriage, in order not to be ashamed, is quite unnecessarily justifying her instinct, and is underestimating herself. By contrast, the unfaithful woman, who generously pours her all into 'the feast of love' [*das Fest der Liebe*] and keeps nothing back from it for 'building houses', instead of splitting like the man (and to some extent, the marriage-insistent woman), remains wholehearted, whole-spirited, and yet also makes a contribution to culture, for her 'erotic power' flows into all the ready-made relational and cultural forms. It seems to be implied that she is the vigour and the animation of it all.[57]

A later entry[58] links up with this thought. Again it was prompted by a discussion, this time with Tausk. Tausk had said something Lou found inspiring: that all negative attitudes to life are related to a lack of felt life. Lou agrees, and comments: rationally we can step back and judge life negatively, but every intuitive moment is bound to be an affirmation as it senses that the very power to criticise life, to be negative about it, is thrown up *by* it. (This is rather like Tolstoy, in his *Confession*, reasoning that he must kill himself, yet realising that the reasoning itself is a process produced by life.) The example of criticism of life Lou has in mind is the Nietzschean and Freudian idea that culture is a decline, a product of the weak. The weak here means men, she thinks, for men are the weaker sex from woman's life-affirming point of view: the idea of culture in decline is itself the decline. She announces woman as the animal of happiness ['*Die Frau als das Glückstier*']. Comparing women with neurotics – she finds them just as narcissistic though not neurotic; they are 'regressives without a neurosis' – she declares: 'Fundamentally the neurotic's wish to be a woman would be a wish to be healthy. And it is always a wish to be happy.'[59]

The same entry reflects on female infidelity and makes the startling statement that women have always to choose between infidelity and being only half of themselves. A woman is like a tree with two destinies: to be struck and cloven by lightning and also to flourish and bear leaves and fruit. If she chooses the flourishing she will live only a half-life, sacrificing the lightning. Alternatively, she could expose herself to the lightning and then repeatedly re-plant the tree, starting afresh from the seed, and this will be called 'infidelity', even though she has probably not abandoned one man for another but has left the man in order to go temporarily back 'home' into herself.

The allegorical and periphrastic style of the passages on infidelity may indicate Lou's caution about any public application of them to herself. There are many places where she does seem, privately, to have herself in mind. Infidelity need not be treacherous or cruel, she says; in fact it may be accomplished with a respectful gesture, a gesture that does not 'reject the man as limited or inadequate but sets him into the midst of life's boundless connections which immediately close up again behind him and take him into their largeness'.[60] She sounds here rather like the mother she described in *The Erotic*, setting the child out into the world. It is difficult not to relate this account (at least *inter alia*) to her dismissal of Rilke in 1901 and her 'Last Message'. In fact, it is frequently interesting to see how Lou's theories, such as these about the nature of woman, derive from her own past feelings and actions – not exactly in justification of them, but as a long meditation on what they must have meant in terms of principle: on what principle can she subsequently discern herself to have acted earlier? Lou was constantly working out her philosophy by reflecting on things she had unreflectingly done and caused, from the way she had lived and was living. Her philosophical world was a direct outgrowth of her lived life, very much as she had explained in her book on him, that Nietzsche's was of his. This is, above all, true of her theory of narcissism.

NARCISSISM

Freud's earliest reference to narcissism was in 1909. He was working on a description of it in the years in which Lou first knew him. He was never quite conclusive about what it meant. At first it meant to him a stage of infantile development coming between auto-erotism and 'object-love'; that is, a stage of love of one's own self which comes *after* the self has been experienced as an entity. In 1914 he devoted a paper[61] to the concept, presenting it in a new way: narcissism was 'the libidinal complement to the egoism of the instinct of self-preservation'; it was thus something that went beyond the infantile stage and was attributable to every living creature. Although libido was mainly directed to objects after the first phase of life, it was normal and necessary, Freud wrote, that some of it should remain attached to the ego. He likened this to an amoeba, which can extend its pseudopodia to reach absorbable objects but is also complete without doing so. The amoeba's completeness is like that of the ego 'cathected' by the narcissistic libido. (The analogy might seem to imply that not to love oneself would be equivalent to not being there at all.)

An intuition of security had always been fundamental to Lou's thoughts about human life. She came now to see both the infant's first self-love and the continuing self-loving (ego-libidinal) element throughout life as primal and repeatable experiences of an original blissful security. She wrote that the growth of the person, unlike that of the animal, proceeds according to the principle of progressive separation, that separation is suffering and that 'the human being can never have suffered so fundamentally, at the very beginning, as from the way his becoming humanly conscious made an abyss open up between himself and all the rest.'[62] From then on, all subsequent hatred derives from the original hatred which was really the anxiety of birth, weaning and the disappointment of 'waking out of total being and finding oneself unable to love totally [all-lieben]'[63] (it is the hatred necessary to the very incipience of the ego). All love felt and encountered in the course of life expresses the happiness that preceded that first separation. Lou considers that to renew that happiness is one of the two basic human desires. As well as the obvious desire to be a separate individual, there is also a lifelong desire to rejoin the world he was formerly at one with. And some people are better able to do this, or perhaps they never quite lose the original bliss as an all-surrounding, all-meaning atmosphere of their existence. The poet, for example, creates from within it; the hero acts within it; women – as we have seen – are generally closer to it; homosexuals are probably closer to it; masochists remember it. (The reference to masochism comes later; Lou wrote, in 1920, that under the hurt from a loved hand 'there revives the blissful memory of the primal undifferentiated state'.)[64] No matter how further advanced the ego-powerful, individualised, unmasochistic, non-poetic and unheroic heterosexual male – the normal man – may be (and he *is* more advanced, further along in evolution, as it were), he is not more fully 'in the real', for the recalled and renewable experience of union *is* reality.

That reality, or the orientation that made it possible, could now be described as narcissism, which Lou said was 'rooted in the deepest naiveté that exists'.[65] Her difference from Freud, in degree of generality and in the very use of the term, was wide. Indeed, her conception of the Unconscious, where these things all happen, was very different from Freud's. He saw the Unconscious mainly as a receptacle for repressed material, whereas for Lou it was important to see it as containing – or as being – far more than that. It was there long before anything had been repressed. Moreover, Freud's accounts of the Unconscious were provisional. He approached it in various ways – descriptively, dynamically, or systematically – and when he likened it to the submerged part of an iceberg or drew it diagrammatically as a space beneath the Preconscious and the Conscious, he did not insist on such representations but apologised for their inadequacy, and was ready to adopt better ones. This was the flexibility Lou admired in him. But her own use of spatial imagery was of a sort that tended to preclude further exploration. When she spoke with delight of the 'all-enclosing ring of the Unconscious, infinitely rounded at all points',[66] she needed just this formulation, suggesting as it did the earth with its curved horizons, the cosmos where parallel lines bend to meet, and perhaps also the female body.

Freud repeatedly called narcissism a limiting concept. He wrote that 'from the vantage-point of psychoanalysis we can look across a frontier, which we may not pass, at the activities of the narcissistic libido',[67] and he told Lou he felt warned not to pursue these problems further 'until light has been shed in other dark places'.[68] She, characteristically, did pursue them further, and made narcissism, which is relatively marginal to Freud's psychology, central to her own. She took the opportunity it gave her to develop and magnificently reformulate the theories about sublime moods and total union that she had long ago put forward in her essays on religion. In an impressive passage in the *Freud Journal* she wrote that, if only the psychoanalytic method permitted,

> if we could approach the analysand in his totality as closely as we approach his fragments – then, instead of encountering the monotony of a few typical basic motifs, when the analysis ends in the depth of his unconscious, we would sink down beyond all that in the mute and solemn miracle of a world which is also our own and which appears inexhaustible just because it is a shared world. The final consequence would then be not something sick and full of guilt, at best to be practically cured, but something guiltless and universal, which would throw a shining white mantle (that of the 'narcissistic') around the poor exposed nakedness of the all-too-human structure. Where so many disguises have been torn off our personal fate, so many falsely idealised circumstances destroyed, it ought to be possible to go with one another far enough to arrive at the place where the individual person quietly makes himself small and can see through himself in his absurd ambitions, because at the same time he is, so to speak, lifted back into his home, into his total value, which remains untouched by them and from which only one judgment on all human doings can be valid: 'they know not what they do'.[69]

The thought of a place beyond the personal and comparatively boring Unconscious, a place shared by all human beings as a kind of home, would seem to have something in common with Jung's later conception of the 'collective unconscious', although no images or symbols appear to belong there. Jung wrote (in 1935)

> The deepest we can reach in our exploration of the unconscious mind is the layer where man is no longer a distinct individual, but where his mind widens out and merges into the mind of mankind – not the conscious mind, but the unconscious mind of mankind, where we are all the same. As the body has its anatomical conformity in its two eyes and two ears and one heart and so on, with only slight individual differences, so has the mind its basic conformity. On this collective level we are no longer separate individuals, we are all one.[70]

Lou also wrote: 'Just as we have *one* anatomy, so we have also *one* common Unconscious'.[71] Yet she never noted any such affinity.

'Narcissism' was a word with solely positive connotation for Lou, and although she spoke of defect ('the erotic defect of the narcissistic person lies in the fact that his own love's outburst almost suffices for him') she also saw narcissistic love as the best love. The gratitude the lover feels for the partner who *taught* him what his own love's outburst could be is a gratitude so warm that it outlasts love itself, 'and in it, in the narcissistic person, it is as if wholly egoistic and wholly selfless ways of loving meet each other.'[72] Where Freud thought the ego needed to attach itself to objects in order to discharge excess of energy, Lou considered that it used objects in order to bring about such excess, for it was in the excess of energy, of feeling, that it found itself most intensely. This high point of discovery of oneself was, she said, identical with discovery of the world.

The passage from the *Journal* quoted above proceeds to distinguish three kinds of narcissism.[73] First, it is the 'particular stage of development to be transcended'. Second, it is the 'persistent accompaniment of all deeper experience' – narcissism in its creative form, which Lou often emphasised in overt criticism of Freud.[74] And finally, there is what she calls 'a third and beautiful meaning of narcissism', seen in the figure of Narcissus 'oriented to himself as a discoverer: Narcissus the self-knower'.

'What a horrible transfiguration!'[75] she had written earlier, of Freud's conception of civilised man as a 'sadly tamed savage' and of the goal of all culture as a 'constant attenuation of instinct'. She had argued against Freud's too-sharp distinction between culture and nature. To her mind, the cultural *was* the natural and, with as simple a basic switch of judgment as she had applied in her translation of Ferenczi's 'death-tendency' into 'life-impulse', she claimed in a later passage in the *Journal*[76] that what we call 'sublimation' and what in Freud's view is in opposition to nature (and hence pushed into 'ominous kinship' with represssion) is actually the natural realisation of our self. She felt that a better word for it would be the word Tausk had introduced: 'elaboration'.[77] This leads her to a rather grand climactic piece on narcissism, an image of noontide, Nietzsche's 'high noon':

Only *that* human being who Prometheus-like has created human existence over again in culture, as a second reality, is also the fully developed Narcissus in front of his own likeness: it is *himself* that he beholds in it; he is not the scourged slave, forced to escape from himself into it. It is wrong to see nature and culture as an opposition like sun and shadow, with regard to our natural desire for happiness and for our own ego; it is wrong when the growth of this shadow appears to coincide with the increased slant of the sunbeams: this is a wrongly chosen image. The right image is rather that of the plant around the hour of the full noon: then it spreads its own shadow vertically down beneath it – a doubling of itself in which it repeats its outline and gazes at it: its finest protection – that the great burning should not consume it before it bears fruit.[78]

Narcissus in love with himself, and therefore with the whole world he has recreated; human culture conceived as a second reality which is equivalent to, and which intensifies and expresses, human nature; worn by it as the plant wears the shadow it is drenched with, and not divergent from it any more than the midday shadow is separately visible; a glimpsed Prometheus tearing fire from heaven for himself and thereby becoming fully himself; self-centredness identical with selflessness; a both comfortable and glorious transformation of the perfect Rilkean intransitive love. In all this, in this 'third and beautiful narcissism', we see Lou Andreas-Salomé at her best: Nietzschean, evolutionist, religious atheist, poetic psychoanalyst, eclectic and original at once, infusing the ideas she has inherited and developed with the profound *joie de vivre* that was wholly her own. In such intensified synthesis of the ideas of others, we see Lou herself, with her certainty of the goodness and marvel of all that has happened to humanity. This is sharply distinct from the strenuously achieved affirmations of Nietzsche, the lamentations and anguished acclamations of Rilke and the scepticism and final misanthropy of Freud.

CONCLUSION

Perhaps the best commentary on Lou Andreas-Salomé's personal experience of psychoanalysis in 1912–13 is the indirect account Rilke gave in a letter to his friend, the Princess von Thurn und Taxis. It was written when he had met Lou that July, just after her half-year of study with Freud:

Then I spent a week in Göttingen at Lou Andreas-Salomé's, there's a lot to tell about this and the most wonderful is what magnificent insights this woman has, how she turns all that books and people bring her at the right moment into the most blessed comprehension, how she understands, and loves, and moves fearlessly among the most burning mysteries – that do nothing to her, only beam at her with pure firelight. I know no one else – and since those far-off years when she first met me and brought such infinite significance into my life I've never known anyone else – who had life so much on their side as she has, recognising, in the tenderest and most terrible things, the one single power, which puts on disguises but, even when it kills, desires to give . . . I'll tell you one day.[79]

CHAPTER ELEVEN

War-time, Psychoanalysis, Rilke and Freud

I like nothing better than to run on your lead – though it has to be a really long one – so that as soon as I go scrambling about too far away you've only got to wind it up to have me standing right beside you.[1]   LOU TO FREUD

If I could only see things for one second from your eyes . . . I would come back to my entanglements with new strength.[2]

RILKE TO LOU

From 1914 onwards, Lou Andreas-Salomé's chief activity was her work as a psychoanalyst. Patients were recommended to her by Freud and others, and soon she could not imagine her life without at least one current analysis. At home she saw few people apart from patients but lived quietly, enjoying her house and garden and surrounding woods, her dog, and the seasons. She was always delighted when spring came, finding it unexpected and astonishing.[3] Often she rose early, to the red glimmer of the stove and red rim of the sun, and everywhere she sensed the miraculous and the magnificent.[4] Meanwhile she still led, at intervals, a fairly vigorous life of travels and society, though after about 1912 all her travelling was connected with Rilke or Freud, or with her professional work.

There were some personal griefs. A great loss had been the death of her friend Frieda in 1909; then her mother had died in 1913 (which she kept sadly to herself among the Viennese psychoanalysts). Now she was stricken by her brother Alexander's death in 1915; in 1919 came the (lesser) shock of Viktor Tausk's suicide. And there were other, less personal, griefs: the war, and the revolution in Russia.

THE 1914–18 WAR

The war had a special pathos for Lou, since fighting on each side was a country that she felt to be her own. Her psychological studies were reflected in the sad and angry notes on the war that began to fill long sections of her diary. It was because they had so long repressed their instincts, she said, that war seemed 'real' to so many men; it appeared to them a sanction for the exploding of an unbearable self-control. But war was not (as Nietzsche had it) something healthy, youthful and virile; it was the stimulant sought by old tired nations. Anyone who lived authentically and productively felt alive without such stimulants. She believed, all the same, that everyone had to join in, because all of us are murderers a thousand-fold, of ourselves and of others. She herself would take part were she a man, or would send her sons to fight if she had any. Guilt united across national frontiers: by putting it this way she was, true to her habit, finding some good within the bad; moreover, the motive to fight, she reasoned, had not to do with state or national interests, nor was it egoism, nor the force of moral argument, but anger, an anger which was really a disguised love, 'for all life proceeds from something positive, however negatively it may be rigged out'. Later, looking back, she disagreed with the often-expressed view that there would be no war if women ran the world: motherhood includes partisanship with not only the loves but the hates and aggressions of one's sons; and in any case psychoanalysis has shown the aggressiveness in us all.[5] At the same time she hated the 'spectrality', the unreality, of the war, and loathed the war-justifying clichés in the press and in common talk. It was not true, she objected, that after the first terrifying moments in a bayonet attack you are roused to your real animal nature and begin wanting to kill – on the contrary, only those first few moments were the real experience; the rest was sheer rhetoric. She was scathing about propaganda that claimed the enemy alone had wicked motives while 'we' fought to show our courage, and so on; no, war was altogether a temporary relapse into a primitive condition.'

Lou took issue with several commentators on the war, grieving over pro-German views put forward by Richard Dehmel and Max Scheler, over Paul Ernst's idea of war as 'truth' and Fritz Mauthner's theory that death had become easier through a kind of general ecstasy. She agreed only with Maximilian Harden, whom she considered the only writer one could read on the subject – except that she thought productiveness, rather than the desire for comfort (as he had it) was conducive to peace.[6]

To Freud, Lou wrote about the war with a certain measure of optimism. Freud wrote to her misanthropically in November 1914, asking her if she still thought the 'elder brothers' (her world full of brothers) were so very good, and giving the melancholy view that as civilisation was afflicted with a monstrous hypocrisy we should resign from it and leave the Great Unknown to repeat the 'experiment of culture some day with another race'.[7] In reply Lou pointed out that, for one thing, the solitude and rest which the war was forcing upon Freud had given him the freedom he wanted for his work; and, for another (here she spoke straight out of her theory of narcissism): 'behind individual human activities and the territory which can be reached by psychoanalysis there lies a depth where the most valuable and also the nastiest impulses indistinguishably condition each other and make any

final [moral] judgment impossible.'[8] In all its woolliness of expression,
this was Lou's equivalent of Nietzsche's 'have you said yes to one joy? –
then you have said yes to all woe'. Freud told Karl Abraham: 'Her
optimism is too deeply rooted to be shaken.'[9]

The same pages of Lou's diary abound in the deaths of her acquaintances' sons, in descriptions of trains full of wounded men and of
mothers proudly walking out with their bandaged soldier sons. Though
her accounts tend to be general, she could also be detailed. She
described, for instance, a crowd of people staring at a soldier's unban-
dageable mouth-wound as if looking at a fallen horse. Characteristically,
in the midst of her horror and gloom about war, Lou could still be
overtaken, in life and in her diary,[10] by outbursts of sheer existential
joy, such as her delight – after the sight of the soldier's wound – at
seeing a spruce tree into which a mass of bright yellow birch leaves had
dropped, so that it seemed to be sprouting oranges.

THE 1917 REVOLUTION

The October Revolution in Russia brought Lou heartache as well. She
had once admired the Russian revolutionaries as Utopians hopelessly
working for Heaven on earth, in tragic contrast to the practical political
interest of other nations. But she was firmly against the Bolsheviks, who
were determined to stay in power by force and dictatorship; the true
heirs of the earlier idealists were the Social Revolutionaries. At the news
of the separate peace treaty between Russia and Germany she was
deeply upset and spent a night in tears,[11] and she wrote to Freud in
May 1918 about 'the tragedy of that land'.[12] In the 'NEP' period she
was quick to feel hopeful again: 'Since the Bolsheviks gave up the
bestiality of their methods (which stood in such gruesome contrast to
their social ideal and goal), since, that is, they were forced to make
concessions to Europe's capitalism, a new generation has been growing
there, full of ardour and purity, determined to achieve that very goal
after all.'[13] But these, she predicted, would be the martyrs of the
following period.

Her family was, of course, affected by the Revolution. Her brother
Robert, for instance, came home in 1921 from the Crimea (where he
had buried his youngest son) to find his house taken over by his servant.
Thenceforth he lived humbly alongside him, often having to pick
berries and mushrooms to stay alive.

CORRESPONDENCE WITH RILKE IN 1914

In her long exchange of letters with Rilke in the years after their
reunion in July 1913, there were for Lou at least two moments of
particular intensity, two high points when she greatly gained from him
and which he must have seen as a belated attainment of the relationship

he had longed for in 1898 – with himself as the 'giver'.

The first may be found in their exchange between February and July 1914. This had two stages: a shared creative moment for them both, and then an important poem of Rilke's leading to a sort of creative climax for Lou. The shared moment was their discussion in February of her book *Three Epistles to a Boy*, and his immense pleasure in it. She incorporated part of his letter of response into the book itself, and he later worked up some of her ideas into two of the Elegies. This is probably the closest identifiable effect of Lou on his work, and of him on hers. The important poem was *Wendung*, the 'turning-point' poem arising out of the crisis over 'Benvenuta' which Rilke had characteristically shared with (or confessed to) Lou. She had wept over his crisis-letter, but replied all the more encouragingly, telling him (as she had done during his Parisian fears of 1903) that his very way of putting his hopelessness into words showed 'exactly, exactly, exactly'[14] his old undamaged power of turning death into life. He had thanked her for this '*good*' letter and a week later had written the poem, which he immediately sent her, for 'you will understand how it is meant',[15] and now in reply she wrote him three long letters, euphoric, triumphant, even prophetic.[16] The first gave a curious psychosomatic interpretation of the poem, evoking from it an 'obscure, heavy, magnificent' mystery which others could not guess at but, she wrote, 'you will *experience* it'. She longed to talk to him about it, not because she knew such a lot but because she was, 'as a woman, somehow at home in those regions'[17] and felt she heard his heart's profound new tones sounding through her whole being. She asked him to meet her, and even made a definite proposal for a meeting, just as *he* had so many times longed to meet her! Her next letter (with inspired thoughts about his poem *Narziss*) was so enthusiastic about his unconscious success in creating happiness out of his misery, that she herself became creative: transported, released into writing well. These three letters might be seen as a good and unselfconscious example of what she always meant by self-transcension through feeling (of which she considered everyone capable). She seemed to be raised aloft by his art, and this meant, paradoxically, by the pain his art was made of: 'For *you* it's pain: I feel through your pain happiness. Forgive me.'[18]

Rilke's reply to this second letter, beginning with the words 'Dear Lou, you *know* and you *grasp* . . .', was yet another of his long, eloquent, confessional lamentations.[19] He was endangered by the external world, he was the anemone that could not close, he was exposed [*preisgegeben*], he could *do* nothing, he was Goethe's opposite, his body was a surface full of traps that snapped shut on tormented impressions and let them wither, he had lost the unity and sensation of his youth, he was ill, tired, split, wasted, guilty, and – 'Is it fine where you are, and lots of roses?'[20]

And Lou's answer (her third letter) was another inspired declaration of belief in him, and especially of belief that, without knowing it, he was happy:

> What you say about it, for instance what you say about the anemone, is nothing other than work, work, the coming about of deepest unities in you! It's true that a great deal of poetic work has arisen out of despairs, but if it arose out of *that* despair, the despair of ever being capable of such unifying work, there'd be a mistake in that, wouldn't there? that's how it seems to your *consciousness* of yourself. Your consciousness is on the side of that which suffers from inhibitions and therefore does not go along with the moments when it repeatedly becomes clear that you *are* not so thoroughly lacking in unity as you feel and think 'you' are ... for one *cannot* write about the anemone as you do without some kind of (simply not working through into full consciousness) happiness![21]

WITH RILKE, 1915 AND 1919

Lou and Rilke met again briefly in Göttingen that July, when she found him cheerful, humorous and childlike, and the next year Lou joined Rilke for two and a half months in Munich, where he was then living with the young artist, Loulou Albert-Lasard. He had told Loulou that she would find in Lou 'a friend and a mother and, you will see, everything will become clear'[22] (meaning the problem of Loulou's impending divorce). What she found, though, was that Lou brought with her a veritable whirlwind of external events. 'From the moment of her arrival our days were filled with her programmes. In the morning a spiritualist seance [Rilke's programme rather than hers], in the afternoon historians or astronomers, finally in the evening psychoanalysts, writers or doctors. Taken separately, each of these gatherings might have been interesting, but this mad pot-pourri made me dizzy.'[23] What was more, Lou took Rilke with her on her numerous visits and long walks, which got him out of breath. Even the dog she had brought with her filled the house with noise.

Loulou summed up Lou as a 'woman of penetrating intelligence and powerful temperament' who 'despite a strong sensuality seemed somewhat too exclusively cerebral',[24] and she wondered how Rilke's friendship with her could have endured so long – two such different beings. It must have been the sheer vitality, the nature force, she felt, in the 'Russian woman'. She noted that Lou's teaching Rilke to walk barefoot was something of the greatest importance to him, taking him away from the old, nervous civilisation he belonged to. She guessed he was drawn by her dynamic way of talking, as well as by her ability to discuss 'the most delicate problems with astonishing assurance'.[25]

Above all, Lou, she realised, was associated with his experience of Russia.

Loulou also gave an account of Lou's physical attractiveness:

Despite her age and although she took no care at all about her appearance [she went around in grey sacks, then called 'reform clothes'], Lou, in her ardent vitality, still had passionate admirers. I recall one of them getting tears in his eyes from a passing word of Lou's, so that in his dismay he dropped his monocle. Her glance radiated a great power.[26]

One evening, when she and Rilke were sitting with Lou and Baron 'G' (doubtless Gebsattel), Loulou was struck by the different beauty of the three pairs of eyes before her: Rilke's, dark-violet and 'all soul'; the Baron's, a penetrating blue of clear intelligence; and Lou's, 'a magnificent tiger-gaze'.[27]

There exists an account of Lou from a time very close to this one, by Kurt Wolff, later a well-known publisher. His account conjures up a timeless peace and quietness about Lou which is wholly different from Loulou's turbulent, tigerish impression; and this confirms our view of her as alternating between two kinds of existence – the active and the contemplative. Wolff had called on Lou in her hotel one afternoon in Leipzig in the summer of 1916, and had a long, soothing talk with her about her life, which seemed to him filled with mystery and significance. He described her manner of talking as 'simple, peaceful, sober', and said of her appearance:

A broad face, a strong-willed chin, a beautifully curved mouth, wise, expressive eyes which always looked full at the listener or speaker. A completely feminine, attractive person, tender and strong.[28]

Lou and Rilke did not meet again for four years. In 1919, despite the difficulty of travelling in those years and the considerable problems of daily life during the postwar unrest in Munich, Lou visited Rilke again in that city as his guest for a fortnight. She saw many of her friends there but she later noted that, when she looked back to Munich, 'I see only Rainer.'[29] His friendship, his poetry, had helped her; once again, he had been the giver – she had needed 'a bit of life' and he had been able to give it.[30] Knowing that he could help her was of course of help to him; it gave him self-confidence, and he thanked her for being there 'with so much closeness and existence and trust!' Their friendship seems now to have reached a new stage, of exchanging mutual comfort on almost equal terms. That year Rilke left to live in Switzerland. Henceforth their correspondence proceeded with gaps, sometimes of a year or more, but when they did write (usually at his initiative), the letters were long and warm, right up to Rilke's death in 1926.

The intensity of the relationship of Lou and Rilke is perhaps best seen in another remarkable moment, the second high point in their later correspondence. This is their exchange of letters about the final accomplishment of the *Duino Elegies*. Lou was among the first Rilke wrote to in February 1922 with news of the completion of the long-awaited work and he wrote ecstatically:

> In this moment, this Saturday, the eleventh of February, at six, I put down my pen, after the last completed Elegy, the tenth ... Think! I have been permitted to endure till this moment. Through everything. Miracle. Grace ... Now I *know* myself again. For it was like a mutilation of my heart, that the *Elegies* were not there. They are. They are ...[31]

Lou's reply was spontaneous and strong:

> Ah, *slava bogu* [Russian: 'thank God'], *dear* Rainer, how he has enriched you and how you have enriched me! I sat and read and howled with joy, and it was far from being merely joy, but was something more powerful, as if a curtain were divided, torn through, and everything all at once had become quiet and certain and present and good.[32]

He had copied out the sixth, eighth and tenth elegies for her. Of the eighth she said: 'O how this is the [poem] of my most secret heart, the unsayably splendid [poem]; *said*, the inexpressible lifted into presence.' And, she continued, at last receptively understanding Rilke:

> And *that's* what it is altogether, what it's about, that we are surrounded, encircled, by presences which are released into existence for us *only* in this way, yet these are the only things we have our life from. But where *is* there anything like this in poetry? ... I imagine you so fabulously distinct as you must now be looking: and as you *then, then,* were sometimes able to look.[33]

Rilke replied:

> That you are there, dear, dear Lou, to confirm it for me, right into my innermost heart! Reading your good letter that shared my knowledge: it all came over me once again, this security on every side, that now it's *there*, it's *there*, the thing that for such a long time, since all time, has been coming about![34]

He spoke of the enormous gratitude he felt, and Lou, replying that it was all like a dream, 'this marvellous certainty that life is so marvellous a thing',[35] took up his feeling of gratitude to exclaim that this was the one valid proof of the existence of God. Now this gratitude of his to

God (as she took it to be) was matched by her gratitude to Rilke, when a few days later she received from him the rest of the Elegies and found she could scarcely read the ninth for the sheer pleasure of it, like being in a garden whose paths one can hardly use

> because each step is held up and stopped by the blossoming and greening all around; everywhere, continually, in every stanza, every part of a stanza, I sit down, I feel I'm in a bower, as if branches must be weaving together above me and making an unheard-of home. Yes, these *are* the gardens of my most secret home from time immemorial, childhood and youth and all existence have always stood in the midst of these gardens and grown eternal there. *This* I shall *never* be able to tell you, what this means to me and how I have been unconsciously waiting to receive what is *yours* as *mine* like this, as life's veritable consummation. I shall be grateful to you for this as long as I live.[36]

Lou was wound up by Rilke's words to a pleasure beyond words, to something like a spiritual conjunction with him. For her it was more than a response to a great work of art; more than emotionally joining him in his triumph; more, even, than her pleasure in the pleasure it must have been to *him* to witness her humble, awed reception of him; and more than being momentarily swung aloft by the power of whatever it was that had seized and swung the poet to the height of writing the poems. More than all this momentary feeling, it seemed the climax to a life-long intellectual preparation. For Lou's most cherished theories about the higher, the sublime, moods, the all-justifying possibility of self-transcension, were proved and fructified by this supreme act of Rilke's. He proved (she thought) the truth that she had always argued, that at the highest moment there is 'home' and also, moreover, the kind of thanking that must imply 'God'. As she had said twenty-four years before in her essay 'On the Religious Affect', the summit moments generate gratitude and our desire to thank means that God is there to be thanked. That it didn't mean this for Rilke made no difference. Rilke's kind of thanking had confirmed the existence of God for *her*. This was how their minds came together.

One cannot leave this rapturous exchange, however, without noting that in the midst of it Lou did not cease altogether to be doctor, mother and adviser to the reckless Rilke. She warned him that after so much uplift he was very likely to experience a reaction, a rebound. 'Don't be frightened by it', she told him, 'when it comes (it is how the Marys feel, too, after the birth that is incomprehensible to their carpenters)'.[37]

DEATH OF RILKE

Three and a half years later, Rilke described his last illness to Lou as that very 'rebound' she had foretold after the writing of the Elegies:[38]

he presented his symptoms to her in relation to 'diabolically obsessive' (masturbatory) activity of his own, and begged her for help. Though he asked if she knew anyone else who could help him, his appeal was also very directly to her. It was, despite his fear that he had a fatal physical disease, very much an appeal for psychological help. And Lou replied in psychoanalytical terms, advising him to see it all (even the lumps on his lips) as the result of guilt feelings about masturbation in childhood: 'Such hypochondria can also be grasped as a kind of amorousness drawn back upon itself in respect of the organ concerned, except that it does not feel like that at all, but feels like aversion, pain, almost hatred for the body ... Ah, this whole picture is so clear.'[39] She blamed herself, for had she understood his trouble earlier she might have known how to prevent it getting worse, and it had got worse. The shift, as she saw it, from anal obsession to oral manifestations meant a shift backward to a more infantile stage. The lumps in his mouth were again that 'too big' which in Rilke's poetry so often expresses a fear of the external world and which Lou (apparently with his agreement) related to his particular sexual anxieties.

But Rilke was developing leukaemia. It is a pity that the last letter we have from Lou to Rilke is one in which she misinterpreted his condition. He did not lose his conviction that she understood everything about him. From his deathbed a year later, he wrote her an anguished and loving letter, and Nanny Wunderly-Volkart, who was then looking after him, told Lou how he said: 'Lou must know everything – perhaps she knows a consolation.'[40] Although Rilke did not want to know about his illness himself, he wanted her to know, and in the week before he died (on 29 December 1926) he said several times: 'Perhaps Lou Salomé will understand what it has all been about.'[41]

WRITING

As a writer, Lou continued to be extremely productive. She still wrote and published fiction, including a number of stories such as 'Siblings', written in 1919 (the study of a hothouse of youthful sexual intensities and disasters), and the idyllic yet horrific tales of childish dreams and desires that appeared under the title *The Hour Without God* in 1922, as well as three plays. Of these she published only one, *The Devil and His Grandmother*, a quasi-expressionist verse-drama full of nightmarish humour and erotic-cosmic philosophy; this was written in 1915 and published in 1922. She also wrote articles about Russia, about poetic creation, and about Strindberg, among others; and numerous reviews. But her main achievement was her series of articles on psychoanalytical subjects, most of which appeared in *Imago*. Between 1914 and 1920 Lou was writing two, and sometimes three or four, substantial works every year. Then, after six relatively unproductive years, came three final full-length books: on Rilke, on Freud and on her own life.

LOU AS PSYCHOANALYST

Scarcity of food after the war had made Lou 'quite thin and quite grey'.[42] At the age of sixty, she temporarily lost all her hair after an illness; she wore a small cap and called herself a 'little old woman'.[43] But her active life was hardly that of an old person. That same year she was doing six or eight hours of analysis a day; at another time Freud had to warn her that ten or eleven hours a day was too much. She needed the money, especially in those days of wild inflation and financial panic. But far more important was the fact that she liked it – 'psychoanalytical work makes me so happy that even if I were a millionaire I would not give it up', she said,[44] and she was remarkably good at it. Her famous ability to listen, to make people feel better, wiser, by the way she listened, and to talk of anything, no matter how intimate, without inhibition, had come into its own.

In the 1920s, Lou had increasing financial problems yet, while often working long hours from sheer need, she often undercharged her patients (Freud intervened over this) and sometimes gave analyses free of charge. Freud himself assisted her a lot from 1922 onwards, enabling her that year to send a parcel to her last surviving brother, Robert, and to get her fur coat repaired. In 1923 he arranged to send her (apparently) fifty dollars every six months from Rome. Later, after the death of her husband, he gave her 1000 marks out of his Goethe prize of 10,000 marks, which – no longer in need – she said she would keep in trust for him.

Lou was never analysed – in those days it was not an essential part of an analyst's training – but her childhood, with its imaginative obsessions, was always a preoccupation and she may have found explanation for some of it in the course of analysing others. At any rate, her great love of the work and her conviction that it did *her* good contributed to her success. She told Freud:

> For me personally there is a permanent strong enchantment in the very basis, the initial grounds, of psychoanalysis; it may well be connected with the actually not very gratifying fact that one (i.e. I myself) has not got so far with oneself, practically, as one has with insights into others, and one feels again and again that the most appropriate place one could possibly be is at the very beginning of the process of psychoanalysing.[45]

Psychoanalysis enabled her, too, to understand something of her own past relationships, or at least something of those with whom she had had them. In 1917 she noted with very great sadness that had psychoanalysis been discovered in time, Paul Rée would have been saved.[46] At the time of their friendship she had realised that some illness lay at the heart of his extraordinary kindness. Only through psychoanalysis did she understand how she might have helped him.

Psychoanalysis helped her not only to think, but also to feel, as she told Freud on another occasion. He had sent her an agoraphobic patient along with a warning that as the woman wasn't very intelligent the work would be difficult and that he was not even sure 'whether the person is worth it'! After getting to know the patient, Lou replied that the work would indeed be difficult because of the patient's lack of intelligence, but that on the other hand she was noticing

> how in my eagerness to understand her and help her I feel more and more well disposed towards her. I know this quiet progress in myself, and for me this belongs to the most warming of pleasures; for in myself I am a cold old animal which is attached to very few people; for this reason I'm so grateful to be able to flow out so warmly within psychoanalysis.[47]

He later warned her not to get too involved. Lou had felt she should intervene when the patient's husband risked spoiling the treatment by forcing his wife to make a decision; but she took Freud's advice and stuck to her contract as analyst. Indeed she asked for and took his advice on many occasions over the years. Although he pointed out that there could not properly be any consultation in psychoanalytic treatment, he usually responded to her requests with commentary and guidance – as in the case of a six-year-old girl with nightmares (whom Lou was able to cure), a woman with a compulsive neurosis whom she wanted to treat by letter (in which she failed), and several others, including a girl with a flatulence phobia though also with a happy, promiscuous sex life. A case in 1929 that gave Lou very great pleasure was that of a hysterical woman whose cure she had first despaired of, but who had then responded to treatment and in the course of it had revealed unsuspected artistic gifts, eventually becoming not only healthy but an accomplished painter.

Rilke had always thought highly of Lou as a psychoanalyst and in 1924 he had told the Princess von Thurn und Taxis, who was dubious about the Freudian method:

> Lou Andreas (who is now a wise old lady) cannot be called a pupil of Freud's, but she is certainly one of his oldest fellow-workers. In her remarkable and personally developed spirituality his (Freud's) important discoveries have acquired a special significance, perhaps the widest and most valid they will ever have and at the same time the most fundamentally helpful. Besides the few Swiss psychoanalysts, Frau Andreas is the only non-Jew who practises this treatment in

particular cases and with a conscience, an empathy and a devotion that are incomparable.[48]

There is no sign that Lou thought of herself as conspicuously non-Jewish, nor that she thought she had any special or unusual method: her theoretical differences do not appear to have affected her practice. From much that she said, though, it is clear that she saw the analytical situation as one shared and enjoyed by analyst as well as patient. The happiness of psychoanalysing is the starting theme of her book *My Thanks to Freud*. No other relationship, she wrote, comes near the special equality between analyst and analysand; nothing else demonstrates so well the significance and dignity of every human being; nothing else offers so deep a knowledge of humanity – and this is all pleasure. She used two domestic similes: one was of Freud describing a case of neurosis, first of all layer by layer, as it were, and then presenting it whole to his audience, so that the description reminded her of suddenly taking a baked cake from the baking-tin, and made her exclaim 'Human life – ah! life altogether – *is* poetry!'[49] The other simile said the analytical approach was related to the artistic (the synthetic) in the way looking at woven cloth towards the left and observing the track of individual threads and knots is related to looking at the same cloth towards the right – and seeing the pattern they form. She felt she was able to do both: thus something of Rilke the artist and also of Freud the analyst met in her, their 'understander'. Above all, the happiness of psychoanalysis was that of freeing the real from the unreal; there was an unparalleled possibility in it of reality meeting reality, instead of – as in so much of our social life – spectre encountering spectre.[50] In none of her writing did she consider that psychoanalysis might fail.

Lou always wished that psychoanalysis could go further than it did, and wished she could treat the insane as well as the neurotic, for she thought she glimpsed in the psychotic, as in the artist, how the circle which in most of us is broken (the break between individual and entirety, between subject and object) is closed up again to a 'perfect round'.[51] In general, her enormous respect for those who were either neurotically or mentally ill led her to define such a sufferer as one who had tried to go

to his uttermost extreme – *this* is why he slipped off the rails, rather than the others. They, the ones who remained healthy, were, in comparison, simply the ones who put up with what they'd got.[52]

And she came to ask not only why the sick person was sick, but, 'just as suspiciously', how the healthy had managed to stay healthy. She got as far as making some of the doctors to whom she was giving 'teaching analyses' in 1924 feel uneasy about their health.[53]

Lou adhered faithfully and constantly to Freud, yet several elements in her thought suggest that had she allowed herself more freedom, and had she known Jung's work more closely, she might have employed her 'synthesising' faculty in combining some of the latter with the former. These elements include her hankering after the study of psychoses, her stress on the active and wholehearted participation of the analyst, and – although she was Freudian in generally conceiving the Unconscious as being determined by infancy experiences – her belief that the glimpses of individual patients' most hidden (repressed) secrets might ideally add up to the vision of a shared and infinite substratum to consciousness, an unmediated sight of reality itself. Her admiration for religion, too, as well as her positive estimation of the nature of woman, and of the psyche in the second half of life, could be accommodated in a partially Jungian psychology.

As well as receiving patients at home, Lou worked at different times in a number of clinics, particularly at the psychoanalytical polyclinic set up for poor patients by Max Eitingon in Berlin in 1921, and one run by Otto Bruns in Königsberg which she helped re-organise on psychoanalytical lines, but where she found among the doctors 'lack of respect for the seriousness of the matter and for him who created it'.[54] She had a 'complete disappointment'[55] from attending an experimental clinic (run by Dr and Mrs Marcinowski in Munich) for a while: this was an attempt at a community of the sick, with doctors and patients living together as one big family.

FRIENDSHIP WITH FREUD

Lou's friendship with Freud lasted from the Vienna years, 1912–13, until her death in 1937. Towards the end of 1921, she stayed in his home for the first time. It was a visit of five weeks, during which she made friends with his daughter Anna, and went for walks with Freud in the evenings. She was his guest on subsequent occasions too (in 1921, 1925, 1928 and 1929), and Anna visited her several times in Göttingen.

Lou Andreas-Salomé was the second woman – and the only woman among his colleagues – with whom Freud kept up a long, continuous correspondence (the first was his sister-in-law, Minna Bernays). More than two hundred letters, many of them extremely long, passed between them. The letters were frequent in the first ten years; after that, partly because they did their talking when Lou visited Freud and partly, no doubt, because of increasing age and absorption in work, they are less frequent, though still regular. It was not a correspondence which, like that with Rilke, recorded a dramatically changing personal relationship, with churning confessions and high peaks of communions. It was a sober intellectual exchange, containing much discussion of scientific topics, on the basis of a firm, unvarying and often-expressed friendship. For Lou, this friendship gave a profound security to the last third of her life.

From the beginning she had told Freud she wanted her relationship with him to remain 'completely free from the usual conventionality and politeness', and he had implicitly agreed; the mutual gratitude and admiration that characterised the whole of their correspondence is therefore all the more remarkable. Freud was consistent in his admiration for Lou through all the twenty-five years he knew her. But his admiring remarks often included a subtle hint at the way they differed: he suggested that she was up to something *he* would not do, and perhaps would rather *she* did not.

Each time I read one of your appraising letters I am surprised by your art of going beyond what has been said, of completing it and making it converge at some distant meeting-point. Naturally I don't immediately go with you. I rarely feel much need for synthesis. The unity of this world seems to me something self-evident which is not worth emphasising. What interests me is the separating and articulating of what would otherwise flow together into a primeval pulp [*in einen Urbrei*]. Even the assurance that is best expressed in Grabbe's *Hannibal*: We shall not fall out of this world, seems to me no substitute for the giving up of the ego-frontiers, which may be painful enough. In short, I am clearly an analyst and I consider that synthesis presents no problems if one has first done the analysis.[56]

Lou herself was apt to use the phrase, 'We cannot fall out of the world', and to praise the Russian character for being rooted in this sentiment. Freud's criticism of her was gentle but definite. A year later he wrote rather similarly, if with more self-criticism:

You are, after all, an understander par excellence, and, what's more, you understand more and better than what has been set before you. I am always specially impressed when I read your comment on one of my works. I know that while writing I have artificially blinded myself in order to gather all the light onto the one dark spot, renouncing coherence, harmony, elation, and everything you call the symbolical ... Then you come along and add what's missing, and build up something on it and put the isolated phenomenon back into its connections. I can't always follow you for my eyes are adapted to the dark and probably cannot stand strong light.[57]

His confidence in her is seen in his openness about the colleagues who deserted him. Of Adler, he wrote to Lou: 'Let's talk plainly: he is a repulsive person.'[58] About Stekel – whose name Lou divided up as *St Ekel* [St Nasty][59] – he spoke of his regret that he could not exterminate him.[60] He shared with her his worries about Rank, who had been 'a

faithful son' for fifteen years but in 1924 was becoming refractory. Thus
Lou shared Freud's enmities and troubles. Much of their harmony
seems to have been due, though, to her tact, or perhaps to a tacit
agreement to keep disagreements out of it. They said very little, for
instance, about Tausk. When the subject came up with great force, in
the news of Tausk's suicide, Lou answered Freud's letter conveying the
news to her with remarkable diplomacy.[61] First she gave Tausk his due
– that is, her affectionate remembrance and a kindly judgment: 'Poor
Tausk. I was fond of him.' She said that what made him a danger to
Freud was also what made him attractive, for he was 'wild-souled and
tender-hearted'. But having said this, she could agree that he was, as
Freud thought, a very real threat to the future of psychoanalysis. That
being said, she once again gave him his further due: he was 'an
enthusiastic and genuine exponent' of it. She took some responsibility
for his despair and death, admitting that, when he had recently wanted
to see her, she had not answered his letter – but this was simultaneously
a way of letting Freud know that she had broken with him after all and
thus that she, like Freud, did not, finally, care; and she could understand, she said, Freud's 'not missing him'. It was a lament for Tausk,
but it was written for Freud, every phrase turned so that something in it
would please him. The letter ended with a shifting of the grief away
from herself onto someone else (Tausk's sister), from which transition
she then turned her attention wholly back to Freud and could go on – as
if Tausk were forgotten – first politely and then lovingly, about her
wish to see Freud again.

To Freud's illness, Lou responded in rather a different way than she
had to Rilke's: not with advice and warnings, but with grief and anger.
It was also different from her response to her friend Frieda's fatal
illness in 1908–9. Then she had made an energetically philosophical
attempt to be of help. Her letters, written between November and
March (when Frieda died), movingly sought to share the pain and fear
and also offered positive ideas: she tried to persuade Frieda to see the
death pains as birth pains – as if one's self were finally to be born.[62]
When Freud first fell ill (in 1923), she said her famous optimism had a
hole in it with regard to physical pain;[63] she told Rilke a year later that
her heart had been burning for a year from knowing of Freud's illness,
which was a 'deep deep calamity for us all and makes even the summer
grey';[64] and after his operation in 1931, Lou spoke so violently about
what he had to bear ('I'd like to find some person who's caused it and
pull off his arms and legs') that Freud was astonished: 'You seemed to
be indignant, thrashing about yourself – why?'[65]

It cannot be said that Freud actually consulted Lou about his ideas.
He received from her innumerable accounts of her reactions to them
and to the publications he sent her, and he discussed her criticisms and

questions. In this respect he was not as attentive as she would have liked, but then she would have liked infinitely much. She sent him several pages of notes she had taken upon reading his 'General theory of the Neuroses'[66] and asked him to send them back with marginal ticks and annotations. He replied merely that he would read it and be affected by it, adding, once again, how she anticipated and complemented him and gave unity to his fragments: 'If I should be in a position to build further on the theory, you will perhaps recognise with satisfaction certain new things as having been long foreseen or even announced by yourself.'[67] This is as far as he went. He did not say she would have influenced him; only that she might have foreseen his next step. In 1917, the year in which this exchange took place, Lou published part of a book she was writing ('The Unconscious', never finished) as an article called 'Psychosexuality', placing it in the more popularly read journal, *Zeitschrift für Sexualwissenschaft* in an attempt to win over its readership for Freud. This was an occasion where Freud was quite critical of her: he told her he did not think it would be understood by the 'stupid multitude' and said, irritably: 'At some points I can only guess what you mean, when you undertake to describe things that I have avoided as being not yet amenable to language. At other points I, as sensitive author, feel that you are making more of an effort to excuse me to the miserable plebs than is necessary.'[68]

But such caution and occasional criticism characterised only the more technical part of their correspondence; more personally, he told her again and again how much he needed her, and it seems that with the years he revised his affectionately sceptical view of her 'synthetic' approach and came to give it more value:

I note with pleasure that nothing has altered in our approach to any theme. I strike up a melody, usually a very simple one, you supply the higher octaves to it; I separate one thing from another, you combine what was separated into a higher unity; I silently take for granted the conditions of our subjective limitation, you expressly draw attention to them. In general, we have understood each other and are of the same opinion. Only that I tend to exclude all opinions but one, and you tend rather to include all opinions, putting them together.[69]

That was in 1930. Lou was then sixty-nine and as capable of youthful enthusiasms and energies as ever. Freud, only six years older but fatally ill and given to melancholy, must have felt moments of rejuvenant hope and happiness from her letters. The next year, after reading her *My thanks to Freud*, he expressed some of this as a matter of sensing her womanliness:

For the first time I am struck by something exquisitely womanly [*etwas exquisit Frauliches*] in your intellectual work. Where I in annoyance at the eternal ambivalences would like to leave everything in a muddle, you tidy things up, you make lovely order and show that it can be comfortable that way too.[70]

A month before this, he had reprimanded her for not telling him of her seventieth birthday. He would have liked to tell her, on her birthday, 'how much I value and love you'.[71]

Sigmund Freud, taken in about 1931
Mary Evans/Sigmund Freud copyrights

CHAPTER TWELVE

Psychoanalytic essays

'Optimists are reverers of emotion.'
'Death from passion is death from life.'
'Pain is the accent upon happiness.'
'To love is to hold high.'[1]   LOU VON SALOMÉ, 1882

Lou Andreas-Salomé's chief contribution to psychoanalytical theory lies in her two long articles, '"Anal" and "Sexual"' and 'Narcissism as Dual Orientation', published three and eight years, respectively, after her half-year in Vienna in 1912–13. But an earlier work belongs here too, although it was conceived not scientifically but personally – the book called *Three Epistles to a Boy*. This consists of three pieces of sexual-philosophical enlightenment which were addressed and sent to a young boy of her acquaintance, Helene Klingenberg's son Reinhold, at three stages of his growing up.

THREE EPISTLES TO A BOY

The book was begun before Lou's encounter with psychoanalysis but not finished until after it; the second and third epistles show the influence of that encounter. Rilke read the book with great emotion[2] and it had an effect upon his own work. Lou said that, for her, Rilke's reading it was its 'legitimation'. Freud, too, admired the book greatly and recommended it to his daughters and patients.[3]

The first epistle, dated 1907, is in Rilke's words (which really summed up Lou's lifelong method and belief) 'the arguing away of the miraculous for the sake of the miraculous'.[4] In fairy-tale manner, it tells the small boy two things: that there is no Father Christmas and that babies are not brought by the stork. Lou relates how she met a little old man on a bench; the bench turned out to be not a bench and he turned out to be the disappearing Father Christmas, who told her that *many* babies have been born since Jesus, so that Christmas is now about and for them all, not just for that one. Storks, too, have long been dismissed from service and the baby now grows under the mother's heart and feeds from her breast. Meanwhile, as the old man became heavy as stone and his words became one with the wind, 'I realised he was only a name for everything friendly in our life.'[5]

The second epistle, four years later, is an 'Answer to a Question' which the boy is asking, upset about dirty information he has got from school-friends. We are not given the question, but if we assume it is

'How can I make all this dirt, that affects me so closely, into something clean?' then Lou Andreas-Salomé's answer is direct and persuasive. It is not so much an exposition of sexual facts as an attempt to turn the boy's attention to life's mysteriousness, so that he will stop thinking any part of it *particularly* weird. She does this without religion or emotion, and with a look at the relation of humans to animals, plants and micro-organisms which succeeds in avoiding the usual embarrassment (of parents digressing into bees and butterflies) through the palpable strength of her own interest.

In an exceptionally limpid and concrete style, good-natured, and as brief as she is able to be, she points out that he wouldn't be distressed to see a pond where the mother-fish has left a mass of eggs for the father-fish to pour fertilising liquid over. For mammals, she says, the same happens inside the female body; and this means that the coming of new life is 'doubly bound to the female: through what she contributes to the conception as well as through the body in which she carries the conceived creature till birth'[6] (her favourite idea of the equal activity and greater importance of the female in the procreative process). Now she explains how, for the sake of the meeting of seed and egg,

> at the same place from which later – about nine months in humans – the child will be born into the world, the female body is therefore accessible to the male; it opens into the special bodily space where the child can germinate and grow big, and at the same place in the man the precious juice of life gathers in two containers (testicles) out of which his strength will push it towards the female egg.[7]

This is the closest she gets to describing the sexual act, but as an account for a child this was very close for its time. Rilke said he wished he could have had it told to him like this in his childhood. She explains the secrecy by saying we are secretive about not only shameful things but also tender and beautiful ones, and that *this* tenderness exceeds all others. There are two ways of looking at it, she says: either with awe as at the most mysterious thing in nature, or with a curiosity that sees no mystery but just a tantalising secret; for the time being his school-friends see it the latter way.

There is a long and fine section on the sexual behaviour of plants. They hold up their sexual organs into the air and the sun, doing all they can to make them conspicuous, yet we don't snigger at them. This is because the entire existence of plants is a secret from us, so we don't suspect a special secret in their sexuality. Still further from us, she continues, are the one-celled creatures, which are immortal through reproducing by splitting (some of which immortality we have, too, in our egg-cell and sperm-cell). Following this, building up a great scheme from our affinity to animals, distance from plants, greater distance from the amoebae and, finally, distance from and disgust with inorganic matter, Lou gets to the proximity of the reproductive and the excretory. She gives in simple terms a Freudian account of the infant's attitude to his excrement, then cleanses the 'dirt' by explaining that it is precisely the inner sexual experience that reveals the vast difference between those similar things: between the stuff that begets and the stuff that is cast out, the acts of embracing and of excreting, love and disgust, life and death. It is all like the fairy-tale in which the hideous frog changes into the prince – in fact this *is* the grown-ups' fairy tale![8]

The third epistle, dated 1913, and addressed to the boy at puberty, is wordier and more patronising, and somewhat too ready to talk of 'eternal' things, although the purpose now is to talk about sexual feelings, which the second letter had avoided going into. Lou is explicit about conveying insights owed to Freud. She gives her philosophy of the body. Body is both 'I' and part of the world; growth is a process of making the body more ourselves and of separating mind from body – all of which, already paradoxical and strange, is still more confused by the onset of sexual sensations. Rilke's experience ('the too big') is doubtless behind the way she puts this: it is, she says, as if someone else began to be living in us, or as if there were some 'second thing' beside us, and (like Rilke in the Third Elegy) she claims that this thing's desires refer not just to us but to our 'eternal existence' [*Daseinsewigkeit*][9] – to something far beyond us.

Now, with judicious reference to the antiquity of sexual pleasure (the baby felt it, people of oldest times made glorious ceremonies around it and created gods for it), as well as careful stress on the necessary involvement of another person, Lou moves into her narcissistic theme. In the 'primal womb' there was undivided unity; the born individual yearns back to that unity. Loving, he identifies the beloved with the All he once enjoyed. The sexual is the highest and deepest act because it overcomes the rift between body and mind and because in it everything becomes 'eloquent of this eternal wholeness'.[10]

The boy might have felt talked down to in this third letter, and perhaps annoyed by its tone of knowing the ultimate truth, but he must also have felt exhilarated by the absence of conventional piety and moralising and by the unconventional glorification of the body.

'ANAL' AND 'SEXUAL'

Freud called Lou Andreas-Salomé's article '"Anal" and "Sexual"' (1916) a 'splendid essay'[11] and twice incorporated a summary of its main argument in work of his own.[12] One of these summaries reads:

> Lou Andreas-Salomé, in a paper which has given us a very much deeper understanding of the significance of anal erotism, has shown

how the history of the first prohibition which a child comes across – the prohibition against getting pleasure from anal activity and its products – has a decisive effect on his whole development. This must be the first occasion on which the infant has a glimpse of an environment hostile to his instinctual impulses, on which he learns to separate his own entity from this alien one and on which he carries out the first 'repression' of his possibilities for pleasure. From that time on, what is 'anal' remains excluded from life. The clear-cut distinction between anal and genital processes which is later insisted upon is contradicted by the close anatomical and functional analogies and relations which hold between them. The genital apparatus remains the neighbour of the cloaca and actually (to quote Lou Andreas-Salomé) 'in the case of women is only taken from it on lease'.

The sentence about the leasehold is quoted again twice by Freud.[13]

In fact Lou argues here not only that anal experiences in infancy underlie the individual's entire psychical development, but that they more generally underlie the whole development of a specifically human-cultural world. 'The first prohibition – the first "ugh!" – is a lesson in disgust which lasts a lifetime,'[14] but it is also more than this. For just as the baby's experience of the breast, that ineffable unity of ego and world when it is in love with and one with the object, is later paralleled in the basic religious idea of the human being as the blessed child of God, so the anal stage – that of hatred and disunity of ego and world – is paralleled by all subsequent unhappy individualisation and by all 'satanism'. The third stage is that of self-control, thus of self-definition, the stage of pleasure in producing, when the disunited world is given back to the infant in the forming of his own (excremental) products. It is related to all cultural creation and production. Again, as ever, Lou Andreas-Salomé is not being reductive about culture, but magnificatory about infancy. 'Only through Freud do we begin to suspect from what heights and depths the child finds itself thrust out into the conscious world of its later years.'[15]

There is a disquisition on shame. Because he has learned so early to distinguish his self from whole provinces of his own body, the child can feel shame and disgust without being harmed by these feelings. It is as if he is not himself the doer of the dirty deed. This separation of self from the filth of the self's body (the sense of the self as clean) makes possible all subsequent youthful idealism, all lofty ideas, all grand aims and notions: success in regulating anal activity is related to success in living altogether. Biologically, life is the taking of substances into the body and the giving out of substances from it; psychically, also, it is this. Achieving it in the biological, one becomes able to achieve it in the psychical and so to develop as a person altogether. And Lou argues that excrement, for which we feel this special disgust, becomes the representative of the disgusting, the alien, the deathly and inorganic, the 'not-us', altogether. Enabled to reject it, we then become able, through our symbolising power, to reject, with the same thoroughness and impunity, everything which would drag us down: death, mere matter. Only when something goes wrong in this process do guilt feelings arise.

The second half of the article discusses 'genital experience'. It is related to the 'anal' both by proximity and by similarity. (Neither Lou Andreas-Salomé nor Freud appears to conclude anything from the greater proximity of genital to 'cloacal' in the female. One might well have expected Lou to say that this indicates the better balance in woman between life/sex and death/excretion.) As control of the anal impulse led to anal pleasure, so struggle against genital desire leads to fullest genital pleasure. Moreover, the proximity of the anal function is entirely to the advantage of the sexual act, in which the primary shame (by which the ego was first defined) joins with the ultimate intimacy (in which the ego is given up). Since the anal symbolises death, so in sex we spur life on by confronting death – that alien side of us which we have rejected – and, 'as in an obstacle race', strength is increased by the overcoming of the resistance to this. All this is unknown to animals and perhaps explains why our sexual feeling is so much stronger than theirs.

There is more in this article but the point to emphasise is this: in accepting the anal, the author sings a hymn to the genital, turning disgust itself into a sort of inspiration.

NARCISSISM AS DUAL ORIENTATION

In her article on narcissism of 1921, Lou Andreas-Salomé gives another and less Freudian version of the relation of culture to feelings originating in infancy. '"Anal" and "Sexual"' referred to Freud's theory of the oral and anal phases in the infant's development and linked them to adult aspirations and cultural life. The later article refers to Freud's concept of 'narcissism' and, with the re-interpretation of it that we have already seen, links this to all human creation.

For Freud, narcissism after the infancy stage tended to mean something pathological or regressive. The far more positive estimation Lou Andreas-Salomé gives it is perhaps concentrated most succinctly in her reading of the original Narcissus legend.[16] Narcissus, she points out, looked not into a man-made mirror but into a forest pool, the mirror of nature, so that what he saw was not just his own face, but his face in union with the outer and boundless world of nature. That union, that entirety, was what he was in love with.

Lou argues that the word 'narcissism' should be used not for bad self-love but for good. It should mean the delighted experience of total union (or the vision of it) that spellbound Narcissus. Starting from

Freud's statement that 'narcissism is the libidinal complement of egoism'[17] she proceeds (as she had already begun to do in her *Freud Journal*) to conclude, far more firmly than Freud intended, that since egoism continues throughout our lives, so does narcissism. She asserts that narcissism is oriented two ways – to separation and to fusion. As Freud said, it consists of ego (separation) and sex (fusion). Neither orientation has priority; but her main concern is to emphasise the aspect of fusion, 'the affective identification with everything, the re-merging with everything as the positive basic aim of the libido'.[18] Becoming an individual is suffering and self-abasement, as if the water of an ocean were being forced to flow along a river-bed, but the individual's sense of identity with the All none the less continues. The abasement is exemplified in a little boy's games which Lou had observed, as well as in her recollection of feeling great loss when she gazed in the mirror at the age of six and was shocked out of her 'sheltering in God' [*Gottgeborgenheit*]. (One wonders whether the re-interpreted image of Narcissus was a conscious replacement and overcoming of her own desolating mirror-experience.) But the continu-ing sense of the identification remains the best and most profound element in everyone's life, and this is what Lou seeks to persuade her reader of. There is a self-love which is good; when you go deep into this, you come closest of all to the truth of things, nearest to what can ever be called 'objectivity'. This is the metaphysical sense of self and the love of self. The thought might be grasped by considering what is implied by 'love your neighbour as yourself' – though this is not Lou's example. Looked at one way, the injunction means: preserve your neighbour just as you preserve yourself, recognise that his individual ego is as valid as yours is. Looked at another way, in implying that you should love him absolutely and wholly, as if he were a world, *the* world, it reminds you that that is how, at your best, you already love yourself.

In the terms of her theory, even the phenomenon of sexual over-esteem (the exaggerations entertained by the lover about the beloved) is narcissistic, for it is the attempt to turn the beloved into a substitute for the underlying, all-embracing unity. She means that in loving someone we try to feel him to be as marvellous, as cerebrally incomprehensible, as totally immersed in our attention (and ourselves in his) as was the All with which we once were, or felt, 'one'. Thus object-libido itself derives from narcissism, and

> The typical disappointments in love are ultimately caused not by love's decline with the passage of time . . . but by the fact that the [love] object is obliged to guarantee with its body that it is much more than bodily and prove with its unique individuality that it is universal. The greater the ecstasy of love, that magnifies its object ever more

luxuriously and unsparingly, the thinner and more undernourished does the object remain behind its symbolical character; the hotter our worship, the more chilling this quid pro quo, until at the right pitch fire and frost feel almost identical.[19]

The loved person loses out in the idealisation process, since the lover realises that the beloved is not the universe. So a happy love relationship is almost less desirable, given this intense conjunction of illusion and disillusion, while an unhappy one is in this respect happier, as the lover will not expect such union from it and can go on being simply warmed by his own state of loving. Lou Andreas-Salomé curiously alters Freud's theory that over-esteeming the beloved impoverishes the lover's own narcissism, which then needs the return of love for its re-enrichment. It does this by saying instead that the element of narcissism in object-love impoverishes the beloved by expecting from him what he cannot provide: the original total union.

Lou's notion of narcissism in the infant is not co-extensive with Freud's narcissistic stage of the infant's development, coming between the stages of auto-erotism and object-love. It seems to mean, more amorphously, a temporally indefinite infantile pleasure, related to the pleasure of the foetus in the womb (which cannot but feel at one, since it is). Nor is her idea of a continuing lifelong narcissism the same as Freud's. His view is somewhat minimal (to her mind, regrettably so): narcissism is the state one keeps returning to, like the amoeba withdrawing its pseudopodia; or it is an attachment of the libido to the ego, whereby the ego is finite, like Narcissus' face in a looking-glass. Lou's 'narcissism' is about the all-reflecting woodland pool, and is conceived as an energy which is more than just a help to the ego and is called 'life-intoxication [Lebensrausch]. Characteristically, she links this intoxication with optimism and states that 'the optimist is eternally right'[20] while the pessimist – the one who judges without intoxication, without love – is always wrong in what he says about life.

The question of sexual estimation leads to the question of estimation, or valuing, in general. 'The problem of value is invariably a problem of libido.'[21] No matter what logic we invoke when we 'prove' something's value, or what modesty we pretend when we say we are only making subjective judgments, really all our valuing is connected with our narcissistic needs. Really we know, in some dark way, both that value cannot be proved, and that what we call subjective value is objective. For it is our point of relatedness to the only thing that is ultimately real. Whenever metaphysics tries to harmonise 'being' with 'God', it is recognising, Lou says, this oneness of subjective and objective.

She now discusses the ego-ideal, again quietly altering Freud. It does not consist chiefly of idealised parent-images and symbolised commands and prohibitions from our milieu. When all those elements are shorn away, the essential remains: the image of ourselves that we have narcissistically projected into an ideal, not from weakness but from delight. This image then works back upon us. Lou here employs the very word she had introduced in her religious essays of the 1890s about the concept of God: it has a 'back-effect [*Rückwirkung*]' upon us, which improves us, stressing in us certain features and erasing others.

The God-value is narcissism's most brilliant achievement. It is the highest manifestation of its dual orientation, towards the assertion of ego and towards the merging in totality, for God is both all-dominant and all-intimate. Idealisation, which harmed the beloved person by hiding him in the obligation to be representative of something more than a person, now produces its beneficial masterpiece when it so intensifies the God-value that 'God becomes a person'.[22]

The last section of the article is concerned with artistic creation. 'Poetry is perfected recollection',[23] and the artist, because he is able – in recollection – to withdraw from the cleavage of subject and object back into their primal oneness, is always coming to us 'from his fulfilments' rather than, like everyone else, in pursuit of them. Indeed, if he did not have to translate them into formal works, he would forever *live* his work, she says, like a happy child at play. But for the risks and anxieties that attend this translation, 'art would be a "guide to the Blessed Life" like nothing else on earth'.[24]

Occasionally, Lou too involves herself in a negative and regretful view of culture: better for the infant to stay in his bliss; better for the artist not to give form to his experience. None the less the thrust of her argument is to praise human culture for its origination in those profound blissful strata. 'The compulsion to objectification', she writes, is 'already given in the narcissistic identification as the basis of all creativity.'[25] She has shown how, just as the child gave value to its toys, setting them up as symbols of the 'one-and-all' it so recently enjoyed, so the lover exalts the beloved and the artist makes works of art. So, on the same impulse, do we all conduct all of our constructive cultural activity.

Thus, if for Freud the mind-made world is a by-product of displaced energies, of 'aim-inhibited libido', a sort of fortuitous excrescence to the basic process of the libidinal drive's ever-futile search for satisfaction, Lou Andreas-Salomé (despite her convoluted style) makes the whole thing far more straightforward. We make or find pictures of – substitutes for – the original Something with which our unconscious self was once bound up, re-binding that self to it through the substitutes, and loving the reconstituted unity with a love that is energy and rich frenzy. The womb was indisputably real and good, and, as far as the unborn child could tell, was all that was real and good. We spend our lives actually, elaborately and admirably remaking that reality.

CHAPTER THIRTEEN

Three Last Books

'I have spent my whole life working, working hard'[1]

LAS, 1937

Between the ages of sixty-seven and seventy-three Lou Andreas-Salomé wrote (in addition to diaries and several as yet unpublished shorter pieces) three books – one about Rilke, one about Freud and one about herself. All are retrospective, composed in grateful mood and seem designed both to express and to contribute to the rounding and perfecting of her whole life.

RAINER MARIA RILKE

A few months after Rilke's death in 1926 Lou told Freud[2] that her feeling about his death was not what it would have been had she been younger. It was not painful only but there was a sensation of seeing Rilke at last whole and clear, in closed outline, and this was like remembering having been with him in a way that she actually hadn't. It was a quite new vision of him, and she longed to tell him about it. Her book *Rainer Maria Rilke*, published in 1928, was perhaps a wishful attempt to tell him about this rounded outline.

Like her book on Nietzsche, it is organised vaguely, without dates or details and using a large amount of quotation from his letters. It traces Rilke's development through Russia, Paris, Rodin, fame, to the Elegies. His career is depicted as a struggle to accomplish something uniquely difficult, in which he succeeded, for he did accomplish the work, yet also failed, for he neglected the one true means of saving himself, and therefore could not be helped by the work; it remained outside him, she thought, so that he died, as she told Eva Cassirer, 'comfortless'.[3]

Lou sees Rilke as not so much a fragile person as a person *carrying* something fragile, something precious that he had to guard against jolts.[4] He himself had a considerable robustness. At the same time, he had his permanent horror of bodily existence; he felt, and was, exceptionally defenceless. Russia was a help against this, as was (she forestalls misinterpretations) his pursuit of aristocracy and lovely solitary places. But he did not solve his problem. He grew increasingly alien to his body, and the work that he finally produced failed to cure him. The Elegies, for example, contain a hope, but no more than a hope, of being able to 'affirm' physical things; they actually lead *down* into the hellish thought of the body with all its ancestral, inevitable horrors. So the physical, because it is the sign of 'not belonging to the angel realm', is for him 'the last word for the horrible'.[5]

To read the Elegies this way is to ignore their sequence, and Lou does in fact quote the first and the third of them last, as conclusive, so that their theses – the terribleness of the beautiful and the ghastliness of the physical – overshadow the release and affirmation that do come later; in this way she underplays what would otherwise seem a triumph. She was of course reading these poems under the impression of the poet's illness and death, which came so soon after their appearance. She understood them not as we might, with our effort to grasp and place their ideas as ideas ('Every Angel is terrible' takes, after all, some effort) but as directly expressing something felt by Rilke the man, and standing in a necessary relation to his ruin. She was reading them too in connection with what she herself had known and shared of his life, and this makes for some unexpected assertions: she interprets the culminant outcry 'Earth, you dear one, I will' as deriving straight from Rilke's experience of Russia ('This is the poet's belonging at home in Russia') and also claims that this cry does not reach the angels, quoting in evidence the failed address to the angels in the first Elegy and not realising that by the ninth he had stopped addressing them.[6]

Lou's response to anyone who felt he had fallen out of the human pattern of things was as to a sick person she longed to cure. Just as she had not gone all the way with Nietzsche's deepest enquiry (into a reality without human shaping), so she did not go along with Rilke's postulating of the Angels (who mark the futility of all human shaping and seeking). She knew the remedy for Rilke's malaise and boldly prescribed it, as she had done in his lifetime: it was, or would have been, the 'unrestrained giving up of himself to his most forgotten memories'.[7] Because he would not do this, she considered, he lost the rapport with what was deepest in himself, and instead of reaching the 'primal ground' he ended up in the 'unfathomable' [*das Bodenlose*] from which nothing could rescue him; at the end of his life he was still the disguised child he had described in *Malte*, staring into the mirror and fainting from terror.

And she gives her new view (in the light of Rilke's fate) of what art is and should be: it has its proper limits, it is 'nothing but' communication, even when its motive is not the wish to convey but the desire to disburden. At the furthest point to which it ought to go, art is still only a bridge: between the sayable and the unsayable. As a bridge it can go a long way, all the way, towards the unknown, but it may not lose touch with the known. If it tries to do more, to be the path in the unknown (which it can only lead to), art will take the place of reality and steal

away the ground of the human. This happened to Rilke. That he
tragically went too far and destroyed his own life is the final message of
her book.

MY THANKS TO FREUD

The book on Freud is explicitly a book *to* Freud, a rambling letter to
him of over a hundred pages, in honour of his seventy-fifth birthday.
His ideas are told back to him like the describing of gifts received at
some lavishly celebrated coming-of-age birthday of her own. Attached
to them, like glamorous subsidiary parcels, are expressions of her own
conclusions and meditations in the areas of psychoanalysis, religion and
art – with conclusive remarks on Nietzsche and Rilke too, so that the
book is a last ranging over all her most held-to and beloved ideas. As
offering, one might compare it with Rilke's 'Florence Diary' of 1898,
but an initial difference is that Rilke had then gone away to define
himself as other than her, while she has here gone not away but deep
into the territory named after Freud, there to define her differences in
the atmosphere of a general obedience – mild factions beneath a
recognised government, idiosyncratic landscapes under his sky, an
elaborate example of the attitude she once expressed as an adolescent
girl towards a vague godhead:

> I want but one thing – only space
> That I might kneel beneath you

the fundamental tone of which, she said, had from that time 'swung
through all my experience and attitudes'.[8] In *My Thanks to Freud* she
writes 'I like nothing better than to run on your lead – though it has to
be a really long one'.[9] Since Freud is addressed throughout in the
respectful second person, the book represents too an affirmation of that
continuing relationship, one such as she had not enjoyed with any
earlier friend.

From the opening address to Freud (which centres her admiration for
him on his having delved *unwillingly* – not gladly, as Thomas Mann
would have it – into the psychic darknesses that his sheer scientific
adventurousness required him to investigate) she moves into a grand
apologia for psychoanalysis. Then there come seventy pages in which
she finds room to expand her main ideas, in each case rounding them off
with a new conclusion or perspective: thus narcissism is set forth again,
with the added point that it makes Freud's 'id' superfluous; the
philosophy of the 'open secret' of the body is summed up under the all-
explanatory concept 'ambivalence'; she adapts her optimism to Freud's
death instinct by recognising that a necessity of our minds to conceive
things as dead stands alongside our knowing that psychoanalysis frees
the trapped person back into 'life'. She also very cleverly saves Freud

for 'Life' by arguing that what his death instinct theory really means is that life is worth living *even* without any illusions about it.[10]

The section on religion is clever too. It puts the finishing touch to her earlier theories, according to which the freethinker had greater religious experiences than the committed Christian. It argues that the best 'faith' is actually a kind of doubt, or the element which surrounds the doubt, an element consisting in our awareness that we ought never to call to God (as if he were a person) or to wish him present (as if he were a thing). It follows from this that 'worship of God' is the name of a *gap* in our piety, 'a way of compelling God because one does not possess him'.[11] So all the Christian (and other) pointings to God, in doctrine and in rituals, actually show a lack of faith in God. Real faith is 'a resting in something that surrounds and holds us',[12] and any anthropomorphising of it must be done in the deep unconscious.

This leads to the final words on Nietzsche.[13] He did his anthropomorphising consciously. Instead of looking into himself, he looked up to himself; instead of finding repose in the impersonal God, he thought he had to make a replacement for God by outbidding the hardest human fate, his own, with the only harder thing, its eternal repetition. He laid his hand on 'millennia' as if on wax and, by measuring himself against God, made himself God. Meanwhile his envy for the 'blond beast' showed his envy for those who could trust in instinct (as Lou knew that she herself did) and who could dispense with the whole monstrous search for 'God'.

Lou's final words on Rilke reinforce the judgement made in her book on him: the Angels of the Elegies usurped his reality, themselves damagingly becoming his 'love-partner', and Rilke was in fact a sacrifice to his work. In the ten years preceding the Elegies the human being in him resisted their 'breaking through', and then he made the work and broke himself.[14]

A grand section near the end sums up Lou's attitude to life altogether. These lines might be read alongside her letter to Gillot at the age of twenty-one and her 'Last message' to Rilke when she was forty. What the three statements share – over all those years – is both boldness and the *declaration* of boldness, a sort of sudden recklessness, and the sense of herself as decider of values just because she consciously lives in relation to something bigger.

The more fully we enter into the 'challenge of the hour', into the present factual moment, into the conditions that hold from one case to another, instead of being trammelled by prescriptions and directives (written by human beings!), the more connectedly do we act in accord with the whole ... If anyone thinks that is immorally presumptuous and high-handed, then it would be truer to call the childish-slavish

obedience to prescriptions which make everything easy a convenient
moral slovenliness!... Yes, the most audacious thing we have
invented for ourselves is our condition of being human: and thus – the
evaluating human being, the sublimest adventurousness of life.[15]

Freud, though he criticised the book for its partial obscurity, and for
not all of it being 'equally worth knowing',[16] admired it for the
'synthesising' gift he had come to respect so much in Lou.

It certainly has not often happened that I have admired a psychoanalytical work rather than criticising it. This time I cannot help doing so.
It is the finest thing of yours that I have read, an involuntary proof of
your superiority over us all, which accords with the heights from
which you came down to us. It is a genuine synthesis, not the senseless
therapeutic kind of our opponents but the genuine scientific kind
which one can trust to transform the collection of nerves, muscles,
sinews and vessels, into which the analytical knife has changed the
body, back again into a living organism. If only it were possible to
coarsen and make tangible all that you paint with such fine strokes of
the brush, one would perhaps have gained possession of some ultimate
insights.[16]

It is quite clear that he did admire both it and her, yet we note once
again – as Lou herself must have noted and smilingly accepted – the
way Freud's very praise of her fineness implies that it is none of it solid
(coarse) enough to amount to usable insights.* He tried hard to
persuade her to alter the title to 'My Thanks to Psychoanalysis'; she
would not, however, and insisted that the whole book was derived from
him.

LOOKING BACK

Looking Back, or, more accurately translated, 'A Look Back at Life', is
the longest of the 'three last books', with over two hundred pages. It is
Lou Andreas-Salomé's retrospective meditation on the main moments
of her own life (if 'moments' can mean both 'times' and 'significant
factors'), as if on the main structures of a house that she had built (or
that had been built around her). It is a leisurely backward look in
gratitude, a counting of blessings. She did not herself publish the book,
but she certainly intended it for publication, at least in its original form
finished in May, 1932, to which she gave the title: 'Ground-plan of
some life-recollections' [*Grundriss einiger Lebenserinnerungen*]. The
word 'ground plan' suggests that she saw her life as spatial, not
temporal, and as rising upward, rather than going linearly. Six of the
ten original chapters are entitled 'Experiences' [*Erlebnis* not *Erfahrung*:
experience lived through rather than experience acquired]. These are

the experience of God, of Love, of Family, of Russia, of Friendship and of Freud. It is notable that, apart from Freud (who is, also, the only experience from her later life), no individual is called an experience; neither Gillot nor Rée is thus honoured but they are introduced under 'Love' and 'Friendship' respectively. The remaining chapters (apart from two with impersonal titles) are named after the two men she evidently thought back to as relationships rather than as such basically structuring experiences: Rilke and Andreas. As for Nietzsche, he has no title-place at all, either as 'experience' or as relationship: the meeting with him is subsumed under the heading of friendship with Paul Rée.[17]

It is difficult to read this book as an autobiography, yet it does to some extent ask to be read as one, since it is chronological and offers quite a lot of concrete detail, particularly about her family, Nietzsche, Rilke (an added piece 'April, our month, Rainer ...' addressing Rilke in the second person), and Andreas (in another added piece).

Some of the things that make it difficult are the absence of all dates and of all historical and circumstantial background, the tendency to see things rosily, and the predilection for compound abstractions. At the beginning, for instance, one has to climb several fences of words like 'all-nativity' [*Alleingeborenheit*], primal-childhood' [*Urkindheit*], 'the happening of existence' [*das Daseinsgeschehen*], 'all-includedness' [*Allesenthaltenheit*], and 'our primal-relatedness to all existence' [*Urbezogenheit zu allem Dasein*]. Another point of difficulty is the recurrent sense of particular omissions: much that one is made to ask about is then withheld, either from discretion or from such immersion of the author in the encompassing meditations that she is unaware of any reader's reactions and questions. 'At first some altercations seem to have taken place between Nietzsche and me', she says of the first Tautenburg days, and practically no more about it.[18] An episode when Andreas, during a conversation with her, suddenly stabbed himself in the chest includes no hint of why he did it or what the conversation had been about.[19] The ostensible point made is the uninteresting one that she *might* have appeared a murderess. In another place she writes that it is not impossible that she felt something about Ledebour[20] and one wonders why anything at all is said about her feelings if it is to stop at this.

The sparsity of reference to Nietzsche is surely an instance of Lou Andreas-Salomé's avoidance of any self-aggrandisement through famous acquaintances. This work could hardly be further from the 'great men in my life' kind of book which she could so easily have written; nor does she lay particular stress on her own importance in the lives of the great. At the same time, the provocatively truncated episodes, and a certain awkward vanity in the examples of self-quotation (several poems, and a letter in full – the one she wrote to

Gillot from Rome in 1882), show an ineptitude that is of a piece with similar self-quotings and self-references in other books. The portions of letters in the Nietzsche and the Rilke books, far as they are apart – 1894 and 1927 – have this in common, and there are references to herself at the beginning of the Freud book. The contrast between these rather clumsy parts and the tact and naturalness in diaries, letters and other more direct instances of self-expression suggests that Lou could write well about herself so long as it was spontaneous; but was inhibited by any attempt at self-presentation. She was no actress, had no clear notion of an audience, did not *see* herself upon life's 'stage'. She never, for instance, criticises, corrects, or laughs at herself.

The absence of anything ironic or humorous, light or delighted in the style of *Looking Back* is at variance with its general theme: the marvel of life and the glad abundance of her own life's content. Despite this, and although there are some turgid, even impenetrable, passages, there are also many memorable reflections and recollections. It is always of interest to see how Lou Andreas-Salomé habitually aspires to the feeling of awe and to the perception, philosophic rather than poetic, of a sort of all-promising immensity in commonplace occurrences. The incident when she and Savely, barefoot in Swiss meadows, suddenly walked onto a mass of low-growing brambles and screamed with pain, gives rise to two such reflections: that her thought, in that moment, was of the birth-plunge out of 'primal blisses' into the hideous exposure to life, and that (contradictorily) when Savely said they ought to beg forgiveness of the brambles for having trodden on them instead of kissing them, she realised that everything bad in the world amounts to this misunderstanding (that we think it's *we* who are injured ones).[21] Another example, also from accounts of her travels in the 1890s, leads to a reflection on the immensity hidden in the ordinary:

The most bewitching landscape impression I had was what I once saw of *three Springtimes* in rapid succession, when I was travelling to the North from Italy through Germany. Never had the South penetrated my senses more triumphantly than then, when, despite the Winter that had been like May, it succeeded in becoming Spring without getting mixed up with Summer: this gave the semblance of something altogether inexhaustible, beyond all visibility, which would always be able to be finished with any season if it wished, and [made me think] that *if* human receptivity were only more capable of nuance and were more deepreaching, the Immeasureable would await us in the most Earthly.[22]

Looking Back is to be read, then, chiefly as a series of meditations. Much of the material has been largely used or duplicated in other parts of the present book and therefore will not be dwelt on here. There is however, a final passage which has not been so used. It contains an unexpected confession and, following this, a very characteristic declaration. Lou writes, as I do not think she has written elsewhere, that not to have been a mother cuts her off from the essential experience of womanhood: 'Beyond all problematics, the passing on of life affirms a great health in woman. Not to be able to experience this doubtless excludes a person from the most valuable female material'.[23] In another piece of writing of that period,[24] pondering her own unusual love-life, Lou recalls Freud telling her that the reason she was always so grateful to any man who made her feel love was her 'non-female' preference of *loving* to *being loved*; in other words (said Freud) her coldness, a description she perplexedly yet emphatically agrees with. Similarly here, in *Looking Back,* she recognises that she has not had any of the three kinds of love-fulfilment which other women have: not a real marriage, not motherhood, and not the 'sheer eros-bond'.[25] But then, more typically of herself, she declares that this does not matter, for she has had 'life', and she explains:

It is rather like this: if someone plunges his hand firmly into a full rose-bush, the blossom will fill his hand. Compared with the abundance of the bush it is only a little, however much it is. None the less the handful is enough for him to experience in it the whole of the blossom.[26]

These words – philosophic, modestly triumphant, and grateful – are virtually her last full statement about her life.

CHAPTER FOURTEEN

Growing Old

Whatever happens to me, I never lose the certainty that behind me arms are open to receive me.[1]

Lou Andreas-Salomé thought a lot about old age before it came to her. For example, in 1901 (when she was only forty) she published an essay entitled 'Age and Eternity'. It foretold how she would approach old age herself.

FORESEEING OLD AGE

Age, she wrote then, must be accepted as the mental and physical decline that it is, as a time without future, and without even the ability to teach, since it takes away the very tools we would have used for teaching. All the same, age can be beautiful, if we let our person express the fact of being at the edge of eternity. Whether this can be done depends on how we have lived, for there is nothing new to learn at the end; there is only the chance of revealing what has been learned. Thus (Lou characteristically draws opposites together) 'being able to die and being able to live are not separate.' Age should not be resisted either by efforts to remain unchanged or by attempts to seem young and adapt oneself to new fashions. Lou develops here a persuasive philosophy of happy dying. It is founded on the thought that the human cultural world is our work of art, and just as an artist serenely withdraws once his work is made, so too can we all. To have raised the natural facts of living and dying to the level of a 'second' order of things, to specifically human events, is our cultural achievement, and while 'youth means giving oneself to life in human work, and youth may go on even into very old age so long as the strength lasts . . . age means understanding with one's heart that the whole of this work is only the peculiarly human expression of a small temporality entering into a great eternity'.[2] Yet age should not be approached with resignation, either, but welcomed as a positive experience in which each moment is sovereign, being released from temporal service and becoming a 'representative of eternity'.

A little after this essay, in April 1902, Lou meditated in her diary that perhaps age brought back the kind of dreaming condition which belonged to childhood, so both the beginning and the ending were rooted in dream. At its best, the life in between communed with it.[3] We have seen how this urge to interpret all things for the best and the happiest, and this likening of the 'highest' and most creative experiences to the 'deepest' ones, were constant elements in all Lou's thought.

THE PLEASURE OF GROWING OLD – DEATH OF ANDREAS

Many years later, Lou exchanged views on old age with Freud. In 1925, when he was sixty-nine, he spoke of a 'crust of insensitivity' that was 'creeping up around' him and called it the beginning of the inorganic: 'some kind of resonance is lacking'.[4] Lou, who was sixty-four, replied life-affirmatively. She conceded that many things do vanish from our life, but she was much more interested in the 'increasing tendency to turn away from the multifarious and attend to what is substantial, essential.' Many of her 'sensations of happiness', she believed, were due to this and to the 'subsequent "grateful" feeling of not having died young'.[5] Age was a fairly frequent topic of their letters in the later years and at sixty-six Lou wrote Freud a particularly confessional letter, telling him that as regards the erotic sphere, which for women is the 'nearest', she had been afraid she would reach her old age too late and thus miss its special gifts. Physiologically speaking, it had set in, she wrote, only when she was sixty. Presumably she had in mind the capacity to feel erotic pleasure, which had come to her late and had also left her rather late. Both times she was grateful for the change. She described her gladness about the second change* like this:

> when one leaves erotic experience in the narrower sense, one is leaving a blind alley which is indeed very wonderful but which only has room for two side by side, and is entering an indescribably vast expanse, the expanse which childhood too belonged to and which we had to forget about for a while . . . Now one can devote oneself to this renewed experience more independently, leaving one's personal self behind (instead of that ghastly dependence of the child on people and their approval, and the way one had oneself so helplessly *ahead* of oneself). One finds nests everywhere, lays eggs everywhere, one becomes lighter and lighter and finally flies away.[6]

Although she added that 'it can't be denied that the body is more and more of a hindrance in this . . . Devil take it', she also declared that if she now had to choose between youth and age she was really not sure how the choice would turn out. So she was confirming in experience her meditation twenty-five years before on the kinship between childhood and old age.

On 4 October 1930 Andreas died, at the age of 84. Lou felt that for years he had been growing into age as if into a special country and that his death was the sort that for once really suited the cliché 'gently fell asleep'. It made her happy, especially as he had not had to know the worst of his illness. Her diary recorded: 'A feeling of purest joy, like a miracle, like a grace, as if – as can happen in late Autumn – light, light, light were breaking through the curtain in the storm of blowing leaves'.[7] She told Freud: 'Here everything is staying as it was; here I am surrounded by rooms and things and people which were arranged for him, and here I myself will meet my end.'[8]

Her seventieth birthday came four months after this. A letter she wrote to a cousin of the same age[9] expresses, more than mere 'acceptance', a positive rejoicing in the age she had reached comparable to the feeling about middle age she had expressed in her letter some thirty years before to Frieda von Bülow. A brief acknowledgement of the more common attitude of complaint (or grief) about age – there are fewer and fewer contemporaries with whom one has shared experience – gives way to an affirmative attitude. Age, she is convinced, brings an increasing capacity for contact with what is universally human, and even with the wider world of animals and plants. She recognises that her almost twenty years of coming close to people through psychoanalysis have enabled her to feel and enjoy this benefit more fully than others can. Later she wrote something similar in *Looking Back*: 'The years went by, age thinned the ranks of one's contemporaries, as war had thinned those of the young: the stranger [*der fremde Mensch*] remained.'[10]

At seventy-two, she found age an increasing 'presentness'.[11] She still occasionally sat down to write, and she never ceased meditating on the meaning of her life, and of life generally, never losing her amazing certainty about it. It is worth noting that although Lou lived for four years under Adolf Hitler's government, she did not record a single word about the political changes in Germany. (The Nazi government paid her no attention either, despite her Jewish connections, though after her death her library was seized by the police.) *All* her thoughts were of religion, psychoanalysis, her own past, and her immediate surroundings. She wrote about the ego, about trust and piety, about the difficult lives of unconventional thinkers, about the analyst's respect for the analysand, and – ever and again – about the security which underlies all being: 'under our hurrying foot *our ground rests*, as it does under that of all the beings around us'.[12]

Her last writings continued to be thoroughly abstract, and while they show the remarkable intellectual energy that Lou retained into her seventies they also show how she never overcame her tendency to vague enraptured polysyllables sufficiently to leave posterity an outline of her personality. Her writing is a thickly diaphanous curtain across a stage; the enacted play is properly visible only to those gazing from close by.

THE SHAPING OF LIFE

Between observing the shape and pattern of one's life and *giving* it shape and pattern, only a fine distinction can be made. Lou found shape in, and gave shape to, her life (from the first to the final dream, with dream-excursions rising up over the long wakefulness between them), which is no more contradictory than her simultaneous belief in total freedom and total obedience. A notable instance of her giving a retrospective shape to her life, apparently unconsciously, may be found in *Looking Back*, in the chapter on Freud. Long before, in 1913, Freud read her 'Hymn to Life' (which he took to be by Nietzsche) and told her he disliked its philosophical dimension and was horrified by its welcoming of pain. 'For me it would be enough to have one really bad cold in the head to be cured of such wishes!' At the time Lou mildly criticised him for this, and connected his disinclination to philosophise with his general lack of euphoria.[13] Now, years later, when Freud was old and suffering terribly, she reminded him of the poem and his remark about it and then, bursting into tears, declared: 'the very thing I once wrote that enthusiastic drivel about – you have done it!'[14] The Nietzschean attitude becomes drivel; Freud's unrhetorical endurance is actuality. Thus Freud becomes the keystone in the arch of which Nietzsche was a foundation stone. In the same moment the presence of Gillot as another foundation stone to that same arch is indirectly suggested, for Freud, instead of saying anything in reply, gave her a hug, and we read as the prominent last words of the chapter: 'I only felt his arm around me.'[15] The arm around her always had great dramatic and emotional significance for Lou, and her account clearly echoes the end of the first chapter of her novel *Ruth* (which was confessedly about herself and Gillot). The emotional young girl has journeyed to the adored teacher's house, longing to be accepted by him and taught the things of the mind, and is accepted, more fully than she ever foresaw. That chapter ends with the single-sentence paragraph: 'He had flung both arms around her.'[16] Not only is Freud, Lou's last friend of genius, set in the very place that Nietzsche, her first friend of genius, once almost occupied, but he is honourably established in the place that Gillot once held and dishonoured. In this way Lou finally linked and ordered the renounced, the rejected and the accepted teachers. Indeed, one can look back, with Lou, at a stage further back than this and note how she conceived of Freud as even more than the corrector of Nietzsche and perfector of Gillot: in one of her last letters to him she told him that his was the 'father countenance over my life'.[17] So the very ground in which the foundation of the arch was laid, her childhood closeness with her father and through that the lost blissful experience of 'God' as father, was taken over, in her mind, by Freud, inhabited now formally by him.

IMPRESSIONS OF LOU AS AN OLD WOMAN

We cannot associate Lou Andreas-Salomé in her seventies with any stereotyped picture of an ageing woman. Ernst Pfeiffer, who first met her when she was seventy-one, recalls her as, above all, unaffected, and the most guileless [*arglos*], most innocent person in the world, unlike anyone else and quite without social orientation. Her clothes were always out of fashion, she did not bother with a hairdresser, did not entertain guests. Yet she was certainly no 'witch' or cultivated oddity. She seemed to have no pretensions or pretences at all. Once when he saw her in public (at an election booth), she struck him as wholly and pitiably out of place, looking as lost as some small animal that had wandered there.[18]

People who visited her in her home found her serious, withdrawn, attentive, wise and childlike. Viktor von Weizsäcker – later known for his work combining scientific medicine with psychoanalysis – first learnt of psychoanalysis through Lou. He had read her book *My Thanks to Freud*, thereupon wrote to her and called on her, and she encouraged him. Later he recorded that at seventy

> she conducted a psychoanalytical practice very quietly in Göttingen and lived the mysterious life of a Sibyl of our own intellectual world ... She knew from the first moment what sort of person she had to deal with and where my needs had their roots. She could not help me, perhaps, but she understood how to love the spirit and was experienced in the worlds of loneliness.

In appearance, he said, she was feminine, her hair still blond, and she walked with

> the supple gait of a wandering young tree. Less monumental than Gertrud Bäumer or Ricarda Huch ... but of a pleasant and seeking or tentative empathy into people, without the all-too-manly weightiness of the brain-worker full of plans and the constructing of works.[19]

Another account of the ageing Lou was left by one of the two writers he mentions here, Gertrud Bäumer, who went to see her five years after Weizsäcker's visit and gave a somewhat more journalistic description. Looking at Lou, she thought:

> How indestructible is her youth! She already had a heart complaint and ought really to have been lying down. But she kept sitting up on the edge of her bed, in very lovely erect posture, with her slim arms pressed for support against the wood on both sides; and her head, with its still reddish-blond gleaming full hair that framed half the length of her face and was brushed back from her powerful forehead – a boyish forehead – made the years forgotten. There seemed to be an intangible

eternal piece of nature in her. The outline of her head, the fine proud line of her neck, always reminded one of the picture of a young girl.[20]

Lou's talk, about Europe's loss of spirituality and of the ability 'to live as from another reality', was still vehement, and Gertrud Bäumer admired her 'sovereign way of going straight to the essential point and talking about this essential thing completely unrestrainedly and without personal reserve.'

LAST FRIENDSHIPS

The most eloquent tribute to Lou in her old age is the way in which Ernst Pfeiffer, who (after his earlier first meeting with her) called constantly on her from May 1934 until her death in February 1937, has devoted his entire subsequent life to preserving her memory and her work. With immeasurably affectionate labour he has edited, annotated, published and re-published her writings.

Ernst Pfeiffer was one of two friends Lou made in her last years. The other was his friend Josef König, who died in 1974. Lou wrote to Freud about Pfeiffer, whom she called a 'splendid acquisition', a Kleist scholar in his early forties with whom she sometimes worked and whom she had to thank for 'very lively stimulation'.[21] She added, 'I find it nice of life that it always, even so late as this, sends something so exquisite for companionship along the way', and expatiated again on the special happinesses of old age (with which Freud replied once again that he could not agree).

The importance she had for this younger friend seems to have been due to that same power so many had noted in her before and which she evidently kept to the very end of her life – her power as 'understander' and listener. Pfeiffer visited her day after day and was quietly encouraged by her to talk about feelings, impressions, experiences. Often during these conversations he would think she had fallen asleep and he would stop talking, but then would hear her wholly attentive voice in the half-dark asking him to go on. Only after a long time, and then only tentatively, did she offer to respond to all he had told her, but what she replied (the words are unrecorded, though the sense and significance can be imagined) was, he felt, such as to give pattern to – or to show the pattern of – his entire life thitherto. Everything acquired clarity for him at once, like a shadowy landscape being wholly transformed by the sunrise.[22]

DEATH

Lou expected to die in the summer of 1935, when she had to undergo an operation to have a breast removed. The words she then said to her two friends in a provisional farewell were 'everything, everything is good.' But she lived another year and a half. In 1937, she fell ill with the uremic infection she was to die of. Ernst Pfeiffer has remembered some of her very last remarks. At one point she said – not complaining, but wondering at the oddness of her life – 'Actually I've spent my whole life working – working hard, and *only* working ... What for?' When she was near death she said, 'If I let my thoughts roam, I find no one'. But then, at the last: 'The best is death, after all.'[23]

She died in the evening of 5 February 1937, a few days before her seventy-sixth birthday. Her ashes were buried in her husband's grave in the Göttingen town cemetery. Her unrealised wish – expressing her lifelong sense of the boundlessness of her home – had been to have them scattered over her garden.

Early Fiction, 1883–95

Lou Andreas-Salomé published twenty long stories, eight novels and one play. She also wrote two other stories and two plays which she did not publish. One group of stories is about childhood; the rest are about a girl (or girlish boy) or a young woman who seems like a projection of herself in her youth. The circumstances are usually Lou's own (a German girl living in Russia, or studying in Switzerland, or married but virginal) and the themes are those she was preoccupied with in diaries, letters and essays. Two central themes recur: the loss of a religious faith felt strongly in early youth, and disenchantment with an `older man after a devoted and subservient attachment to him.

Lou did not learn to write better from her close acquaintance with writers. Her literary gift was slight and she did not try to develop it. What she had, she used without great effort. We have to realise that she did not regard her fictional writing as important. She thought such writing ought not to be central to any woman's life, but should be a luxury, like the fruit growing unexpectedly on a tree planted for its beauty or for the shelter it gave. She did acquire a considerable reputation as an interesting if cerebral woman-writer 'drenched in mind' (*durchgeistigt*), average to good. She saw herself as creative in a general way, but she never called herself a 'creative writer' or an 'artist'. She wrote fluently, sometimes gushingly, offering a lot of dialogue and inner monologue, very little action and still less description. Geographical themes that would seem to promise much, such as Petersburg seen by a German émigrée from it, are made nothing of. One feels she would have done without times and places altogether had this been possible, and have had only inner events: mental processes, emotional shocks and conflicts.

STRUGGLING FOR GOD

It is unlikely that Lou's first book, her novel *Struggling for God* (1885), written in 1883–4

when she was living with Paul Rée, was produced solely in order to persuade her family to let her stay abroad, as she said it was, by showing them that she was not wasting her time there. She could have done this with a shorter and less serious book. *Struggling for God* consists of 317 pages crammed with the most earnestly elaborated reflections on life. Some sentences in it are copied out of the ('Stibbe') notebook she had kept while with Nietzsche; some formulations and ideas derive from conversation with him, and (she said) much was culled from her old writings, from poems which she merely divested of their rhyme. But although the whole thing does look patched together, it is a great deal more sincere, and solemn, than her remarks about it suggest. The book was published under a pseudonym, 'Henri Lou'. (Gillot's first name was Hendrik, so that 'Lou' – the name he gave her – becomes, as a surname, provocatively masculine.)

It purports to offer memoirs written by its hero, Kuno (the bold one?), in his old age. Kuno is the son of a parson. As a child he has fiery religious experiences, but, growing up, he starts theorising and loses his faith, which makes him gloomy for years with a sense of having murdered God. As a student, he goes in first for asceticism, then for debauchery, and realises he can never be like his carefree fellow students; for him there is only 'tyranny or unrestraint'. Back in the village of his childhood he resumes friendship with his childhood playmate, Jane, now married to a dull man, and they spend wonderful evenings together, becoming happier, he through her healing nature, she through having him to heal. This relationship is wound up by Lou von Salomé (as she then still was) to a pitch of bliss and holiness which becomes almost unbearable for the reader and even for the characters. It turns out that they have neglected the danger of eros and at a peak in a conversation about women and love Kuno, deeply moved, grasps Jane's hands and kisses them. He is seized by a passion in which all lofty feelings are reduced in an instant to an insatiable, destructive sexual excitement:

> At her touch something shot through me like an electric shock, stormily the blood pressed to my heart and I trembled in overpowerful passion[1]

He resolves to leave, but the noble Jane, saying to herself 'His happiness at any price', throws herself into his arms, and a sexual union (which is not described) takes place, after which Kuno, 'benighted' and feeling like a criminal, rushes off to foreign lands, while Jane, ' a fallen angel', pines away in a state of mental 'rupture', all her naiveté and spontaneity gone, and dies after giving birth to his daughter.

This theme was to become familiar in Lou Andreas-Salomé's early fiction: an intense, quasi-erotic, 'holy' love explodes into or collides with the fact of 'eros' and instantly topples into disaster.

Kuno now follows spiritual aims, becomes a professor in a university and temporarily finds his vocation in devotion to a group of young followers. But another love relationship again leads to the woman's death. He offers to marry Margherita, whom he long ago seduced and who has consequently had a hard time, her reputation in ruins. She loves him but, being in her own way as ineffably noble as Jane, refuses him. She pretends it is because she is too immoral for the domestic life, while really it is so as not to hinder him from the freedom she knows he wants. Relieved, Kuno goes away and Margherita poisons herself, happy to think she has at last done a great deed. The point is not so much that Kuno is worth the sacrifice of these lives – though there is a strong hint that he is – as that the best thing about women is their capacity for self-sacrifice.

In the last part of the book Kuno destroys yet another woman, this time his daughter, who has been brought up in a far away village. She is a wild, timid, delicate, capricious girl, scornful of people, happiest among rocks and fields. He names her Märchen ('Fairy-tale') and supervises her upbringing for six years without telling her who he is. The tuition starts with his having to tame her, breaking her resistance with authority and cruelty, whereupon he becomes her 'god'. He, however, does not notice this, as his aim is precisely to help her direct her great store of passionate feeling towards something *other* than religion. As her teacher, he must inspire her 'to fight with life, with promethean defiance, for an ideal of her own'[2] – success in this will make up for the wrong he did her mother. His failure is catastrophic: she loves him more and more, and hopes to become his wife. The climactic moment occurs when, on her seventeenth birthday, he is to tell her the secret of her parentage. He starts to confess, then stops, thinking she has understood. His 'Can you still love me?' is answered by her rapturous 'I love you', and he begs her to call him (on his next visit) by the name he longs to hear. Thinking he means 'husband', she is radiant with joy and ready for the wedding; when instead he says 'Call me father', she utters it wanly, and goes out in the night to drown herself.[2] Meanwhile Kuno's brother, a melancholy, atheistic priest who has had a big role in the novel, also falls ill and dies for love of Märchen. Kuno alone does not fall ill, but lives to grow old and write his memoirs. Restless with the 'powerful painful unrest of the creative spirit', he goes on believing in life, and the last word of his memoirs is that the best life is a 'moving from God to God'.[3]

The struggle for God means the struggle to find out what to do with overwhelming, onward-driving emotions which once, in the trusting Christianity of childhood, were directed to 'God' but which lost that object when intellect developed. Kuno plunges through his life like someone in a fever, looking for – not a purpose, and not an explanation, and not peace either, but – a dynamic repository for himself, something in which his feelings can be engaged and be creative. It may be love for a woman – provided this doesn't become sexual or domestic – or it may be teaching, either a group of young people or a single pupil. He keeps finding it, but it doesn't last and he plunges on, leaving destroyed people in his wake. He is himself *never judged*, except implicitly as one whose life was worthwhile because he insisted on freedom, was ready for anything, felt strongly and loved life as absolutely as Christians love God. Perhaps he is intended as a Faustian figure, since one of his women is called Margherita, and God's words in *Faust*, 'who always strives and labours on, he can be redeemed',[4] would apply to him; but there is no devil present any more than there is a God – everything is man-made, and all religion is a big mistake. In this and other attitudes (such as the glad endurance of pain) Kuno is Nietzschean, and the final word about him heralds Lou's judgment of Nietzsche.

Kuno also seems to represent the author herself, for there is nothing very male about him, and the break with the family, the glorification of freedom, the switch from pious religious fervour to pious fervent cerebration, the mixture of devotion with principled infidelity, the very deliberate and conscious amorality, the highly charged sexuality along with horror of sex – all these things belong to the author's own biography. There are part-images of her, too, in Jane, who longs only to devote herself to a man and live for him; in Margherita, with her problem of whether to have the conventional home life or to resist it; and – most of all – in Märchen, a copy of herself in the relationship with Gillot: the young girl learning everything she knows from a godlike teacher who takes her on his knee, combining infinite love with infinite knowledge, and who finally disappoints her infinitely. Märchen is also the occasion for introducing the image of her appearance than Lou most liked: the farouche, sprite-like solitary, the dreamer and imaginer, stubborn and with something violent in her (she stabs herself to escape her lessons), but also with fine talents to be revealed.

Erwin Rohde, who found a lot of Nietzschean melancholy in the book, said of it:

> For all the novel's big defects – its very boldness and spectral intellectuality – it is very attractive for the pure flame of inwardness, truth and feeling that flares forth everywhere.[5]

The 'spectral' narrative is a structure for containing ideas as well as feelings. Perhaps one could liken this novel to a greenhouse: its thin, transparent walls keep all breezes out; inside, in the heat, a mass of thoughts grow unnaturally close to one another and their watering equipment is visible. As for the ideas, they grow from two rooted themes: the differences in the ways women and men love, and the nature of religious experience. There are discussions on both these subjects.

It is also a eulogy of the feeling of freedom, and justification of whatever leads to this. Feeling of freedom is not the same as actual freedom of choice. 'Where I am wholly, there the feeling of compulsion is taken from me, there I feel freedom. But least of all in freedom of choice.'[6] In Rudolf, who has never felt free and expects to feel it only when dying, we see Lou von Salomé arguing against conventional morality: he has spent his life respecting his parents, behaving kindly, keeping even self-destructive promises, giving up the girl he loves, practising chastity – and has found happiness impossible. Meanwhile Kuno disobeys the parents, goes in for every excess, and causes the deaths of three women, but he keeps his belief in himself and in 'life'. The strange thing is that what justifies him is his faith in his ideal and yet we scarcely know what the ideal is: it does not seem to have a verbal form, but has to do with the quality and intensity of his feelings. Intensity justifies all, as the Tautenburg diary said.

RUTH

It was nearly ten years before Lou (now *Andreas*-Salomé) wrote her next work of fiction: *Ruth*, which was begun in 1893 and published in 1895. In the interim she got married, lost Rée, knew Ledebour, met writers, scholars and artists, did a lot of studying, and made a name for herself with her book on Ibsen and many articles; in 1893 (when she was working on this second novel) her Nietzschean book was with the printer. For the next ten years, much of her time was spent in writing fiction.

Ruth is entirely and avowedly about its author and her experience with Gillot. Again it is a hothouse of thick-stemmed, fast-blooming plants, but this time the plants are all emotions. Instead of general statements, or typical behaviour, it is the recalling, selecting and manipulating of the remembered material, in order to bring about intense and – it is implied – unique moments of feeling. But the atmosphere is that of immature erotic reverie and, despite the desire for uniqueness, it is all rather platitudinous. All the same, it is not rubbish, not written to please a slovenly-minded public; and it was seriously reviewed, though mostly with strong criticism. For instance, one reviewer wrote that it was clever and deep but also 'spoilt by brooding, by dreaming; unrealistic and then again childishly naive'.[7]

There is an Anne-of-Green-Gables pathos about Ruth, the schoolgirl who is 'different from the others' – orphaned, living a life of imagination, inventing tales about wonderful men and getting other girls to live them with her. The great thing about her is that she believes dreams can be *lived*. Her teacher – Erik – is charmed by an ecstatic essay she writes. He gets to know her, and we see her as the slight boyish figure in simple grey clothes, with long hair escaping from its ribbon, and face expressing courage and desire for life – a 'Bacchus youth'. She realises he is the one for her to worship. She slips out one evening to his house and there is the dramatic meeting – 'Do you come to me?' – with trembling, weeping, his stroking her hair, her kneeling to him, and finally his arms around her. He takes over her education (starting with a will-breaking episode like the one between Kuno and Märchen) and she moves into his house. She has lessons morning and evening and no thought for anyone but him:

> He occupied her thoughts so strongly, he set her in such astonishment that she herself dropped out of her thoughts and she only gazed at him.[8]

Now the teacher falls in love with the pupil and, being a decent man, worries that he might take advantage of her frequently expressed willingness to obey him in absolutely everything. 'I'm your child' is her cry. It seems – though this is immensely vague – that Ruth obscurely knows about sexual feelings and is willing for all that to be done to her, provided only that is is *done to* her, and that her part remains that of an adoring obedience:

> I will do anything, anything! right or wrong, good or bad – anything! I will be obedient to

the death. Test me. But I must be allowed to obey you.[9]

Erik sends her abroad to study, and the most intense of their several shared moments of emotion occurs on the eve of her departure. In a close embrace with her, he declares his love, she gazes at him with 'roguish' joy, and he is overcome with a voluptuous bliss 'far finer' than anything sensual. When he tells her he'll be close to her wherever she goes, she replies, in a pert but not ironic manner, 'like God', and he reflects that 'she was never so near to love, complete love, as in this most childlike confession – the most presumptuous.'[10]

Months pass, exercise-books are sent to and fro. Then, without warning, Ruth returns. She comes across Erik's son, Jonas, who falls upon her in senseless raving, mad with love for her, and bites her hand. Paying no attention, she goes on to a meeting with Erik in the garden and finds catastrophe: Erik has divorced his wife, assuming Ruth has grown up, and now he welcomes her as a woman! She shies away from the unconcealed sensuality as well as from something that is even worse – his looking up to her. No use his reminding her how he helped her throw off her fantasies, and telling her the one last fantasy to throw off is the one about him: Ruth is having none of this. She feels 'a boundless alienation and horror' and when Erik's 'Be my wife!' is overheard by the luckless Jonas and the father has to go and minister to the fainting son, she nimbly departs, keeping intact her last fantasy, for she says as she goes: 'I'm not going away. I'm going and remaining your child.'[11]

We can note four main elements in the image of herself which Lou projects in *Ruth*. There is the 'Bacchus youth', brimming with genderless life and possibilities. There is the young woman who thrives on the expectation of love but is not ready to receive it. There is the sojourner in dreams who intends to stay in the dream right through her liberation from the illusions that constitute it. (This parallels her account of Nora's going away at the end of Ibsen's *Doll's House*. Nora has suddenly grown up, become disillusioned about her husband, freed herself wholly, yet goes away in order to preserve her dream and her belief that miracle is possible and that she can find something perfect and wonderful. To stay with the demiraculised husband would have been lamentably to recognise reality.) And finally there is the pupil who, while enjoying being a pupil, aspires to being the teacher. When Erik's wife tells Ruth that the greatest bliss is to serve God, she rejoins: 'If that were true, God would be worse off than people – no, God has the better lot.' Similarly, when Erik tells her a parable about a lonely gardener cherishing a small plant and hoping it will become a big beautiful tree, she replies, realizing that she

is the tree, that she'd rather be the gardener. These are tendrils of emancipatory ambition, and a hint as to why the author herself remained as yet fastened to her problem: she both wanted to stay the child and be forever taught, and wanted to be God, the teacher, the gardener, not just someone's garden.

FROM ALIEN SOUL

Struggling for God and *Ruth* belong together with Lou Andreas-Salomé's third novel, *From Alien Soul*, for the way they all present love as worship. *From Alien Soul* (begun in 1895 and published the following year) was admired by Rilke, who even wrote a poem about it. But there is little new to say, as it largely repeats the two preceding novels. Method and manner are much the same: *tête-à-têtes* in indistinct localities (handled rather better in this book), an atmosphere of humourless, yearning passion, the winding up and up of emotional encounters to their climax of union or more often of just-avoided union and shock.

The protagonist is the foster-son (though not made convincingly male) of a pastor, whom he adores. Again it is the story of how a younger person's worshipful love for a masterly elder comes to grief when the beloved turns out to be faulty. When he loses his belief in God, Kurt assumes miserably that he has lost what he shared with the pastor. But something far more terrible happens – he loses faith in the pastor himself, when he learns that the pastor long ago lost his own belief and has spent his life preaching without believing. Far from feeling glad that he can now share atheism with his idol, Kurt feels he has lost his real God, the deified person; so he shoots himself, though he does not die at once. In an effort to win him back, the pastor confesses the damaging truth to his congregation, but the boy dies unforgiving, and the pastor goes mad.

Rilke's poem implicitly shows up the lonely individualism of the novel. He tells the story, but gives it an ending of his own: the pastor's tombstone should have an inscription saying that he gave great joy to many, then, like gently taking off a robe:

He rejected the great lie
And went – a great man – into the night.[12]

AN ENCLOSED WORLD OF EMOTION

When, in *Wuthering Heights*, Catherine declares that she *is* Heathcliff, and when, in Goethe's *Elective Affinities*, we are told of the strange oneness of Ottilie and Eduard, we don't feel anything perverse in these identifications. They seem to belong to some greater normality, to be supported by a sense that this is how the natural world is made, that real laws lurk here somewhere, governing not only people but chemicals and weathers. But when

Lou Andreas-Salomé says of Ruth and Erik that

'only in him did she grasp and sense herself. The same life-urge slumbered powerful and joyous in them both'[13]

and when she describes all the yearnings, worshippings, sovereignties and subserviences that fill her stories, we find ourselves in a world of emotion only, where there are no rocks, trees or natural laws, and therefore somehow neither normality nor mystery. In this enclosed world there is often a morbid element, as when Kuno's father prays with ghastly cruelty for God to bring his infidel son back to the faith:

Punish him, wake him, re-cast him in your purifying fire of pain, my God . . . come to him with your terrible weapon, make him unhappy, make him miserable, make him ill and full of wounds, but let him *change his ways*.[14]

Or when Erik enjoys his ambiguous possession of Ruth:

It intoxicated him, a voluptuousness finer than any that can be communicated through the senses filled him with powerful pleasure. He could not make Ruth his own more unconditionally, more strongly, than in this moment when he was letting her go from him . . . Union and separation, selfless renouncing and selfish intervening, protecting and violating, serving and commanding, entwined indistinguishably in a single knot of feeling, a single moment of inebriating experience.[15]

These first novels present a torrid dream-world of dire sexuality, full of an inescapable desire for things that scarcely exist.

Fiction, 1896–98

Lou's next two short novels, *Fenitschka* and *An Aberration*, written in 1896 and 1897–8 (in her mid-thirties, just before and during her time with Rilke) are, except for some conspicuous contrival at their conclusions, more skilfully written than the three earlier ones. They are also more pleasant, no longer stifling with lack of air and excess of heat. The pent-up eros of romantic, inhibited youth is no longer the main inspiration, and the emphasis on 'God' has largely gone as well; instead of the breath-held effort of transforming the admired person into a godhead, the theme becomes the recognition of the misguidedness of such efforts, and the assertion of a personal freedom through considerable difficulty, more like Lou in her letters to Gillot and in the impression she made on Nietzsche. In each book the main character is a young woman.

FENITSCHKA

The eponymous heroine of *Fenitschka* is a young Russian woman. She is unconventionally serious and she regards the world as consisting of her brothers. Max, a young psychologist, comes across her one evening in a café in Paris giving moral support to a prostitute insulted by others. He suspects that she is less nunnish than she seems, accompanies her home, falls a little in love with her on the way, cannot believe she cares only about her studies and tries first to embrace her and then to lock her in his room. Faced with her contempt, he yields up the key and begs forgiveness. A year later, he meets her in Russia. She is changed. The 'sisterliness' of her behaviour is now recognisable as a Slav quality, and she now has a lover – yet she has not become less pure, for in her self-confidence, in the freedom she arrogates to herself, in her contempt for the conventional, there is 'an icy undoubtable purity'. Unlike Lou's previous heroine, Fenitschka thinks of love as simple and righteous, undemonic and healthy like 'good blessed bread eaten each day, the fresh stream of air we open our windows to',[16] and not something to make phrases about. Of course these *are* phrases, but he is very moved (and in his rather slippery male way, attracted, despite having a fiancée back home) by her openness and her anger about the secrecy forced upon women:

Yes, it may be necessary, as the world now is, but it's the most humiliating thing I have ever heard. To have to deny and conceal something which one does with one's deepest heart! To be ashamed where one ought to be jubilant![17]

Although he dislikes all this 'emancipation of women and student life . . .' he thinks her splendid, especially when he finds her veiled upon a stairway one night in a hotel and, ripping the veil off, she makes him a great speech about the marvel of sexual passion: 'spirit' and 'soul' are not, as we're taught, the highest things: what *is* noble and rare is something else:

Then something comes, and carries you away, and you give yourself up, and you stop calculating, and you hold nothing back, and you're no longer content with half measures, you give and you take, without considering, without thinking, almost without consciousness; laughing at danger, forgetting yourself, with wide, wide soul and swooning mind – and this, oughtn't *this* to be the higher thing?[18]

This speech holds one half of the story's message. Passion is nobler than intellect, because uncalculating and indivisible. The other half is that this is only so while passion remains undivided and whole, which it cannot be in the framework of marriage. 'Love and marriage are just not the same thing.' When her lover insists on marrying her, her feelings disappear, she gives him up, and begins to think she was whorish after all. The story ends here, with her sending the lover away and making the obedient Max overhear her doing so, as a lesson to him (for he thinks love and marriage go well together).

It is not subtle. But as praise of spontaneity, as a rather rough and unromantic acknowledgement of the coming and going of erotic feeling, it is impressive: speedy, forceful, a sort of long éclat, a burst of defiance and certainty. It prefigures some of what Rilke says in his 'Letter of the Young Worker', which declares that it is incomprehensible and terrible that just where we are purest we are made to feel dirtiest: 'Why has sex been made homeless instead of being celebrated as our natural right?' Rilke continues, 'I will admit that it shouldn't belong to us, who can't control and be responsible for such inexhaustible bliss. But why don't we belong to God at *that* very point?'[19] In *Fenitschka*, though the absence of the previous religious sensuality is just what makes this book refreshing, the heroine retains her nun-quality to the very end, giving herself first to intellect and then to sex with exactly the same fierce religiousness. One reviewer read the book in quite another way: Fenitschka forfeits some of her humanity by loving like a man, that is with only half of herself, 'differentiating a function out of' herself, and therefore having to renounce love at the end.[20] This seems to me to be a wrong reading.

AN ABERRATION

An Aberration (published 1898) is in part a second treatment of the Gillot affair. Ruth departed from her novel determined to be the 'child' for ever, and paradoxically triumphant. Adine, the heroine of this next novel, gives up being the child to her masterly suitor quite early on, and shows somewhat more sympathy to him when the wretch confesses his human sensuality.

Lou von Salomé declared – to Nietzsche and to Rée, and then no doubt to Andreas (and perhaps to Ledebour) – that her love for Gillot and its disappointment had closed off her love life for ever. But what did this mean? Here she tries to explain it, seeing it from the viewpoint of one who has either come to be capable of love after all, or at least (the point is not quite clear) acquired more insight into the matter. The theme is masochism.

'A long aberration made me incapable of full, serious love', the first-person narrator, a young artist, tells the male friend who wants to hear the story of her life. This starts with a memory of being held by her nurse while the nurse, gazing humbly and happily at him the while, was being beaten by her husband in the bright sunshine. There follow details that suggest identity of heroine with author: her parents' perfect marriage, the way 'mother did all father wanted while father did all I wanted', the mother's disapproval but tolerance of the freedom with which she is brought up; then the fact that at seventeen she falls in love with an older man (Benno), whose attitude to her is didactic; there is, too, one of the descriptions in which we recognise the author's account of her own appearance – of the heroine's walk, her 'carefree rocking stroll', as Benno calls it: 'only you walk like this, as if over the whole world there were nothing but smooth paths, or as if an invisible being were walking ahead of you, smoothing them'.[21]

Adine gets engaged to cousin Benno, and both his mental hospital and the local prison become associated with her future as wife of the man she loves: domestic bliss is prison and lunacy. Yet – this is the extraordinary theme of the first part of the book – in forcing herself to bow to this hated fate for the sake of the love she will indubitably enjoy through it, there is a kind of glamour, not moral, but voluptuous, an increase of passion. The deliberate self-subordination of a woman to a man to whom she is not inferior has an intoxicating effect, it seems, and can be a 'fearful spice to love, such an enormous whipping up of her nerves that mental balance must be forfeited'.[22]

Adine is well aware of what she is doing. Her confronting of reality saves her from Ruth's debilitating absorption into girlish trance – but *what* a reality. In it, sensual joy comes from spiritual humiliation; delight is to be won from giving one's life to what is trivial and soul-destroying. That this is not a matter of love as affection or as security, but love as sensual passion, is clear from the inebriate language in which Adine recalls all this, as well as from the effect a certain painting has upon her. The painting (Klinger's *Time Destroying Fame*) shows a young man in armour with an expression of omnipotence kicking a woman who has fallen before him; Adine associates this with Benno holding her in his arms and teaching her 'the first intoxication of love and the first shudder at the dependence of love', as well as with the moment in her infancy when her nurse blissfully accepted the blows. It seems this is the one way, for her, that passion can be compatible with marriage!

However, the discerning Benno notices her masochism and dissolves the engagement. She goes abroad to study art instead and sets up a studio in Paris, thus successfully becoming the person that she had been going to deprive herself of being. Yet that painting still represents the 'real' for her, and remains a kind of dark truth underlying all, as something she will never escape. No matter how she might criticise Benno or see through him (she now sees him as pedant and moralist), something has been learned through him which must dominate her life – sexual love is so strong that, once one feels it, one can only be a slave to it, and if this means destroying important parts of oneself, then the enslavement will be enhanced, and the joy will be greater. So now that she has her free life of moderate artistic creativity, Adine is resolute never again to let herself risk that subjection. This is how, through being taught the feeling of love, she has become forever 'incapable of love'.

All the same, when she meets Benno again after some years she is afraid his old instinctual tyranny will conquer her once more. The irony is, however, that he has changed. No longer the man in armour, he has grown adaptable, kindly, a better man altogether – and thus has lost all hope of getting her back. Far from welcoming the offer of a new kind of love, one between equals, Adine is disappointed, 'as if this love did not mean me at all, but he were loving, as it were, past me into the void'. Now that he is no longer the type to kick a woman down, she feels for the first time close to him as a human being, while irremediably distanced from him 'as a woman'. After all, he is no abyss, only a flat meadow, 'and yearning and disappointment and a revulsion against everything that did not seek abyss and danger awoke in me'. There is a scene where she allows him to embrace her while she gazes at the ceiling and imagines she is giving the breast to a crying child, at the same time wondering at the egoism and loneliness of his love. 'The passion of love is like the ultimate and most extreme solitude.' Then she escapes Benno by telling him the untruth that she already has a lover, thus (like Margherita in the earlier novel) self-sacrificingly ruining her reputation, yet reflecting that the self-slander is in a way true, for 'whatever I might achieve as an artist, the seriousness was gone from my love life, from my life as a woman'.[23]

So 'virginity' can be lost in other ways than sexual. In *Struggling for God*, Margherita was robbed of her maidenliness through giving herself to intellectual studies – a thought expressed in other stories too, and a sad thought, as it is not about release into maturer pleasures but about forfeiture of innocence: the girl who studies becomes tough and blasé, and all too knowing. It can also be lost through excessive romantic love early in life, and *this* is Adine's peculiar 'aberration':

Why didn't one regret . . . the frantic waste of feeling, the wearying emotional aberration, in the romantic Marlittiades [Marlitt was a popular sentimental novelist of the time] of us others? Were they less harmful just because

we weren't physically damaged by them and because their subtler and more intimate corruptions of the spiritual life were less noticeable from the outside? Actually it may be less dangerous to be distracted by superficial enjoyments than to sink down into all kinds of sultry obscure elements of feeling, against whose over-excitement the healthy warm charms of life cannot prevail.[24]

MASOCHISM AND VIRGINITY

The idea of 'normal' marriage as a masochistic temptation to the woman is treated most prominently in this novel, but it is present in other works too (such as *The House* and 'Dance of Girls'[25]). It is also expressed in a review Lou wrote of a performance of Wedekind's *Spring Awakening* in 1906. She regrets the omission of the scene in which the boy Melchior gives a beating to the girl, Wendla, for the beating makes her feel a mixed happiness and fear which she had never known in her spoilt life at home and this explains *why* she felt bound to him from that moment on. In that beating, Lou writes, Wendla became aware of 'the destiny of woman, which would bind her to the man who . . . first showed her who was the stronger.'[26]

The traditional masochistic situation is that in which a man enjoys being 'powerless victim of the furious rage of a beautiful woman'.[27] When Adine offers herself as wife like a sensualist offering her body to flagellation, this is a case of a woman enjoying being in the power of a beautiful man whom she could not in any circumstances physically overcome. Her wish to be overcome by him has its clear relation to normality. But the outcome is that she acquires power over *him* – this is the strange cunning of the theme in Lou Andreas-Salomé. The deified man, a civilised fellow, will not take advantage of the deifying woman's offer of herself and feels obliged to let her go (as in *Ruth*). When she comes back to find he is an ordinary human being begging her to be his *without* the melodrama, it turns out that this was all she wanted in order to reject him. Now he is at her mercy – his entire personality in detumescence. She sees through him: he is, and was, only a man, with nasty little male desires. So of course he cannot have her. The male masochist seeking the *femme fatale* regarded knowledge of her body as an unsurpassable goal; Lou's heroine seeks an *homme fatal* in order to defatalise him.

So virginity, in Ruth and Adine, is both protectively and destructively powerful, and there are other examples of the power of virginity, like Fenitschka's influence upon the prostitutes and her escape from the man who tries to trap her.

CHILDREN OF MAN

Written in the period 1895–8, this is a collection of ten stories about young women in love. They appeared as a book in 1899, though most had been published separately before. They were much praised by reviewers and show their author getting somewhat outside herself to depict a range of female types – all, reviewers said, instances of 'the new woman' and of 'woman's suffering from man'. Three stories in particular seem most interestingly to present aspects of Lou Andreas-Salomé herself.

The virgin wife Edith, in 'Before the Awakening', married to a man who is old enough to be her father and is lame in one leg, spends a day in Lübeck, where, walking in the streets, she senses the mighty presence of the sea. Town and sea seem a metaphor for the heroine herself: the lovely, tasteful, cold woman with something immense and wild all around her, part of her, yet unseen. What is this immense forceful thing? One would think, reading most of the narrative, that it means passion, the desire of love. But Edith evades surrender to a desirable and handsome artist who scatters rose petals over her in her bed, and finally even evades all desire to surrender to him, and moves away, it seems to something else. As she leaves Lübeck by train, she forgets her lover, even while he is risking his life jumping onto the train step to catch her handkerchief. She falls asleep and dreams of tobogganing down dazzling slopes of snow, a downward plunge which might be read as a dream of the hitherto evaded surrender, yet much more strongly suggests a real preference for the world of nature and the cold giving of oneself only to what is non-human.

Anyuta, the young literary career-woman in 'Incognito', is one of those who have lost their innocence through studying; neither virgin nor non-virgin. She, too, is roused to love by a handsome stranger and considers giving up her independence and responding to the demand for the traditionally feminine made by her anti-feminist wooer, until she notices a petty ill-humour in his face as he learns of her career, whereupon she slips away back to her journalism. But not only to journalism. The ending suggests that she unwittingly prefers (to the man) something more universal and splendid: a hot ray of sunshine 'kisses' her neck, and she pulls off her scarf and bows her head, yielding to the impersonal element: it replaces the man and points to a wider world altogether than that of emotions.

This plunge into snow and sun's kiss are taken up into the explicit theme of the most interesting story of the collection, 'Return to the All'. Here for the first time Lou Andreas-Salomé depicts a woman, Irene, who does not want human relationships at all, wants none of the female life of home and children, or the usual give-and-take of affection, but seeks solitude and indifference and a cool, silent union with the world of animals and vegetation.

The message is not straightforward. There is also Ella, who represents the opposite – the normal – values, and is just as sympathetically presented. But Irene is the interesting one. She is a woman all passers-by turn to look at: slender and fine, with a face expressing indifference. She runs a landed estate which she expects to inherit, and she plays the piano, yet believes herself to be 'a wholly unproductive person' because she doesn't compose. She is visited by the sincere, excited Ella, her friend of long ago, now engaged to be married. There is also a visit from a corpulent Frau Doktor in a man's waistcoat who is working for feminism in Germany and expects Irene, who dislikes men, to be on her side. To this, Irene remarks that disliking men doesn't mean liking women. She has no wish to take part in anything at all. She admits that she has something deathly in her and believes the feminists recognise this and are therefore drawn to her, since they too have in themselves the smell of death. All Irene's behaviour is noble and cold. She repulses Ella's affection, countering her talk of love with 'I don't believe love releases us from our separateness'. She makes remarks like 'all proximity makes me feel nauseous', and almost kicks a servant whom she is dismissing for pregnancy. Yet she works hard at getting a calf to feed, takes an interest in the virtue of duck-dung for growing hazelnuts, and plays in a field with a young filly. Ella is surprised. Irene explains that only in animals and plants does her disgust with living beings relax, 'and then I actually do, perhaps, a little of what all of you are trying to do in endlessly new sensations and passions and trying in vain: I merge with what is around me'.[28] She is grave and reverent as she says this and now it seems that her values prevail: even Ella understands how it might be more pleasant to let a cool flower slide through one's fingers than to embrace a human being.

In the end, Irene yields the estate to Ella to let her live there with her future children and fill the place with love and merriment: these things are *right*. She herself goes mysteriously away to be united with the eternal and universal – 'I shall find what I need in every blade of grass, in every cloud.' Just what she will do we cannot imagine: set up a farm? become a tramp? commit suicide in field or ditch? She merely gives the astonished Ella a chilly kiss and goes off quietly through sunset and trees, a noble vision.

The admission that love cannot save us from solitude was to be Rilke's theme. Irene adds a disgust for love, an aristocratic distaste for the pressing and panting of human relations, for all teeming procreation and for the whole human bother of offering, accepting, adapting, cohabiting, or pleading and thanking, of feeling, opining, debating, participating. She asserts her right to be uninvolved and separate. (At the same time she confesses her barrenness – not that she wants children, but she would like to be an artist, and her desire to get away and be united with the cosmos is presented as an artist's desire, only without the art.) The main thing is, she is right – she has the right – to be what she is: alone. She seems to elude moral judgment. Rough dismissal of the pregnant maid is not 'unkindness', it is an expression of her necessity; and giving the estate to Ella is not 'generosity', it is again her necessity. It is all an impassioned demonstration that, while Ella's way is obviously right, Irene's is, if mysteriously, also right.

LOU ANDREAS-SALOMÉ AND 'WOMEN'S WRITING'

'Return to the All' offers an idiosyncratic answer to the question of women's emancipation, suggesting a female possibility which does not overlap either with wife-and-mother or with career-woman. Wise about the nature of the universe, a woman may withdraw from the whole business, simply not take part. It is an extreme version of the notion that women should 'be' and not 'do'; for Irene, rejecting not only the doing of men and of liberated women, but also the doing of ordinary maternal women, prefers to be something she wilfully chooses for herself alone, which is not chosen for her by men.

Lou Andreas-Salomé's fiction is related, of course, to the 'women's writing' of her time – the many tales written by women, for women and about women, which, without being greatly talented, were an important new phenomenon and part of the growing women's movement in the later nineteenth century. Gabriele Reuter, for example, shares with her the subordination of character, dialogue, plot and setting, to a sole main concern with the woman who is the story's protagonist. She too, as author, lingers in the heroine's mind, explores her emotions and thoughts, tells us what it is like to be a woman. She also shares the elements of protest: women ought not to have to endure such restrictions and privations. But here is the big point of difference. For Reuter and others, the protest is the main thing: society must be changed, it is unjust that woman is helpless and forced to succumb in a male-made world.[29] Lou Andreas-Salomé's women do not and cannot succumb. In one way or another, they get clear of their men and discover their freer self. Because she is interested in the women who can do this – by definition the extraordinary ones – she is less concerned with the social question and with the liberation of women who, even if quite gifted and vital, are weaker and tied to men. She is not concerned with the loneliness of marriage but with the acceptance of unmarried solitude. And where the others write somewhat daringly of the feeling of sexual love as an overwhelming and magical feeling leading to the coy row of asterisks, Lou describes it as something even more overwhelming but which it is wiser to resist or, once had, to renounce, and which then will always lead, not to a man, but to something else, something more distant and abstract, private and vast. She depicts women without any ties (like Irene), avoiding ties (Fenitschka), or permitting a tie but mentally going beyond it (the heroine of 'Dance of Girls'), or else (several heroines and the women in *Struggling for God*) women who are destroyed by allowing or expecting a tie to take central place in their lives.

THE ALL AND JUGENDSTIL

The title 'Return to the All' contains a concept that was always important to Lou Andreas-Salomé. Whatever it means: the entire experienced earth, or the cosmos, or some other conception of totality; and whether or not it is to suggest some spiritual or quasi-spiritual presence brooding over or in or beneath, or perhaps some great abyss, the All is a notion that has excited and exalted many minds. Not an invention of Lou Andreas-Salomé, it was cultivated by the adherents of *Jugendstil*. The critic J. Hermand has shown how, unhappy with the life of the modern industrial city, artists sought a new 'unity of life', producing numerous images of it until

wherever one looks there is talk of primal images, the fundamental, the elemental, the thing in itself. On all sides people are dreaming again of states of affairs derived immediately from the Absolute.[30]

The characteristic view of woman promoted by *Jugendstil* writers was of 'a biological primal being'. From the slightly earlier femme fatale, she has developed into the Undine-figure, the water-nymph, the naked sylph-like haunter of forest pools and secluded, leafy springs; and woman herself somehow represents the All or merges with it, so that while she is sought by men, loved by men, theorised about by men, she is also raised to such a biological and cosmic marvel that she is actually robbed of intellectual and personal dignity. The idea that woman has a special relation to the All is close to some of Lou Andreas-Salomé's theories as well as to the title and theme of the story we have discussed. But in her there is an utterly different *estimation* of woman. Lou characteristically takes a male image of woman, rids it of the silliness with which the cavalier, the Faustian, the Jugendstilist, has invested it, takes it seriously (not to say solemnly) and dignifies it. Yes, we *are* the Eternal-Feminine, we are the one thing you seek in your endless restlessness; you lack us but we lack nothing. Or: Yes, I *am* the femme fatale if that's what you want to call me, and I shall sit back and enjoy being it, having invented and finally discredited my own homme fatal. Or: Yes, I *am* Undine, she says, and proceeds to explore in the figure of Irene what it might mean to have the Undinian capacity for immersion in the infinite of the nonpersonal. It does not mean being naked and floating from the beginning of time in a reedy twilit pond. It means choosing (with a necessitous determination men think only they can show) to go alone into the world of ponds and fields. A part of the 'total' biology and cosmos, yes, but not mindless: on the contrary, very intellectual and conscious about it.

THE THEME OF INCEST

There is a recurrent, though not prominent, motif of incest in Lou Andreas-Salomé's fiction. Märchen prepares to marry her father; Ruth tells her beloved teacher she is his 'child'; Kurt is in love with his foster-father with an intensity verging on voluptuousness, and the father feels much the same towards him; and there are other instances. To these hectic father-child relationships, all leading to disappointment or tragedy, a series of cool, constructive brother-and-sister loves is contrasted, and these all lead to success and happiness. In a 'A Death', love for a foster-brother is a more passionate matter than love for a husband, but it is happily transmuted into admiring recognition. The marriage between cousins in 'Paradise' will be affectionately happy. When Anyuta's love-relationship fails, she goes back to friendship and work with the man who represents her dead beloved brother. In 'Jutta', a story Lou did not publish,[31] a young girl gets distressingly involved with a young man on holiday, but always has her brother in the background, from whom she came and to whom she returns.

Lou's relations with her own father and brothers were very important to her, but there is certainly not enough evidence to psychoanalyse them. What seems clear is that by making all the father-child loves in her fiction lead to disaster, she is turning her back firmly (though with difficulty – it has to be done so many times!) on the Gillot-type relationship; and by making the sibling or cousin loves happy, and either unsensual or else able to transcend sensuality, she is welcoming an equality between man and woman that is never to be wrecked again by sex.

Fiction, 1902–04

The stories Lou Andreas-Salomé collected in 1902 under the title *The Land Between* are a return to the cult of adolescence, and are mainly a repetition of previous themes. Young girls grow up through the painful transition from dream to reality. If the dream contains worship of a famous, authoritative or fatherly man, the reality will consist in the discovery that he is not worth it; siblings in childhood may be comfortingly close but this will be lost as reality impinges; the male is a dangerous beast, all force and charm and the cause of despair or death. But the longer novels which belong to the first years after Rilke and the early years in Göttingen are all about marital, maternal or otherwise grown-up emotions and concerns, and they reflect the author's achieved balance and peace. Lacking the erotic urgency and problematic quality of the works of her earlier period, they are also considerably duller, full of a placid gratitude – for maturity, for a home, for a country and for the ability to be oneself. *Ma* is about sticking to one's chosen identity against all temptation; *The House* is largely about people becoming more fully themselves through disturbing experiences; *Rodinka* places the peacefully achieved self in the womb-like and alien kindred setting of Russia.

MA

Begun in 1899 and published two years later, *Ma* is a novel infuriating to read slowly. The style is somehow sticky underfoot and if one slows down one hardly proceeds at all. But it is quite rewarding to read fast – one flies across the verbiage and constructs from the whole thing the firm, original outline of a woman in a crisis of development. The theme is widowhood and motherhood. The heroine, whose name is Ma, and who has defined herself as the essential mother, feels her identity threatened when, with the second of her two grown-up daughters planning to leave home, she is offered a new marriage and unmaternal happiness. This temptation is far more frightening than the departure of her children. She rejects it and goes on into a kind of higher (now childless) motherliness.

Summarised, it may sound silly, and perhaps partly is. Ma's character is overdone: she is wholly self-sacrifice and good taste, is heroic in all griefs, is a wonderful teacher whose pupils model their lives on hers. The daughters go off to the real world in Berlin and the Women's Movement, but are devoted to her and are presented as her inferiors in that *she* created the conditions for their freedom. To them, she will always symbolise everything big and generous. Her friend, a doctor, is the same lordly, all-understanding, advice-giving, and always-right man who appears in so many of Lou's books. In this one, where the erotic is scarcely evoked at all, the heroine has worked out a perfect relationship with him. For twenty years he advises, respects and loves her, at a distance. At the crisis – is she to let the younger daughter leave home? – she accepts once more his severe, educative, wonderful advice and the calming medicine he slips into her tea – she accepts his authority so long as it is good for her. But when he proceeds to offer love, marriage, pleasure, a happiness that is even described by the word so important to Lou Andreas-Salomé: 'festival', she fights down an initial response of joy, realising it would mean she would be woman rather than mother, and tacitly says no (whereupon he retains his reliable lordliness by understanding perfectly that it has to be like this). Back in the primordial loneliness she knew when first widowed, she collapses onto a bench (in Moscow, with church bells ringing and the sun setting), suffocating and inwardly struggling. Then she rises (it is described as a resurrection) to walk away in a sort of glory – watched, incidentally, by an awestruck young poet – into a new life that is not described but which will certainly have in it fidelity to herself as mother, final independence of the man, and acceptance of solitude.

The book is all about love, and the statement it makes, I should say, is this: without love, a woman does not live, but she does not have to love a man, she can love her children, and when they are gone she can just *love*. As for the man, he is a necessary friend, and always has to be looked up to, but one should not bind oneself to him at the price of one's sense of identity.

THE HOUSE

Though not published until 1919, *The House* is closely connected with the move to Göttingen. It was started soon after the move there in 1904 and the house is the Andreases': it 'lay on the slope of the hill and looked down at the town in the valley.' This is Lou Andreas-Salomé's only book about a happily married couple and, of the three 'mature' novels, the only one set in Germany. The house is described down to details of the dog; the dog is named 'Salomo' – a strange name, she comments, since the dog was female but the name 'male and kingly'. Another point that relates the dog (an infinitely merry and uncomplicated inhabitant of the house) to herself is the description of it watching the birds on the grass as a 'spoiled child of the house watches the begging street-folk' – one of her intense though guiltless memories of childhood.

The married couple in the house represents a norm: happy together and with a 'sibling' feeling. The doctor husband, Frank, is again the strong, encouraging, understanding male, and (like Fred Andreas) is gifted with great intellectual concentration while 'dramatically' unable to be comprehensive in his work. The wife, Anneliese, is taller than her husband but not obviously modelled on Lou. She is a musician who gave up music in order to be absorbed in love of home and family. The perfect marriage, the book says explicitly, has this brother-and-sister quality and, it implies, consists of a strong, thinking male and devoted, emotional female.

This is only one of the ideals presented. The book is built up on a system of contrasts, of polarities and affinities, perhaps learned from Goethe's *Elective Affinities*. Other marital and erotic possibilities are introduced through the device of having visitors arrive, one by one, to alter the pattern of relations already set up and to provoke thought about opposites.

First comes Gitta, the daughter: spontaneous, unruly, seeing her father as God but offending him by marrying a Jew, Markus – a bad thing since it cannot, in her father's eyes, lead to the sibling-type marriage. Gitta is temperamentally unsuited to marriage, and to Markus in particular. He likes old buildings, whereas she likes swimming, and this seems connected with her remaining virginal (in fact the dog Salomo comes to live with them in their house) – which doesn't mean the marriage is a failure; neither does the fact that she tends to go wandering on vague, wild escapades.

Second comes Balder, Gitta's brother and boyish counterpart (at least in his instinctive opposition to the father's discipline and morality of hard work), but her opposite in being unstable, with high moods of confidence and horrible depths of self-annihilation. When he talks to his father, he loses his willpower. But the mother is delighted to discover that the boy feels at home writing poetry. Balder is modelled on Rilke, but one can see the author herself in him (her idea of herself in childhood and adolescence as alien to her parents, living in imagination, writing poems, needing to go away) as well as seeing her in the mother.

Third comes Renate, a friend, modelled on Frieda von Bülow and, like her, suffering from the tired nerves of an old family. Renate represents a contrasting erotic type. Herself noble, she is attracted to an unworthy and violent working man. She longs to subjugate herself to him, and talks crazily about this:

For even being trodden on – if we *love* the one who does it, then we've *wanted* him to do it. He is only apparently the lord who subjects us, in reality he is our tool, tool of a most hidden pleasure – servant of a longing – what do I know.[32]

This kind of desire has been met with in Lou's earlier works, especially in *An Aberration*. There it was central, here it is marginal and disapproved of by the central female character, Anneliese, so it seems to be rejected. All the same, she not only writes of it compassionately, even voluptuously, but in Anneliese she gives merely a more conventional version of the

same thing, since Anneliese in another way –
the way called 'normal' – goes in for wholesale
subjugation of herself to men: to husband and
son.

Fourth is Markus, Gitta's husband, drawn
to Frank by profession and admiration and to
Anneliese through music (though with defined
oppositeness); and Balder is drawn to him
through shared knowledge of self-doubt, fear
of cowardice.

The story proceeds through intensification
and variation of these attractions and clashes,
but with little incident. Balder and his mother
are spiritually united in art, and in a sort of
rapture; Balder and his father are disastrously
alienated by that same art. Anneliese and
Frank are thus thrust into disagreement.
Balder leaves for foreign parts, and writes
passionate letters to his mother. Gitta leaves
Markus and turns up at her parents' house
with Salomo (having 'lost Markus and kept the
dog'), but goes back to him. Tolerant Markus
is the opposite of disciplinarian Frank, who has
to go through such self-discipline (to endure
his son's behaviour) that he is forever slightly
estranged from his wife. Each ends up corrob-
orating his original nature and also making
something more of it. Balder, far away, has
become wholly what he had to become: a poet.
Gitta is acknowledged as virginal and wayward, a self-seeker, still wandering about in
autumn fields. Markus somehow becomes the
wonderful Jew, for Jewishness means not only
brave work for others – 'because a Jew may not
be private in anything' – but also devotion to
ideas of freedom and equality (perhaps this is a
homage to Paul Rée). Frank takes in students
at home and re-establishes himself as teacher
and father. Anneliese accepts Markus as son,
becomes pregnant (the young wife, Gita, of
course does not) and seems to expand to
become everyone's mother. The book ends
with Anneliese's trance of happiness, and the
last word is of the faithful dog.

RODINKA

Rodinka, though written in 1901–4, was published in 1923 and dedicated to Anna Freud.
The first-person narrator seems to be Lou
Andreas-Salomé herself, slightly fictionalised.
In the first half she is a German girl growing
up in her family in Petersburg, with the Russian name Musya (rather as Lou was called
Lyolya, though 'Musya' also echoes Muschka,
the name Lou used of her mother), and surrounded by brothers. In the second half she is
the same girl grown up and now a visitor to
Russia – its observer, critic and lover, observing the countryside and life on a landed estate.
Although there are well-delineated characters
and something of a story, it is too leisurely for a
novel. It is more like a gathering of places,
atmospheres, characters, conflicts, fates and

ideas, which could have been shaped and
sharpened into a novel, but with no sign that
the author wished to do so. It seems written for
herself alone, a homage and reminiscence; or
perhaps it was also for friends whom she
wished to remind of shared experience, like a
discursive and very full diary, or even like a
rough, large painting, for it is all visual and
still, scene after scene. It is a book that could
be read out with probable success to an
imaginative insomniac: an invoker of sleep and
good dreams. Although more neatly and
laconically written than many of her things,
with every sentence well formed (but too many
of them), the whole is too unbounded, loitering
and lingering, for it to be called art.

A typical paragraph describes how Vitaly (the
admired, rather enigmatic, secretly revolutionary, all-benevolent hero) arrives home:

> Once at night a dog's long, long, drawn-out
> howl of joy struck suddenly through the
> quiet. Then it went silent. But the joy in it
> somehow enchanted my heart. Without
> understanding, without interpreting, I sank
> back into slumber as into festivity – with
> wide-open soul, through which moved lights
> and sounds and they all seemed to celebrate
> something that had broken forth from the
> very mouth of the animal as a cry of joy.[33]

Rest, silence, distance (suggested by the dog),
the festive, the implication that there is no
need to be dynamic or purposeful so long as
one is restfully open and welcoming – these are
the book's mood and message. In its meander-
ingly descriptive way, it is the most political of
all her books, since a part of its concern is to
depict and praise revolutionary Russian youth,
as well as those (like Sofya Shil) who worked to
bring literacy and improved conditions of life
to Russian workers – workers who needed to
begin to think, not in a harmful collision with
sudden ideas from the West, but in their own
Russian way.

Maternity, and the loss of children, are met
with in several of this book's characters. Not
with the desperate centrality of *Ma*, but as
recurrent elements of individual fates, all are
overshadowed by the general evocation of Holy
and holy-atheistic Russia. There is wild
nomadic Ksenia, pregnant and frightened;
sorrowing Hedwig, whose husband and child
have died; sad, fat, motherly Tatyana, one of
whose children is likely to die; and the beautiful, irresponsible poet, Dmitri, who has left
Tatyana for a great love. Towering over them
is the tyrannically possessive, superstitious,
old-style 'babushka', head of the house, powerful, unselfconsciously alternating between the
extremes of confessional humility and legisla-
tive severity. She prays endlessly, stubbornly
disowns her errant son Dmitri, lets the local
people see her as healer and wise woman, rules,

judges, forbids, tells long, weird tales and (one of the few strands of developing action in the book) conducts a passionate war of wills with her son Vitaly.

Vitaly is the Russian version of the masterly male. In his youth, he ran off to war and came back missing an arm; he lives in secret contact with terrorists, he teaches peasants and workers, and at the end he goes away to some terrible fate amid talk of printing presses and danger. He is the great understander. He understands how the peasants can believe they have no one over them but God; why the poet has to leave home (like Rilke's Prodigal Son); the way women need men as brothers; and what the cattle feel when they are let out for the summer. He is a healer (another doctor) and adviser. He is the man of great feeling and great hope for Russia. He is also, and this is important for Lou's image of herself, mentally in close relation to Musya, and a counterpart to her. For not only is she the only one he tells of his dangerous activities, but he also assures her that he and she 'have the same relation to life – one without deception'.[34] The ending is reminiscent of that of 'Return to the All', with Vitaly vanishing into the immense Russian fields to an unknown fate, leaving wife, family, unborn child, affections and love – irresponsible yet nobler than them all. Indirectly, it is saying something about how Lou thought of herself: stable, settled and domiciled, she was yet romantically free, with the whole world hers to roam.

Late Fiction, 1915–19

While the fiction Lou Andreas-Salomé wrote before about 1900 might be described as 'fiction of desire', and the narratives of her second period – from about 1901 until her involvement in psychoanalysis – as 'fiction of fulfilment', the imaginative works of her third, post-psychoanalysis period differ from all the earlier ones. First, instead of concentrating on her own present desires and fulfilments and offering projections of her own psyche, they offer applicable generalisations of her experience. Second, they are concerned with probing psychical depths and establishing a final control over them. These 'depth-control' writings must count among her best. They are varied in genre: a series of tender tales of childhood fantasy; a long, turbulent story about a group of adolescents; and three plays. The only play she published (in 1922) is a half-expressionist, half-classical drama about the Devil.

THE DEVIL AND HIS GRANDMOTHER

This play was written in 1915, at a time when Lou had been practising as an analyst for two years. The title means, idiomatically, something like 'every man and his wife' or 'everyone and his brother'. It has been called her 'most successful work'[35] and, indeed, among her fiction it is; it is also her most unexpected and weird. But to say merely that 'the meaning of this strange parable in which religious and psychoanalytical elements are grotesquely mixed is that love conquers death. Even the outcast is reborn in love',[36] is to miss its extraordinariness. The truth is that, for once, its author is not being nebulous. Its real concerns are both concrete and analytical, rather than nobly moral. Lou had once been greatly cheered by Wilhelm Bölsche's showing her how the animal world, with all its slimy, ugly creatures (not only spiders, snails, rats and frogs, but also the life going on in the human belly, gut and womb), is worthy of endless admiration; Freud had furthered this work of release by showing how one could look with unflinching interest at the most ghastly preoccupations of the mind. Some of the materials liberated for decent consideration by Freud's theories are the subject matter, the stuff – it is extremely physical – of this play. The importance of their liberation is its message; the theme is the redemption of the body, especially of anality and physical sexuality.

It is an allegorical play. The Devil represents that badness we customarily impute to the lower functions of the body, especially the way we think of them in childhood; or rather, he is that imputation, so that the final elimination of it means his disappearance. 'With every slandering of the earthly something diabolical is born,' as Lou was to write later in her book about Freud.[37] Her Devil is a bored, talkative, playful fellow who can only be seen in the dark and is thus not really there at all, not really anything, an unnecessary suffering.

The reader gets two initial surprises. One is that Lou Andreas-Salomé could write, if somewhat derivatively, skilful humorous verse. The play opens:

Devil (yawns)
What boredom – boring boringest of dullness,
So *that*'s the 'pleasure of eternity'.
One zealously inspects the freshly dead,
Yet scarcely are they in the hellish slough –
Scarce have they seen their fire flare up
    around –
I know already how it licks and laps
And how they'll anxiously contort
    themselves.
A rotten lot of wretched callow souls!
No chance of getting any fun from them.
Nearby I see one of them surfacing:
Long-haired and in a girlish shift. The dung
Makes its grimacing shadow almost blind.

(Starts)
What – is it stretching out its hands to me – ?

Poor Little Soul
Stars!

Devil
Well, that I call a healthy confidence,
To think the slough of hell is roofed with
    stars!
– You seem to have arrived here quite
alive.[38]*

These pentameters are a world away from the
solemnity of Lou Andreas-Salomé's earlier
poetry and suggest she had a comic gift which
she might have developed.

The second surprise is the ubiquitous and
undisguised imagery of excrement. The scene
opens in a cesspit. This, we see, is what Hell is:
everywhere liquid shit, steaming and stinking;
worms crawl in it, flames start up in it because
'garbage burns well'; we are, in fact, in the
bottom of an old woman. It turns out that the
whole world – as we, with our fears and prejudices perceive it – is the body of the Devil's
grandmother. Her faraway head is Heaven,
with angels and other inhabitants peering
longingly downwards, and her bottom – the
bottom of all our minds – is Hell. This is the
one place God never looks into, not having one
himself and being altogether too prudish. As
for Heaven:*

Only when weakened by strong purgatives,
Almost de-arsed, does he admit the blessed.[39]

The newly arrived Soul is disgusted, but the
Devil tells her he will seduce her out of her
self-deception (meaning she is only pretending
not to enjoy the shitty scene?) and he becomes
so charming to her that her blood spurts out in
flames and fills the Devil himself. He explains,
in voluptuous pleasure: 'Nought am I but the
space in which you flame.' So it seems that the
Soul has been seduced into enjoying what she
thinks she ought not to enjoy. She quickly
regrets it and calls her blood (now wrapped
around the Devil's neck in two red ribbons)
'unfaithful', at which he proclaims, rather like
Mephistopheles in *Faust*:

The meaning of 'unfaithful', even to humans,
Swings between Heavn's deception and
    Hell's truth,
And aren't all things, in any case, to us,
In spirit and in truth *one* holy thing?[40]*

She prays to him, and he lifts her up out of the
muck ('so that the ground gurgles') and turns
her into a Child, tastelessly telling her that this
is *'our'* version of the birth of Jesus. The baby
is indeed Lord of the world, both infant and
wise, but instead of martyrdom it shall have a
wealth of wish fulfilments. When the Child
demands 'Heaven', he gives her visions of it
between his horns. In it she sees blissful people
who are one and the same person endlessly
multiplied; angels who have hooves and wear

billowy dresses so as not to look down at
themselves; and attractive animals who have
human beings attached to their backs in endless copulation. She also sees a baby born –
excreted undigested by the grandmother.
Probably this refers to Freud's article on
childhood sexual researches which establish
that babies are born through the anus. The
Child is delighted – she has a companion – but
the Devil makes the baby vanish, at which the
Child screams and pees on him, so he sets her
upon a golden chamber pot. Thus infancy is
acted out: the infant's first sense of total power
yields to the forcible discovery of the filthy
underside of beauty and to toilet training. Yet
the pot is golden, the Child accepts it, and here
begins individual dignity.

The Devil now climbs laboriously up his
grandmother's spine towards her head, the
place of the Creators. He meets some workers
on the way, invites them to his wedding, and
gets them to make him a gift of their potency,
after which he expands to the size of the world.
The scene changes to a cinema. On the screen,
the Devil's marriage with the Soul (the Child)
is performed (she comes straight from the pot
to the wedding!). He chases her onto a vast
purple bed, sharpens his tail with a tableknife
pulled from under his dinner jacket, violates
her by plunging it into her navel, then chops
her up; the pieces of her body are strewn about
in heaps. Once again we are being shown
children's theories, which establish that sexual
intercourse is violent and takes place through
the navel.

Now comes the Devil's transformation. He
begs his grandmother to resurrect his bride.
Huge in size, lurking among vast rocks, he
listens while her scornful voice reverberates
through the universe. She says that her old
womb might just manage it, and tells him
important truths, such as that she – who is the
earth – only exists through God; were He to
look away, she would not be there. Confronted
with such grandeur and nobility, the Devil
now realises that God had to load all his own
filth onto him in order to remain clean for the
sake of people who could not bear an unclean
God. People thus brought about the existence
of both Devil and Hell. He is furious, but sees
that he can get out of it by agreeing to cease to
exist. Magnanimously (he is good humoured
throughout, though the grandmother-earth is
irritatingly splendid), he commits suicide by
willingly entering the light. It makes holes in
him until he disappears altogether, reassured at
the end that he will not be forgotten and that
he is actually entering a world of love. Presumably this means that he becomes united with
the 'All', so here is, indeed, 'the conquest of
death by love'. But all the sentimental and
grand sequences at the end, including the
rebirth of the Soul and an epilogue with non-

allegorical people (we have been allowed at last out of the world of the body into the world of personalities), talking beautifully about it all, are far less powerful than the main part of the play, with its filthy language and filthy images.*

SIBLINGS

Another late fictional piece, 'Siblings', begun in 1919 and published in 1921, is a story about dark passions raging beneath the jocular surface of a houseful of adolescents (five siblings), with whom their maiden aunt Adele comes to live *in statu parentis*. The five were once eight, three having died. All are boys, except the youngest. This one girl, Jutta, hero-worships an infinitely attractive, authoritative, forty-year-old doctor who rents the flat above, and secretly visits him. All these things show Lou Andreas-Salomé's own adolescence as a starting point for the story. That the marvellous man up above is at last publicly exposed as a sensualist, guilty of 'moral crimes', suggests that she is working at a final resolution of the still painful and dominant memory of Gillot. That Jutta is the same gamine, sparkling with spontaneity, burning with self-devotion, as her forerunners (from Märchen and Ruth on), suggests that, under all her maturity and success and changed image, the author still felt continuous with the ideal self of her youth. But it would be nonsensical to read more than this into such references.

The story represents a return to the impetuous, vague, morbid fictions of desire and disappointment of her earliest works, along with a greater control. This happens not just in the idolised but suspect teacher meeting his destruction, but in the way passion is distributed among as many as six characters (including Aunt Adele), and in its being placed in lucid relationship to a set of 'appearances': the tomboyish young people rollicking home from a day in the country, the homely accounts of baking and sewing, the scenes where the good-willed Aunt listens at her nephews' doors to check on their evening activities. The author is saying that under our everyday social lives are untamed loves and hates, a whole 'polymorphous perverse' range of them.

By any respectable literary standards, this is still a poorly written piece, or rather a pre-literary work, a hotchpotch presentation of materials that might conceivably have been shaped into a brilliant work. Among its awkwardnesses is the fact that we cannot know whether the half-titillating, half-irritating indefiniteness about what actually goes on is a deliberate tactic, a habitual obeisance to the convention of discretion, or merely vagueness.

Three kinds of passion are revealed: homosexual, normal heterosexual, heterosexual-incestuous; and perhaps teacher-love should be added as a fourth – the peculiar voluptuousness of prostrating oneself before a leader, and the most exciting and dangerous kind of sexuality. Stefan (or 'Fanny') is nineteen and makes secret visits of an exalted and unspecified nature to Klaus-Trebor, the man above. Erwin is eighteen and makes nightly visits of a more easily discernible nature to Elfrieda, friend of the housemaid. Herbert, a year younger, puts on his best clothes and goes upstairs for an ecstatic nocturnal meeting with the much-made-up Bella Belloni. He is so sobered and changed in the morning that one supposes this, too, is a normal male sexual experience. The last two children, the twins, Gottlieb with the misshapen chest, and Jutta (an hour younger), are more sibling even than the other siblings, because they once shared the primal pre-birth harmony. They cling to each other in a way that comes over as incestuous yet mysteriously righteous – as if they are driven by some force, or law, to return to each other. When away from Gottlieb (whose name suggests there is something divine about their relationship), Jutta is very individual. Not only does she, like her brother, slip upstairs to Klaus-Trebor, but she is drawn to Stefan, especially in a climactic scene when he demands to know why she goes upstairs and she answers that it is for the same reason as he does. They stare at each other for a long, tense, shuddering moment:

Her gaze opened into his, depth upon depth, without restraint, raising up the profoundest things . . . Stefan yielded to this gaze, a shudder went over him. The same upward looking, the same experience, the same love? – because the best of love. – That which lay upon him like the secret of all dread and all bliss, with primal suddenness loosened, released itself to become the simplest and commonest thing, as if to become something which wasn't talked about only because it was the life-giving breath from the breast's depth. She stood before him . . . like one who shared the knowledge of all mysteries and sacraments of the world.[41]

He warns her of the danger she is in, which is not that she might love the older man, but that he might love her. How can you hint such things about your friend? cries Jutta, not understanding what it is all about. Because, says Stefan, I *know*, and love is not always something exalted. At this he stands close before her and says that

she should never learn what it meant to be loved without being loved – confounded with one's own body – not to be distinguished any more from beauty, from attractiveness – to have to fight with shame.[42] [All this is printed in widely-spaced type for emphasis.]

He puts his arms around her for a long and passionate, dream-like moment. She then goes to say goodbye to Klaus-Trebor, but he repulses her, and she rushes to her twin to tell him *he* must help her. Gottlieb, who has been boiling with jealousy of Stefan, is overjoyed and the twins weep, talk and embrace for the rest of the story.

Now comes crisis after crisis. Stefan realises that his jealousy is not of Jutta for having Klaus-Trebor, but of the latter for having Jutta, and after waiting up for Klaus-Trebor he stabs himself with a blunt dagger and slowly bleeds to death. In the morning the papers tell of Klaus-Trebor's arrest; Stefan is discovered dead; Jutta realises that all her life every man she loves she will love as a brother; and Aunt Adele, sitting by the corpse, confesses to herself that she had been in love with her dead sister's husband.

There is something subterranean about all Lou's fiction, but most especially about this last piece; everything seems to take place in a reddish half-light, on the verge of dream. Perhaps the annoying absence of clarity about the incidents should be forgiven as part of an attempt to depict impulses and impulsive behaviours before their naming – to show the narcissistic, the wombish, the languageless, furiously passionate, helpless landscape of infancy. Here eros is everywhere, not in many forms but in many semi-forms: the homosexual merging into the leader-follower (then lusting to be the leader), thence into incest (and *Liebestod*?); the incestuously-inclined pupil-voluptuary falling into sensuality with the elder brother and an almost otherworldly union with him, thence back to the darkness of twin-love, a mumbling, sobbing, inscrutable union between creatures nearly identical. All depends on the blurring of edges, on lack of outline and name. Even Aunt Adele is *strangely* female, strangely alluring and emotionally potent, right from the beginning. And yet there is nothing sinister in any of it. On the contrary, everything is held firmly within a sense of home, in fact by the house they all live in – a sort of nest, out of which no one can fall. Even the dead Stefan remains thoroughly at home, as if he has died into the womb. All the others, drifting in their several yet collective passions around him, are devoted to the mysterious urging of the blood in just the same way as he was.

THE HOUR WITHOUT GOD . . .

Three stories about childhood, collected as *The Hour Without God and Other Children's Stories*, were published in 1922, though they were written in 1909, 1913 and 1919. They are a reaffirmation of the bliss of primal security. Revolts, fears, encounters with the incomprehensible, never suffice to destroy the original paradisal order – at least in the fortunate lives depicted here. The little girl central to each tale is called Ursula, which surely means not so much 'little bear' as an Ur-creature – belonging to the primeval, genuine, incontrovertible origin of all things.

In the first tale, 'The Hour Without God', there are Freudian concerns: the great importance of infancy, the child's interest in sex, an instance of the primal scene, a close experience of happiness with her father, self-identification with the mother in the father's absence; and a horror-laden scene where an aunt leaves a snake on the bedside table – it is a plait of false hair, but Ursula's revulsion is extreme and associated with hatred of her own body. The sexuality has the true childhood quality of illicitness and uncertainty, yet infinite meaning and possibility. At the same time, there is another theme, more defined and controlled by Ursula's thinking: that of God. Lou Andreas-Salomé recounts here the actual incident (of the snowmen) through which she lost her childish faith. There is the crisis Lou herself went through when God had failed to answer her, worsened by the realisation, when the father reads from the newspaper, that no God could have allowed such misery as there is in the world. She thinks up ways of restoring him, but cannot, until the story ambiguously ends with her coming to some greater happiness than she had had before: in the burgeoning spring countryside of the family estate, climbing trees, overwhelmed by summer, hearing God's voice in the voices calling her from the house.

The story has some charm and it seems to promise literary achievement, had the author had such ambitions. It is written with ease, is talkative, gentle, rhythmic, like a long story told by firelight. It moves from paradise to paradise, through despair and hints of the diabolic. But the whole devil-world is excluded, perhaps through being banished to the play. The childhood fantasies which there take the form of violated navels, knife-sharp penises, splitting bellies, excreted babies, drownings in urine, here turn up in a purified and safe form: the snake which is only a plait of hair, the pretence of baby-making for which the girl is satisfactorily punished by the all-knowing parents.

In 'The Tales of the Daisies and the Clouds', Ursula and her baby brother enter a flower and experience happiness: she marries him, they have hundreds of children. Their love lasts a millenium, till a world-disaster sends them searching for the 'invisible presence', which is rightly hidden behind locked doors – 'for the greatest love and the greatest secret are surely always one' – and which they later realise is embodied in their mother. Then they have a similar adventure in the sky, as streaks of water, endangered but finally rescued.

In 'The Alliance between Tor and Ur', little Ursula meets little Torvald (Ur and Tor: the Origin and the Fool). He involves her in an adult-defying make-believe of lordship, servility and elemental magic. The story starts with Ursula engaged in making up people from features of passers-by (Lou's own childhood preoccupation) and following along behind the unknown boy, who turns out to be running away from 'culture' to a realm of his own that he has established down by the river. Although she is socially acquainted with the schoolmaster to whom he is obsessively hostile, the boy lets her join his daily game. He is the wild man of the forest, the ferocious lord, and she becomes his slave and wears a necklace of wild beasts' bones. While delighted to call him Master, she is always aware that it is a pretence. As she invents people, he is inventing an alternative life and character for himself. In each case, the pretence takes over a large part of actual life, but while hers is an enriching and embellishing of reality, his is a protest against it. As woman, she understands what he's doing and plays along with him, knowingly; as man, he cannot tolerate what he calls her 'lying'. So the savage, idyllic life in the cave is continually invaded by uncertainty about the status of the pretence and by the boy's unsolved worries about his relation to the people outside. Ur has no such worries; she *is* security. The idyll is finally invaded by some hostile boys and Tor is nearly defeated, but Ur happens to know some of them and saves him by bringing the whole civilised world into the scene:

Even before Tor was flung to the ground, she threw herself into the midst of them. 'Richard!' she shouted piercingly, and seized one boy by the hair, almost tearing out the lofty black tuft. 'Don't you dare! I'll murder you! I'll get you chucked out of the whole boarding-house!' and saying this she thumped with her other fist at the face nearest to her, while her primaeval necklace provided the military music.[43]

There then comes the reconciliation of Tor with civilisation – that is, with the grown-ups. As in 'The Hour without God', the grown-ups are not enemies. They may spoil things, but finally they love and are loved. The hated headmaster turns out to be friendly and invites the vanquished Tor to tea.

The story teaches that rebellion is a disguised form of longing for love from the authority figures, and that the girl – cleverer, stronger and unrebellious – is fulfilled in two roles: as servant and as saviour of the boy.

This judgment is, of course, only a part, not the whole, of Lou Andreas-Salomé's view of the relation between male and female. Here she is writing of children. In general, she does show that the girl-child and the girl-adolescent has to go through some kind of enslavement, however conscious it is and however much it may involve a deliberate restraining of one's superior knowledge and talents. But the stories of children and adolescents point forward to the stories about adult women, all of whom, having gone through that fascinated stage of enslavement, emerge into autonomy and self-sufficiency.

Appendices

APPENDIX A

Nietzsche's 'Columbus' Poem

In November 1882 Nietzsche handed Lou the final version of an eight-line poem that had gone through many versions. Its evolution, of which Ernst Pfeiffer sets out the several stages in *Dokumente* (pp. 458–68), shows in miniature the whole process by which Nietzsche tried to make Lou a part of his life: both how the vision, the ambition, the self-certainty, were there before he met her, and how she none the less became for a while necessary to that vision and confidence.

The first version, written before he met her, ran:

Dorthin will ich; und ich traue
Mir fortan und meinem Griff.
Offen liegt das Meer, – in's Blaue
Treibt mein Genueser Schiff.

Alles glänzt mir neu und neuer,
Mittag schläft auf Raum und Zeit,
Nur dein *Auge – ungeheuer*
Blickt mich's an, Unendlichkeit!

This describes both a real and a metaphorical journey – the one he made by boat that March from Genoa to Messina, and the one he was making, mentally, as a Columbus of the spirit, from *The Gay Science* to an unprecedented philosophical adventure. It is an adventure of his own: the pronoun 'I' dominates (seven occurrences, counting the variants); while the only 'you' is not a person but 'eternity'.

Meeting and loving Lou, who was clearly no Muse or Beatrice but a possible companion and collaborator, Nietzsche began writing her into the poem. One variant had her at the helm of the boat and addressed as '*lieblichste Victoria!*' But she was, above all, his friend, and 'friend' now became the first word of the final poem:

Freundin – sprach Columbus – traue
Keinem Genueser mehr!
Immer starrt er in das Blaue,
Fernstes zieht ihn allzusehr!

Wen er liebt, den lockt er gerne
Weit hinaus in Raum und Zeit –

Über uns glänzt Stern bei Sterne,
Um uns braust die Ewigkeit.

This is a better poem – more supple, lighter, with a more fluent combination of the dramatic, the explanatory and the declaratory; and it is no longer egocentric.

Overt subject-matter overlaps remarkably little between the two poems: in both there are *trauen*, *glänzen*, *blau*, *Genueser*, *Raum*, *Zeit*, infinity, but sea and ship have to be inferred in the second (the final) poem, and the journey is much more abstract (*fern*, *weit*). Though both culminate in cessation and radiance, the second ending is very different: the monstrous watching eye has been replaced by the sounding of that eternity into which the traveller has come. Moreover, it is the shining of the stars, not of the sun. Perhaps the biggest difference is that the journey is now for two people: '*uns*' is now the important pronoun.

So the poet-adventurer arrives in the realm of glorious, dangerous eternity with his special *Freundin*. Or does he?

The way in which the poem is a true account of Nietzsche's relation with Lou is that it includes a deep doubt and ambiguity: self-doubt and the actual ambiguity of their situation. '*Traue/Keinem Genueser mehr*': she is first of all to beware of him, not because he wants to seduce or mislead her but because he is himself all too greatly lured away by distant things, things that are more distant than herself and that make it difficult for him to have an ordinary, reliable friendship. And she should also beware because he (or any such Genoan) will try to take her with him and she will face the risk of leaving familiar shores. So far, it might be read as a warning to a person who has not gone with the traveller: next time, don't trust such a man as me, because he'll be off into the distance and you won't want to accompany him.

But the second stanza, especially its last two lines, could also be read either as indicating that the other person has gone with him or as describing the magnificent experience he and she would have found had they made the journey together (that is, if we understand the present indicative as standing in for the past conditional). Yet again, if these two lines are taken as referring to the regular state of things – the condition in which we are all always surrounded by eternity and starry distance, which explains (in some) the desire for such travel – there would seem to be still a possibility of their setting off together.

Whichever it is, the tone is exalted, self-knowing and strangely jubilant. And whichever it is – an offering of great risk and great awareness, a withdrawal of that offering, or a recognition that the offering isn't wanted – it remains a very fine love poem.

APPENDIX B

Rilke's Letters to Lou compared with his other Letters

Rilke's letters to Lou after the first period of their acquaintance were consistently darker and more tormented than those he wrote to other friends. His biographers have commented on this, some saying that, as a great letter-writer, he skilfully assimilated himself to each correspondent, and so in this case, 'overemphasised the sorrowful aspects of his thought' (Wydenbruck, p. 54); others that Lou was actually the only person he felt he could turn to when 'violently troubled in spirit' (Butler, p. 150), and that he therefore wrote her his most significant letters. The latter seems the more probable reason, though one may wonder whether Lou's unfavourable reception of Rilke's 'Florence Diary', with its sunshine, pleasure and self-assertiveness, initially increased his tendency to relate only his 'sorrowful aspects' to her.

Other women were important to Rilke later on. But he wrote to them differently: to Katharina Kippenberg with some authority and equilibrium; to 'Merline' (Baladine Klossowska) emotionally and warmly but with an insistence – that Lou would never have provoked – on the inviolable separateness required by his work; to Nanny Wunderly-Volkart, the friend of his later years (and companion in his last illness), extremely frankly and trustingly, yet keeping hidden even from her the deepest levels of his feeling; and he wrote differently again to his most significant female friend after Lou, the princess Marie von Thurn und Taxis, whom he met in 1909 and was close to for many years. She, too, was a 'motherly friend', twenty years older than he; but she, unlike Lou, was 'a great lady, a lady of the world' (Buddeberg, p. 203), who patronised the arts, travelled in great style, was at home in the most cultivated society, and was 'genuinely cultured' and 'gifted at conversation' (epithets one would not need to stress regarding Lou). It was she who lent Rilke her castle at Duino, where he began the Elegies. 'A romantic nature' (Kassner, quoted by Buddeberg, p. 203), she addressed him as 'Dottor Serafico' and revered him as a great poet in need of protection and promotion. To her, too, he wrote many letters of a confessional type, but these typically contained a measure of cheerfulness and lacked the infinitely probing introspection of the letters to Lou. Only to Lou, who did not idealise but criticised him, could

he tell his fears and existential anguishes. Buddeberg considers that the correspondence with the Princess was healthier for Rilke; 'Perhaps it was essential for Rilke that he could express himself within this warmth [of her friendship for him] – up to a certain limit, and that this self-expression did not attain the relentlessness, even laxity, of those to Lou. This definite, final reserve in the communication is a positive factor able finally to lead to the recovery of self-possession.' (209) Here one has to note that it is just the 'lax', unrestrained, relentless quality of his letters to Lou which led to the full expression of those same 'modern fears' that Buddeberg sees as Rilke's great task.

It is interesting to note that Rilke could write cheerfully to others at the very same time as writing despairingly to Lou. He resumed contact with her in 1903 and wrote of his terrors and feeling of unreality, pleading and begging like a child, looking up from his low place to her in her high one, humble, ignorant and lamenting. He was simultaneously writing his *Briefe an einen jungen Dichter*, in which *he* is the older and wiser person, authoritative, condescending, measured and kind. Be patient, he advises the young poet, accept all that comes; learn to love the questions that bother you; don't torment the people around you with your doubts and joys. This suggests that the outflow of fear in the letters to Lou may have enabled Rilke to preserve the steadiness which he required in his often benevolent and helpful relationships with other people.

APPENDIX C

Lou Andreas-Salomé's influence on Rilke's Work

Lou's influence on Rilke was so prolonged and so manifold that one is inclined merely to repeat what he said to Marie von Thurn und Taxis in 1924: she was 'one of the most wonderful people who have come my way . . . without the influence of this extraordinary woman my whole development would not have been able to take the paths that have led to many things.' But several instances of her influence on his work can be noted.

His many love poems up to at least Autumn 1900 are addressed to her, some explicitly (such as the 'Lieder der Sehnsucht, Gedichtkreis für Lou Andreas-Salomé' and the fifteen or so poems that he sent her in letters, now published as part of the correspondence) and others without name (like the hundred or so poems of *Dir zur Feier*, written in 1897–8). Her influence has been seen in 'Die Weise von Liebe und Tod des Cornets Christoph Rilke'. She greatly influenced the *Stundenbuch* (Book of Hours) which he said was 'hers' and which was dedicated to her: 'laid in the hands of Lou'. Then there are tokens of her in many poems beyond the period of their closest acquaintance. She may have spurred him on to try to master Rodin's method and thus to write his *Neue Gedichte* (New Poems), since after calling her approval of his book on Rodin its 'recognition by reality' Rilke firmly declared that he must learn from Rodin. She was also an indirect helper with the prose of that time: her friendship helped inspire the *Geschichten vom lieben Gott* (Tales of the Dear Lord); her encouragement was vital to his writing the books on Worpswede and on Rodin, both of which were composed with her in mind as their recipient ('read them . . . as you read these letters, for I wrote much in them to you and in the consciousness *that you are*').

Her presence is also discernible in the *Duineser Elegien*, which were written many years after their love relationship and the first intense resumption of their correspondence. On the copy of them that he sent to her he wrote: 'for Lou, who has always possessed it with me – this work now finally formed.' She is diffusely present, for example, in the Third Elegy, as knower of the ancestral sexual terrors, and more centrally there, as the Mother, the comforting (if temporary) barrier against those terrors. Probably, too, something of what she was to him contributed to his conception of the 'Angel', that narcissistically perfected, self-mirroring being, far above his anguished struggle; perhaps also to that of the 'hero', incapable of fear and always in mid-action; and even to the splendid lion in the Fourth Elegy who has never heard of faintness and knows only how to be real. For in this sense Rilke applied, many times, the adjective 'real' to Lou: 'You alone are real', he told her, and once, when she had read and liked his work, he responded (as already quoted above) that this meant it was at last 'recognised by reality'.

The Seventh and Eighth Elegies actually incorporate ideas due to her or shared with her. Certain thoughts expressed in her book *Drei Briefe an einen Knaben* had closely met Rilke's own, and, spelling them out, he wrote to her, on 20 February 1914:

I've understood it beautifully, as it was never presented to me before . . . : the way the creature as it comes into being is set further and further inwards, out of the world and into the inner world. Hence the fascinating situation of the bird, on this path towards the inner; his nest is indeed almost an external womb permitted him by nature . . .

(The bird's special confidence in the outer world lets his song sound in *our* most inward mind and makes the whole world an 'Innenraum' for us.) Rilke reminded Lou of the question he had once asked – 'Whence comes the inwardness of the creature?' – and found he could now answer it, with the help of her book:

From this fact, that it did not mature within a body, which has as consequence that it actually never leaves the protective body . . .

He re-read Lou's *Drei Briefe* many times and he reflected further on them four years later (20 February 1918) when he wished she would write something similar for his present age – with an account of

the death experience that would correspond to that she had given of the love experience; and he wrote yearningly once more of the tiny creatures which feel at home all their life long and 'do nothing but jump for joy in their mother's womb like the little Johannes.' This bird idea reappeared a year later in a piece he wrote straight after his fragment 'Erlebnis', and then, climactically, both bird and gnat reappear in the Elegies – in the opening passage of the Seventh about the voice of the bird, and in these lines in the middle part of the Eighth:

O Seligkeit der kleinen Kreatur
die immer bleibt im Schosse, der sie austrug;
o Glück der Mücke, die noch immen hüpft,
selbst wenn sie Hochzeit hat: denn Schoss ist alles.

More generally, Lou Andreas-Salomé's influence on the early Rilke was a determining one in two main areas – religion and Russia.

The importance of Russia to Rilke – and incidentally of Lou introducing it to him – has been studied by a number of writers in considerable detail. (For example, K. Azadovsky in a number of studies, including 'Russkie vstrechi Ril'ke', 'R. M. Ril'ke i L. N. Tolstoi', 'Ril'ke perevodchik "Slovo'o polku Igoreve"', 'R. M. Ril'ke i A. M. Gorki' (*Russkaya literatura* 1967, no. 4, pp. 185–91); S. Mitchell, 'Rilke and Russia', *Oxford Slavonic Papers*, 1957, vol. 9, pp. 138–45, Marion Böhme, *Rilke und die russische Literatur*. On Rilke's own influence in making Russian art known in the West one should also read Azadovsky's studies, e.g. 'Briefe nach Russland', which show Rilke in 1899–1902 as an active propagandist for Russian culture and single out the artist Malyutin as one who became known in Germany through him.) See Bibliography.

There are several aspects of this worthy of further investigation. One is the visual imagery of Russia in Rilke's work, from landscapes to such particular things as the horse he and Lou saw by the Volga, struggling along with a block of wood tied to its foot, which became the subject of one of the *Sonette an Orpheus*. Another is the conception of God (his friend the painter Heinrich Vogeler noted that 'The underground churches of Kiev fertilised his tendency to mysticism further'). A third is the more general benefit the experience of Russia was to Rilke's development.

Russia certainly meant for him a release into greater creativity and a period of mental peace, it gave him a feeling of home (he shared Lou's home there), and perhaps freed him from the oppressive feeling he had about that other Slav city, his actual home, the alienated and anguished city of Prague (according to H. Politzer in *Modern Language Quarterly*, 1955, vol. 16, part 1, pp. 49–62). His emotional connection with Lou – who was part of Russia for him (and altogether in his love for Russia there was something of love for a woman) – helped him to endure the 'big' without a disabling fear, for he found that in Russia one re-learned all dimensions:

Land is big, water is something big, and big above all is the sky. What I have seen hitherto was only an image of land and river and world. But here is everything itself. (Letter of 31 July 1899)

But this is a wide subject and it must be enough here to quote Rilke's words to Lou Andreas-Salomé in 1903:

That Russia is my home belongs to those great and mysterious certainties from which I live

and his words of seventeen years later when, although he had begun breaking off Russian contacts by the beginning of the 1910s, he still said Russia had 'made me into that which I am – from there I inwardly set out; all the home of my instinct, all my inner origin is *there*!'

In the matter of religion Rilke already sensed a coincidence of ideas before he and Lou met, when he was so struck by the similarity of the ideas in her essay 'Jesus der Jude' to those in his 'Christus-Visionen'. The foolish grey vagrant of Rilke's poem-cycle is not really much like the 'religious genius' of Lou's essay, but there are important affinities. To start with, there is the merely human Christ who undergoes exceptionally intense experience. Then there is the fact that both dwell on the question Jesus puts to God from the Cross and understand it as an expression of extreme loneliness due to loss of faith – not so much of faith that God exists as that He will manifest Himself. There is, further, the sharp distinguishing of Christ from the crowd: Rilke includes an idea, like Lou's, that God has a history and is created by man out of need. Very clearly, there were wide grounds for agreement and kindling of thought between them. Rilke must have read her other essays on religion after this, and there are many points in his later work of probable influence in this sphere.

More largely, Lou's writings on religion influenced Rilke in two ways. One is the emphasis on exceptional and emotional states of yearning for some all-culminating experience, along with the 'Russian' intimacy and tenderness towards 'God' (God as a lonely neighbour, for instance). The other is the conception of God as always in process of growth – thus Rilke's 'We're building you . . .', 'God ripens . . .', 'And your coming contours dawn' – to take examples from *Stundenbuch* I, of which they are characteristic and in which the influence of Lou's religious views is not to be separated from that of her view of Russia.

Book II of the *Stundenbuch* derives less immediately from the relation with LAS, but her ideas, or ideas that they had together, still recur throughout it, especially that of the growing God, the God who is there only for the individual ('Thou *art* not in any union' ['Du *bist* nicht im Verein']). And when Rilke writes of the experience in which the passionate egoism of the one (the 'I') confronts the 'All' (which is 'God') and becomes so confounded that neither pride nor humility makes sense any more, he does it very much as Lou had done (in her 'Realismus in der Religion' and elsewhere):

Bist du denn alles, – ich der Eine,
der sich ergiebt und sich empört?

Bin ich denn nicht das Allgemeine,
bin ich nicht Alles, wenn ich weine,
und du der Eine, der es hört?

Lou Andreas-Salomé influenced the *Stundenbuch* in another way too. There seems to be in it a conjunction of herself with the idea of God, for the devotion to God in these poems is very similar to that addressed to her in letters, diaries and other poems: in the letters, she became something of a divinity; in the poems, God became mixed with her. The clearest example is the poem 'Lösch mir die Augen aus', written first as a love poem and laid on a table for her to find in Wolfratshausen, and later included, with a few changes, in the second book of the *Stundenbuch*, as a prayer to the Deity. Stripped one by one of all powers of perception and relation, the poet says he would still remain a vehicle for the beloved, with his blood: it is as much an act of love as of prayer. (As Buddeberg says (p.32): 'On the one hand it reveals the comprehensive significance of this love-relationship for Rilke; on the other it makes clear the very narrow limits within which the Stundenbuch may be taken as a strictly religious work.') Other poems, addressed to God, contain the same images as are elsewhere used of Lou.

. . . dir war das Nichts wie eine Wunde,
da kühltest du sie mit der Welt . . .

echoes ghastlily the poem he wrote about her years later:

Wie man ein Tuch vor angehäuften Atem,
nein, wie man es an eine Wunde presst . . .

In another the lines

ich geh doch immer auf dich zu
mit meinem ganzen Gehn

recall many such utterances made to Lou, as in the 'Florence Diary' (a prose example):

Du bist nicht ein Ziel für mich, Du bist tausend Ziele
. . . und ich . . . führe Dir alles zu bei meinem Dir-entgegengehn.

And he seems to be speaking straight to Lou when he says, to God:

[ich] sehne mich nach einem Bande,
nach einem einigen Verstande,
der mich wie ein Ding überschaut, –
nach deines Herzens grossen Händen –

So often hands, especially big ones, are frightening for Rilke, yet here they are thought of as moulding, as they also are in his 1913 poem that looks back on their relationship.

Finally, the very melodiousness of these poems, all the heavy, shapely play with vowels, the successful singing mode that is so distinctive of the *Stunden-buch*, may well spring (it is hard to think it does not) from Rilke's enchantment with the Russian language which, with its ubiquitous vowel-endings, is so sensitive to the uses of emotion, poetry and song, and is used so easily and fluently by Drozhzhin; this enchantment was mainly transmitted and encouraged by Lou Andreas-Salomé.

APPENDIX D

Lou Andreas-Salomé on Hauptmann

Among her many writings on drama, Lou Andreas-Salomé's reviews of two plays by Gerhart Hauptmann – *Hanneles Himmelfahrt* (1892) and *Michael Kramer* (1901) – are of some interest for their relation to her developing philosophy and conception of herself. Two kinds of subjectivity important to her prompt these two separate articles. Her delight in *Hannele* is that of someone in whose childhood the most important pastime was an inventive and manipulative daydreaming.

Hannele was generally received as an unexpected move away from Naturalism by the most outstanding Naturalist dramatist and was seen by many as an indulgence in sentiment and falsity. A girl of fourteen, dragged out of the pond where she has thrown herself, lies dying in the paupers' refuge. The play consists of her dreams or hallucinations: her cruel stepfather is dispatched to Hell, her dead mother is combined with the sister of mercy and welcomed in Heaven, there are the black angels of death and the golden angels of bliss, Hannele's schoolmates begging forgiveness for their mockery, and the kind schoolmaster, merged with Christ, to whom she kneels. Herself she sees in a crystal coffin, with radiant robes and music; but then, at the end, she is merely dead, in her pauper's rags. As recently as 1971, Lou Andreas-Salomé's view of the play has been appreciatively quoted: John Osborne (*The Naturalist Drama in Germany*, p.130) writes: 'In her review of the play, Lou Andreas-Salomé stressed the subjective nature of Hannele's dreams: "we encounter here a child of this earth and her earthly longing. If we are prepared to adopt this standpoint, then the 'sentimentality' of the play is no longer a fault, but part of its overall consistency".' That is to say, one should not regard the dreams as some kind of would-be mystical reality but should see them, as LAS does, as a magnifying glass showing what is really there, *in* the girl's mind and life. Thus, Hannele sends herself to Heaven to satisfy her real need for significance, and she reveals a first adolescent eroticism 'in the confounding of her teacher with the Saviour and in the exaltation with which she kneels before this dual figure.' Lou finds in the play a view of religion like her own. She believes religion is nourished solely by human impulse and finds that Hauptmann, too, shows the originating impulse of religion in a 'free-working creative correction and completion of the reality of human life'.

In 1900, after she and Rilke had been sole spectators at the final rehearsal of Hauptmann's new play *Michael Kramer*, both of them wrote about it, he in his diary, she in an article called 'Ein Dank an einen Dichter.' The aspect of Lou's self-awareness that comes out in what she wrote here is that of realising oneself through loss. She concentrates her praise on the artist father's (Kramer's) discovery at the end of the play of a new language that at last expresses his

own personality – he discovers this through the death of his artist son and makes a big speech about how he can now understand, admire and love his son as he could not do before. Lou points to the signs of individuality: his halting repetitions, the gaps in his speech that let in 'air and light and colour', the way all he now says is '*his*', unprecedented. This is what matters, she implies. She adds what is a foretaste of the main theme of her later years: we can all understand the father's unique experience because it comes from that wisdom, that non-intellectual origin of thoughts, that Something, out of which we all live and which at some other level unites us all. 'Yes, it is basically that same piety of soul with which Michael Kramer goes back behind the consciously knowing mind and also behind religion, back to those warm depths from which all life streams into all things.' Her review ends with the thought that the bells interrupting Kramer's speech are a 'call to our souls', either to open up to the immense festival of joy and resurrection, or else to close off from it, and she climactically links this with the Easter bells she heard that year in the Moscow Kremlin which some, she says, listened to joyfully but others turned away from. She seems here to be committed to an idea of conversion. Truth is good and truth is 'bell-hard' and will sound out like a summons. All this may sound emotional, but there *is* a hardness in it, and by 'bell-hard' she means something she has known, something like Heidegger's 'muffled bell' that sounds at least once in each man's life, telling him of how things really *are*; the typical difference is that for Lou it isn't muffled but very loud and from a Russian church.

APPENDIX E

Lou Andreas-Salomé's writings about Russia

Lou Andreas-Salomé took up Russian studies in the year she met Rilke, sixteen years after her emigration from Russia. She had grown up in Russia, spoke Russian, had 'Excellency' in her passport thanks to her belonging to the Russian nobility, and in Germany carried with her an exotic quality – often she was referred to as 'the Russian'. In taking up these studies she was thus going back, at once visitor and native, to the place where everything had begun for her.

In *Ma* she describes how the German heroine is welcomed in a Moscow house, going in from the snow to soothing indoor light, three kisses, soft Russian language, icons in the corner, shining samovar, tiled stove, comfortable disorder, a general trustfulness and 'Russian carefreeness'. This is emphatically Moscow, not Ma's own city, Petersburg. 'In Petersburg one is neither abroad nor in

Russia', whereas Moscow is all piety, pilgrims, homeliness and the simple folk tiptoeing up to paintings in the art galleries in their heavy boots. In *Rodinka*, too, a novel directly about Russia, she depicts herself as both coming from home and coming home. ('Everywhere at home because nowhere completely so,' she once wrote in her diary.)

Two things especially Lou won for herself by her return to Russia: contact with a class the opposite of her own, the Russian people, the 'narod', and an understanding of 'God' which complemented her childhood one. Her Protestant and private God had been hers alone and when she lost Him she thought she was united with the universe in a shared deprivation. The Russian God was ubiquitous, with no need for individual adherence to Him, and her feeling of unity, through the later encounter with Russia, became that of unity through a sharing in the divine presence.

Lou began writing about Russia when that country was starting to matter urgently to many thinking people in Europe. As with so many other things, she was on the stage just as the scenery was being put up. She was now among the earliest exponents of the idea that the Russia people were close to great truths that had been lost by the rest of Europe, an idea which informed the western conception of the 'Russian soul' during two decades of Russia-enthusiasm. Russians were held to be childlike, spontaneous, passive and compassionate. Lou wrote:

> . . . in the simple people the feeling for music and poetry, for plain and melancholy tunes . . . a childlike immediacy between person and person, and . . . that kindness that lets the Russian describe 'criminals' as 'unfortunates' and imbeciles as 'those insulted by God'; a largeheartedness alien to everything trivial, that prefers spending to hoarding, lack of understanding for rules, duty, constancy, legality, responsibility; lack of power to take action except in intoxicated states of ecstasy or fanaticism.
> ('Russische Dichtung und Kultur', Russian Poetry and Culture, p.574)

The West raced ahead, the East waited and endured, the West had gone on and had left behind what the East had preserved. Rilke too wrote that the Russian is essentially a waiting person, 'perhaps so made that he will let the whole of human history go by, in order that he may later drop into the harmony of things with his singing heart'. (Letter to LAS 15 August 1903, *LRBW*, p.112).

(Somewhat contradictorily, the same dichotomy can present the West as old, and the East as young; Lou wrote in her diary of the 'intact youth-soul' of the Russian intelligentsia.)

Lou's articles on Russia (which are all turgidly written and hard to read) fall into two groups: four long pieces written in 1897 and 1898 (which must have affected Rilke), in which years she was relying, with due acknowledgement, on the help of Akim Volynsky, with whom she worked in Wolfratshausen; and a series of later, mostly shorter, pieces which are of less interest (a review of Russian drama in 1909, a review of Tolstoy's correspondence in 1913 and five articles in 1919–21 which for the most part repeat ideas that had been worked out earlier).

Volynsky (real name Akim Lvovich Flekser, born 1863) was one of the early theorists of the Symbolist movement in Russian poetry, a polemicist against the subordination of literature to 'civic' purposes. He earned a lot of hostility and is called by D. S. Mirsky (in his *History of Russian Literature*, p.409) 'a martyr in the cause of emancipation' from the civic view of Literature. It is telling that LAS did not use her acquaintance with Volynsky to find her way into the world of Russian Symbolism, and did not take much interest in the work of poets like Balmont, Bryusov and the Merezhkovskys. The second half of her long article of 1897, 'Russische Dichtung und Kultur', is a survey of Russian criticism avowedly taken straight from Volynsky. Another piece directly inspired by him is her 1898 article 'Russische Philosophie und semitischer Geist', which is about the poverty of Russian philosophy and how Jews (who look at ideas with love and enthusiasm) and not Germans (who take hold of them with conceptual tongs) are best adapted to helping the Russians in this sphere, so that, she concludes, there ought to be more places for Jewish scholars at Russian universities.

The first group of articles was thought of as introducing Russian culture to Germany – not a completely new project: she was writing after Melchior de Vogüé's pioneering book, *Le roman russe* (1886) which was known in Germany; after the introduction of Tolstoy to the German theatre and the first translation of Dostoyevsky's novels into German; and after the appearance of a handful of books on Russian culture. But Merezhkovsky had not yet written his *Tolstoy and Dostoyevsky* (1901), nor Shestov his *Dostoyevsky and Nietzsche* (1903), and the great period of translation from Russian and of enthusiasm for Russian spirituality had not got under way.

Lou has two recurrent themes and one central figure. The figure is that of Tolstoy. One of the themes is 'brotherliness', which she sees, for example, in the Russian preference for love-relationships that recall family ones and in the absence from sexual love in Russia of the exaggerations and tensions that characterise it in Western Europe. The other theme is the Russian God, who is all kindness, simplicity and closeness. Lou liked to quote a sentence from Leskov saying that Russians did not see God as omnipotent: He 'cannot do everything, but when He sees the grief of a child he creeps to him and stays under his left armpit' (Leskov, *On the Edge of the World*; quoted by LAS in 'Der geistliche Russe', The spiritual Russian, and elsewhere).

Lou was little interested in Dostoyevsky. In fact she came to appreciate his work only when, after reading it for years in German translation, she read it in the original for the first time in 1917. (This is recorded in her diary of the time, where she also made some very perceptive notes on *The Idiot*.) But she would never have gone very far in company with contemporary Russia-enthusiasts who set an inaccessibly 'Russian' Dostoyevsky at the centre of their cult, and she would have found excessive Berdyaev's claim that 'the structure of the Russian soul is all its own and quite unlike that of Westerners' (in his book on Dostoyevsky). For all its special qualities, she thought it very accessible to us. Nor did she go anything like as far as Hermann Hesse, for example, who in 1919 welcomed the way Europe, 'old and tired, ready to submerge itself in oriental chaos', was being taken possession of by 'the Russian symbol'. There was nothing pessimistic in Lou's views. She saw the relation of East and West rather as a happy meeting of two extremes, each with much to offer; indeed, in both Rilke's and her own experience she saw examples of this.

The two novelists she wrote most about were Leskov (the most 'Russian' of them all, unfortunately little known in the West, now as then) and Tolstoy, in whom she saw the great conflict between western rationality and eastern religiousness. She has been called (by K. Azadovsky) 'one of the most notable and independent interpreters of Tolstoy in Germany', one of the first to note the melancholy and death-preoccupied aspect of his thought, which she saw as the modern, Western, element in him, while he also had a deeply secure, 'eastern' religiousness. In dragging the Byzantine embellishment off Orthodox Christianity, she believed Tolstoy was getting back not to an original Christianity in particular but to the original religiousness itself, a Russian pre-Christian oneness with God, which merely coincided with aspects of the Gospel.

Her view of Tolstoy was first put in 'Russische Dichtung und Kultur', then expanded in another article the same year: 'Leo Tolstoi unser Zeitgenosse'. Here he is seen as the culmination of the development which started with Pushkin listening to his nurse's folktales, that is of the return to the 'people', not to teach but to learn. Tolstoy's *What is Art?* had just come out and she looks at it in this light, suggesting that we should read it with the imaginative effort we make when reading a novel and follow the author far enough back in his longing for simplicity to see him as a peasant in the field, dreaming of what will answer his peasant needs. Thus she tries to save it for us, to stop us from rejecting this angry and paradoxically art-hating treatise on art by a great artist, by seeing it as the (doubly fictional) product of a character in a Tolstoyan work of fiction. From such a position, she believes, we shall get an enlightening vision of civilisation and see that Tolstoy's hope for total 'religious' union among all people is his Russian way of seeing things. Even if we cannot do this, we can still look at the sheer massiveness of human power in him, which reminds us that art always comes from a *depth* and that the genius, Tolstoy, is 'a poet by God's grace even when he wants to be a thinker'.

As regards her own development, Lou's whole exaltation of Russia and things Russian might be seen as a tacit countering of Nietzsche's cultural

philosophy. The religious and conflict-torn genius of Tolstoy with his striving for humility is implicitly preferred to the godless, self-entire Zarathustra, and a new ideal of the primitive is set up. Her 1894 essay on Islam had promoted Nietzsche's conception of an amoral natural grandeur that preceded the coming of an otherworldly and pitying religion; now she counters this, finding in the Russian peasant a primitive who was pious from the beginning. Had she looked more inquisitively and less expectantly into the Russian past she might have found some natural grandeur there, as well as some thoroughly worldly bestiality, and might have wondered whether the humility of the peasants were not due to their helplessness after the Mongol conquest and centuries of tsarist absolutism. Still, her picture of the pre-civilised soul is scarcely more arbitrary than Nietzsche's. My suggestion that she was setting the Russian peasant against the Superman arises from her essay 'Der geistliche Russe' (1919), which explicitly argues that Russian Christianity contains the *opposite* of the pre-Islam Arabs' sense of the divine, and that the Russians were fitted for Christianity by their native qualities. Where the Arabs had urge to mastery [*Herrschsucht*], the Russians had urge to love [*Liebessucht*]; they neither deified, nor fought against, any original feeling of strength and glory (which they had not had) but started from holiness: earth, criminal, sinner, imbecile, child, congregation – all were holy. And it was of the greatest significance that the Russian church (though often used by the State) did not seek power, but encouraged an equal relation with God, as though with someone living among us 'as if it were only for lack of space that we did not put God up in our private houses'.

APPENDIX F

Lou Andreas-Salomé's writings on Art

Soon after meeting Rilke, Lou Andreas-Salomé wrote an essay ('Grundformen der Kunst,' 1898) on what distinguishes artist from non-artist. There are three main points to be noted in it. First, although she describes the artist in terms suggesting immaturity and a deficiency of some kind, she does not mean to point to any inferiority: the most developed thing is not *ipso facto* the best thing. True, if the artist's 'embryos of sensation don't, so to speak, finish growing, they don't reach clarity about themselves and are not able to be resolved into actions under the practical stimuli of . . . everyday life.' However, instead of this they enter into union with the imagination and 'form a new world of their own'.

Secondly, she stresses that it is not the emotions apparently expressed in the work of art but 'other', darker vibrations underneath them that make it valuable.

Thirdly, her guiding thought throughout is that we, too, we non-artists, are capable of feelings and 'vibrations' equivalent to the artist's – only that we don't go ahead and turn them into 'works'. 'It is only through our relation to them that things, *all* things, become the world they are for us': ordinary feelings sustain an ordinary world, extraordinary ones an extraordinary world, and the artist merely does, in his special way, what the rest of us are also doing.

The important distinction is not between artist and non-artist but between the ordinary and the extra-ordinary in experience altogether. 'Being an artist is only a form of being human . . . and all art is, finally, only one of the hidden little paths which lead from the sanctuary of the human upward to its Hallelujah . . .'

It is possible that LAS has in mind here something very interesting about the nature of perception, such as that the kind of forming which percepts undergo in the process of being collected into a single image for recognition and for retention in the memory is the same as that which, more deliberately, the diverse elements of an artistic image are subjected to in the mind of the artist. But, as usual, she does not present any examples or elucidations of her general thesis and the argument remains almost unusably abstract and unfocused.

There are echoes of Nietzsche here. The dark vibrations beneath the poem's subject-matter recall his explanation of the Dionysian lyricist in *The Birth of Tragedy*. 'Little paths' [*Weglein*] seems an echo from one of Nietzsche's letters to Lou – the letter of 16 September 1882, where he proposes a *Weglein* on which the two of them might together reach immortality. But in all her writings on art Lou is really writing about Rilke. His artistry, and at the same time his humanity, were there in her life, in him the transition from uncreative to creative was enacted again and again before her eyes, his experience prompted her to think about these things; and her closeness to him is expressed in these theories – in their lack of envy, their certainty that poet and non-poet share one cosmos, their consistent rejoicing.

In a short article called 'Erleben' ('Experiencing', 1899), the kinship of the ordinary (but deep-feeling) person to the artist is spelt out more centrally, and the suggestion is made that life can be consciously lived as if it were art, or the stuff of art, with the only difference that its ecstasies and patternings do not obtain permanence in verse or paint (it is doubtful if she ever thought of music). We can all, she repeats, have moments of intense feeling, and, like the artist, 'in such moments we are not greedy for the happiness or fearful of the pain that must be mingled with them, but we are obedient to the one single urge: to bring our work to maturity'.

Subsequently Lou wrote many pieces about art – more than fifty if we count, along with essays and books, her reviews of works published or performed – but most of these are best read under the headings of Religion, Psychology, Russia or Woman. She was never concerned with what the formalists have called the 'literariness' of a work of literature.

That she did not draw on her own creative experience indicates an appropriate modesty and reflects her view that her own writing was not 'art' but part of her 'life'. But then art, she said, *is* only life. Perhaps the most frequent phrase in her utterances on this subject is 'nothing but'. 'Art is nothing but life-content.' 'In the last analysis all poetry, both as productivity and as enjoyment, is nothing but an enormous participation in someone else's existence.' She relates art to the rest of life, showing that there is just a small extra element in it; art is like love, *except that* the artist fashions something finished while the lover's act starts up something that continues growing outside him; or – the artist is like the neurotic, *except that* he works his own therapy: 'the creative person, the great man of health, cures himself'.

After studying psychoanalysis, Lou compared genius to insanity: both start with the readiness to take a risk, to lean out over the abyss – except that a tiny margin prevents the genius from falling in, while the madman does fall in. This image fits awkwardly with another she often used later on. The artist, in touch with primal realities [the *Urschoss*] is like the child; if he didn't have to translate this condition into forms, he would live all his life in happy childish play, which would be really preferable (she does seem to suggest, at least at this point), for art would then be a 'guide to blessedness like nothing else on earth'. So the first image says it is a matter of boundless danger; the second, a matter of absolute security. But perhaps she meant three stages: all is risk while the poet waits for the creative moment, rejecting other holding-points for the sake of the one that *might* present itself; if it does, he enters the second, the happily infant-like, condition; a third comes when he spoils the bliss by putting it into words.

This account is similar to that given by many poets – by Alexander Blok, for instance, in his poem 'The Artist' (although Blok there has 'boredom' where Lou has 'risk'), and indeed the conviction that 'life' at its highest, in the supreme moments of feeling and knowing, is superior to – preferable to – 'art', is a chief theme of the Russian Symbolists: they too would rather stay up on high in the wordless experience of merging with the 'world-soul' than descend to the level of language and 'kill' it by expressing it. All the more striking, by comparison, is Lou Andreas-Salomé's contentment with merely knowing, without trying to give perfect expression to what is known. There does seem to have been – as in the case of music – a gap in her actual awareness. She seems blithely, strangely, unaware of what it would mean to get it all finally into words, and probably would not at all have appreciated another Russian Symbolist's (Vyacheslav Ivanov's) remark that 'many go up but few know how to come down'.

APPENDIX G

'HYMN TO LIFE'

The German text of the *'Hymnus an das Leben'*, or *'Lebensgebet'*, written by Lou von Salomé in 1881 or early 1882 and subsequently set to music by Friedrich Nietzsche.

Gewiss, so liebt ein Freund den Freund,
Wie ich Dich liebe, Rätselleben –
Ob ich in Dir gejauchzt, geweint,
Ob Du mir Glück, ob Schmerz gegeben.

Ich liebe Dich samt Deinem Harme;
Und wenn Du mich vernichten musst,
Entreisse ich mich Deinem Arme
Wie Freund sich reisst von Freundesbrust.

Mit ganzer Kraft umfass ich Dich!
Lass Deine Flamme mich entzünden,
Lass noch in Glut des Kampfes mich
Dein Rätsel tiefer nur ergründen.

Jahrtausende zu sein! zu denken!
Schliess mich in beide Arme ein:
Hast Du kein Glück mehr mir zu schenken –
Wohlan – noch hast Du Deine Pein.

NOTES

CHAPTER TWO

Page 15

Resident Germans had been influential in Russian urban life (and especially in education and technological development) since the seventeenth century; Peter the Great (tsar from 1696 to 1725) actively encouraged the immigration of skilled Germans, Swedes and Dutchmen; for a time the eighteenth century court was dominated by Germans; Germans held high positions in education, the Civil Service and the army throughout the nineteenth century.

CHAPTER THREE

Page 32

Malwida von Meysenbug was born in 1816 and spent her youth with her wealthy and distinguished family in Kassel; she sympathised with the 1848 revolutions; at thirty-two she freed herself from her family and went to teach in a girls' school in Hamburg; she read and heard Wagner with enthusiasm, met leading intellectuals, and became a vigorous fighter for women's rights. In time she not only became a friend of Wagner, but also developed close connections with such prominent thinkers as Mazzini, Garibaldi and Gottfried Kinkel (German poet, journalist and revolutionary). In 1852 she was forced to leave Germany. She lived in exile in London, working as tutor and companion to the motherless daughters of the émigré Russian revolutionary journalist Alexander Herzen, whose memoirs she translated into German. When Herzen died, she adopted his daughter Olga. In Paris too she met some of the best known men of her day: Renan, Michelet, Baudelaire and Berlioz. Volume I of her first book, which won her great acclaim, first appeared in French (in 1869) as *Mémoires d'une Idéaliste (entre deux révolutions, 1830–1848)*. All three of its volumes were published in German six years later. Malwida made friends with Nietzsche in Bayreuth in 1872, at the founding of the Wagnerian opera-house. Nietzsche sent her all his works as he wrote them, discussed his plans and anxieties with her, and said he felt a good influence from her 'mellow, harmonious character'. Although she was known as a rebel, there was nothing aggressive about her; her later photographs reveal a serene, attentive face, kind and, in a small way, matronly. In her memoirs, which Nietzsche called health-giving and containing 'something of the highest *caritas*', there are statements like 'I have to believe that the feeling of reverence was innate in me', and she wrote to Lou von Salomé about male-female friendships: 'I consider that the only progress and the only thing worth aspiring to is that people should meet freely and openly in intellectual realms, and should strive, learn and enjoy together, but without that kind of behaviour which provokes playing games with feelings or at the least a kind of momentary excitement, such as used to be common in the past.' (25 May 1882, *Dok*, p111)

Page 33

The London periodical *Mind*, then newly founded, reviewed this work in 1877, noting its 'boldness of thinking' and calling it 'a rather striking specimen of the pessimistic vein of thought now prominent in Germany'.

Whereas Darwin had shown that – far from being created once for all by a Divine Being – human bodies, characters and habits came about in a long process of development, so that everything 'higher' is a product of continuous evolution from something 'lower', Rée set out to demonstrate something similar in the realm of morality. Where do ideas of 'good' and 'bad' come from? They have no ultimate sanction but have developed, through time, from such base things as advantage and disadvantage. Rée also spends a lot of space arguing, pleasantly, that there is no free will. Everything has *had* to be exactly as it has been. No less than is a stone or a donkey, a man and every one of his actions are subject to the law of causality. Consequently guilt and merit are unreal notions. Nor is there mystery anywhere, nor any 'other' way of seeing things. He does not actually prove the absence of freedom, but expounds it as something self-evident to the clear mind. He sums it up in a later work called *The Illusion of Free Will* (1885): 'That I am sitting in this place at this moment, holding my pen in just this way and writing that every thought is necessary, is necessary; and if the reader holds the opinion that this is not so, that thoughts ought not to be regarded as effects, then it is equally necessary that he should hold this false opinion'.

Page 34

Nietzsche's and Rée's letters to each other were full of affection. 'How gladly, gladly, would I fly to you', Rée could write, and when Nietzsche sent him Part 2 of *Human All Too Human* he was 'quite beside myself with delight and I immediately flung myself on it like a hungry animal'. Although he sent sober and perspicacious appraisals of his friend's new works, his feeling for Nietzsche the man was nearly always rapturous in those years. The friendship seems to have been a great release for him: at last he had someone to whom he could tell everything, with whom rules could be broken and politeness neglected. There was great affection in Nietzsche's letters too. He sent Rée advice, information, notes of others' good opinions of Rée's work, and of his own feelings. He too, used strong imagery: 'Whenever I hear of your studies, my mouth waters for your company' (see their correspondence in *Dok.*, pp9–90).

Page 35

It appears from Rée's letter to Nietzsche of 20 April 1882 that this was Lou's idea, or at least her desire. That it was so is also clear from Malwida von Meysenbug's letter to her of 6 June 1882. When Lou writes in *Looking Back* (fifty years later) that Nietzsche, hearing of the plan she and Rée had made to share a home, 'unexpectedly' made himself the third in their group, she had either forgotten the circumstances or else she meant that Nietzsche's making himself the third was both desired by her *and* (as he seemed to have been going in an opposite direction) unexpected.

Page 36

See especially *The Gay Science*, §276, which runs: '*At the New Year.* – I still live, I still think: I must still live, for I must still think. *Sum, ergo cogito: cogito, ergo sum.* Today everyone allows himself to express his wish and dearest thought: well, so I too will say what I would wish myself as a gift from myself and what thought first ran across my heart this year; what thought is to be the ground, guarantee and sweetness of all my further life! I want to learn more and more to see the necessity of things as their beauty: – thus I shall be One of Those who make things beautiful. *Amor fati*: let this henceforth be my love! I do not want to make war against the ugly. I do not want to accuse, I don't even want to accuse the accusers. May *looking away* be my sole denial! And, all in all: I want to be some day nothing else but a yea-sayer!'

With regard to Nietzsche's probable influence on Lou, it is worth noting some other ideas in *The Gay Science*. He has discovered, he says, the 'liberating' thought that life can take the form of an experiment by the one who gains knowledge '('ein Experiment des Erkennenden') (§324) and this thought cheers him absolutely. Laughing, he scorns those who

assume that intellectual work has to be solemn. This gaiety of Nietzsche's is of course linked with pain, including the pain of knowing that this world and this life (eternally repeated) are all our doing and all there is. People shall be judged according as they accept the infinite insecurity of this insight. There is also a powerful optimism in Nietzsche's assertion that those who think *do* more than those who act: 'We first created the world *which concerns human beings!*' (§301) The life of the mind is full, rich, all-encompassing, sufficient for the whole life, if lived by one who constantly overcomes himself in order to become himself. *The Gay Science* abounds in injunctions: don't seek comfort, don't value stability, value the vita contemplativa, don't yield to pity, 'live dangerously'. It foresees and describes the very moods that the Superman, Superphilosopher, will feel: 'a continual movement between high and deep, and the feeling of high and deep, a continual As-if-climbing-stairs and, simultaneously, As-if-resting-on-clouds' (§288).

Page 39

'Peter Gast' was the *nom-de-plume* taken at Nietzsche's suggestion by Heinrich Köselitz (1854–1918), a musician who went to Basel in 1875–6 to hear Nietzsche's lectures, and later became his indispensable friend, secretary and helper in many ways. He orchestrated Nietzsche's setting of Lou's 'Hymn to Life'. He admired Lou at the time of her participation in Nietzsche's life, but later made disparaging remarks. In 1897, for example, he said of her in a letter: 'To have lived for a while close to Nietzsche and, instead of becoming kindled, to be only an observer and cold registering machine, that's really something'. (Quoted by Pfeiffer, Dok., p371). After Nietzsche became insane, Gast worked closely with Elisabeth Förster-Nietzsche on her brother's archive.

Page 43

Heinrich von Stein (1857–1887) had written his first book, *The Ideals of Materialism*, a work of 'lyrical philosophy', at the age of twenty. He was one of those who lectured to Malwida von Meysenbug's circle in Rome and he became something of a protégé of hers; she sent him to Bayreuth and there he became the tutor of Wagner's son Siegfried. Rée discovered Stein in 1876 and praised him to Nietzsche as a youth 'with a soul of fire, a noble appearance, shining eyes and a profound receptivity for everything great in every genre, especially music!' This 'model of splendour' (*Dok.*, p13) took a different philosophical path from Rée's: what set him thinking, he explained to Rée in 1881 in a noble and exquisitely near-static style which shows up the virtues of Rée's own quick unpretentious writing, was the 'ideal meaning of mind' ('die ideelle Gemüts-Bedeutung') by contrast with which everything external was 'a worthless game'. How vain was the endless alternation of fates in the world with baseness always winning, how tragic and glorious the transient apparitions of the great heroes!

Clearly, parody him though he (unwittingly) might, Stein felt himself to be with Nietzsche, and in fact his letter (28 October 1881) proceeds to explain that as an artist Nietzsche *had* to go through a sceptical phase, which would not last: he could never fall away from the 'grace' he had once been in (*Dok.*, pp86–8).

Page 44

In Book 4 of *The Gay Science* (before meeting Lou) Nietzsche had written: 'I want to have my lion and eagle near me so that I shall always have hints and omens that help me to know how great or small my strength is ...'. W. Kaufmann writes (in the Vintage Books edition of *The Gay Science*, 1974, page 50) that 'Lion and eagle never turn up again as a pair' in anything Nietzsche wrote. They do, then, *only* in this description of Lou von Salomé.

Page 47

Lou did not, apparently, read the essay on Schopenhauer. She had undoubtedly read parts of *Human All Too Human* with Rée, she was reading *Dawn* during the months of her acquaintance with Nietzsche, and she certainly knew much of *The Gay Science* – Nietzsche had just finished writing this book when he met her (he received the publisher's proofs of it with the same post – on July 2nd – as her letter of agreement to visit him in Tautenburg). In fact she records that it was the only work of his she had read at the time of Tautenburg, and he must certainly have urged her to read the fourth section, 'Sanctus Januarius', of which he said: 'There stands in sum my private morality, as the sum of *my* conditions of existence' (to Rée, *c.* 1 September 1882, *Dok.*, p224).

CHAPTER FOUR

[*N.B.* For much of the notes to this chapter given below, especially those on lesser-known persons, I am greatly indebted to Pfeiffer's notes to *LRB*]

Page 59

Besides Haller, the philosophers in the group were Heinrich von Stein and two friends of Nietzsche and Rée from an earlier period: Paul Deussen and Heinrich Romundt. Deussen, who had known Nietzsche from his schooldays and who must have been very attached to Lou, as he wrote in December 1884 that upon reading her book *Struggling for God* 'my love for Lou flared up in bright flames' (quoted by Pfeiffer in notes to *LRB*, p249), was a Schopenhauerian interpreter of Indian holy scripts; his *Elements of Metaphysics* was finished in 1877 and *System of the Vedanta* in 1883. Romundt, who had originally introduced Nietzsche and Rée to each other, was a Kantian scholar who had published *Human Knowledge and the Essence of Things* in 1872 and a series of works on Kant including *The Establishing of the Teaching of Jesus through Kant's Reform of Philosophy*, 1883. Heinrich von Stein's *Ideals of Materialism* had appeared in 1877. Representatives of less strictly learned professions were the Public Prosecutor, Max Heinemann, whom Lou ceased liking after she learnt that he had been

present at an execution; Hugo Göring, a doctor; Paul Gussfeldt, an explorer; Baron Carl von Schultz; Julius Gildemeister. Other scholars were the historian Hans Delbrück; the philologist W. Halbfass; a Sinologist, Wilhelm Grube; Rudolf Lehmann, an educationist; Georg Runze, a Protestant theologian; Ferdinand Laban, librarian of the Berlin Royal Museums.

Georg Brandes (1842–1927) has been called 'the most eminent Scandinavian critic of his time' and 'a true cosmopolitan'; Nietzsche called him 'a good European' and missionary of culture. He was at that time writing his six-volume work *Main Currents in the Literature of the 19th Century*. He wrote books on Lassalle, Shakespeare, Goethe, Voltaire, Michelangelo, Disraeli and Julius Caesar. Later, in Copenhagen, he was the first ever to lecture on the work of Nietzsche and to try to make Nietzsche known to a wide educated public. His book on Nietzsche is called *An Essay on Aristocratic Radicalism*.

Ferdinand Tönnies (1855–1936) was a man of wide learning: he had studied philosophy, history, classical languages, archaeology, economics and statistics, in five universities, and he took his doctorate in classical philology. He is now best known for his first book *Community and Society*, which is still regarded as 'one of the most influential books in modern sociology' (Cahnmann and Herberle in their introduction to *On Sociology ...*, Chicago, 1971), the first draft of which he had finished two years before meeting Rée and Lou. Tönnies too wrote a book on Nietzsche – *The Nietzsche Cult*, 1897.

Hermann Ebbinghaus (1850–1909), to whom Lou felt intellectually closer than to Rée, was at that time a university lecturer in Berlin (he later taught at Breslau and Halle). He was to become known for his work in experimental psychology, being the first to apply experimental techniques to 'higher-order' processes such as memory. His book, *Über das Gedächtnis*, 1885, was translated into English in 1964 as *Memory*.

Page 64

Andreas had studied at Halle, Erlangen, Göttingen, Leipzig, and again Erlangen; he took his doctorate in 1868. When the Franco-Prussian war began in 1870, Andreas returned from Copenhagen (where he was then pursuing his Iranian studies) and took part in the battle of Le Mans in 1871. After the war he went to Kiel to study Pahlavi but interrupted his studies in 1875 to accompany a Prussian government astronomical expedition to Persia as its epigraphic and archaeological expert; despite getting there too late to join the expedition (and despite misunderstandings with the organisers, which left him without any finance) he then stayed on in Persia for the six years mentioned.

Page 66

Gerhart Hauptmann (1862–1946) brought about the emergence of literary 'Naturalism' in Germany with his social drama *Before Sunrise*, first performed on 20 October 1889 by the Freie Bühne. Arne Garborg, who came to Germany in 1890, was one of the most important Norwegian writers of the time. Hulda Garborg translated LAS's book on Ibsen into Danish (1893). Bruno Wille founded in 1890 the 'Freie Volksbühne' which was to give workers a relationship to the arts; he was author of novels which enjoyed considerable fame in their time. Wilhelm Bölsche (1861–1939) published *The Scientific Foundations of Poetry* in 1887; he wrote novels and he was for three years editor of the periodical *Die Freie Bühne*. Heinrich and Julius Hart, who were critics and poets, were prominent theorists of Naturalism for a number of years. Ola Hansson-Marholm, who lived in Friedrichshagen from 1889 to 1900, was writer and spokesman for Danish poets; he wrote a study of Nietzsche in 1890. His wife, Laura Marholm, wrote plays and novellas. August Strindberg, the already famous playwright (1849–1912), had come from Switzerland to Friedrichshagen when LAS got to know him in 1892; two years later he went to Paris. Max Halbe had great success with his play *Youth* in 1893. Arno Holz was a significant Naturalist dramatist and his play *The Selicke Family*, 1890, is often regarded as a model of Naturalism. Walter Leistikow was an artist especially known for his pictures of the Grunewald landscape. John Henry Mackay, who was of Scottish origin but lived in Berlin from 1898, was an 'individualistic anarchist' and wrote a novel *The Anarchists*, 1891, arguing his views. Richard Dehmel, poet, was bringing out his first collections of poems at that time – 1891 and 1893.

Fritz Mauthner (1849–1923) was a co-founder of the *Freie Bühne* periodical; he called himself a 'godless mystic' and published in 1901–2 his *Contributions to a Critique of Language*. Maximilian Harden was first an actor, then founder of the important periodical *Die Zukunft* in 1892; he wrote disguised attacks on the Kaiser and court society. Otto Erich Hartleben was a prominent playwright. Eugen Kühnemann, literary historian, wrote *The Life of Herder* (1895), which he told LAS was 'her book'. Otto Brahm was at first a critic and literary historian; from 1889 he was president of the Verein Freie Bühne and first editor of the periodical; from 1894 he took over the Deutsches Theater, which grew out of the Freie Bühne.

Max Reinhardt (1873–1943) was Director of the Deutsches Theater after Otto Brahm and, in 1906, founder of the smaller theatrical group, the 'Kammerspiele'.

Page 67

Ledebour was elected to the Reichstag in 1900 (until 1918 and again 1920–24). For a quarter of a century he was known as one of its best men, becoming Germany's leading socialist expert on foreign policy. He excelled both in debates and in popular speeches, had enemies among his colleagues and was much loved by the workers. He was particularly brilliant in defending himself in a treason trial brought against him in 1919. For forty years Ledebour was in the forefront of major political debate. He was one of the

founders of the Independent Social Democratic Party which separated from the S.P.D. (on the issue of peace) in the First World War but rejected union with the Communist Party. In 1924 he founded the Pacifist Socialist Union. When Hitler came to power he emigrated to Switzerland. He died in 1947.

Page 69

An article by Johannes Schlaf entitled 'Prudery' rather cheerfully invoked 'Dionysian man' as a salvation from constrictive prejudices of the present, and there were many articles welcoming the 'new morality', including its division of people into masters and slaves, and stressing how the *Übermensch* accords with modern science. There were also articles sharply opposing all this – e.g. by the socialist Paul Ernst.

Page 72

Frank Wedekind (1864–1918), became famous for his play *Spring Awakening*, 1891, with its forthright demonstration of the need for the sexual enlightenment of schoolchildren. The play was written in Munich; shortly afterwards Wedekind went to live in Paris. The misunderstanding, which Lou dealt with (as Pfeiffer relates, *LRB*, p258) by saying 'The fault is mine, Mr W., for I have never met an indecent man before', was depicted by her in the novel *Fenitschka*. It seems that Wedekind visited Lou the next day wearing his best clothes and with an apology; Pfeiffer showed me a card from Wedekind to Lou with the words '*Ich muss die Demütigung über mich ergehen lassen*' ('I must submit to the mortification'). They became good friends after this, and for a time worked on a drama together, which Lou later finished alone (this work is lost).

Page 73

In a letter of 15 May 1895 Hofmannsthal told Beer-Hofmann that he was hoping for a lasting and pleasant relationship with 'Frau Andreas-Salomé' and that he valued her opinion of his work since she was someone accustomed to a remarkable intellectual and moral atmosphere and would judge from within it. Beer-Hofmann wrote back on 22 May that 'Frau Lou' was still in Vienna and spending many hours each day with them. He went on to say that she seemed to be 'very fond of us – i.e. Arthur [Schnitzler] and you and me – and I think we signify something in her life to her or are a symbol for something, we can't know for what. She is becoming fond of many things in Vienna – for our sake – but she feels that a lot of it is especially ours, whereas it is only Vienna itself. She calls us "lucky people" and means we're also lucky because we love the town we live in and because it is the town we were born in, and because we have one another.' He told Hofmannsthal he had given her his (Hofmannsthal's) works: 'The Fool and Death', 'Gestures', the d'Annunzio pamphlet, and some poems; that she liked and respected Gerhart Hauptmann but 'feels we are "richer"'. He also wrote that her 'eyes and laughter are so young that we only recently discovered how much younger we feel her to be now than at the beginning'. This communal friendship continued through the summer. In August, Hofmannsthal was glad to hear that Schnitzler was in the company of Richard Goldmann and Lou, for 'Goldmann, who lives in journalism, and has protected himself so completely from all mesquinerie, and Frau Dr Salomé are altogether the right atmosphere for believing in the idea of the youth of the soul' (Letter to Schnitzler, 21 August 1895). Olga Schnitzler wrote in her memoir, *Richard Beer-Hofmann*, how 'Lou Salomé, the friend of Nietzsche', was fascinated by the three young poets: 'She admires Loris [Hofmannsthal] most, she said; she found Schnitzler the most interesting and would like to be like him; but she is fondest of Beer-Hofmann'. In relation to this it is interesting to see how this memoirist goes on to sum up each of the three: Hofmannsthal is interpreter of the world in its 'magic mirror' of art, Schnitzler is the one who knows human nature in all its 'errors and sufferings', Beer-Hofmann is herald of the divine-eternal in everything ephemeral. In later years LAS was to meet them all again, most often Schnitzler and Beer-Hofmann.

CHAPTER FIVE

Page 75
Well before Nietzsche's famous announcement, there had been a growing tradition of Bible criticism in nineteenth-century Germany, important moments in which were the publication of David Strauss, *The Life of Jesus*, 1835–6, and Ludwig Feuerbach, *The Essence of Christianity*, 1853. In England Charles Hennell, who had not read Strauss, published his *Inquiry Concerning the Origin of Christianity* in 1838 (an important influence on George Eliot), but the mainstream of Bible criticism remained in Germany, even if it was true, as Strauss said of Hennell, that 'our English author often succeeds in seizing in one quick grasp the essence of problems which the German first approaches with many slow learned formulae'. (Introduction by D. Strauss to the 1840 German translation of Hennell's book.) For some, Strauss' book was the beginning of a demolition of religion, for others (as for Strauss himself) it was not against religion but to demonstrate that, even after the destruction of its foundation upon miracle and the supernatural, religion remains valuable as myth. Feuerbach went further and denied the value of the myths too, saying that Christianity had now lost all meaning for our time, now we realise that it is nothing other than compensatory fantasy.

CHAPTER SIX

Page 87
The eight early articles on drama were the following: a long piece called 'A Dutch Judgment of Modern German Drama', which appeared over six editions in 1891 and reported in detail an article by a Dutch critic, J. Simons, in praise of the 'Freie Bühne' dramatists; a critique of the acting of Eleanora Dusa

in 1892; five theatre reviews; and an essay in 1893 entitled 'Ibsen, Strindberg, Sudermann'. Five years later an article by LAS on 'The Drama of "Young Germany"' appeared, in Russian, in the Petersburg periodical *Severny Vestnik*; in 1901 her essay on Hauptmann's *Michael Kramer* appeared in *Der Lotse* in Hamburg; in later years she wrote several more theatre reviews, and in 1915 and 1919 two pieces on Strindberg.

CHAPTER SEVEN

Page 100
Rilke was born in Prague in 1875, as the only child of Catholic parents who believed they belonged to the oldest aristocracy, and was brought up by his mother after the parents' marriage ended – a coddling upbringing which could hardly have been a worse preparation for the military academy he was subsequently sent to for four unhappy years; he left it in 1891. Receiving a small monthly income from an uncle, he matriculated in 1895, began studies at the Philosophical Faculty of the German University of Prague, and then moved to Munich.

Rilke's collections of poems before he met Lou were *Leben und Lieder* and *Larenopfer*, both 1894; *Traumgekrönt*, 1896; *Advent*, 1897.

Page 108
This Moslim movement which arose in Persia in the 1840s, preached rebirth, scorn for death, the changeless essence of an unknowable God, progress and international brotherhood, a certain amount of equality for women (restrictions on polygamy, abandonment of the veil), kindness to children, the prohibition of smoking and the mystical value of the number 19; Tolstoy found in it quite a lot to agree with.

Page 114
Details of the arrangements made for this visit, including the arrest of a working-class writer, N. A. Lazarev-Temny, for 'unreliability' by the tsarist police (who had searched his house and found a letter from Drozhzhin mentioning an expected visit from 'distinguished foreigners', which the police assumed to be a cover for revolutionary connections) are given in Chertkov, *Rilke in Russland*, pp9–10.

Page 115
One of the people Rilke met in Petersburg was the art critic of the Petersburg German newspaper, Fyodor Ivanovich Groes, and another, through him, was a journalist named Vasily Grigorovich Janchevetsky, who left this account of meeting Rilke: 'Groes introduced me to Rainer Maria Rilke, a God-seeker who had come to Russia; when he heard that I had "wandered all over" Russia, he wanted to make my acquaintance without fail. Rilke held the view that the truth ("pravda") would come from Russia. Laboriously and badly he learnt the Russian language, but tried all the same "to wander over Russia". Rilke spoke of Christ wandering through

Russia as though of something completely real. He had also spoken to Tolstoy of this and Lev Nikolayevich had replied: "What do you think then? If Christ had appeared in one of our villages he would have been jeered into the ground by the hussies ('devki') there!" Rilke read my notes on Russia, translated some of them and took them to Germany to be printed. The conversations I had with him at that time were shattering to me, his speech and his whole personality were so filled with deep mystical power, and his "search for truth" made a big impression on me.' Chertkov, *op. cit.*, p11.

CHAPTER EIGHT

Page 125

Lou's judgment of Rilke's attitude to his body was noted down on several occasions and with changing emphases. In 1913, in her *Freud Journal*, she wrote a number of passages about Rilke, dwelling on the attractive combination in him of vulnerability with maleness. The most interesting is her comparison of him with her friend Poul Bjerre, with whom he had in common, she said, a 'delicate sexual disposition'. Her pathological account (he was a 'sickly aristocrat', a 'typical hysteric') is infused with admiration: unlike Bjerre he had the ability to 'give of himself unrestrainedly' and his 'deficiencies', which were 'directed externally onto the surface of his own person as abuses or weaknesses', were 'no secret to *him*'. He could afford to admit all, since 'the hour of genius extends its grace to him on just such occasions of failure'. In her book on Rilke fourteen years after this, Lou wrote less admiringly about the way the body was for Rilke an agonising problem. She held that in artistic creativity 'the natural maturing of the body finds . . . a dangerous rivalry, it sees its strength claimed by the direction towards work instead of towards the reality of the partner. Assigned to compromise, it yields an all the stronger numbness . . . There are sheer manifestations of aversion which are repressed yearnings for pleasure and thus produce melancholy and hypochondriac over-sensitivities.' Still later, about 1934, Lou wrote a play, *The Hood of Darkness* (*Die Tarnkappe*), in which Rilke (apparently) was represented as a dwarf who could do two magical things – disappear by wearing a hat of darkness and wave a wand that would make people, entranced, tell the truth about their feelings. The dwarf meant an incomplete human being, somewhat absurd, being small and childlike, but this was ambivalently compensated by the ability to work magic.

Page 126

Much later, writing to 'Merline' in 1921, Rilke wrote 'Don't worry, there is no guilt in what has happened to us, it was simply something *too big*', underlining the words 'too big' as if still lightly hearing their horrid echoes. But these words nearly always meant to him something of immediate horror, as in 'the deep anxiety of the over-big towns' (*Stundenbuch* III, 1903), and 'Suddenly I'm as if thrust out/ and

this solitude becomes a thing too big for me' (*Neue Gedichte* I, 1906).

Page 132

At the end of 1911 and beginning of 1912, Rilke gave serious consideration to psychoanalysis as a possible remedy for his trouble. This was just at the time that Lou was becoming involved with it through her friendships with Gebsattel and Bjerre. His decision against it seems to have been closely linked to his relation with her. When he said (28 December 1911, *LRBW*, p240) 'Psychoanalysis is too fundamental a help for me, it helps once and for all, it clears you up and to find myself cleared up one day would perhaps be even more hopeless than this disorder', this was in the midst of his fervent turn back to her. In the same breath he rejected psychoanalysis and begged for her help. Three weeks later he sent on to her Gebsattel's letter to him suggesting he undergo a course of analysis, and explained his own reluctance: 'You can understand that the idea of undergoing an analysis now and then occurs to me; true, what I know of Freud's writings is disagreeable to me and I find some parts of it outrageous; but the matter itself that runs away with him has its genuine and strong aspects and I can imagine that Gebsattel uses it with caution and influence. As for me, I have already written to you that I intuitively shrink from this clearing-up process and, with my character, could scarcely expect anything good from it. Something like a disinfected soul emerges from it, a monstrosity, a living thing that has been corrected in red like a page in a school exercise-book' (20 January 1912, *LRBW*, p250). At the same time he was not sure, he had indeed just asked Gebsattel whether psychoanalysis might be right for him, he admitted that he did have serious problems which perhaps did need this treatment; true, unlike his wife Clara, who was already being analysed by Gebsattel, he saw his own art as 'a kind of self-treatment', but he also realised that someone going in for the immense exaggerations of art needed to rely on a body which did not do likewise ('My physical self runs the risk of becoming the caricature of my mind') and he asked Lou to advise him finally what to decide. She replied with telegram and letter – both lost – advising him against analysis, and, although he had more or less already decided against it himself, he answered her with warmest thanks and now felt clear, with a certainty unusual for him, that analysis would only help him if he had decided not to write any more: only then could he dare, in the driving out of his 'devils', to risk the loss of his 'angels'. If he was right about the effect it would have had on him, we may have to thank this moment (and Lou's part in the making of it) for the existence of the *Duino Elegies* – it was only a month later that he began writing them. This reply of Rilke's is an uncharacteristically happy one. He ends: 'It's wonderful for me, anyway, that you know psychoanalysis so exactly and, on top of that, have seen Gebsattel . . . I shall read your letter many times'. For a full discussion of this subject, see Pfeiffer, 'Rilke und die Psychoanalyse'.

CHAPTER NINE

Page 133
The movement had officially begun in 1865 with the formation of the '*Allgemeiner Frauenverein*'. Milder than similar movements in other countries, it rejected Hedwig Dohm's proposal for a German Woman's suffrage society in 1876 (the British suffrage movement had got going ten years before this). Not until 1894, with the organisation of the '*Bund der deutschen Frauenvereine*', did a more radical movement come into being, and the demand for female suffrage was not raised until 1902. Greater political restrictiveness in Germany had the result that the moderate feminists were very moderate, the radical ones – when they did find themselves – very radical.

Page 135
Much of what happens in us, she says, can be grasped 'if one dreams oneself back into the realm of the smallest organisms, of creatures not yet different-iated as plants or animals.' The word 'dreams' is conspicuous and it is fair to emphasise that Lou Andreas-Salomé was perfectly aware of the dreaming tendency of her science. She was not claiming to be a biologist, and if much of the detail of what she had to say had been proved wrong she would probably have reconstructed the 'dream' from the revised facts.

Page 137
For example, Ruskin, in 'Of Queen's Gardens' (*Sesame and Lilies*, 1864), writes: 'Wherever a true wife comes, this home is always around her. The stars only may be over her head; the glow-worm in the night-cold grass may be the only fire at her foot, but home is yet wherever she is' (quoted by Elaine Showalter, *A Literature of Their Own*, p184).

Page 140
Gertrud Bäumer (1884–1954) was President of the *Bund der deutschen Frauenvereine* 1910–1919 and its guiding spirit for far longer. She regarded woman as belonging in a different sphere from man's 'and one must simply leave it to her to seek out this sphere'. Devotion to house and family could, in her view, be seen as an act of emancipation. Under Bäumer's leadership the BDF mounted a big campaign against the 'New Morality' (see R. Evans, *The Feminist Movement in Germany 1894–1933*, pp153ff).

CHAPTER TEN

Page 148
Ellen Delp was a young actress in Max Reinhardt's theatre company in Berlin when Lou made her acquaintance in 1912. Ellen, who had read Lou's novel *Ruth*, had written her an enthusiastic letter, whereupon Lou, liking the letter, immediately arranged to meet her. She remained Lou's com-panion in Vienna until April 1913 and also went with her to Budapest. In a letter to Lou of 1 August, 1913, Rilke referred to Ellen as 'your "daughter"'

(*LRBW*, p292) and addressed her in a letter as 'Lou's daughter, morning-like Ellen'.

Page 149
Members who customarily attended at that time were, besides Freud: Federn, Ferenczi (when he came from Budapest), Hitschmann, Jekels, Marcus, Nepallek, Rank, Rosenstein, Sacks, Sadger, Silberer, Steiner, Tausk, Weiss, Winterstein. Among the most frequent attenders, Federn, Jekels, Rank, Sadger, Silberer and Tausk were mentioned by Lou Andreas-Salomé as people she talked to. On one evening, 8 January, there were as many as eight guests, with three women among them.

Page 149
The Interpretation of Dreams (1901), *The Psycho-pathology of Everyday Life* (1904), and *Three Essays on Sexuality* (1905).

Page 152
Lou heard Freud lecture on (*inter alia*): the descrip-tive, dynamic and systematic aspects of the Uncon-scious (2 November); dream symbols (16 November); wish-fulfilment in dreams; defiance and anal erotism (30 November) (which gave rise to an interesting commentary by her); therapy of the neuroses and transference (?14 December); then, in the 1913 session: fairy tales (11 January); children's lies – a lecture later printed in his *Complete Works* – (18 January); neurotic types (25 January); the traumas of childhood (8 February), and bisexuality (15 February). In discussion she heard him talk about a multitude of subjects, including sado-masochism, penis-envy, magic – a paper at a Wed-nesday discussion which later became the third part of *Totem and Taboo* – the story of his scientific relations with Fliess, and how he first arrived at the theory of childhood sexuality.

Page 155
Viktor Tausk was born into a Jewish family in Slovakia in 1879, grew up in Serbia, was baptised a Christian in order to marry a Christian (his wife, a distant relative of Martin Buber, later held important posts in the Social-Democratic party), studied law, because medicine was expensive, but did not enjoy practising as a lawyer because of the pressure to help rich criminals evade punishment – in fact it seems he acted instead to help penniless defendants. He left his wife in 1905 and was divorced three years later, but felt so guilty about this that he suffered a serious depressive illness. His discovery of Freud in 1909 was a rescue for him, and he now began the study of medicine – as many did – in order to practise psychoanalysis, finishing his studies in 1914. One work of his subsequently became well known: 'On the Origin of the "Influencing Machine" in Schizo-phrenia', published in 1919.

Page 155
On 12/13 February 1913 (*FJ*, p98) LAS noted, after

a late-night conversation with Freud: 'Freud acts with complete conviction when he proceeds so sharply against Tausk, there is no doubt about that. But along with this "psychoanalytic" circumstance (with regard to Tausk's originally neurotic disposition) it is also clear that any independence around Freud, especially when it is aggressive and shows temperament, worries and wounds him in his egoism as investigator, that is in his noblest egoism.' Another of her talks with Freud about Tausk is briefly recorded in a way that suggests she had some positive influence in this matter: 'Before supper and then again later, Freud talked readily and at length about the whole Tausk problem. At the end he spoke kindly and tenderly' (12 and 14 March 1913, *FJ*, p120).

Page 156
By its title this poem appears close to LAS's main theme, but in content it is little related. Rilke's Narcissus feels the *loss* of his face in the water: 'Nothing binds us enough'. [*Nichts bindet uns genug*]. But LAS did underline three lines in it about the reflected face: '*it could have inwardly arisen perhaps/within a woman; it could not be reached,/however hard I fought into her for it.*'

CHAPTER THIRTEEN

Page 193
Freud's obituary of Lou Andreas-Salomé is wholly laudatory. He wrote:

'I am not saying too much when I acknowledge that we all felt it as an honour when she entered the ranks of our co-workers and co-fighters, and simultaneously as a new weapon for the truth of the analytical teachings. . . . She was of an unusual modesty and discretion. She never spoke of her own poetic and literary productions. She obviously knew where the real values of life are to be sought. Whoever came close to her received the strongest impression of the genuineness and the harmony of her being and could see, to his astonishment, that all feminine, perhaps most human, weaknesses were foreign to her or had been overcome by her in the course of her life. . . . My daughter, who was in her confidence, heard her lament that she had not made the acquaintance of psychoanalysis in her youth. Indeed, at that time it didn't exist.'

Yet one group of sentences, of which each in isolation is a piece of praise, reads quite strangely in sequence. Starting 'She was of an unusual modesty . . .' [*Sie war von ungewöhnlicher Bescheidenheit und Diskretion. Von ihren eigenen poetischen und literarischen Produktionen sprach sie nie. Sie wusste offenbar, wo die wirklichen Lebenswerte zu suchen sind*], sentences one and two together imply the undisplayed great merit of her fiction, while sentences two and three together imply her good sense in realising that it was worthless. Is this a Freudian slip? I suspect it is no lapse, or that if it began as one it then became intentional. He meant both things quite straight: she

was a writer and was modest about it; she knew her work was far from great but it did not matter because she was great in other ways – and anyone who met her could understand this. And yet it remains a strange series of remarks, perhaps not perfectly kind.

CHAPTER FOURTEEN

Page 198
In Chapter Four there was occasion to relate Lou's view of love to that of Socrates; it is interesting to note another coincidence here between her attitude and Socrates': [Socrates is reporting his conversation with Cephalus] 'Some of us old men often meet . . . Most of our company are very sorry for themselves, looking back with regret to the pleasures of their young days, all the delights connected with love affairs and merry-making. They are vexed at being deprived of what seems to them so important; life was good in those days, they think, and now they have no life at all. Some complain that their families have no respect for their years, and make that a reason for harping on all the miseries old age has brought. But to my mind, Socrates, they are laying the blame on the wrong shoulders. If the fault were in old age, so far as that goes, I and all who have ever reached my time of life would have the same experience; but in point of fact, I have met many who felt quite differently. For instance, I remember someone asking Sophocles, the poet, whether he was still capable of enjoying a woman. "Don't talk in that way," he answered, "I am only too glad to be free of all that; it is like escaping from bondage to a raging madman." I thought that a good answer at the time, and I still think so; for certainly a great peace comes when age sets us free from passions of that sort. When they weaken and relax their hold, most certainly it means, as Sophocles said, a release from servitude to many forms of madness.'
I was charmed with these words.
(Plato, *Republic*, Book 1, transl. F. M. Cornford.)

FICTIONAL WRITINGS

Page 216–17
TEUFEL (gähnt):
Langweile, – lange, lange, längste Weile,
Das also heisst hier: Ewigkeitspläsier.
Begierig inspiziert man Frischgestorbne,
Doch kaum sind sie im Höllenpfuhle drin
Kaum sehen sie ihr Feuer vor sich lohen:
Weiss ich bereits, wie's züngelt und wie's leckt,
Wie angstvoll sie sich drehen und verrenken.
Ein Seelenkropzeug! miserabliges!
Unmöglich, sich damit zu amüsieren:-
Dort drüben auch taucht solch Armseelchen auf;
In langem Haar und Mädchenhemd. Die Jauche
Macht ihm beinah sein Schattenfrätzchen blind.
(Stutzt) Doch – streckt es nicht nach mir die Hand
aus –?

ARMSEELCHEN:
> ... *Sterne!*

TEUFEL:
> *Das nenn' ich noch robuste Zuversicht,*
> *An Sterne überm Höllenpfuhl zu glauben!*
> *Recht sehr lebendig scheinst du angelangt ...*

Page 217
> *Nur stark geschwächt von schweren Purgativen*
> *Fast ganz entarscht, lässt er die Sel'gen zu.*

Page 217
> *Was 'untreu' heisst, schwankt selbst der Menschenwelt*
> *Schon zwischen Himmelstrug und Höllenwahrheit.*
> *Sint überdies nicht alle Dinge uns*
> *In Geist und in der Wahrheit heilig-eines?*

Page 218

Although it is wordy and would-be classical, *Der Teufel* can be compared with some of the Expressionist plays of the time in respect of its embrace of the violent and dangerous, in its visual representation of horrors normally kept in the mind, and in its mixing the funny and the serious. Its cinematic sequence may be an imitation of the mode of, say, Kokoschka's *Murderer Hope of Womankind* (splendour of rape, unrestrained cruelty, lopping off of limbs and releasing of primal screams, all absurdly exaggerated) and in the same part of the play there occurs a petrified scream, which may owe something to Edvard Munch's lithograph 'The Scream' and to that kind of contemporary drama that has been called 'scream-drama' [*Schreidrama*] (see J. M. Ritchie, *Seven Expressionist Plays*).

TRANSLATIONS AND ABBREVIATIONS OF TITLES

Aus fremder Seele = From Alien Soul
Eine Ausschweifung = An Aberration
Drei Briefe an einen Knaben = Three Letters to a Boy
Die Erotik = The Erotic
Fenitschka = Fenitschka
Friedrich Nietzsche in seinen Werken = Friedrich Nietzsche in his Works
Das Haus = The House
Henrik Ibsens Frauen-Gestalten = Henrik Ibsen's Female Characters
Im Kampf um Gott = Struggling for God
Im Zwischenland = The Land Between
In der Schule bei Freud = The Freud Journal [FJ]
Lebensrückblick = Looking Back [LRB]
Ma = Ma
Mein Dank an Freud = My Thanks to Freud
Menschenkinder = Children of Man
Rainer Maria Rilke = Rainer Maria Rilke [RMR]
Rodinka = Rodinka
Ruth = Ruth
Die Stunde ohne Gott und andere Kindergeschichten = The Hour Without God and Other Children's Stories
Der Teufel und seine Grossmutter = The Devil and his Grandmother
Friedrich Nietzsche, Paul Rée, Lou von Salomé: Die Dokumente ihrer Begegnung = Friedrich Nietzsche, Paul Rée, Lou von Salomé: The Documents of their Meeting [Dok.]
Rainer Maria Rilke – Lou Andreas-Salomé Briefwechsel = Rainer Maria Rilke – Lou Andreas-Salomé Correspondence [LRBW]
Sigmund Freud – Lou Andreas-Salomé Briefwechsel = Sigmund Freud – Lou Andreas-Salomé Correspondence [LFBW]

References given are to the 1977 edition of *LRB*, the 1975 edition of *LRBW* and the 1910 edition of *Die Erotik*.

REFERENCES

Except where otherwise indicated, unpublished materials referred to are in the possession of Dr E. Pfeiffer

CHAPTER ONE

1   Kurt Wolff, 'Lou Andreas-Salomé', p1191 (in 1963)
2. The phrase used by Ernest Jones in his Freud biography.
3. Reported by Ernst Pfeiffer.
4. J. J. Spector, *The Aesthetics of Freud*, Penguin, 1972, p16.
5   Ernest Jones, *Life and Work of Sigmund Freud*, Penguin, p428.
6   Tautenburg diary of 1882, in *Dokumente* [*Dok.*], p189.
7. Reported by Gertrud Bäumer in *Gestalt und Wandel*, p470.
8. Letter to Peter Gast, 13 July 1882, *Dok.*, p159.
9. Letter to Princess M. von Thurn und Taxis, 19 July 1913, *LRBW*, p568.
10. 'Lou Andreas-Salomé', p.237.
11. In a letter to Pfeiffer, quoted here by kind permission of Miss Freud and of Dr Pfeiffer.
12. 'Ungedeutetes Geheimnis', p55.
13. *Wege mit Rilke*, p55.
14. Letter to LAS, 25 May 1916, *LFBW*, p50.
15. Stanley Leavy, introduction to the *Freud Journal*, p17.
16. E. Brausewetter, 'Lou Andreas-Salomé' in *Meisternovellen deutscher Frauen*, 1898, p14.
17. *Dok.*, p183.
18. Letter to Freud, 18 March 1918, *LFBW*, p105.

CHAPTER TWO

1. *LRB*, p43.
2. Diary 18 January 1904 (unpublished).
3. Letter to Frieda von Bülow, *LRB*, p260.
4. *LRB*, p61.
5. *LRB*, p60.
6. *LRB*, pp49f.
7. *LRB*, p47.
8. *LRB*, pp48f.
9. 'Die Stunde ohne Gott', pp31ff.
10. Letter to Nietzsche, 10 November 1882, *Dok.*, p245.
11. *LRB*, p43.
12. *Freud Journal*, p93.
13. Diary 1917 (unpublished).
14. 'Gottesschöpfung', p169.
15. As autobiography in *LRB* and as fiction in 'Die Stunde ohne Gott'.

16. Diary 21 August 1882, *Dok.*, p188.
17. 'Von frühem Gottesdienst', p466.
18. For example, in 'Das Bündnis Zwischen Tor und Ur', 'Im Spiegel', *LRB*, chapter 1.
19. 'Tor und Ur', pp117f.
20. Diary 1917 (unpublished).
21. *LRB*, p13.
22. 'Im Spiegel'.
23. 'Der Gott' (unpublished), p13
24. *Im Kampf um Gott*, p264
25. *LRB*, pp47f
26. *LRB*, p12
27. *LRB*, p24
28. *LRB*, p43
29. *LRB*, p61
30. *LRB*, p48
31. *LRB*, p62
32. Related by Pfeiffer, *LRB*, p221
33. *LRB*, p28
34. This unpublished letter is here quoted from for the first time, with thanks to Dr Konstantin Azadovsky, of Leningrad. The letter is dated 1/13 May (presumably 1878)
35. *Ruth*, p51
36. *LRB*, p28; and see account by Pfeiffer, *LRB*, p223
37. Quoted; *LRB*, p223
38. Diary of her journey back to Russia in 1900 (unpublished)
39. *Freud Journal*, p69
40. *Ruth*, p177
41. Related by Pfeiffer in *LRB*, pp222–3
42. *LRB*, p29
43. Quoted in full in *LRB*, p32
44. *LRB*, p39
45. *LRB*, p55
46. *LRB*, pp30–31
47. *Ruth*, p215
48. Diary-note of 31 October 1888, *LRB*, p289
49. Letter to Lou von Salomé, 20 September 1881, *Dok.*, p84
50. Letter to Frau von Salomé, 7 July 1883, *Dok.*, p319
51. Quoted in full in *Dok.*, p436
52. *Dok.*, p159
53. 'Der Kampf ist's, der die Grösten gross gemacht,
    Der Kampf um's Ziel, auf unwegsamen Bahnen'
54. *Dok.*, p450; also *LRB*, p40; the German text of this poem is given above as Appendix G
55. 'Herr, schicke was Du willt,/Ein Liebes oder Leides;/Ich bin vergnügt, dass beides/Aus Deinen Händen quillt ...'

56. 'Das Lebend'ge will ich preisen,/Das nach Flammentod sich sehnet.'
57. Peter Gast, 7 November 1882, *Dok.*, p242
58. Ludwig Hüter, 31 March 1883, *Dok.*, pp309–10.
59. An acquaintance in Hamburg, 13 June 1882, *Dok.*, p143
60. Ferdinand Tönnies, 11 July 1883, *Dok.*, pp321–2
61. Franz Schoenberner (a nephew of LAS), *Confessions . . .*, p44

CHAPTER THREE

1. Nietzsche of Lou, *Dok.*, p159
2. Letter to Rilke, 9 November 1903, *LRBW*, pp122–3
3. 14 March 1882, *Dok.*, p96
4. 8 January 1883, *Dok.*, p286
5. 25 May 1882, *Dok.*, p113
6. On 21 August 1882; see *Dok.*, p186
7. Rée, *Psychologische Beobachtungen*, p103
8. See *LRB*, p76
9. 25 May 1882, *Dok.*, p114
10. *LRB*, p231
11. *Dok.*, p210
12. *LRB*, p76
13. *LRB*, p79
14. This letter is printed both in *Dok.*, pp102–3 and *LRB*, pp77–9
15. 21 March 1882, *Dok.*, p100
16. 27 March 1882, *Dok.*, p104
17. 20 April 1882, *Dok.*, p106
18. *LRB*, p80 ('*Von welchen Sternen sind wir uns hier einander zugefallen?*' She also recorded the words in a slightly different recollected form: '*Von welchen Sternen gefallen sind wir uns hier einander zugeführt worden?*' *Dok.*, p108)
19. LAS, *Friedrich Nietzsche . . .*, p12
20. 2 July 1882, *Dok.*, p155
21. 19 or 20 July 1882, *Dok.*, p161
22. LAS, *Friedrich Nietzsche . . .*, p222
23 Quoted by LAS in diary 14 August 1882, *Dok.*, p183
24. Bernoulli, *Overbeck und Nietzsche*, p336
25. See LAS, *Friedrich Nietzsche . . .*, p87
26. 10 November 1882, *Dok.*, p244
27. Letter to F. Tönnies, 7 December 1904, quoted by Pfeiffer in *LRB*, p231
28. 17 or 18 August 1882, *Dok.*, p219
29. 7 June 1882, *Dok.*, p135
30. 4 June 1882, *Dok.*, p130
31. 18 June 1882, *Dok.*, p147
32. 13 July 1882, *Dok.*, p159
33. 26 June 1882, *Dok.*, p152
34. 13 July 1882, *Dok.*, p159
35. To Ida Overbeck, Whitsun 1882, *Dok.*, p126
36. To Rée, 29 May 1882, *Dok.*, p128
37. ('Stibber Nestbuch'), *Dok.*, p200
38. 2 July 1882, *Dok.*, p154
39. 2 August 1882, *Dok.*, p170
40. 29 January 1883, *Dok.*, p294
41. 13 July 1882, *Dok.*, p159
42. 4 August 1882, *Dok.*, p174
43. 4 August 1882, *Dok.*, p175
44. *LRB*, p240
45. Elisabeth N. to Clara Gelzer, September–October 1882, *Dok.*, p254
46. Nietzsche to Overbeck, mid-September 1882, *Dok.*, p229
47. 24 September 1882, *Dok.*, p254 (etc.)
48. Nietzsche to Gast, 20 August 1882, in *Nietz-sches Briefe an Peter Gast*, Leipzig 1924, pp94–5; see also Nietzsche's letter to Lou, December 1882, *Dok.*, p263
49. Quoted by LAS in diary 14 August 1882, *Dok.*, p183
50. Diary 14 August 1882, *Dok.*, p182
51. Mid-September 1882, *Dok.*, p229
52. Letter to Overbeck, mid-September 1882, in *Dok.*, p229
53. Letter to Lou, 16 September 1882, *Dok.*, p231
54. *Im Kampf um Gott*, p108
55. For example, in *Die Erotik*, p9
56. *Sämtliche Werke*, vol. 10 (1980), p37, *Dok.*, p211
57. Reported by Elisabeth in a letter to C. Gelzer, September–October 1882, *Dok.*, p252
58. *Overbeck und Nietzsche*, p352
59. Brann, *Nietzsche und die Frauen*, chapters 1 and 7
60. To Gast, 13 July 1882, *Dok.*, p159
61. To C. Gelzer, September–October 1882, *Dok.*, p258
62. Diary 18 August 1882, *Dok.*, p184
63. *Sämtliche Werke*, vol. 10, 'Tautenburger Aufzeichnungen', *passim*
64. Letter to C. Gelzer, September–October 1882, *Dok.*, p255
65. Diary 18 August 1882, *Dok.*, p185
66. *Ibid*
67. *LRB*, p25
68. 13 July 1882, *Dok.*, pp159–60
69. Reported by Lou, diary 18 August 1882, *Dok.*, p185
70. Reported by Lou, diary 14 August 1882, *Dok.*, p182
71. *Sämtliche Werke*, vol. 10, pp38–9, *Dok.*, pp212–13
72. *Dok.*, pp190–211
73. *Sämtliche Werke*, vol. 10, pp41–2; *Dok.*, pp215–16
74. Diary 21 August 1882, *Dok.*, pp186–8
75. *Dok.*, p189
76. *Dok.*, p190
77. *Dok.*, pp200, 202 (Stibbe Nest-Book)
78. Letter to Lou, 16 September 1882, *Dok.*, p231
79. Nietzsche to H. Romundt, October–November 1882, *Dok.*, p240
80. To Overbeck, November 1882, *Dok.*, p246
81. End of November 1882, *Dok.*, p259
82. *Sämtliche Werke*, vol. 10, p24
83. *Dok.*, pp262–3
84. To Overbeck at the end of 1883, *Dok.*, p349
85. End of November 1882, *Dok.*, pp261–2
86. *Dok.*, pp281–2
87. Draft of letter to Rée's brother Georg, July 1883, *Dok.*, p325
88 *Dok.*, p293
89. To Ida Overbeck, mid-August 1883, *Dok.*, p338
90. From draft of letter to Elisabeth, probably January 1884, *Dok.*, p351
91. Letter to Overbeck, 7 April 1884, *Dok.*, p355
92. *Dok.*, p353–4
93. Letter to H. v. Stein, 15 October 1885, *Dok.*, p362
94. *Sämtliche Werke*, vol. 6, p336
95. *Dok.*, p224
96. *Sämtliche Werke*, vol. 4, pp143–4
97. Letter to Peter Gast, late August 1883, *Nietz-sches Briefe an Peter Gast*, pp136–7
98. *Das Leben Nietzsches*, 1904; *Der Einsame*

Nietzsche, 1915; *Nietzsche und die Frauen*, 1935
99. *LFBW*, p216
100. See Gertrud Bäumer, 'Lou Andreas-Salomé' in *Gestalt und Wandel*, p470
101. See *Die Fröhliche Wissenschaft*, §290
102. *Die Fröhliche Wissenschaft*, §295
103. 'Von der schenkenden Tugend' in *Also sprach Zarathustra* (my italics)
104. *Jenseits von Gut und Böse*, §260

CHAPTER FOUR

1. Words in which LAS summed up her attitude to life, as reported by Pfeiffer
2. *Psychologische Beobachtungen*, p68
3. *LRB*, p88
4. Letter of Tönnies to Paulsen in July 1883 (see F. Tönnies, F. Paulsen, *Briefwechsel*, where LAS is mentioned, pp185f and 190)
5. *LRB*, p86
6. *LRB*, pp88–91
7. See the account by Pfeiffer, *LRB*, p254
8. *LRB*, p255
9. *LRB*, p93
10. *LRB*, p199, and see Pfeiffer's comment p290
11. *LRB*, pp202–3
12. 31 October 1888. This diary note is given by Pfeiffer in the Notes to *LRB*, pp287–9
13. *LRB*, p200
14. *LRB*, p202
15. Diary note of 1888, *LRB*, p288
16. In 'Neue Frauentypen'. The following quotations are from pp621 and 632
17. *LRB*, p205
18. 'Das Leibfremde', *LRB*, p201
19. *LRB*, p201
20. *LRB*, p197
21. *LRB*, p191
22. *LRB*, p192
23. *LRB*, p193
24. *LRB*, p203
25. *LRB*, pp193–4
26. *LRB*, p205
27. *LRB*, p206
28. *LRB*, p207
29. *Das Haus*
30. Rilke to Lou, 26 June 1905, *LRBW*, p207
31. *LRB*, p96
32. Anna Siemsen in *Georg Ledebour*, p8
33. *LRB*, p208
34. *LRB*, p98
35. Janz, *Friedrich Nietzsche*, Vol. 2, p116
36. *Ibid.*
37. 'Der Mensch als Weib', p225
38. Phrase taken from Roy Pascal, *From Naturalism to Expressionism*
39. From 'Bekanntmachung an das kunstliebende Publikum Berlins', 1890
40. In 1894 it changed its name to *Die neue deutsche Rundschau*, and in 1904 to *Die neue Rundschau*, as which it still appears
41. 'Zum Beginn', p1 of first issue of *Die Freie Bühne* in 1890
42. *Ibid.*, p5
43. Bölsche, *Die naturwissenschaftlichen Grundlagen der Poesie*, p3
44. 'Das Ende der Religion', *Die Freie Bühne*, 1891, p11
45. *Das Liebesleben in der Natur*, 1898–1901
46. For example, in *Introductory Lectures on Psycho-analysis*, lecture 22

47. ('In dem Urbazillus steckt schon der Mensch') *Liebesleben . . .*, p103
48. *Naturwissenschaftliche Grundlagen . . .*, p45
49. *LRB*, pp98–9
50. L. Chertkov, p5
51. *LRB*, p106
52. *Jahrhundertwende*, p32
53. *LRB*, p110
54. This follows the interpretation given by Pfeiffer

CHAPTER FIVE

1. *Jenseits von Gut und Böse*, §212
2. Remarks made in 1859 and 1862, quoted by Basil Willey in *Nineteenth Century Studies*, 1949
3. 'Jesus der Jude', pp342–3
4. Kerényi, *Umgang mit Göttlichem*, p19
5. In *Das Heilige*
6. 'Realismus in der Religion', p1028
7. *Ibid.*
8. *Ibid.*, p1029
9. *Ibid.*, p1058
10. In Part II, 'Von den Tugendhaften'
11. *Op. cit.*, p1082
12. Adolf Harnack, *Das Apostolische Glaubensbekenntnis* (44pp), Berlin, 1892
13. 'Jesus der Jude', p347
14. *Ibid.*, p350
15. *Ibid.*, p351
16. 'Religion und Cultur', pp5 and 6
17. *Die fröhliche Wissenschaft*, §125
18. 'Aus der Geschichte Gottes', p1215
19. 'Lines composed above Tintern Abbey'
20. 'Vom religiösen Affekt', p149
21. *Ibid.*, p154
22. *Nutzen und Nachteil der Historie*, p91
23. 'Vom religiösen Affekt', p154
24. *Ibid*, p152
25. *Op. cit.*, p6
26. Russian Diary, 1900 (unpublished)
27. *The Varieties of Religious Experience*, lectures 4 and 5
28. *In der Schule bei Freud*, p69; *Freud Journal*, p75
29. *Ethics*, Part III

CHAPTER SIX

1. *Menschliches-Allzumenschliches*, I, §513
2. 'Die Wildente' in *Die Freie Bühne*, 1890, pp849–52 and 873–5
3. *Henrik Ibsens Frauen-Gestalten*, p86
4. *Ibid.*, p41
5. *Ibid.*, pp46–7
6. *Ibid.*, p212
7. Bölsche, 'Sechs Kapitel Psychologie nach Ibsen', *Die Freie Bühne*, 1891, vol. 2, pp1272–4
8. Mauthner, 'Henrik Ibsens Frauen-Gestalten', *Das Magazin für Litteratur*, February 1892, p135
9. Löwith, *Nietzsches Philosophie der Ewigen Wiederkehr*, p200
10. Hillebrand, *Nietzsche-Rezeption in Deutschland*, p114
11. Of *c.* 16 September 1882, *Dok.*, p231
12. *F.N. in seinen Werken*, p4
13. *Ibid.*, p17
14. Letter of Rohde to Overbeck, 13 March 1891, quoted in Bernoulli, *Overbeck und Nietzsche*, p390
15. *F.N. in seinen Werken*, p42

16. *Ibid.*, pp42–3
17. *Ibid.*, p42
18. *Ibid.*, p169
19 *Ibid.*, p118
20. *Ibid.*, p169
21. *Ibid.*,
22. *Ibid.*, p146
23. *Ibid.*, p193
24. *Ibid.*, pp205–6
25. *Ibid.*, pp262–3
26. *Zarathustra* I, 'Vom Lesen und Schreiben'
27. *F.N. in seinen Werken*, p7
28. *Jenseits von Gut und Böse*, §9
29. Tönnies in *Die Philosophie der Gegenwart in Selbstdarstellungen*, p214
30. *LRB*, pp90, 91
31. W. Bölsche, 'Das Geheimnis Friedrich Nietzsches'
32. H. Albert in the *Mercure de France*, February 1893, quoted in Bernoulli, *Overbeck und Nietzsche*, p389
33. Bernoulli, *ibid.*
34. According to Bernoulli
35. 'Noch einmal Friedrich Nietzsche und Frau Lou Andreas-Salomé'
36. Bernoulli, *Overbeck und Nietzsche*, p390

CHAPTER SEVEN

1. 'Sei du mir Omen und Orakel/und führ mein Leben an zum Fest'. From the cycle *Dir zur Feier* of 1897–8, *Sämtliche Werke*, vol. 3, pp171–198
2. Letter of 13 May 1897, *LRBW*, p7
3. 31 May 1897, *LRBW*, p10
4. *LRB*, p221
5. Ernst Zinn, note in Rilke, *Sämtliche Werke*, vol. 3, p827
6. Florenzer Tagebuch (in *Briefe und Tagebücher aus der Frühzeit* ...), quoted *LRBW*, p30
7. Letter of 8 June 1897, *LRBW*, pp16–17
8. Letter of 9 June 1897, *LRBW*, pp20–21
9. July 1897, *LRBW*, p22
10. *LRB*, p138
11. *LRB*, p114
12. 'Lösch mir die Augen aus: ich kann dich sehn' – from Book I of the *Stundenbuch* quoted, in slightly different version, in *LRBW*, p26 (and see Pfeiffer's note, pp496f)
13. *LRBW*, pp399f
14. *LRB*, p210
15. *LRB*, p114
16. *LRB*, p116
17. June 1914, *LRBW*, p337
18. 'So ausgesetzt dem Übermass von Einfluss' – line from poem starting 'Warum muss einer gehn und fremde Dinge' written January 1913
19. Florenzer Tagebuch, p79
20. *Ibid.*, p114
21. *Ibid.*, p117
22. Rilke, *Sämtliche Werke*, vol. 3, p196
23. By E. M. Butler
24. By R. Binion
25. Florenzer Tagebuch
26. Florenzer Tagebuch
27. *LRB*, p116
28. *LRB*, p150
29. *LRB*, p141
30. Pasternak, 'Avtobiograficheski ocherk' in University of Michigan edn of *Sochineniya*, vol. 2 ('Proza') p6 (or see English translation by Manya Harari, *An Essay in Autobiography*, p39)

31. 'The Slavery of our Times'; 'Patriotism and Government'
32. LAS, *Rainer Maria Rilke*, p19
33. F. C. Andreas, *Die Babi's in Persien*, 1896
34. Rilke, *Zwei Prager Geschichten* and LAS, *Menschenkinder*
35. Letter of 13/25 September 1899, quoted in *Zaidenshnur*
36. Letter of 31 March 1904, *LRBW*, pp142–3
37. H. Nostiz
38. Mandel'shtam, 'Shum vremeni' in the Struve and Filippov edn of his works, vol. II, p54 (or see English translation, 'The noise of time' in C. Brown, *The Prose of Osip Mandelstam*, p78)
39. Quoted in Chertkov, pp4 and 5
40. The *Peredvizhniki*, generally translated as 'Wanderers', were a group of young Realist painters in revolt against the Academy and concerned to bring art to the ordinary people
41. See Rilke, *Briefe und Tagebücher*, p420
42. This memoir, which is kept in a Leningrad archive, was made known to me by Konstantin Azadovsky, in whose forthcoming book *Rilke und Russland* it is extensively quoted. Parts of it are also quoted in Azadovsky's essay 'Russkie vstrechi Ril'ke', published in the Russian edition of some of Rilke's prose works; Rilke, *Vorpsvede ... etc.*
43. LAS, *Rainer Maria Rilke*
44. *LRB*, p119
45 LAS's name and patronymic in Russian manner (Louise, daughter of Gustav)
46. Quoted in Azadovsky, 'Russkie vstrechi Ril'ke', pp368–9
47. 'Okhrannaya gramota' in Pasternak, *Sochineniya*, University of Michigan edn, vol. II, pp203f (see also English translation of this work by A. Livingstone in Pasternak, *Collected Prose*, Praeger, pp21f)
48. L. Pasternak, 'Vstrechi s Ril'ke'
49. In 'Aus dem Briefwechsel Leo Tolstois' (1913), and her books *Rainer Maria Rilke* and *LRB*, as well as in the Russian diary of 1900
50. 20 May, 2 June 1900, *Briefe und Tagebücher*, pp37–42
51. Rilke, *Tagebücher aus der Frühzeit*, pp234–7
52. Betz, *Rilke vivant*, pp154ff
53 Du Bos, *Extraits d'un Journal*, pp285ff
54. Russian diary, 1900 (unpublished)
55. Drozhzhin, *Zhizn' poeta-krestyanina*, pp98–103
56. S. Brutzer, *Rilkes russische Reisen*, p7
57. LAS to S. Shil 24 June/7 July 1900 (unpublished)
58. 11 August 1900, *LRBW*, pp41ff
59. Russian diary, 1900 (unpublished)
60. *Ibid.*
61. In 'Der Mensch als Weib'.
62. Russian diary, 1900 (unpublished).
63. *LRB*, p146
64. 19 December 1900, 'Schmargendorfer Tagebuch', in *Briefe und Tagebücher*, p421
65. 26 February 1901, *LRBW*, pp53–5
66. *LRB*, p147
67. *LRBW*, p55

CHAPTER EIGHT

1. Lou to Rilke, 5 July 1903, *LRBW*, p62
2. 23 June 1903, *LRBW*, p56
3. 27 June 1903, *LRBW*, p57
4. Unpublished letter
5. 30 June 1903, *LRBW*, pp57ff

6. For introduction of this term and discussion of Rilke's correspondence with Lou in relation to his correspondence with others see the doctoral thesis by Joachim Storck, *Rainer Maria Rilke als Briefschreiber*
7. 5 July 1903, *LRBW*, pp62ff
8. 18 July 1903, *LRBW*, p65
9. *Ibid.*, *LRBW*, pp74–5
10. 22 July 1903, *LRBW*, p76
11. 25 July 1903, *LRBW*, p78
12. Quoted from Lou's unpublished diaries by Pfeiffer, *LRBW*, p513
13. 1 August 1903, *LRBW*, p86
14. 7 and 8 August 1903, *LRBW*, pp87–90
15. E. Buddeberg, *Rainer Maria Rilke*, pp31–50, 74–83 and *passim*
16. *Ibid.*, p77
17. *Die Aufzeichnungen des Malte Laurids Brigge Sämtliche Werke*, vol. 3, p165
18. *LRBW*, p59
19. 10–16 October 1913, *In der Schule bei Freud*, p209
20. 19 October 1917, *LFBW*, p74
21. Simenauer, *R. M. Rilke, Legende und Mythos*
22. 10 August 1903, *LRBW*, p103
23. See *LRBW*, p34
24. *Ibid.*
25. Printed in *LRBW*, pp55f
26. Unpublished diaries of 29 November 1900, and 1 January 1901
27. Unpublished diary note of 31 December 1903
28. 21 May 1905, *LRBW*, p204
29. 23 May 1905, *LRBW*, p205
30. 23 November 1905, *LRBW*, p214
31. Unpublished 'Tagesnotizen'
32. Pfeiffer's words
33. Unpublished diary of February 1905
34. Unpublished diary of 4 June 1903
35. Unpublished letter undated, but filed with letters of 1901
36. According to Pfeiffer in conversation
37. See *LRB*, p36
38. 'Geschwister', p35
39. 28 December 1911, *LRBW*, p238
40. Letter to Lou, '3 Kings Day' 1913, *LRBW*, p280
41. For example in letters of 17 June 1909, 28 December 1909 and 6 November 1910 (*LRBW*, pp226, 235 and 236)
42. August 1909, *LRBW*, p228
43. Quoted by Pfeiffer in *LFBW*, p234

CHAPTER NINE

1. *Jenseits von Gut und Böse*, §175
2. LAS, 'Gedanken über das Liebesproblem', p45
3. *A Room of One's Own* (Triad/Panther edn, 1977) pp92 and 106
4. 'Die moderne Frau'
5. 'Frauen in ihrem Schaffen, p391
6. 'Mensch als Weib', p225
7. *Ibid.*
8. 'Mensch als Weib', p234
9. 'Mensch als Weib', p232
10. Quoted by G. Bäumer in *Die Frau und das geistige Leben*, pp6–7
11. 'Study of Thomas Hardy' (1914–15) in *Lawrence on Hardy & Painting*, 1973 edn, p63
12. 'Gedanken über das Liebesproblem', p1013
13. *LRB*, p212
14. 'Gedanken über das Liebesproblem', p1016
15. *Ibid.* p1015
16. *LRB*, p34

17. 'Gedanken über das Liebesproblem', p1025
18. *Ibid.*, p1026
19. Unpublished letter of 10 February 1910; quoted by Pfeiffer in his 'Nachwort' to LAS *Die Erotik*, 1919 edn, p188
20. *Die Frau und das geistige Leben*, p247
21. *Die Erotik* 1979 edn, pp98–9
22. *Ibid.*, p109
23. *Ibid.*, p111
24. *Ibid.*, p119
25. *Ibid.*, p124
26. *Ibid.*, p125
27. *Ibid.*, p126
28. *Ibid.*, p127
29. 'Dass aber unsere Liebesträume uns nur so hoch entrücken, um wie von einem Sprungbrett, diesen Sprung zu tun von ihrem Himmel auf die Erde hinab, das bekommt ihnen desto besser, je machtvoller sie als Träume waren. Denn als ursprünglich blosse Begleiterscheinungen, Überschüsse, an den leiblich bedingten Vorgängen, und dadurch ins Wahnhafte verflüchtigt, sind sie ja schon ihre eignen Wirklichkeitsvorläufer, Lebensverlanger, Zukunftszeichen, Versprechen; ihr Lebensinstinkt muss in die ganze Breite des 'Wirklichen', Simplen, Grobgegebenen greifen, wie ins Gespensterhafte Verzauberter nach seinem Leibe greift, und wär es die unscheinbarste Leibhaftigkeit, um daran zu sich selbst zu kommen' (*Die Erotik*, p138)
30. *Die Erotik*, p143

CHAPTER TEN

1. Letter to LAS, 9 November 1915, *LFBW*, p38
2. *LRB*, p151
3. Pfeiffer, 'Rilke und die Psychoanalyse', p253
4. 'Nietzsche with Rée' in *Friedrich Nietzsche . . .* (Part 2); 'Nietzsche with Haller', an unpublished essay of *c.* 1887 from which Pfeiffer quotes in the introduction to his forthcoming new edition of LAS, *Friedrich Nietzsche . . .*; 'Andreas with Rée' in her 1888 diary; 'Rilke with Bjerre', in *Freud Journal*, pp148ff (May 1913); one could add 'Rilke with Kleist' in *Eintragungen*, 1934, pp43–61
5. *Dok.*, p190
6. For example, 'Gedanken über das Liebesproblem', p1013
7. Nietzsche, 'Tautenburger Aufzeichnungen' 1882, *Sämtliche Werke*, vol. 10, p10
8. *FJ*, p223
9. *FJ*, p69
10. From letter to Frieda von Bülow in winter 1908–9, quoted by Pfeiffer in *LRB*, p260
11. *Mein Dank an Freud*, p28
12. *LRB*, p153
13. *LRB*, p163
14. Letter to Freud, 28 April 1912, quoted by Pfeiffer in *LFBW*, p234
15. 27 September 1912, *LFBW*, p7
16. 1 October 1912, *LFBW*, p7
17. *FJ*, p13
18. *LRB*, p167
19. *LRB*, p166
20. *FJ*, p70
21. *FJ*, p89–90
22. 27 February 1913, *LFBW*, p13
23. 9 April 1916, *LFBW*, p44
24. The affair with Bjerre: according to H. F. Peters, *My Sister, my Spouse*, although Pfeiffer

(in conversation) considers Peters' version greatly exaggerated; with Gebsattel: according to R. Binion, who quotes from letters I have not seen.

25. *LRB*, p179
26. 20 November 1912, *FJ*, p38
27. 22 January 1913, *FJ*, p78
28. 13 November 1912, *FJ*, p30
29. 30 October 1912, *FJ*, p18
30. E. Jones, *Life & Work of Sigmund Freud* (Penguin Edn) p474
31. Letter of Jung to Freud, 2 January 1912, *Correspondence between Sigmund Freud and C. G. Jung*, translated by Ralph Manheim, pp477–8
32. 10 November 1912, *FJ*, pp27–8
33. 28 October 1912, *FJ*, p14
34. *Studie über Minderwertigkeit von Organen*, 1907
35. 28 October 1912, *FJ*, p15
36. 16 August 1913, *FJ*, p180
37. 7 November 1912, *FJ*, p26
38. 29 June 1914, *LFBW*, p19
39. Freud to Abraham, 10 July 1914 in *A Psycho-Analytic Dialogue* translated by B. Marsh & H. Abraham, p182
40. 7 November 1912, *FJ*, p27
41. 10–11 September 1913, *FJ*, pp193–4
42. *Ibid.*, p195
43. 30 October 1912, *FJ*, p18
44. P. Roazen, *Brother Animal*
45. K. Eissler, *Talent and Genius*
46. 26 November 1912, *FJ*, p43
47. Quotations in latter part of this paragraph are from the diary entry made at the end of August 1913; *FJ*, pp188–9
48. Unpublished letters
49. 2 April 1913, *FJ*, pp140–1
50. 6 April 1913, *FJ*, p143
51. LAS, unpublished diary of April–May 1913
52. 9–21 July 1913, *FJ*, p170
53. Ernest Jones, *Life & Work of Sigmund Freud* (Penguin edn), p413
54. Freud, 'Female Sexuality' (1931), *Standard Edition . . .*, vol. XXI, p224
55. 12/13 February 1913, *FJ*, p100
56. 21 January 1913, *FJ*, pp75ff
57. *FJ*, p77
58. 12 and 14 March 1913, *FJ*, pp123ff
59. *Ibid.*, pp132f
60. *Ibid.*, p132
61. 'On Narcissism', an Introduction
62. 11 May 1912, *FJ*, p167
63. 8 February 1913, *FJ*, p94
64. Letter to Freud, 10 January 1915, *LFBW*, p25
65. *Mein Dank an Freud*
66. Letter to Freud, 20 July 1920, *LFBW*, pp113f
67. 'The Libido Theory' in the third of the 1905 *Three Essays on Sexuality*
68. 31 January 1915, *LFBW*, pp29f
69. 11 December 1912, *FJ*, pp66–7
70. Jung, *Analytical Psychology*, p46
71. 14 December 1912, *FJ*, p65
72. 5 March 1913, *FJ*, p113
73. *Ibid.*, pp114ff
74. For example 29/30 September 1913, *FJ*, p198
75. 26 November 1912, *FJ*, p43
76. 11 May 1913, *FJ*, p160
77. *Aufarbeitung*
78. 11 May 1913, *FJ*, pp160–61
79. Letter of 29 July 1913, quoted by Pfeiffer in *LRBW*, p568

CHAPTER ELEVEN

1. *Mein Dank an Freud*, p47
2. Letter of 26 June 1914, *LRBW*, p336
3. Unpublished diary, 1914
4. See for example her letter to Rilke of 5 December 1913, *LRBW*, p308
5. *LRB*, p180
6. Unpublished diary, 1914
7. 25 November 1914, *LFBW*, p23
8. 4 December 1914, *LFBW*, p24
9. Letter of Freud to Abraham, 11 December 1914, *A Psycho-Analytic Dialogue*, p205
10. Unpublished diary, December 1914
11. Unpublished diary, 12 February 1918
12. 18 May 1918, *LFBW*, p87
13. Letter to Rilke, 18 January 1923, *LRBW*, p461
14. 11 June 1914, *LRBW*, p327
15. 20 June 1914, *LRBW*, p329
16. 24 June 1914, *LRBW*, pp332–3; 27 June 1914, *LRBW*, pp334–6; and 2 July 1914, *LRBW*, pp342–4
17. *LRBW*, p333
18. *LRBW*, p346
19. 26 June 1914, *LRBW*, pp336–42
20. *LRBW*, p342
21. *LRBW*, pp342–3
22. L. Albert-Lasard, *Wege mit Rilke*, p55
23. *Ibid.*, pp55–6
24. *Ibid.*, p56
25. *Ibid.*, p57
26. *Ibid.*, p59
27. *Ibid.*, p59
28. Wolff, Lou Andreas-Salomé, p1181
29. Quoted by Pfeiffer in *LRBW*, p408
30. Letter of Lou to Rilke, 6 June 1919, *LRBW*, p409
31. 11 February 1922, *LRBW*, pp444–5
32. 16 February 1922, *LRBW*, p446
33. *Ibid.*, pp446–7
34. 19 February 1922, *LRBW*, p447
35. 24 February 1922, *LRBW*, p449
36. 6 March 1922, *LRBW*, p453
37. 16 February 1922, *LRBW*, p447
38. 31 October 1925, *LRBW*, pp475ff
39. 12 December 1925, *LRBW*, pp479ff
40. Quoted by Pfeiffer, *LRBW*, p618
41. Quoted by Pfeiffer, *LRBW*, p619
42. Letter to Rilke, 17 February 1919, *LRBW*, p393
43. Letter to Freud, 6 September 1921, *LFBW*, p118
44. Letter to Rilke, 4 January 1922, *LRBW*, p442
45. 14 June 1917, *LFBW*, p64
46. Unpublished diary, 1917
47. Letter to Freud, 15 February 1925, *LFBW*, p166
48. 24 May 1924, *LRBW*, p617
49. *Mein Dank an Freud*, p14
50. *Ibid.*, p17
51. Letter to Rilke, 22 September 1921, *LRBW*, p435
52. Letter to Rilke, 16 March 1924, *LRBW*, p464
53. *Ibid.*
54. Letter to Freud, 25 February 1924, *LFBW*, p144
55. Letter to Freud, 6 September 1921, *LFBW*, p118
56. 30 July 1915, *LFBW*, p36
57. 25 May 1916, *LFBW*, p50
58. 7 July 1914, *LFBW*, p21

59. Letter to Freud, 18 December 1916, *LFBW*, p62
60. 14 March 1924, *LFBW*, p145
61. 25 August 1919, *LFBW*, pp109–10
62. Parts of these letters are published by Pfeiffer in *LRB*, pp259–63
63. Letter to Freud, 2 May 1923, *LFBW*, p135
64. 26 May 1924, *LRBW*, p474
65. Letter to Lou, 9 May 1931, *LFBW*, p210
66. 2 July 1917, *LFBW*, p65
67. 13 July 1917, *LFBW*, pp68–9
68. 22 November 1917, *LFBW*, p75
69. 23 March 1930, *LFBW*, p202
70. 9 May 1931, *LFBW*, p211
71. 3 April 1931, *LFBW*, p208

CHAPTER TWELVE

1. From the *Stibber Nestbuch*, *Dok.*, pp193, 195, 198, 206
2. Letter to Lou, 20 February 1914, *LRBW*, p314
3. Letter to Lou, 17 February 1918, *LFBW*, p83
4. Letter to Lou, 20 February 1914, *LRBW*, p314
5. *Drei Briefe . . .* , p23
6. *Ibid.*, p30
7. *Ibid.*, p31
8. *Ibid.*, p47
9. *Ibid.*, p58
10. *Ibid.*, p77
11. Letter to Lou, 18 May 1916, *LFBW*, p49
12. In 'The Sexual Life of Human Beings' (*General Theory of the Neuroses*) Freud, Standard Edition, vol. XVI, p315, and as footnote to 'Infantile Sexuality' (*Three Essays on Sexuality*) vol. VII, p187. The latter is quoted here.
13. In the text of 'Anxiety and Instinctual Life' (vol. XXII, p101) and in 'On Transformations of Instinct as exemplified in anal erotism' (vol. XVII, p133)
14. '"Anal" und "Sexual"', p249
15. *Ibid.*, p252
16. LAS, 'Narzissmus . . .', pp366–7
17. Freud, 'On Narcissism . . .', vol. XIV, p74
18. LAS, 'Narzissmus . . .', p363
19. *Ibid.*, p371
20. *Ibid.*, p373
21. *Ibid.*, p373
22. *Ibid.*, p376
23. *Ibid.*, p380
24. *Ibid.*, p386
25. *Ibid.*, p385

CHAPTER THIRTEEN

1. Quoted by Pfeiffer in *LRB*, p308
2. Letter of 20 May 1927, *LFBW*, pp182–3
3. See Pfeiffer, 'Denn Rainer starb "trostlos"'
4. *RMR*, p9
5. *Ibid.*, p103
6. *Ibid.*, p107
7. *Ibid.*, p110
8. *LRB.*, p20
9. *Mein Dank an Freud*, p47
10. *Ibid.*
11. *Ibid.*, p58
12. *Ibid.*, p61
13. *Ibid.*, pp62ff
14. *Ibid.*, p83
15. *Ibid.*, pp96–7
16. Letter of Freud to Lou, *c.* 10 July 1931, *LFBW*, p213
17. The chapter titles are: Das Erlebnis Gott; Liebeserleben [Hendrik Gillot]; Erleben an der

Familie; Das Erlebnis Russland; Freundes Erleben [Paul Rée]; Unter Menschen; Mit Rainer [+Nachtrag: 'April, unser Monat, Rainer']; Das Erlebnis Freud [+Nachtrag: 'Erinnertes an Freud']; Vor dem Weltkrieg und seither; F. C. Andreas; Was am 'Grundriss' fehlt.
18. *LRB*, p83
19. *LRB*, p203
20. *LRB*, p208
21. *LRB*, p103
22. *LRB*, p108
23. *LRB*, p35
24. *Eintragungen*, p65
25. *LRB*, p39
26. *Ibid.*

CHAPTER FOURTEEN

1. Quoted by Pfeiffer in *LRB*, 300–1
2. 'Alter und Ewigkeit', 149–50
3. Unpublished diary
4. Letter of Freud to Lou, 10 May 1925, *LFBW*, p169
5. Letter of Lou to Freud, 18 May 1925, *LFBW*, pp170–1
6. Letter of Lou to Freud, 20 May 1927, *LFBW*, p181
7. Unpublished diary
8. Letter to Freud, 10 October 1930, *LFBW*, p206
9. Unpublished letter to Lotte Reinecke, 14 February 1931, in the Deutsches Literaturarchiv in Marbach am Neckar
10. *LRB*, p182
11. *Eintragungen*, p24
12. *Ibid.*, p25
13. *FJ*, p107
14. *LRB*, p168
15. *Ibid.*
16. *Ruth*, p59
17. Letter to Freud, 4 May 1935, *LFBW*, p225
18. Conversation with Pfeiffer
19. Weizsäcker, *Natur und Geist*, p128
20. G. Bäumer, *Gestalt und Wandel*, pp469–70
21. Letter to Freud, 3 May 1934, *LFBW*, p219
22. Conversation with Pfeiffer
23. Recorded by Pfeiffer, *LRB*, pp308–9

FICTIONAL WRITINGS

1. *Im Kampf um Gott*, p129
2. *Ibid.*, p242
3. *Ibid.*, p313
4. 'Wer immer strebend sich bemüht, den können wir erlösen'
5. Quoted in G. Bäumer, *Gestalt und Wandel*, p491
6. *Im Kampf um Gott*, p304
7. Review by E. M. Hamann, 1901
8. *Ruth*, p101
9. *Ibid.*, p183
10. *Ibid.*, pp224–5
11. *Ibid.*, p299
12. Rilke, *Sämtliche Werke*, vol. 3, p569
13. *Ruth*, p153
14. *Im Kampf um Gott*, p51
15. *Ruth*, p224
16. *Fenitschka*, p39
17. *Ibid.*, p54
18. *Ibid.*, p66–7
19. Rilke, *Sämtliche Werke*, vol. 6, p1124.
20. Arthur Erloesser, 1899
21. *Eine Ausschweifung*, p121

22. *Ibid.*, p114
23. *Ibid.*, p177
24. *Ibid.*, p167
25. 'Mädchenreigen' in *Menschenkinder*
26. LAS, 'Frühlingserwachen' (published 1907), p98
27. Lafourcade, quoted by M. Praz, *The Romantic Agony*, p278
28. 'Zurück ans All' in *Menschenkinder*, p351
29. For a comparison of LAS's fictional themes with those of G. Reuter and other contemporary writers, see L. Müller-Loreck, *Die Erzählende Dichtung Lou Andreas-Salomés*
30. Jost Hermand, 'Undinen-Zauber. Zum Frauenbild des Jugendstils', in *Wissenschaft als Dialog* (1969), p10
31. Published by Pfeiffer in *Drei Dichtungen*, 1981
32. *Das Haus*, pp206–7
33. *Rodinka*, p101
34. *Ibid.*, p174
35. H. F. Peters, *My Sister, my Spouse*, p287
36. *Ibid.*, p286
37. *Mein Dank an Freud.*, p55
38. *Der Teufel und seine Grossmutter*, p3
39. *Ibid.* p7
40. *Ibid.*, p11
41. 'Geschwister', p46
42. *Ibid.*, p48
43. 'Das Bündnis zwischen Tor und Ur', in *Die Stunde ohne Gott*, p151

BIBLIOGRAPHY

A. WORKS BY LOU ANDREAS-SALOMÉ

(arranged chronologically   f = fiction, r = short review, c = correspondence; posthumous publications are listed separately)

BOOKS

Im Kampf um Gott (f), [by 'Henri Lou'], Leipzig/Berlin, 1885 (317pp)
Henrik Ibsen's Frauen-Gestalten 'nach seinen sechs Familien-Dramen', Berlin, 1892 (238pp)
Friedrich Nietzsche in seinen Werken, Wien, 1894 (263pp)
  also published (incomplete) in Russian as 'Fridrikh Nitsshche v svoyikh proizvedeniyakh: Ocherk' (transl. by Z. A. Vengerova) in *Severny Vestnik*, nos. 3–5, 1896, and in French (complete) as *Frédéric Nietzsche* (transl. by J. Benoist-Méchin), Paris, 1932 (263pp)
Ruth ('Erzählung') (f), Stuttgart, 1895 and 1897 (304pp)
Fenitschka. Eine Ausschweifung ('Zwei Erzählungen') (f), Stuttgart, 1898 (178pp) [republished in 1983]
Menschenkinder ('Novellenzyklus') (f), Stuttgart, 1899 (364pp)
Aus fremder Seele ('Eine Spätherbstgeschichte') (f), Stuttgart, 1901 (162pp)
Ma ('Ein Porträt') (f), Stuttgart, 1901 (202pp)
Im Zwischenland ('Fünf Geschichten aus dem Seelenleben halbwüchsiger Mädchen') (f), Stuttgart and Berlin, 1902 (412pp)
Die Erotik, Frankfurt, 1910 (63pp) [republished in 1979]
Drei Briefe an einen Knaben, Leipzig, 1917 (78pp)
Das Haus ('Familiengeschichte vom Ende des vorigen Jahrhunderts') (f), Berlin, 1919 and 1927 (334pp)
Die Stunde ohne Gott und andere Kindergeschichten (f), Jena, 1921 (164pp)
Der Teufel und seine Grossmutter (f), Jena, 1922 (59pp)
Rodinka ('Russische Erinnerung') (f), Jena, 1923 (260pp)
Rainer Maria Rilke, Leipzig, 1928 (125pp)
Mein Dank an Freud: Offener Brief an Professor Sigmund Freud zu seinem 75 Geburtstag, Wien, 1931 (109pp)

ARTICLES

This list includes stories which were published but not included in a collection; also some of her book and theatre reviews. It excludes separate appearances of poems, and of articles or stories subsequently collected in book form. The list of scholarly and other articles is, as far as possible, complete.
'Ein holländisches Urteil über moderne deutsche Dramen', in *Die Freie Bühne*, 1891 (pp521–4, 541–6, 571–4, 592–5, 670–3, 696–701)
'Der Realismus in der Religion', in *Die Freie Bühne*, 1891 (pp1004–9, 1025–30, 1057–9, 1079–83)
'Ossip Schubin', in *Vossische Zeitung* (Sonntagsbeilage), 10 and 17 January 1892 (pp10–12; pp11–12)
'Gottesschöpfung', in *Die Freie Bühne*, 1892 (pp169–79)
'Emil Marriot', in *Vossische Zeitung* (Sonntagsbeilage), 7 and 21 August 1892
'Harnack und das Apostolikum', in *Die Freie Bühne*, 1892 (pp1214–22)
'Die Duse', in *Die Freie Bühne*, 1893 (pp76–81)
'Ibsen, Strindberg, Sudermann', in *Die Freie Bühne*, 1893 (pp149–72)
'Hannele', in *Die Freie Bühne*, 1893 (pp1343–9)

'Von der Bestie bis zum Gott (Über Totemismus bei den Ursemiten)', in *Neue Deutsche Rundschau*, 5, 1894 (pp398–402)

'Das Problem des Islams', in *Vossische Zeitung* (Sonntagsbeilage), 22 and 29 July 1894 (pp4–8; pp3–6)

Ricarda Huch, 'Erinnerungen von Ludolf Ursleu dem Jüngern', in *Die Frau*, October 1895 (pp32–6)

'Von Ursprung des Christenthums', in *Vossische Zeitung* (Sonntagsbeilage), 22 December 1895

'Jesus der Jude', in *Neue Deutsche Rundschau*, 1896 (pp342–51)

'Ein überlebter Traum' (f), in *Westermanns Illustrierte Deutsche Monatshefte*, 82, April–September 1897 (pp644–59, 761–78)

'Sovremennye pisatel'nitsy', in *Severny vestnik*, 11, 1897 (pp28–40)

'Russische Dichtung und Kultur', in *Cosmopolis*, August and September 1897 (pp571–80; pp872–85)

'Aus der Geschichte Gottes', in *Neue Deutsche Rundschau*, 1897 (pp1211–20)

'Amor' (f) [with A. L. Volynsky], in *Severny vestnik*, 9, 1897 (pp1–6) [published only in Russian until *Drei Dichtungen* (published posthumously)]

'Das russische Heiligenbild und sein Dichter', in *Vossische Zeitung* (Sonntagsbeilage) 2, 1 January 1898

'Russische Philosophie und semitischer Geist', in *Die Zeit*, 15 January 1898 (p40)

'Drama "molodoi Germanii"', in *Severny vestnik*, 2, 1898 (pp53–69)

'Religion und Cultur', in *Die Zeit*, 2 April 1898 (pp5–7)

'Vom religiösen Affekt', in *Die Zukunft*, 23 April 1898 (pp149–54)

'Missbrauchte Frauenkraft', in *Die Frau*, June 1898 (pp513–16)

'Leo Tolstoi, unser Zeitgenosse', in *Neue Deutsche Rundschau*, 1898 (pp1145–55)

'Physische Liebe', in *Die Zukunft*, October 1898 (pp218–22)

'Grundformen der Kunst', in *Pan*, November 1898–April 1899 (pp177–82)

'Ketzereien gegen die moderne Frau', in *Die Zukunft*, 11 February 1899 (pp237–40)

'Der Mensch als Weib', in *Neue Deutsche Rundschau*, 1899 (pp225–43) (republished in *Die Erotik*, 1979)

'Vom Kunstaffekt', in *Die Zukunft*, 27 May 1899 (pp366–72)

'Erleben', in *Die Zeit*, 19 August 1899 (pp120–2)

'Der Egoismus in der Religion', chapter in *Der Egoismus*, ed. Arthur Dix, Leipzig, 1899

'"Essais" von Ellen Key' (r), in *Das Literarische Echo*, 2, 1898–1900 (pp66–7)

'Gedanken über das Liebesproblem', in *Neue Deutsche Rundschau*, 1900 (pp1009–27) (republished in *Die Erotik*, 1979)

'Ein Dank an einen Dichter (Zur Würdigung des 'Michael Kramer' von Gerhart Hauptmann)', in *Der Lotse*, 1:29, 20 April 1901 (pp71–9)

'Alter und Ewigkeit', in *Die Zukunft*, 26 October 1901 (pp146–50)

'Der Graf von Charolais', in *Die Zukunft*, 18 February 1905 (pp286–93)

'Das Glashüttenmärchen', in *Die Zukunft*, 17 March 1906 (pp399–404)

'Frühlings Erwachen', in *Die Zukunft*, 19 January 1907 (pp97–100)

'Lebende Dichtung', in *Die Zukunft*, 22 February 1908 (p262)

'Die Russen', in *Die Schaubühne*, V:39, 23 September 1909 (pp305–8)

'Im Spiegel', in *Das Literarische Echo*, 15 October 1911 (pp86–8)

'Elisabeth Siewert', in *Das Literarische Echo*, 14, 1911–12 (pp1689–95)

'Realität und Gesetzlichkeit im Geschlechtsleben', in *Das Literarische Echo*, 1 September 1912 (pp1672–6)

'Von frühem Gottesdienst', in *Imago*, II:5, October 1913 (pp457–67) (posthumously published in French in *L'amour du narcissisme*)

'Aus dem Briefwechsel Leo Tolstois', in *Das Literarische Echo*, 1 October 1913 (pp4–8)

'Zum Typus Weib', in *Imago*, III:1, February 1914 (pp1–6, 6–14) (posthumously published in French in *L'amour du narcissisme*)

'Kind und Kunst', in *Das Literarische Echo*, 17, 1914–15 (pp1–4)

'Zum Bilde Strindbergs', in *Das Literarische Echo*, 1 March 1915 (pp648–53)

'"Anal" and "Sexual"', in *Imago*, IV:5, 1916 (pp249–73) (posthumously published in French in *L'amour du narcissisme*)

'Angela Langer', in *Das Literarische Echo*, 19, 1916–17 (pp329–33)

'Psychosexualität', in *Zeitschrift für Sexualwissenschaft*, 4, 1917 (reprinted in *Die Erotik*, 1979)

'Insekt und Krieg', in *Die Tat*, April 1917 (pp48–53)

'Expression', in *Das Literarische Echo*, 1 April 1917 (pp783–90)

'Luzifer. Eine Phantasie über Ricarda Huchs Buch "Luthers Glaube"', in *Die Neue Generation*, May 1917 (pp210–15)

'Karl Nötzels Tolstoi', in *Das Literarische Echo*, 20, 1917–18 (pp1268–76)

'Strindberg. Ein Beitrag zur Soziologie der Geschlechter von Leopold v. Wiese', in *Das Literarische Echo*, 21, 1918–19 (pp692, 693)
'Der russische "Intelligent"', in *Die Neue Rundschau*, 1919 (pp127–8)
'Der geistliche Russe', in *Der Neue Merkur*, May 1919 (pp380–6)
'Des Dichters Erleben', in *Die Neue Rundschau*, 1919 (pp358–67)
'Agnes Henningsen', in *Das Literarische Echo*, 22, 1919–20 (pp455–64)
'Waldemar Bonsels', in *Das Literarische Echo*, 1 October 1920 (pp8–17)
'Gott gegen Gott', in *Der Neue Merkur*, 4:1, 1920–21 (pp173–81)
'Narzissmus als Doppelrichtung', in *Imago*, VII:4, 1921 (pp361–86) (posthumously published in French in *L'amour du narcissisme*)
'Geschwister' (f), in *Deutsche Rundschau*, October 1921 (pp24–63)
'Tendenz und Form russischer Dichtung', in *Das Literarische Echo*, 1 January 1922 (pp398–401)
'Eros', in *Faust*, 9, 1922–3 (pp1–6)
'Zum sechsten Mai 1926', in *Almanach des Internationalen Psychoanalytischen Verlages*, 1927 (pp9–14) (posthumously published in French in *L'amour du narcissisme*)
'Was daraus folgt, dass es nicht die Frau gewesen ist, die den Vater totgeschlagen hat', in *Almanach des Internationalen Psychoanalytischen Verlages*, 1928 (pp25–30) (posthumously published in French in *L'amour du narcissisme*)

Works published posthumously

Lebensrückblick. Grundriss einiger Lebenserinnerungen, ed. E. Pfeiffer, Zürich and Wiesbaden, 1951
 Reprinted 1968. Revised and published as 'Insel-Taschenbuch 54', Frankfurt, 1977
 Published in French as *Ma Vie* (transl. by D. Miermont and B. Vergne, preface by Jacques Nobécourt), Paris, 1977
Rainer Maria Rilke Lou Andreas-Salomé Briefwechsel (c), ed. E. Pfeiffer, Zürich and Wiesbaden, 1952 and 1975
 Published in French as *Lou Andreas-Salomé et Rainer Maria Rilke, Correspondance* (transl. by Philippe Jaccottet), Paris, 1975
In der Schule bei Freud, 'Tagebuch eines Jahres 1912/1913', ed. E. Pfeiffer, Zürich, 1958
 Published in English as *The Freud Journal of Lou Andreas-Salomé* (transl. by Stanley Leavy), New York, 1964; London, 1965
'The Dual Orientation of Narcissism' (transl. by S. Leavy of 'Narzissmus als Doppelrichtung'), *Psychoanalytic Quarterly*, vol. 31(1–2), 1962 (pp1–30)
'Zu Besuch bei Freud' (excerpt from Lou Andreas-Salomé's diary), ed. E. Pfeiffer, *Almanack*, 'Das neunundsiebzigste Jahr, S. Fischer Verlag', 1965 (pp136–9)
Sigmund Freud Lou Andreas-Salomé Briefwechsel (c), ed. E. Pfeiffer, Frankfurt, 1966
 Published in English as *S. Freud and Lou Andreas-Salomé, Letters*, ed. E. Pfeiffer, transl. by W. & E. Robson-Scott, London, 1972
Friedrich Nietzsche, Paul Rée, Lou von Salomé Die Dokumente ihrer Begegnung (c), ed. E. Pfeiffer, Frankfurt, 1970
'Mitleben: Tier und Pflanze' (part of the unpublished work 'Der Gott'), in *Alles Lebendige meinet den Menschen* 'Gedenkbuch für Max Niehans', Bern, 1972 (pp129–35)
'Anal und Sexual' e altri scritti psicoanalitici (transl. by Margherita Novelletto), preface by Cesare Musatti, Rimini-Firenze, 1977
Die Erotik, 'Vier Aufsätze', ed. E. Pfeiffer, München, 1979
L'amour du narcissisme, 'Textes psychoanalytiques' (transl. by Isabelle Hildenbrand), preface by Marie Moscovici, Paris, 1980
Drei Dichtungen (f) (contains 'Amor', 'Jutta' and 'Die Tarnkappe'), ed. E. Pfeiffer, Frankfurt, 1981
Eintragungen. Letzte Jahre, ed. E. Pfeiffer, Frankfurt, 1982
Fenitschka. Eine Ausschweifung (f), ed. E. Pfeiffer, Ullstein Taschenbuch, 1983

B. WORKS ABOUT LOU ANDREAS-SALOMÉ

(arranged alphabetically r = short review, u = unpublished, o = not devoted solely to LAS)

BOOKS AND THESES

Bab, Hans Jürgen. *Lou Andreas-Salomé*, 'Dichtung und Persönlichkeit' (doctoral dissertation) (u)
Binion, Rudolph. *Frau Lou, Nietzsche's Wayward Disciple*, Princeton, 1968
Koepcke, Cordula. *Lou Andreas-Salomé, Ein Eigenwilliger Lebensweg*, 'Ihre Begegnung mit Nietzsche, Rilke und Freud', Freiburg i. Br., 1982
Mackey, Ilona Schmidt. *Lou Salomé, Inspiratrice et interprète de Nietzsche, Rilke et Freud*, Paris, 1968

Müller-Loreck, Leonie. *Die erzählende Dichtung Lou Andreas-Salomés: Ihr Zusammenhang mit der Literatur um 1900* (doctoral dissertation, 1972), Stuttgart, 1976.

Peters, H. F. *My Sister, My Spouse*, London, 1963

Podach, Erich F. *Friedrich Nietzsche und Lou Salomé: Ihre Begegnung 1882*, Zürich and Leipzig, 1938

ARTICLES, CHAPTERS OF BOOKS, REVIEWS

Bassermann, D. 'Ungedeutetes Geheimnis, Zu Lou Andreas-Salomés Lebensrückblick', in *Der neue Schweizer Rundschau*, 20, May 1952

Bäumer, Gertrud. 'Lou Andreas-Salomé, in *Die Frau*, March 1937 (pp305–11)
  Reprinted in Bäumer, G., *Gestalt und Wandel*, Berlin, 1939

Bernecker, Senta. 'Lou Andreas-Salomé', a chapter of Senta Bernecker, *Frauen im Hintergrund*, Berlin, undated (pp364–404)

Bernoulli, C. A. 'Nietzsches Lou-Erlebnis', in *Raschers Jahrbuch für Schweizer Art und Kunst*, I, Zürich and Leipzig, 1915 (pp225–60)

Bölsche, W. 'Das Geheimnis Friedrich Nietzsches', in *Neue Deutsche Rundschau*, 1894 (pp1026–33)
  'Sechs Kapitel Psychologie nach Ibsen', in *Die Freie Bühne*, 1891 (pp1272–4)

Brausewetter, E. 'Lou Andreas-Salomé', in E. Brausewetter (ed.), *Meisternovellen deutscher Frauen* (zweite Reihe), Berlin, Leipzig, 1898 (pp3–14)

Dehn, Fritz. 'Nietzsches und Rilkes Freundin', in *Zeitwende*, 24, 1952/3, pp551–2

Dohm, Hedwig. 'Reaktion in der Frauenbewegung' (o), in *Die Zukunft*, 11 November 1899 (pp272–91)

Eloesser, A. 'Neue Bücher' (r, o), in *Neue Deutsche Rundschau*, I, 1903 (p268)
  'Neue Bücher' (r, o), in *Neue Deutsche Rundschau*, May 1899 (pp495–6)
  'Neue Bücher' (r, o), in *Neue Deutsche Rundschau*, October 1899 (p1175)

Flex, Konrad. 'Der überstiegene Kopf oder Lou auf Abwegen' (u)

Frowen, Irene. 'Rilke und Lou Andreas-Salomé – neu betrachtet' (u) (paper given at the conference, 'Rilke um 1900', in Worpswede, 25–28 September 1980)
  'Lou Andreas-Salomé', in *Duitse Kroniek*, 32, nos. 1–2, 1981 (pp4–21)

Förster-Nietzsche, E. 'Der "Hymnus an das Leben"', in *Das Inselschiff*, Leipzig, 1920 (pp209–16)

Gallwitz, S. 'Die Freundin von Nietzsche und Rilke', in *Die Frau*, October 1928 (pp12–16)

Günther, Joachim. 'Die Lou-Affäre in Dokumenten', in *Neue Deutsche Hefte*, 18, 1971 (pp124–9)

Hamann, E. 'Lou A-S, Ruth' (r), in *Allgemeines Literaturblatt*, Wien, 1 July 1901 (p414)

Heilborn, Ernst. 'Lou Andreas-Salomé', in *Die Frau*, October 1898 (pp25–9)
  'Frauen in ihrem Schaffen' (o), in *Die Frau*, April 1897 (pp385–91)

Heine, Anselma. 'Menschenkinder' (r), in *Die Zeit*, 5 August 1899 (pp90–1)
  'Drei Briefe an einen Knaben' (r), in *Das Literarische Echo*, 20, 1 May 1918 (pp940–1)

Heissenbüttel, Helmut. 'Das Vatergesicht', in *Der Monat*, 19, 1967 (pp67–70)

Heuss, Theodor. 'Lou Andreas-Salomé', in *Der Kunstwart*, 21, 1908 (pp9–13)

Klingenberg, Helene, 'Lou Andreas-Salomé', in *Deutsche Monatsschrift für Russland*, 15/28 March 1912 (pp237–52)

Koegel, Fritz. 'Friedrich Nietzsche und Frau Lou Andreas-Salomé', in *Das Magazin für Litteratur*, 23 February 1895 (pp225–35)

Leavy, Stanley. 'Introduction', *The Freud Journal of Lou Andreas-Salomé*, London, 1965 (pp1–27)

Mauthner, Fritz. 'Lou Andreas-Salomé, Henrik Ibsens Frauen-Gestalten' (r), in *Das Magazin für Litteratur*, nr. 8, 20 February 1892 (p135)

Meyer-Benfey, Heinrich, 'Lou Andreas-Salomé', in *Die Frau*, February 1931 (pp304–7)

Moortgat, Pierre. 'Lou Andreas-Salomé et Simone de Beauvoir' (o), in *Revue d'Allemagne*, 5, 1973 (pp938–43)

Moscovici, Marie. 'Une femme et la psychanalyse', introduction to *L'amour du narcissisme*, Paris 1980

Nobécourt, Jacques. 'Lou Andreas-Salomé et le narcissisme' (r), in *Le Monde des Livres*, 26 September 1980

Pauli, Hans. 'Frauenliteratur' (r, o), in *Neue Deutsche Rundschau*, 7, 1896 (pp277–8)

Peters, H. F. 'Rilke's Love Poems to Lou Andreas-Salomé, in *Modern Languages Quarterly*, 21, 1960 (pp158–64)

Pfeiffer, E. 'Hexe von Hainberg? Vier Lebensbilder der Dichterin Lou Andreas-Salomé', in *Göttinger Monatsblätter*, August 1978 (pp12–13)
  'Die Historie von der Lou', in *Neue Deutsche Hefte*, May/June 1965 (pp111–19)
  'Denn Rainer starb "trostlos". Eine Betrachtung', in *Literaturwissenschaftliches Jahrbuch*, 23, 1982 (pp297–304)

The 'Nachwort' to each of his editions of her works

Platzhoff-Lejeune, E. 'Im Zwischenland' (r), in *Das Literarische Echo*, 15 August 1903 (pp1583–4)

Roazen, Paul. 'A Curious Triangle (Freud, Lou Andreas-Salomé and Victor Tausk)', part of his book, *Brother Animal* (see below) in *Encounter*, October 1969 (pp3–8)

Romundt, Heinrich. 'Noch einmal Friedrich Nietzsche und Frau Lou Andreas-Salomé', in *Das Magazin für Litteratur*, 27 April 1895 (pp523–6)

Salzer, P. 'Lou Andreas-Salomé, Menschenkinder' (r), in *Allgemeines Literaturblatt*, 1 July 1901 (p414)

Stöcker, Helene. 'Neue Frauentypen' (o), in *Das Magazin für Litteratur*, 8 July 1899 (pp630–3)
'Lou Andreas-Salomé, der Dichterin und Denkerin, zum 70ten Geburtstag', in *Die Neue Generation*, January, February, March 1931

Storck, Joachim. 'Gutachten über H. F. Peters, My Sister, My Spouse' (u)

Weizsäcker, V. V. 'Mein Dank an Freud ... von Lou Andreas-Salomé ...' (r), in *Der Nervenartzt*, vol. 15, January 1933

Wolff, Kurt. 'Lou Andreas-Salomé. Ein Porträt aus Erinnerungen und Dokumenten', in *Gehört, gelesen*, no. 10, October 1963 (pp1180–90) (broadcast 4 September 1963)

Wurmb, Agnes. 'Lou Andreas-Salomé, Rodinka' (r), in *Die Frau*, March 1925 (pp164–6)

Zepler, Wally. 'Die neue Frau in der neuen Frauendichtung' (o), in *Sozialistisches Monatsheft*, I, 1914 (pp53–65)

C. SELECTIVE LIST OF OTHER WORKS CONSULTED

Albert-Lasard, Lou. *Wege mit Rilke*, Frankfurt, 1952

Alexander, F., *et al.* (eds.). *Psychoanalytic Pioneers*, New York, London, 1966

Andler, Charles. *Nietzsche, sa vie et sa pensée*, vol. 4, Paris, 1928

Andreas, F. *Die Babi's in Persien*, 1896

Azadovsky, K. 'R. M. Ril'ke i L. N. Tolstoy', in *Russkaya literatura*, 1, Leningrad, 1969 (pp129–51)

Azadovsky, K. 'Briefe nach Russland (S. W. Maljutin im Briefwechsel zwischen Rilke und Ettinger)', in *Rilke-Studien*, 1976 (pp197–208)

Azadovsky, K. and Chertkov, L. 'Russkiye vstrechi Ril'ke', in Rilke, *Vorpsvede, Roden, Pis'ma*, Moscow, 1971 (pp357–89)

Bassermann, D. *Der andere Rilke*, Bad Homburg vor der Höhe, 1961

Bäumer, Gertrud. *Die Frau und das geistige Leben*, Leipzig, 1911

Beauvoir, Simone de. *Old Age* (transl. by Patrick O'Brian), London, 1972

Bernoulli, C. A. *Franz Overbeck und Friedrich Nietzsche Eine Freundschaft*, Jena, 1908

Betz, M. *Rilke vivant*, Paris, 1931

Binder, Elsa. *Malwida von Meysenbug und Friedrich Nietzsche*, Berlin, 1917

Böhme, Marion. *Rilke und die russische Literatur. Neue Beiträge mit besonderer Berücksichtigung der Rezeption Rilkes in Russland* (u) doctoral dissertation, Wien, 1966

Bölsche, W. *Das Liebesleben in der Natur*, Jena, 1906

Bos, Charles du. *Extraits d'un Journal 1908–1928*, Paris, 1931

Brann, H. W. *Nietzsche und die Frauen*, Leipzig, 1931

Brockdorff, Baron C. von. *Zu Tönnies' Entwicklungsgeschichte*, Kiel, 1937

Brome, Vincent. *Freud and his Early Circle*, London, 1967

Brutzer, Sophie. *Rilkes russische Reisen*, Darmstadt, 1969

Buddeberg, Else. *Rainer Maria Rilke, 'Eine innere Biographie'*, Stuttgart, 1955

Butler, E. 'Rilke and Tolstoy', in *Modern Language Review*, vol. 35, 1940 (pp494–505)
Rilke, Cambridge, 1946

Čertkov, L. 'Rilke in Russland' (auf Grund neuer Materialien), in *Veröffentlichungen der Kommission für Literaturwissenschaft*, no. 2, Wien, 1975

Cassirer-Solmitz, Eva. *Rainer Maria Rilke*, Heidelberg, 1957

Chronik der Georg-August Universität zu Göttingen für die Rechnungsjahre 1927–1930 [section on Andreas], Göttingen, 1931

Clark, R. *Freud. The Man and the Cause*, New York, 1980

Dettmering, Peter. *Dichtung und Psychoanalyse*, München, 1969

Drozhzhin, S. *Zhizn' poeta-krestyanina S. D. Drozhzhina*, Moscow, 1915

Eissler, K. *Talent and Genius: The Fictitious Case of Tausk Contra Freud*, New York, 1971

Evans, Richard. *The Feminist Movement in Germany, 1894–1933*, London and Beverly Hills, 1976

Festschrift: Friedrich Carl Andreas: Zur Vollendung des siebzigsten Lebensjahres am 14 April 1916, dargebracht von Freunden und Schülern, Leipzig, 1916

Förster-Nietzsche, Elisabeth. *Das Leben Friedrich Nietzsches*, Leipzig, vol. II(i), 1897; vol. II(ii), 1904

'Nietzsche-Legenden', in *Die Zukunft*, 28 January 1905 (pp170–9)
Der einsame Nietzsche, Leipzig, 1914
Friedrich Nietzsche und die Frauen seiner Zeit, München, 1935
Freud, S. *Standard Edition of the Complete Psychological Works of Sigmund Freud* (ed. J. Strachey), London, 1953ff
Freud, S. and Abraham, K. *A Psycho-Analytic Dialogue: The Letters of Sigmund Freud and Karl Abraham, 1907–1926* (ed. H. C. Abraham and E. L. Freud, transl. by B. Marsh and H. C. Abraham), London, 1965
Freud, S. and Jung, C. G. *The Correspondence between Sigmund Freud and C. G. Jung* (ed. W. McGuire, transl. by R. Manheim and R. F. C. Hull), London, 1974
Gilman, Charlotte P. *Women and Economics*, London and Boston, 1905
Halévy, Daniel. *La vie de Frédéric Nietzsche*, Paris, 1909 (republished Paris, 1944)
Hillebrand, Bruno. 'Nietzsche-Rezeption in Deutschland', in *Literaturwissenschaftliches Jahrbuch*, 17, 1976 (pp99–127)
Hofmannsthal, H. v. and Beer-Hofmann, Richard. *Briefwechsel*, Frankfurt, 1972
Hofmannsthal, H. v. and Schnitzler, A. *Briefwechsel*, Frankfurt, 1964
Hollingdale, R. *Nietzsche, The Man and His Philosophy*, London, 1965
Janz, Curt P. *Friedrich Nietzsche* (Biographie in drei Bänden) (vol. II), Wien and München, 1978
Jones, Ernest. *The Life and Work of Sigmund Freud* (edited and abridged by Lionel Trilling and Steven Marcus), London, 1964
Jung, C. G. *Analytical Psychology: Its theory and practice* (The Tavistock Lectures, 1935), London, 1968
Kaufmann, Walter. *Nietzsche* (third edition: revised and enlarged), New York, 1968
Kerényi, Karl. *Umgang mit Göttlichem*, Göttingen, 1955
Kolle, Kurt. 'Notizen über Paul Rée', in *Zeitschrift für Menschenkunde*, Heft 3, September 1927 (pp168–74)
Krieger-Wimpf, Johanna. 'Frauen über Rainer Maria Rilke', in *Monatsblätter des Literarischen Bundes*, no. 5/6, 1936 (pp 51–4)
Kunisch, Hermann. *Rainer Maria Rilke: Dasein und Dichtung*, Berlin, 1944 and 1975
Ledebour, Minna (ed.). *Georg Ledebour: Mensch und Kämpfer*, Zürich, 1954
Leppmann, Wolfgang. *Rilke, Leben und Werk*, Bern and München, 1981
Lessing, Theodor. *Der Jüdische Selbsthass* [chapter on Paul Rée], Berlin, 1930
Löwith, Karl. *Nietzsches Philosophie der Ewigen Wiederkehr*, Hamburg, 1934ff
Mason, Eudo C. *Rilke*, Edinburgh and London, 1963
Meysenbug, Malwida von. *Memoiren einer Idealistin*, Berlin, 1882
Individualitäten [chapter on Nietzsche], Berlin and Leipzig, 1901
Minutes of the Vienna Psycho-Analytic Society (ed. H. Nunberg and E. Federn, transl. by M. Nunberg), New York, 1962ff
Molostvov, N. *Volynsky i noveishie idealisty*, Petersburg, 1905
Morawski, Charlotte. *Der Einfluss Rées auf Nietzsches neue Moralideen*, Breslau, 1915
Newman, Ernest. *The Life of Richard Wagner*, vol. 4, New York, 1960
Nietzsche, F. *Sämtliche Werke* (Kritische Studienausgabe in 15 Bänden), (ed. G. Colli u. M. Montinari), Berlin/New York, 1967ff
Friedrich Nietzsches Gesammelte Briefe (5 vols), Berlin and Leipzig, 1900ff
Pascal, Roy. *From Naturalism to Expressionism*, London, 1973
Pasternak, Leonid. 'Vstrechi s R. M. Ril'ke', in Rilke, *Vorpsvede, Roden, Pis'ma*, Moscow, 1971
Pfeiffer, Ernst. 'Rilke und die Psychoanalyse', in *Literaturwissenschaftliches Jahrbuch*, 17, 1976
Pfleiderer, Otto. *Religionsphilosophie auf Geschichtlicher Grundlage*, Berlin, 1878
Ratz, Ursula. *Georg Ledebour, 1850–1947*, Berlin, 1969
Rée, Paul. *Psychologische Beobachtungen* (published anonymously), Berlin, 1875
Der Ursprung der moralischen Empfindungen, Chemnitz, 1877
Die Illusion der Willensfreiheit, Berlin, 1885
Die Entstehung des Gewissens, Berlin, 1885
Philosophie 'Nachgelassenes Werk', Berlin, 1903
Rilke, R. M. *Sämtliche Werke* (herausg. vom Rilke-Archiv in Verbindung mit Ruth Sieber-Rilke, besorgt durch Ernst Zinn) (6 vols), Wiesbaden, 1955ff
Tagebücher aus der Frühzeit (ed., Ruth Sieber-Rilke and Carl Sieber), 1942 and 1973 [contains 'Das Florenzer Tagebuch']
Briefe und Tagebücher aus der Frühzeit 1899 bis 1902 (ed. Ruth Sieber-Rilke and Carl Sieber), Leipzig, 1931
Gesammelte Briefe (6 vols), Leipzig, 1936ff
Rilke, R. M. and Thurn und Taxis, Marie von. *Briefwechsel*, Zürich and Wiesbaden, 1951
Roazen, Paul. *Brother Animal* 'The Story of Freud and Tausk', Harmondsworth, 1970

Salis, J. von. *R. M. Rilkes Schweizer Jahre*, Leipzig, 1936
Schmidt, Dr. Raymund (ed.). *Die Philosophie der Gegenwart in Selbstdarstellungen* [chapters on Tönnies and Mauthner], Leipzig, 1922
Schoenberner, Franz. *Confessions of a European Intellectual*, New York and London, 1965
Selle, G. von. 'F. C. Andreas', in *Indogermanisches Jahrbuch*, Berlin and Leipzig, 1931 (pp366–76)
Simenauer, Erich. *Rainer Maria Rilke: Legende und Mythos*, Frankfurt, 1953
Soergel, Albert and Hohoff, Curt. *Dichtung und Dichter der Zeit: Vom Naturalismus bis zur Gegenwart*, Düsseldorf, 1961
Sonns, Stefan. *Das Gewissen in der Philosophie Nietzsches*, Winterthur, 1955
Steiner, Jacob. *Rilkes Duineser Elegien*, Stockholm, 1962
Stern, J. P. *A Study of Nietzsche*, Cambridge, 1979
Stöcker, Helene. 'Die moderne Frau', in *Die Freie Bühne*, 4, II, 1893 (pp1215–17)
Storck, Joachim. *Rainer Maria Rilke als Briefschreiber* (u) (doctoral dissertation), Freiburg, 1957
Tausk, Marius. 'Victor Tausk as seen by his son', in *American Imago*, vol. 30, no. 4, Winter 1973 (pp322–35)
Tönnies, Ferdinand. 'Paul Rée', in *Das freie Wort*, vol. 4, Frankfurt, 1904/5 (pp666–73)
Tönnies, F. and Paulsen, F. *Briefwechsel*, Kiel, 1961
Weizsäcker, Viktor von. *Natur und Geist*, München, 1964
Wollheim, Richard. *Freud*, London, 1971
Wurmb, Agnes. *Rückschau auf den Lebensweg*, Hamburg, n.d.
Wydenbruck, Nora. *Rilke*, London, 1949
Zaidenshnur, E. 'R. M. Ril'ke u Tolstovo', in *Literaturnoye nasledstvo*, nos. 37–38, Moscow, 1939

D. UNPUBLISHED SOURCES

SEEN AT THE HOUSE OF DR E. PFEIFFER IN GÖTTINGEN

A large number of manuscripts, including several letters from Lou Andreas-Salomé to members of her family; letters between Lou Andreas-Salomé and Frieda von Bülow; letters from Georg Ledebour to Lou Andreas-Salomé; one letter from Martin Buber to Lou Andreas-Salomé; some 30 pages of diary entries from 1888 and 1892–3; miscellaneous Tagesnotizen; a number of school exercise books; notes taken from Gillot's teaching (dated 1883); notes on Biedermann's lectures in 1880.

Also a number of typescripts made from some of Lou Andreas-Salomé's diaries of 1900–07, 1910–12, 1913, 1917–18, including the 63-page diary of the journey to Russia in 1900 entitled 'Russland mit Rainer'; also 120 pages entitled 'Der Gott'.

SEEN IN THE DEUTSCHES LITERATURARCHIV AT THE SCHILLER NATIONALMUSEUM IN MARBACH-AM-NECKAR

A large number of letters from Lou Andreas-Salomé and from F. C. Andreas to her publisher, dated 1895 and 1896; several letters from Lou Andreas-Salomé to K. Kippenberg, 1927–35; letter from Lou Andreas-Salomé to Lotte Reinecke, dated 14 February 1931.

GIVEN TO ME BY DR K. M. AZADOVSKY IN LENINGRAD

A copy of the first letter from Lou von Salomé to Pastor Gillot, dated 1/13 May (presumably 1878), which Azadovsky had discovered in a Leningrad archive. Also shown to me by K.M. Azadovsky: transcripts of six letters from Lou Andreas-Salomé to Sofya Shil (in Russian), dated June–July 1900.

INDEX

Aberration, An, 63, 107, 134, 208–10, 214
Abraham, Karl, 148, 151, 153, 154, 166
Adler, Alfred, 150, 153, 154, 177
'Age and Eternity', 197
Albert, Henri, 97
Albert–Lasard, Loulou, 11, 168, 169
Alexander II, Tsar, 23
Altenberg, Peter, 72
'"Anal" and "Sexual"', 181, 183–5
Andreas, Professor Fred Charles (later Friedrich Carl), 10, 60–65, 67, 72, 79, 100, 102–3, 107–8, 110, 129–30, 145, 194, 198, 209, 214, 231
Andreas, Marie, 130

Bangs, Hermann, 72
Bassermann, 11
Bäumer, Gertrud, 140, 144, 201, 202, 235
Bayreuth, 43, 44, 229, 230
Beer-Hofmann, Richard, 73, 150, 232, 233
Benois, Alexander, 109
Berlin, 11, 40, 59, 60, 64–6, 69, 72, 103, 109–10, 129–30, 133, 157, 176, 235
Berliner Volkszeitung (newspaper), 67
Bernays, Minna, 152, 176
Bernoulli, C.A., 46
Betz, Maurice, 113
Beyond Good and Evil (Nietzsche), 46, 58, 95
Biedermann, Professor Alois, 27, 74
Binion, Rudolph (*Frau Lou*), 12
Birth of Tragedy, The (Nietzsche), 43
Bjerre, Poul, 132, 145, 150, 234
Bölsche, Wilhelm, 66, 70–72, 90, 97, 135, 140, 216
Bonaparte, Marie, 152
Book of Hours (Rilke), 110, 119, 121, 222
Brahm, Otto, 66, 232
Brandes, Georg, 50, 150, 231
Brenner, Albert, 32, 35
Bruns, Otto, 176
Buber, Martin, 140, 235
Buddeberg, Elsa, 124–5, 222, 224
Bülow, Frieda von, 65, 102, 110, 121, 130–31, 164, 178, 199, 214

Cassirer, Eva, 189
Children of Man, 100, 128, 210–12
'Christ Visions' (Rilke), 99
Christianity, 51, 92, 94, 103, 108

Darwin, Charles, 60, 75, 229
Dawn (Nietzsche), 41, 231
'Death-plea' ['*Todesbitte*'], 26–7
Dehmel, Richard, 66, 165, 232
Delp, Ellen, 148, 235
Deussen, Paul, 231
Devil and his Grandmother, The, 172, 216–18, 236–7
Diaghilev, Sergei, 109
Dohm, Hedwig, 134–5, 235

Dostoyevsky, F.M., 16, 79, 110, 226–7
Drozhzhin, Spiridon, 110, 114–15, 224, 233
du Bos, Charles, 114
Duino Elegies (Rilke), 103, 127, 142, 170–71, 189–90, 192, 222–4

Ebbinghaus, Hermann, 59, 66, 231
Ebner-Eschenbach, Marie von, 73, 150
Ecce Homo (Nietzsche), 54, 90
Eitingon, Max, 151, 157, 176
Emerson, Ralph Waldo, 55
Endell, August, 73, 102
Erotic, The, 129, 133, 140–44, 146, 159

Fenitschka, 138, 208–9
Ferenczi, Sandor, 151–2, 154–6, 162, 235
Feuerbach, Ludwig, 233
Fiedler, Fyodor (Friedrich), 109, 116
'Florence Diary', 103–6, 191, 222, 224
Förster-Nietzsche, Elisabeth, 43–7, 52–4, 56, 97–8, 230
Freie Bühne, Die, 69–70, 87, 134, 232
Freud, Anna, 11, 176, 215, 236
Freud Journal, 12, 126, 146, 151, 154–5, 157, 161–2, 186, 234
Freud, Sigmund, 9–11, 13, 56–7, 61, 70, 98, 126, 132–3, 139, 145–66, 173–9, 181–9, 191, 193–6, 198–9, 202, 216, 234–6
Friedrich Nietzsche in his Works, 90–98
Friedrichshagen, 66, 69
'From the History of God', 80–81
From Alien Soul, 128, 207
'From the beast to the God', 79

Garborg, Arne, 66, 231
Garborg, Hulda, 66, 232
Garshin, V.M., 118–19
Gast, Peter (Heinrich Köselitz), 39, 41–2, 44, 48, 230
Gay Science, The, (Nietzsche), 38–9, 55, 221, 230–31
Gebsattel, Emil von, 150, 156, 169, 234
'General theory of the Neuroses' (Freud), 179
Gillot, Pastor Hendrik, 10, 23–7, 30, 33–5, 46, 49, 56, 58, 61, 63, 64, 70, 74, 89, 119, 147, 192, 194–5, 200, 204, 206, 208, 209, 213, 218
God, 18–20, 22–7, 29–30, 49–50, 64, 68–9, 74–82, 84–5, 89, 91–2, 95, 113, 120, 124–5, 128, 141–2, 147, 170–71, 184, 187–8, 192, 194, 200, 203, 207–9, 214, 217, 219, 223–4, 226, 233
Goethe, J.W. von, 28, 141, 167, 173, 214, 217, 231
Goldmann, Richard, 233
Göttingen, 8, 64, 122, 130, 156, 163, 168, 176, 201, 203, 213

Haeckel, Ernst Heinrich, 71
Halbe, Max, 66, 73, 232
Haller, Ludwig, 59, 145, 231
Hamsun, Knut, 72

Hansson–Marholm, Ola, 66, 232
Harden, Maximilian, 150, 165, 232
Hart, Heinrich, 70
'Harnack and the Apostolic Creed', 77–8
Hart brothers, Heinrich and Julius, 66, 232
Hartleben, Otto Erich, 66, 232
Hauptmann, Gerhart, 66, 87, 117, 130, 225, 231–2, 233
Hennell, Charles, 233
'Heresies against the modern woman', 134
History of the Psychoanalytic Movement (Freud), 154
Hitler, Adolf, 199, 232
Hofmannsthal, Hugo von, 73, 232–3
Holz, Arno, 66, 232
Hour Without God, The, 172, 219–20
House, The, 129, 210, 213, 214–15
Human All Too Human (Nietzsche), 230
'Hymn to Life', 55–6, 200, 229, 230

Ibsen, Henrik, 30, 69, 87–90, 145, 207
[Henrik] Ibsen's Female Characters, 87–90, 134, 207
Imago (periodical), 150, 153, 172
Italy, 32, 104, 106, 117, 130, 195

Jahrbuch, 153
James, William, 85–6
Janchevetsky, Vasily Grigorovich, 233
Janz, C.P., 68, 102
Jekels, Ludwig, 148, 157, 235
Jena, 44, 52, 56
'Jesus the Jew', 75, 77, 79, 80, 99, 224
Jones, Ernest, 152
Joukowski, Paul von, 43–4
Jung, C.G., 150, 153–4, 157, 161, 176

Kant, Immanuel, 25
Kerenyi, Karl, 76
Key, Ellen, 132, 134–5
Klingenberg, Helene, 11, 66, 181
Klingenberg, Reinhold, 181
Kögel, Fritz, 97–8
Kollwitz, Käthe, 131
König, Josef, 202
Kühnemann, Eugen, 66, 232

Land Between, The, 110, 118, 213
Ledebour, Georg, 67, 72, 100–101, 194, 206, 209, 232
Leipzig, 51–2, 169
Leistikow, Walter, 66, 232
Letzter Zuruf (letter to Rilke), 118–20, 121, 159
Life of Nietzsche, The (Förster-Nietzsche), 56
Lonely Nietzsche, The (Förster-Nietzsche), 56
Looking Back [*Lebensrückblick*], 9, 12, 19–20, 22, 25, 48, 62, 67, 97, 117, 139, 193–6, 198, 200, 230
Love-Life in Nature (Bölsche), 70
Lucerne, 39, 53

Ma, 107, 110, 213, 215, 225
Mackay, John Henry, 66, 232
Mann, Thomas, 191
Marholm, Laura, 135, 232
Mauthner, Fritz, 90, 165, 232

Messina, 37–8, 221
Meysenbug, Malwida von, 32–7, 41, 43, 52, 57, 229, 230
Michael Kramer, 117
Monte Carlo, 34
Monte Sacro, 39, 53
Morike, Eduard, 28
Moscow, 107–9, 114–16, 225–6
Munich, 11, 60, 72–3, 97–8, 100, 103, 129, 150, 155, 156–7, 168–9, 176
My Thanks to Freud, 175, 179, 191–3, 201

'Narcissism as Dual Orientation', 181, 185–8
Narziss (Rilke), 167
Naumburg, 52
Nicholas I, Tsar, 16
Nietzsche and Women (Förster-Nietzsche), 56
Nietzsche, Elisabeth, *see* Förster-Nietzsche
Nietzsche, Friedrich, 9–11, 13, 26, 28, 32–61, 68–70, 74, 77–9, 81, 83, 86–8, 90–100, 104–6, 123, 128, 133–4, 136, 139, 144–8, 153, 158–9, 162–4, 166, 189–92, 194–5, 200, 204–6, 208–9, 221, 227–33
'Nietzsche Legends' (in *Die Zukunft*), 56
Nizovka, 114, 115
Notebook of Malte Laurids Brigge (Rilke), 103, 125, 127, 131, 190

'On Early Worship of God', 153
'On Narcissism' (Freud), 149
'On the Origin of Christianity', 79
'On the Religious Affect', 80–82, 171
Organ Inferiority (Adler), 153
Orta, 39, 53
Otto, Rudolf, 76
Overbeck, Franz, 98
Overbeck, Ida, 42, 45, 54, 57

Paris, 11, 40, 72, 121, 123, 125, 127, 129, 189, 229
Pasternak, Boris, 107, 112
Pasternak, Leonid, 107, 112
Pastor Dalton, 23, 24
Persia, 63–4, 108, 231, 233
Peterhof, 16, 18, 19
Petersburg, 11, 15–16, 20–23, 26, 30, 56, 65, 104, 108, 109, 114–16, 130, 204, 215, 225, 233
Pfeiffer, Dr Ernst, 8, 45, 201–3, 221, 230–34
Pfleiderer, Otto, 25
Philosophy of Religion on a Historical Foundation (Pfleiderer), 25
'Physical Love', 71
Pineles, Dr Friedrich (Zemek), 10, 118–21, 130–31, 151
Prague, 100
'Prayer to Life' ['*Lebensgebet*'], 28–9, 41, 43, 52
Prince Igor, 122
'The Problems of Islam', 79, 227

Rank, Otto, 152, 177, 178–9, 235
'Realism in Religion', 75–7
Rée, Dr Paul, 10, 32–42, 44–6, 48–57, 59–61, 92, 97, 100–101, 104, 137, 145, 173, 194, 204, 206, 209, 215, 229–31
Reinhardt, Max, 66, 232, 235

'Religion and Culture', 80–81, 84
Repin, Ilya, 109
Resurrection (Tolstoy), 108
Rilke, Rainer (René) Maria, 8–11, 61, 66, 73, 79, 98–133, 139, 145, 147, 156–7, 159, 163–4, 166–76, 178, 181–3, 189–92, 194–5, 207–9, 211, 213–14, 216, 222–8, 233–6
Rodin, Auguste, 10, 120, 124, 126, 129, 189, 223
Rodinka, 117, 129, 213, 215
Rohde, Professor Erwin, 91, 98, 206
Rome, 32, 34, 37–8, 53, 119, 173, 230
Romundt, Heinrich, 97, 231
Rongas, 115
Russia, 15, 21, 74, 110, 111, 112
Ruth, 20, 24–7, 70, 89, 128, 200, 206–7, 210, 235

'Safe Conduct, A' (Pasternak), 112
Salomé, Alexander von, 15, 16, 17
Salomé, Evgeny von, 16, 17, 20, 40, 59, 104
Salomé, Gustav von, 15, 16, 17, 26, 117
Salomé, Robert von, 16, 17, 166, 173
Salten, Felix, 73, 150
Savely, Dr, 72, 195
Scandinavia, 130
Scheler, Max, 165
Scientific Bases of Poetry (Bölsche), 71
Schiller, Johann Christoph Friedrich von, 23, 25
Schlaf, Johannes, 232
Schmargendorf, 65–6, 72, 103, 107, 110, 115, 117
Schnitzler, Arthur, 10, 73, 130, 150, 232–3
Schnitzler, Olga, 233
Schopenhauer, Arthur, 47, 231
Shil, Sofya, 110–13, 115, 116, 215
Siberia, 108
'Siblings', 131, 172, 218–19
Sils Maria, 38
Socrates, 68, 236
Sonnets to Orpheus (Rilke), 127, 223
Sorrento, 32, 35
Spain, 130
Spinoza, Baruch, 25, 85–6, 146, 155
Stein, Heinrich von, 43, 230, 231
Stekel, Wilhelm, 150, 152, 177
Stibbe, 40, 43, 54
Stibbe Nest-Book, 49–50, 136, 145, 204
Strauss, David, 233
Strindberg, August, 10, 172, 232–3
Stöcker, Helene, 63, 130, 133–4
Struggling for God, 20, 46, 54, 60, 83, 204–6, 210, 212, 212
Superman [*Übermensch*], 57–8, 69, 94, 95, 232
Swoboda, Hermann, 152

Tales of God the Father (Rilke), 107, 110
Tausk Viktor, 61, 150–51, 155–6, 158, 162, 164, 178, 235–6

Tautenburg, 43–50, 52–4, 77, 90, 95, 104, 145, 195, 206, 231
Tempelhof, 65
The Devil and his Grandmother, 172, 216–18, 236–7
The Erotic, 129, 133, 140–44, 146, 159
The Gay Science (Nietzsche), 38–9, 55, 221, 230–31
The Hour Without God and Other Children's Stories, 172, 219–20
The House, 129, 210, 213, 214–15
The Land Between, 110, 118, 213
'Lay of the Love and Death of the Cornet Christopher Rilke, The', 110, 220
'Thoughts on the Problem of Love', 110, 133, 138–9
Three Epistles to a Boy, 12, 167, 181–3
Thurn and Taxis, Princess Marie von, 163, 175, 222
Thus Spoke Zarathustra (Nietzsche), 38, 54–5, 77, 88, 91, 94, 96, 98, 104, 227
Tolstoy, Leo, 10–11, 16, 69–70, 85, 108, 110, 112–14, 130, 158, 226–7, 233–4
Tolstoy, Nikolai, 115, 117
Tönnes, Ferdinand, 59, 96, 231
'To Pain' ['*An den Schmerz*'], 28, 42, 53
Totem and Taboo (Freud), 149, 152, 235
Trubetskoy, Prince Pavel, 107–8, 110–11

Vienna, 11, 59, 72, 73, 148, 150–51, 153, 176, 181, 232, 235
Vienna Psychoanalytical Society, 149
Volga, 116–17, 129, 223
Volynsky, Akim (Akim Lvovich Flekser), 102–3, 226
Vorwärts (newspaper), 67

Wagner, Cosima, 43, 57
Wagner, Richard, 33, 39, 43–4, 52–3, 92, 141, 229–30
Wasserman, Jakob, 73, 99, 102
Wedekind, Frank, 72–3, 150, 210, 232
Weimar, 132, 148–9, 153
Weininger, Otto, 134
Weizsäcker, Viktor, von, 201
Wendung (Rilke), 167
Westhoff, Clara, 118
Willie, Bruno, 66, 232
Wolff, Kurt, 169
Wolfratshausen, 102, 118–19, 129, 224, 226
Worpswede, 117–18, 122, 223
World of Art (periodical), 109
Wunderly-Volkart, Nanny, 172, 222

Yasnaya Polyana, 112, 113
Yeats, W.B., 51

Zasulich, Vera, 23
Zola, Emile, 69
Zoppot, 104, 106
Zurich, 26, 27, 40, 72